Library of
Davidson College

STUDIES IN CLASSICAL ANTIQUITY - Band 3

1979

PLATO: TRUE AND SOPHISTIC RHETORIC

by

KEITH V. ERICKSON

AMSTERDAM 1979

© Editions Rodopi N.V., Amsterdam 1979
Printed in the Netherlands
ISBN: 90-6203-591-4

This book is affectionately dedicated to Mira T. Erickson, Rosamond E. Erickson, and Keith M. Erickson.

TABLE OF CONTENTS

PREFACE   7
INTRODUCTION   9

ARTICLES

1. The Growth of Plato's Perception of Rhetoric, by Rollin W. Quimby 21
2. The Relation of the *Apology of Socrates* to Gorgias' *Defense of Palamedes* and Plato's Critique of Gorgianic Rhetoric by James A. Coulter   31
3. To Make the Weaker Argument Defeat the Stronger, by Alexander Sesonske   71
4. *Gorgias,* by Paul Friedländer   91
5. The Self-Reference of the *Gorgias,* by Adele Spitzer   129
6. Plato and Conjurers, by Jacqueline de Romilly   153
7. Plato's View of Rhetoric, by Edwin Black   171
8. The Unity of the *Phaedrus,* by Paul Plass   193
9. The Non-Lover in Plato's *Phaedrus,* by Stanley Rosen   223
10. The Middle Speech of Plato's *Phaedrus,* by Malcolm Brown and James A. Coulter   239
11. *The Attack on Isocrates in the* Phaedrus, by R.L. Howland   265
12. Irony and Allegory in the *Phaedrus,* by V. Tejera   281
13. Plato's Conception of *Dispositio,* by Floyd Douglas Anderson and Ray Lynn Anderson   299
14. Rhetoric as Seduction, by William G. Kelley, Jr.   313
15. The *Symposium:* A Neglected Source for Plato's Ideas on Rhetoric, by Wayne N. Thompson   325
16. Plato's Conception of Persuasion, by Glenn R. Morrow   339
17. True and False Speech in Plato's *Cratylus* 385 B-C, by W.M. Pfeiffer   355
18. Genuine Speech vs. Chatter: A Socratic Problematic, by Stephen Skousgaard   375
19. Plato on the Rhetoric of Poetry, by Morris Henry Partee   385

BIBLIOGRAPHY   399
INDEX   417

PREFACE

Numerous studies of Athenian society reflect the spoken word's influence in the ancient world. The early Greeks quickly recognized the impact of persuasive discourse upon man's social, legal, and political affairs. Soon, logographers and sophists capitalized on the need for articulate communicators by teaching and composing rhetorical discourse. Concomitant with the increased attention afforded rhetoric there emerged debate concerning its value, ability to articulate truth and falsehood, and its influence on courtroom and legislative decision making. The abuses of sophistic oratory, for instance, did not escape the philosopher's attention, who perceived the sophists' τέχνη as a threat to reason. The fundamental chasm separating dialectic and rhetoric as means of knowing kindled exchanges and attacks seldom paralleled in the history of philosophical disputes. Plato, for one, time and again railed against the basic tenets of sophistic oratory, which he perceived to be shallow, deceitful, and the product of ill-thinking. The purpose of this anthology is to examine Plato's numerous arguments against sophistic rhetoric and those enunciating the requisites of a "true" rhetoric. Basically, true rhetoric is interpreted as an ideal rhetoric practiced by principled rhetoricians/dialecticians with pure motives, while sophistic rhetoric is viewed as false or sham persuasion, lacking in art, and practiced by self-serving men with base purposes. In the main, this bi-polar vision of rhetorical discourse and its practitioners bespeaks Plato, a point which this book establishes both philologically and philosophically.

As an overview, this book examines Plato's concept of true and sophistic rhetoric, the maturation of his rhetorical theory, amatory persuasion, poetry, Isocratean rhetoric, Socratic chatter, dialectic, writing, and specific evidence of rhetorical theory in the *Apology, Meno, Gorgias, Phaedrus, Symposium, Republic, Cratylus,* and *Protagoras.* Several criteria dictated the inclusion or deletion of each essay. Overriding considerations were an article's general scholarship and interpretation of Plato. In addition, each article was scrutinized for evidence of originality, significance, relevance, and philological probity. The articles anthologized here consistently meet these criteria. Not every theme or issue related to Platonic rhetoric is included, however, as certain topics skirt the book's intended focus; neither the influence of Plato's theory nor its later historical development, for example, are evident. Articles which strayed too far from the book's audience (scholars and advanced students of ancient rhetoric and/or Plato) were likewise excluded. Moreover, the articles reprinted here are exceptional specimens of English language research on Plato's theory of rhetoric. While the authors occasionally disagree with one another or even develop contradictory positions, they invariably are engaging and pursue avenues of investigation which enlighten the reader. A bibliography of approximately 450 items concludes the book. The bibliography was collected with the objective of providing the multi-lingual researcher with additional resources.

This anthology represents not only the collective wisdom of its authors but their generous cooperation as well—which the editor wishes to acknowledge. Without the authors' consent to reprint copyrighted materials this anthology would not have been published. Further, the editors and publishers of the *Canadian Journal of Philosophy, Classical Philology, Classical Quarterly, Harvard Studies in Classical Philology, Journal of Aesthetics and Art Criticism, Journal of the History of Philosophy, Kinesis, Man and World, Philosophical Review, Philosophy and Rhetoric, Quarterly Journal of Speech, Southern Speech Communication Journal, Symbolae Osloenses*, and the Harvard and Princeton University presses were courteous and efficient in their handling of reprint requests. A special "Thank you" must be extended not only by myself but by the reader to Mr. Fred van der Zee of Editions Rodopi N.V. for his faith in this project.

Keith V. Erickson   Texas Tech University Complex

PLATO: TRUE AND SOPHISTIC RHETORIC

Introduction

Numerous practioners and philosophers in the ancient Greek world authored a theory of rhetoric. Plato's works represent the major philosophical, as opposed to scientific, approach delineating the worth and parameters of rhetorical discourse. Steeped in symbolism, metaphor, double *entendre,* and multiple themes, his works outline an incredibly thoughtful and innovative theory of true and sophistic rhetoric. Plato's perception of rhetoric and its relationship to knowledge, language, art, philosophy, and human interaction, while ranking among the more engaging theories, is exquisitely difficult to interpret. Thus, philological investigations of Plato's theory of rhetoric reflect a wide diversity of opinion and competing explanations. Each new emendation, it has been observed, seems to lend itself to further speculation and philosophical leaps into the metaphysics of symbolic meaning. Hopefully, this anthology will minimize confusion and facilitate understanding with regard to Plato's estimate of utterance designed to affect human behavior.

Plato voiced the concern that unprincipled sophistic rhetoricians were capable of persuading naive individuals to untruthful positions. His disdain for sophistic rhetoric is documented repeatedly in the *Euthydemus, Gorgias, Phaedrus, Protagoras* and *Meno.* Rollin W. Quimby, "The Growth of Plato's Perception of Rhetoric," recounts the progressive, general changes in Plato's theory of rhetoric. In the *Euthydemus,* for example, Plato attacks the sophists' claim of teaching virtue and that rhetoric constitutes an art (although he did not exclude rhetoric from a list of subjects thought to possess utility). The *Protagoras'* examination of sophistic pedagogical principles indirectly discusses rhetoric by criticizing certain persuasive strategies. In the *Meno,* like the *Protagoras,* rhetoric is a peripheral subject criticized as the persuasive instrument of particular practitioners. Rhetoric is one of the major themes of the *Gorgias,* however, and it expounds lucidly upon the function, purpose, and value of persuasive discourse. The *Phaedrus* also evaluates rhetoric and clarifies many unanswered questions posed by the *Gorgias*. Here, Plato explores at considerable length distinctions between a true and false rhetoric. In sum, Quimby assesses Plato's theory of rhetoric as it evolved and matured over time.

James A. Coulter's "The Relation of the *Apology of Socrates* to Gorgias' *Defense of Palamedes* and Plato's Critique of Gorgianic Rhetoric," examines, as the title suggests, Plato's estimate of Gorgianic rhetoric. Coulter notes initially the verbal parallels between the *Apology of Socrates* and Gorgias' *Defense of Palamedes* and the lack of scholarly attention given the issue. The paradox of Plato's indebtedness to Gorgias is puzzling in light of his apparent abhorance of Gorgianic rhetoric. Coulter's arguments attempt a proof of the hypothesis that the *Apology* rejects the particular assumptions upon which the *Palamedes* was built. "Now, the proposition that the *Apology* represents, at least on one level of its meaning, an effort to subject one of the works of a leading sophist to a fundamental critique by means of an adaptation with polemic intention is not itself surprising in view of what we are otherwise familiar with in Plato's literary treatment of his contemporaries and immediate predecessors." Moreover, previous scholars have noted and cataloged the parallels between the two works but have failed to account for Plato's motive for imitating Gorgias' work, an omission Coulter laments. His analysis of the two speeches notes the absence of *dispositio* normally associated with forensic oratory, parallels in *erotesis*, and three clever *topos* of character; their similarities and disimilarities are carefully drawn. Coulter's conclusions support the thesis that Plato's refutation in the *Apology* is a conscious attempt to criticize the implied philosophy of Gorgias evident in Palamedes' rhetorical methods. The arguments in support of this claim are numerous and need not be elaborated upon here; suffice it to say that, in Coulter's estimation, the basis of Gorgianic rhetoric may be deduced from Palamedes' philosophical position. The establishment of this position, Coulter contends, suggests that the *Apology* is, in one of its aspects, "an implicit critique of Gorgianic rhetoric." Further proof is substantiated by an examination of the *Gorgias* and *Phaedrus*. Moreover, Coulter draws for us a vision of Socrates' rhetoric where truth, not probability, is supreme; a man who has "transcended all need to employ a rhetoric which aims at imparting the semblance rather than the substance of truth."

Perhaps the most famous criticism of rhetoric is that it is capable of making a weaker argument defeat the stronger. This fundamental indictment of sophistry is examined by Alexander Sesonske. In the *Sophist,* he notes, Plato defines the sophist as a "dissembling imitator of appearances, creating a shadow-play of words, the illusion of sound argument." In addition, many sophists claimed that they could defend or defeat any argument whether it be true or false. The sophist, therefore, was concerned more with victory and appearances than with establishing truth. While the dialectician/philosopher sought truth, the sophistic rhetorician sought only agreement. Plato suggests that while the philosopher's superior perceptual abilities enable him to discern sophistic oratory for what it is, merely verbal skill — an exercise in literary gymnastics — ordinary men cannot, and inevitably fall victim to the well turned phrase, moved by what is pleasant to the ear rather than by what conforms to logical processes. As such the sophist is a word combatant, wishing to exercise his skills without regard to resolving particular exigencies. "He is a performer, not an inquirer, wholly concerned with the manner of his speech and its immediate effect upon an audience." The *Apology,* Sesonske argues, establishes this point. At his trial, for instance, Socrates addressed himself to every charge, particularly the accusation that he was able to make weaker arguments defeat stronger ones, which emerges as the major issue of the *Apology.* The trial also symbolizes a contest between the oral tradition and the new, characterized by literary records. Socrates' opening statement accuses his detractors of employing weaker arguments capable of defeating the stronger, and insists upon a distinction of truth and persuasion. He claims to possess meager rhetorical skills, that he speaks in plain and truthful words only, while his accusers orate falsely, "decked out in fine words and phrases." Socrates' line of defense consisted largely of absurd or suicidal positions. If these arguments had swayed the jury he would have been guilty of making weaker arguments appear stronger. As it was, the Athenian jury, so influenced by the oral tradition, was unable to see this paradoxical position and found Socrates guilty, their decision proving that Socrates was incapable of making weaker arguments defeat the stronger!

Paul Friedländer's interpretation of the *Gorgias* follows. Friedländer places the work in perspective, both with regard to Plato's philosophy and his other works. Moreover, the theme, purpose, and significance of the work are carefully examined. Friedländer opens with a contrast of the *Gorgias* and *Thrasymachus* and a demonstration of how Gorgias, the man, represents sophistic rhetoric. The *Gorgias* is dramatistically presented, he observes, with minimal symbolic background, sophistic oratory being the primary subject matter. Friedländer next contrasts the *Gorgias* with the *Protagoras* and elaborates upon the dialogue proper. Carefully observing Gorgias' definitions of rhetoric and art Friedländer concludes that Gorgias had an elevated and exaggerated sense of self and an imprecise concept of rhetoric. Socrates, too, observes Gorgias' shallowness and considers oratory limited as "it does not deal with areas of life in which experts are competent and ... rhetoric can make no claim to knowledge." Moreover, Socrates attacks rhetoric on several levels established by Gorgias' blundering replies to Socrates' premises. In addition, Friedländer reviews argument by argument Socrates' attack on sophistic oratory found in the *Gorgias*. He points out that the dialogue establishes a vision of moral principles and of different ways of life combined with an ideal rhetoric aimed at making good citizens.

A more recent investigation demonstrates the self-referential quality of the *Gorgias*; that is, it demonstrates through the words and actions of the principal characters the nature and defects of sophistic oratory. Adele Spitzer, "The Self-Reference of the *Gorgias*," contends that Gorgias, Polus, and Callicles are symbolic of the three branches of rhetoric evident in Athens. Gorgias is viewed as an exponent of an aesthetic rhetoric concerned with literary techniques and having no particular ends. Polus, whose rhetoric is polemic, is concerned with an ethical rhetoric as a "self-conscious study aware of its ability to gain wealth and power for practitioners." Callicles represents political rhetoric, the art of winning support. Socrates' successful refutation of the premises advanced by Gorgias suggests that rhetoric lacks true knowledge. Moreover, by defeating Polus, Plato argues that rhetoric cannot help a man attain his advantages, and through Callicles, rhetoricians are shown to be unjust and unable to make others just. Spitzer also illustrates how Plato, by contrasting the "lowly" Socrates against the supposed virtues and superior reputations of his adversaries, demonstrates the superiority of dialectic over rhetoric. Ever so subtlely, the characteristic each principal prizes most about himself evaporates as they fall victim to Socratic dialectic. Spitzer concludes her article by outlining the principles of the "true speaker statesman" (his speech, attitude, audience, and concept of self).

Jacqueline de Romilly develops the concept that Plato analogized sophistic rhetoric to magic, a comparison first developed in Gorgias' *Helen*. "Indeed, he returns to it over and over again, in order to cast discredit on the ways of the sophists." He insists that rhetoricians, like magicians employing deception; can make people believe in the existence of things which do not exist. Plato believed, for example, that when two sides of an issue are argued at least one side is illusionary. The comparison of rhetoric to magic is made in the *Euthydemus Republic, Phaedo, Protagoras, Menexenus, Sophist,* and *Politicus*. In addition, the *Gorgias,* while not specifically calling rhetoric magic, labels it as artless deception and compares it unfavorably to medicine. Somewhat surprisingly, Plato likens Socrates to a magician in the *Meno* and *Symposium*. Socrates' magic is not the sophists', however: "Whereas the magic of the sophists aimed at producing illusion, Socrates' magic rests on the obstinate destruction of all illusions." Thus, the confrontation of unyielding logic and deception arose. Gorgias represented the seductive (magical) quality of style, imagery, and the emotional arrangement of arguments, while Socrates stood for implacable truth generated by the power of reason and discussion. The article concludes with an analysis of the *Gorgias'* comparison of rhetoric to medicine, a proposition Socrates systematically discredits.

Edwin Black's "Plato's View of Rhetoric" contrasts, in the main, the *Gorgias* and *Phaedrus* and resolves conflicting opinions regarding (1) whether or not Plato had a unified theory of rhetoric, (2) principle notions of a true and sophistic rhetoric, and (3) the conduct of the true and sophistic rhetorician. Black observes that a major problem in resolving the apparently antithetical philosophical positions in the *Gorgias* and *Phaedrus* may be attributed to the former's satirical and refutative posture as opposed to the latter's poetic, constructive and affirmative judgments. Black further argues that the *Gorgias* is a refutative thematic dialogue aimed at refuting Gorgian rhetoric only, and that it concerns itself with ethics only in so far as it applies to rhetoric. The *Phaedrus'* speeches, Black contends, are rhetorical "courtship" addresses expressing Plato's counterpart of sophistical education. Moreover, the three specimen speeches can be taken as Plato's advice to audiences, or as a discussion of a speaker's moral attitude toward the speeches, or as divine and malign "madness". Black also examines several issues of Platonic epistemology as it applies to rhetoric. He concludes that Plato despised the rhetorical excesses of the sophists but recognized the value of rhetoric when properly applied. In addition, he advances the idea that Plato became entangled with questions of morality which strangled his theory of rhetoric.

The philosophic description of rhetoric eloquently delineated in the *Phaedrus* is taken up next. Of all the issues embodied in Plato's *Phaedrus* the most enduring question, perhaps, concerns the work's theme, whether it is unified or multi-leveled. One of the more articulate essays addressing itself to this issue is Paul Plass' "The Unity of the *Phaedrus.*" Because of the controversial nature of the *Phaedrus,* the author notes the necessity of explaining how Plato combined the numerous issues, devices, and ideas posed by the work; how, moreover, rhetoric and love are thematically reconciled and, by their symbolic unification, explained. At the outset, dialectic dialogue is recognized by Plass for its unequaled flexibility and capacity for simultaneously entertaining and interchanging diverse topics, thus explaining Plato's gifted synthesis of rhetoric and love. Plass' remarkable acumen with regard to interpreting the symbolic meaning of Socrates' speeches offers the reader a truly insightful understanding of Plato's conception of rhetoric. Plass sees the dialogue "held together by the movement of Plato's thought toward progressively greater insight into what is really involved in rhetoric." He sees rhetoric as a magic "conjuring" with souls, demonstrated by Plato's vivid and erotic *mania.* Moreover, Plass addresses himself to nearly every issue generated in the *Phaedrus,* including the speeches, divine madness, writing versus speaking, divine audiences, characteristics of the true rhetorician, Lysian oratory, style, *paideia,* the central myth, words, and the erotic nature of rhetoric.

Another issue raised by the *Phaedrus* is the function of the non-lover, introduced first in the opening passages of the work. Stanley Rosen "The Non-Lover in Plato's *Phaedrus*," sees the beginning of the *Phaedrus* returning the reader to the *Symposium*, its setting directly antithetical to the *Phaedrus* in mood, atmosphere, sobriety, and purpose. Moreover, the speakers in the *Symposium* lack divine madness and as a result *Eros* fails to transcend philosophy. In addition, Socrates' speech fails to convert auditors to philosophy and

Alcibiades, the object of his attention, appears barely responsive. Another important distinction between the works is that the *Symposium*'s speeches are delivered as a consequence of *Eros* whereas the speeches in the *Phaedrus* are addressed to the writing of speeches about love. Rosen develops his thesis regarding the non-lover by a close analysis of Phaedrus, the individual, and Plato. The initial evaluation of Lysias' speech contrasts Phaedrus, who wishes to memorize Lysias' speeches, and Socrates, who prefers merely to listen to them. Rosen suggests that Plato began the work with Lysias' speech in order to indicate the defective nature of the *Symposium*. Moreover, he sees the Non-lover taking pride in his autonomy and industrious efficiency, devoting his energies to the benefit of the lover, and acting as a humanist. The relationship of the lover and non-lover to divine madness and rhetoric is developed also.

The *Phaedrus* is further examined by Malcolm Brown and James Coulter in their essay "The Middle Speech of Plato's *Phaedrus.*" The authors suggest solutions to two problem questions generated by the *Phaedrus*: (1) Is the middle speech faulty or merely a bridge to Socrates' final address? (2) Is the *Phaedrus* unified through a connection between eros and rhetoric? In addition, they address the proposition that Plato sketches a particular kind of rhetorical sophist, best identified with Isocratean thought. The middle speech is believed to occupy, they tell us, "a middle position between those speeches of Lysias and Plato conceptually as well in the structure of the dialogue," whose speaker is an educator with rhetoric as his medium. Moreover, the organization, content and philosophy of the particulars reflect Isocrates. Specifically, the speaker's ambiguity regarding the genus of love, the absence of Plato's *logistikon* as a ruling element of the soul, unPlatonic descriptions of *ousia*, the relationship of accurate knowledge and *philosophia,* and compositional strategies including *amphiboly* and double *entendre* are offered as proof of the proposition. Also advanced are the several reasons why love was not chosen simply as a companion theme to advance an elucidation of rhetoric. The authors conclude by locating generically the character of the middle speaker.

The sophistic rhetorician disdained by Plato in the *Phaedrus* is reasoned by R. L. Howland to be Isocrates. In his "The Attack on Isocrates in the *Phaedrus*," Howland illustrates how Plato argued that Isocrates' reputation was at best unmerited and misleading. Isocrates, of course, saw rhetoric as the fundamental cornerstone of education and citizenship, a position which Plato attacked in the *Protagoras* and *Gorgias*. Isocrates was not one to ignore such attacks, however. In the introduction to Isocrates' *Helen* there appears what is believed to be direct slaps at Plato. "The whole dialogue must be considered primarily as a direct and comprehensive attack on the educational system of Isocrates, in which Isocrates' own words and methods ... are turned against himself." The arguments include the issues of written and spoken discourse, the pleasures of discourse, *techne,* definition, and the worth of rhetorical discourse.

V. Tejera examines "Irony and Allegory in the *Phaedrus."* His essay is not confined, however, to stylistic nuances but entails the relationship of rhetoric to philosophy, dialectic, and writing. Lysias' speech, under Tejera's scrutiny, is visibly sophistic and not philosophic. The speech is considered deceitful and impious by Socrates, an offense against God. In Socrates' first speech, which opens with a purifying palinode to offset the effects of Lysias' speech and Socrates' criticism of it, he "expatiates with wit but not without reverence." Both speeches of Socrates are analyzed for their ironic and allegorical qualities, especially with regard to "normal" madness and formless essence. Tejera sees Socrates entreating Phaedrus to become a philosophical lover, and not a pretender to rhetoric such as Lysias, who he characterizes as a rhetorical speaker and an insincere lover. Socrates' critique of speaking and writing is, Tejera suggests, directed at poor utterance, not speaking or writing themselves. Arguments such as (1) "knowledge does not guarantee persuasiveness," (2) "speakers must distinguish between similarities and differences," (3) "rhetoric must begin with clear ideas," and (4) "rhetoric must be organized," are explored. Moreover, dialectic's relationship to rhetoric is scrutinized since Plato suggests that it encompasses nearly all of rhetoric. The importance of dialectic is further underscored by Socrates' insistance that without a knowledge of dialectic a proper definition of rhetoric cannot be achieved. Phaedrus, entranced by Socrates' innovative approach to rhetoric, inquires where one might acquire such training in rhetoric. Socrates defers mentioning himself by detailing the requirements of a prospective rhetor. Pericles, however, is cited as a contemporary example of an outstanding orator, an aside which Tejera concludes was made strictly in the context of "greatness." In the *Gorgias,* for example, Pericles illustrates that "the successful politician cannot, in the nature of the case, practice the true science of rhetoric because his rhetoric does not serve the true art and science of statesmanship." The author concludes with a discussion of writing and its ironic and allegoric qualities.

The "living creature" image developed in the *Phaedrus* is investigated by Floyd Anderson and Ray Anderson in "Plato's Conception of *Dispositio.*" The essay observes first that scholars have traditionally envisioned the living creature image as a formalized schema of *dispositio* or as a declaration in behalf of "organic unity" of rhetorical and literary composition. The authors believe that these prevailing interpretations are essentially incorrect. "Rather, Plato's 'living creature' analogy alludes to a deeper, philosophical-psychological notion of rhetorical form." For Plato, *dispositio* aids men in obtaining right opinion and persuades them according to the make-up of their souls. The Andersons note that Platonic rhetoric requires the orator to be a philosopher, psychologist, and dialectician capable of practicing the "art of deception" so as to avoid blinding the ignorant when confronting them with truth. The authors add that while Socrates' second speech evidences an introduction, body, and conclusion, its arrangement pattern is a philosophical-psychological knowledge of rhetorical exigencies and not a reflection of close adherance to an artificial system of *dispositio.* Moreover, the "living creature" image encompasses a broader context than spatial representation; the *dispositio* of rhetorical discourse corresponds to an auditor's soul. The authors conclude by drawing comparisons between the "living creature" image and the "winged charioteer" figure. The winged charioteer represents reason reigning two steeds, one symbolizing the will and the other passion. Thus, the "living creature" image implies that discourse must adapt to the auditor's soul, for only then can reason guide "those parts of the soul which are in the beast."

William G. Kelley, Jr., examines "Rhetoric as Seduction," evident in Plato's *Phaedrus* and *Symposium.* These works develop a sophisticated notion of erotic communication, one analogous to "love sharing" or love-making, achieved as one approaches truth. Kelley examines this sex-talk relationship and concludes that Plato saw communication as an erotic encounter. At the *Symposium*'s banquet, for instance, Socrates announces wistfully a wish to speak of love; he flatters his host and expresses a desire for an intercourse of wisdom with Agathon. Pausanias' speech also elucidates the sexual nature of communication, a rhetoric analogous to courtship. The strongest evidence, Kelley believes, is Alcibiades' appearance at the banquet and his drunken protestation that Socrates has usurped the sitting space immediately adjacent to Agathon. Alcibiades accuses Socrates of accomplishing with words the compelling acts of the satyr. "There is no clearer statement of the link between rhetoric and seduction in the *Symposium* than this analogy between Socrates' eloquence and the satyr's cunning." The *Phaedrus* is fraught with illusions to an erotic theory of rhetorical communication. The work opens erotically with Socrates sexually aroused by the presence of Phaedrus and the setting symbolizing numerous sexual matters. Early on, both seduction and the thesis that lovers are preferable to non-lovers are pursued. In addition, both Lysias' and Socrates' first speech are flagrant and sarcastic arguments against rhetoric as seduction. The second speech bespeaks the erotic nature of communication, particularly in the winged charioteer figure. Kelly concludes that "seductive rhetoric is . . . insidious for it arises from a philosophical stance endorsing deceit or shame, . . . it loves the body and not the soul, it seeks and creates the ephemeral and not that which endures."

Wayne N. Thompson's essay, "The *Symposium*: A Neglected Source for Plato's Ideas on Rhetoric," examines rhetorical theory developed in the *Symposium*. Essentially, Thompson supports the conclusions that (1) the *Phaedrus* insists on truth, (2) the *Symposium*'s theories of rhetorical arrangement and content correspond to Aristotle's, (3) Plato's theory of *inventio* is consistent with those of later Athenian rhetoricians, and (4) the Socrates-Diotima address is Plato's example of an ideal speech. The contest of ideas between Socrates and the sophists is also present in the *Symposium*. Thompson observes, for example, that Agathon's speech is a rhetorical masterpiece by sophistic standards. In the *Symposium*, like the *Phaedrus*, Socrates discredits sophistic rhetoric for its inability to achieve truth and, following a critical dialogue, offers advice on speech writing. Moreover, Thompson examines Plato's theory of arrangement for the speech of praise, invention, style, enthymemes, and the qualities of the ideal speaker.

Glenn R. Morrow's "Plato's Conception of Persuasion," addresses the question of how rhetoric might have served the Republic Morrow suggests, contrary to some, that Plato not only distinguished the ideal rhetorician from the sophistic, but advocated using his skills in molding human nature. And, by an examination of the *Laws,* he argues that Plato's theory of "enchantment" may bring "about conformity to the laws, not merely in the public relations of citizen to citizen, but in all details, even the most intimate, of private life." Moreover, Morrow notes that Plato distinguished between compulsion by force and by conviction, the latter achieved by persuasion. In Plato's *Republic,* for instance, it would be necessary to frequently re-affirm each citizen's beliefs lest they question their expected role and the social order. Thus, rhetoric, as enunciated in the *Phaedrus,* was valuable to the philosopher.

William Pfeiffer explores the concept of "True and False Speech in Plato's *Cratylus* 385 B-C." The passage does not deal, as previously assumed, with sentences or the independent existence of true and false names. Rather, the work articulates a correspondence theory of truth for discourse and names spoken within the context of uttered speech. Pfeiffer demonstrates that "Truth is no longer something the attainment of which is physically outside the sphere of human competence, and dependent on the disclosure of things in regions thought of as being elsewhere in space and time; but rather it is present in the things that are to be discovered by the powers of the intellect operating here and now, and to be expressed in utterances which can be evaluated in terms of their correspondence with the things that are available to all men." Like other works of Plato, the *Cratylus* attempts to disassociate truth and falsity from rhetoric, a view holding truth and falsity as characteristics of uttered discourse. The article concludes with a discussion of man's propensity to say a name falsely rather than truely, contending that such behavior is discourse specific and incapable of independent occurence.

Stephen Skousgaard asks the question: "Genuine Speech *vs.* Chatter: A Socratic Problematic? " Shedding new light on the role of language and philosophy within a political community, the author contrasts the genuine speech of Socratic dialogues with sophistic oratory. Skousgaard sees the Platonic dialogue as a ritual having a two-fold effect. In the *Apology*, for instance, Socrates' self-examination through dialogue constitutes his wisdom and the corruptness of the Athenian community. Socrates, in effect, employs dialogue as deliberative rhetoric. "As such it is genuine speech; dialogue is the new speech form for order because it is through this linguistic *activity* that Socrates constitutes himself as wise . . . . Dialogue by its very essence is a political act." Skousgaard believes that in the *Apology* dialogue is on trial, with rhetoric as its accuser; the trial is to decide what constitutes genuine speech. Socrates appeals to the judges to listen to dialogue (wisdom and order) and to cast from their consciousness rhetoric (base and foul), the language of disorder. Socrates' decision to take hemlock, Skousgaard believes, forced the judges into the open which allowed a political victory and a victory for dialogue as a new literary genre. The *Euthydemus* also supports this distinction with its enunciation as to whether the philosopher or rhetorician should teach the young. Again, dialogue and oratory as ways of life are contrasted, the two sophistic brothers who aim to confute, and Socrates, who wishes to lead youth to wisdom. Moreover, Skousgaard notes that the trial of Socrates is a "grim reminder of the corruption resulting from the community's acceptance of rhetoric over dialogue." The *Gorgias,* which has especial political import regarding the corruption of speech, is also examined for evidence of the author's thesis.

The concluding article is Morriss Henry Partee's "Plato on the Rhetoric of Poetry" which examines the rejection of poetry from the Republic because of its alleged ability to obfuscate truth. Plato believed that poetry cannot legitimately express human values, only imitate them. He therefore analogized the poet to the sophist since both use stylistic devices calling attention to their literary creations. Literary poets and logographers, he tells us, engage merely in word games. Although Plato identifies writing with eloquent speaking and its attendant disadvantages, it is, at best, an echo of verbal communication. The poet's problem lies with the inherently seductive power of language "which interferes with both philosophical activity and true poetic response." In sum, Partee interrelates Plato's theories of language, poetry, and rhetoric.

The combined impact of the aforementioned articles is not insignificant. The extensive scholarship and frequently astounding acumen demonstrated by the authors provide the reader with an exceptional view of Plato's theory of rhetoric and its relationship to dialectic, love, truth, poetry, sophistry, and philosophy. The articles are not always easily read, but they are consistently revealing, provocative, and insightful investigations of the ancient world's most intriguing theory of rhetoric. This anthology, however, does not supplant the reading of Plato's works in the original, for only by their examination may the beauty and eloquence of his thought be appreciated.

THE GROWTH OF PLATO'S PERCEPTION OF RHETORIC*

Rollin W. Quimby

Much has been written about Plato's attitude toward rhetoric, and the majority of writers have believed that Plato disdained it throughout his life. Everett Lee Hunt asserted that Plato's treatment of rhetoric was based on his dislike of Athenian culture in general and the Sophists in particular. Hunt dismissed the ideal rhetoric described in the *Phaedrus* as being "as far from the possibilities of mankind as his Republic was from Athens."[1] G. M. A. Grube also reported Plato's antipathy toward rhetoric. He did think, however, that Plato's program for teaching his ideal rhetoric was "not impractical, and rhetoricians could follow it for some way, at least," if they also mastered philosophy.[2]

Neither did Oscar L. Brownstein interpret the description of an ideal rhetoric as an endorsement. To him the definition was simply dialectics broadened "to subsume the whole area of scientific human discourse, not rhetoric expanded to include dialectics." Nothing could persuade Plato to endorse rhetoric because his objections "are as fundamental as his objections to poetry, and for much the same reasons — by his standards of truth they both lie."[3]

In contrast to the above, Edwin Black developed the thesis that Plato favored rhetoric when it was properly used. In presenting his argument, Black stated a major problem of accurately interpreting Plato's opinion of rhetoric. "We discover what troubles the commentators the moment we compare the *Gorgias* with the *Phaedrus*: the former, satirical, contentious, and refutative, the latter emerging with a constructive, affirmative judgment clothed in the most

---

*Reprinted by permission. *Philosophy and Rhetoric,* 7 (1974), 71-79.
 1. Everett Lee Hunt, "Plato and Aristotle on Rhetoric and Rhetoricians," *Studies in Rhetoric and Public Speaking in Honor of James Albert Winans* (New York, 1962), p. 42.
 2. G. M. A. Grube, *Plato's Thought* (London, 1958), p. 215.
 3. Oscar L. Brownstein, "Plato's *Phaedrus*: Dialectic as the Genuine Art of Speaking," *Quarterly Journal of Speech,* 51 (1965), 392-398.

majestic poetry.... Have we here irreconcilably contradictory views of rhetoric expressed by the same author? ... The commentators have responded by maintaining either that Plato changed his mind or his definition of rhetoric."[4] The remainder of Black's essay supports his thesis that Plato was opposed only to incompetent rhetoricians, not to the art itself.

Most writers have focused their attention on the *Gorgias* and *Phaedrus*, which contain Plato's lengthiest statements on rhetoric and which include seeming differences of opinion that must be denied or explained. Most have not examined Plato's statements about rhetoric in other dialogues. Plato wrote dialogues throughout his adult life, and "it would certainly be curious if there was no point on which Plato's views were developed, modified, or even perhaps changed altogether in the course of that long period."[5] The development of Plato's thought and method on other subjects has been profitably noted. For example, his abandonment of eristic for a theory of ideas, the disappearance of Socrates, and changes of style and emphasis are thought to demarcate the progressive, general changes in Plato's thought.

Plato was first interested in rhetoric because it was the Sophists' method and substance for inculcating the qualities of virtue and leadership in their disciples; and Plato was concerned about the development of virtuous leaders. Several of his early dialogues probe the nature and teachableness of virtue. The *Euthydemus* (c. 390 B.C.) shows the opinions Plato expressed at this stage. In this dialogue, Socrates told Crito of the time he and his young friend, Clinias, had talked with two sophists who were well known as teachers of rhetoric and the arts of war. The sophists said rhetoric and war were

---

4. Edwin Black, "Plato's View of Rhetoric," *Quarterly Journal of Speech*, 44 (1958), 362-363. Footnotes for the passage identify a number of scholars who held this view.

5. Guy C. Field, *Plato and His Contemporaries*, 3rd ed. (London and New York, 1967), p. 57.

6. Exact dates of the dialogues are impossible to determine, but there is general agreement on which works belong to the early, middle, and late periods, and such considerations as those noted here figure strongly in these determinations. See Grube, pp. xi-xiii; Field, ch. V; Richard S. Bluck, *Plato's Life and Thought* (London, 1949), chs. I-IV. For a book-length discussion of the growth of Plato's ideas and methods, see Gilbert Ryle, *Plato's Progress* (Cambridge, 1966).

secondary with them for they now taught virtue, a claim which made Socrates incredulous. Throughout the dialogue, the sophists "proved" their assertions with false arguments consisting of loose word play, shifting definitions, and irrelevant analogies. By this process they arrived at the position that there were no such things as falsehoods or ignorance.[7] Socrates was perplexed. "If there is no such thing as error in deed, word or thought, then what, in the name of goodness, do you come hither to teach?" (287).

Socrates insisted that a student should seek for knowledge which would do him good (288E). He must learn both the subject and how to use it beneficially.[8] Having established his criteria, Socrates asked if one could become happy by learning to compose speeches (298C). Clinias thought not, for there were skillful theorists who could not deliver acceptable speeches and worthy performers who must ask logographers to compose their orations (289D). Socrates agreed, and added that "composers of speeches . . . always appear to me to be very extraordinary men . . . and this art of theirs is lofty and divine" because it was part of the great art of enchantment which charmed and pacified large assemblies of men (289D-290).

The talk now turns to a search for the highest art. It is tentatively decided that all other arts render up control of their "products" to the royal (governing) art, for it was the only one which can use them. While exploring this idea, Socrates states that each art has a supreme authority in its own field; e.g., medicine produces health, and husbandry supplies the fruits of the earth. The art of statecraft, therefore, ought to be useful in something and ought to confer some good.

After Socrates has finished his account of the conversation, Crito

---

7. The Sophists' absurdities read like a parody of logic. Jowett believed that Plato was caricaturing arguments expressed more subtly and plausibly by certain philosophers. Benjamin Jowett, *The Dialogues of Plato: Translated into English with Analyses and Introductions,* 4th ed. (Oxford, 1953), I, 200. Except where noted, quotations are from this edition. To reduce the number of footnotes, Stephanus numbers are inserted into the text.

8. According to Field, pp. 98-99, the Greek word for "good" had various meanings, but none of them included moral obligation. The reference was to a purpose — good for something — "and the task of moral philosophy is the development and refinement of this idea." I have added the word "beneficially" because, as we shall see, Plato included that dimension of "good" as a distinction between true and false art.

tells of hearing a logographer denounce philosophers as drivelers and philosophy as naught (304E-305C). Socrates replies that such men are on the border line between philosophers and statesmen. They believe themselves wiser than either, yet if one ranks between something good and something bad, he will be less than the first and more than the second. In this case, if a man has only *parts* of philosophy and statecraft he will be less than either the philosopher or the statesman. The dialogue draws to an end with Socrates' observation that in every profession the inferior sort are numerous and good for nothing, while the good are few and priceless. Gymnastics, rhetoric, the acquisition of wealth and the military arts are all noble; the presence of inferior performers should not lead one to shun these pursuits (307).

In the *Euthydemus* Socrates opposes the Sophists not because they teach rhetoric, but because they expound an erroneous philosophy and hold an inflated opinion of their ability to improve mankind. Although Socrates denies that rhetoric is a true art (because there is little correlation between those who study it and those who can practice it) he includes rhetoric among the subjects worthy of attention despite the inferiority of its adherents.

The *Protagoras,* written about the same time as the *Euthydemus,* contains Plato's inquiry into sophistry and into men's ability to teach such things as virtue and wisdom. Rhetoric is mentioned only because it is central to the work of the Sophists. Socrates notes that men who desire to learn medicine or sculpture study under physicians or sculptors. He questions Hippocrates about the subjects his prospective teacher, Protagoras, could teach as a Sophist. Hippocrates replies that Protagoras knows wise things. Socrates asks which branch of wisdom and which arts Protagoras knows. The art that makes men eloquent, says Hippocrates. Eloquent in what? Something which the Sophist understood. What is that? Hippocrates does not know (312).

When they arrive at the house where Protagoras is staying and ask him to explain the benefits of studying under him, Protagoras declares that Hippocrates will become better every day, for he will learn prudence in both private and public affairs and will be able to speak and act powerfully in matters of state (316B-C, 318). Socrates expresses doubt that anyone can teach virtuous citizenship or the art of governance, as the experience of Pericles shows (319D-E). Protagoras holds a contrary view. Certain things can be taught by anyone. Children learn to speak Greek from adults in general, not teachers (328). All men reprove, chide or reprimand others in order to teach them. Rational punishment is not given to change past wrongs, but to correct future behavior (323-324B). In presenting his opinions, Protagoras expresses a subjective view of truth, relating it to belief Socrates rejects this line of thought, as always.

Rhetoric is never the direct object of discussion in the *Protagoras*; Plato's attitudes toward rhetoric appear only incidentally. For example, Protagoras sometimes states his ideas in long persuasive speeches and the rhetorical method makes Socrates uncomfortable. After a lengthy answer by Protagoras, Socrates says *he* could not express himself in that form. If the audience wishes the discourse to continue, it "must ask him [Protagoras] to shorten his answers and keep to the point, as he did at first if not, what sort of thing is our discussion to be? For discussion is one thing, and making an oration is quite another (336B). Socrates' objection ultimately leads to an agreement that discussion will follow his dialectical method (338D). This is Plato's only direct criticism of rhetoric in the *Protagoras*. It has no significant bearing on the outcome of the dialogue, for Protagoras holds his ground even in the new format. Socrates himself admits that the argument ends in a draw (361).[9] Here, then, certain rhetorical practices are indirectly criticized but not rhetoric itself.

Another brief glimpse of Plato's attitude toward rhetoric is found in the *Meno,* possibly written in 387 following his first visit to Sicily.[10] In the *Meno* Plato continues his inquiry into whether or not virtue could be acquired by instruction and practice. Socrates' first speech contains a reference to Gorgias as the philosopher who taught the Thessalonians wisdom and the habit of "answering questions in the grand and bold style which is natural to those who know, and may be expected from one who is ready to be questioned on any subject by any Hellene, and answer all comers" (70B). The context and the subsequent argument give the words an ironic tone. More-

---

9. The longer speeches of Protagoras contain accepted rhetorical arrangements and other devices for achieving audience acceptance, yet they do not always answer Plato's questions. This could be an implied criticism of rhetoric, but if so, the charge is never expressed and Protagoras' longest speech *is* a direct reply to Socrates. Furthermore, before beginning the speech, Protagoras offers to cast his thoughts in the form of a myth or to argue out the question (320C).
10. Bluck, p. 72.

over, Plato immediately charges that Gorgias' definition of virtue was a mere list of types (72). But no more did Plato approve of philosophers who gave impromptu answers in a grand style to questions on every subject, as the *Euthydemus* and *Protagoras* make clear.

Later in the *Meno* after Anytus has declared angrily that the Sophists are unworthy of teaching virtue to public leaders, Socrates asks who, then, should be the teachers of future governors. Step by step he leads the others to the position that Athens' great leaders did not act out of wisdom or knowledge, but out of inspiration. They were not philosophically knowledgeable men, but divines and prophets. Virtue, at least in governance, is an instinct given by the gods to certain men. Since it is not accompanied by reason it is unteachable. This is why such leaders as Pericles could not impart greatness to others (99-100).

Rhetoric is again an undefined, peripheral topic mentioned only because its practitioners claim to make men wise. Plato's criticisms are not criticisms of rhetoric itself, but of Gorgias and his like. The situation is much like that in the *Protagoras*: persons and specific methods, not an art, are negatively criticized.

It can be argued from these dialogues written before the *Gorgias* that Plato held a temperate opinion of rhetoric. It might not fully qualify as an art, but it was worthy of attention. Plato was annoyed at the unnecessary verbosity of the Sophists, and he chided them for concealing their lack of answers to his questions in copious language and irrelevant thoughts; yet the fault is not attributed to rhetoric but to the speakers' defective philosophy and ignorance of the dialectical method. That he finally allows Protagoras to reply briefly and to the point indicates that Plato did not believe men trained in rhetoric *must* have the failings he was criticizing.

Plato probably wrote the *Gorgias* after his return from Sicily, when he was preparing to settle down to administer his academy.[11] Rhetoric is again a side issue, even though the subject takes up a good deal of the dialogue. The arguments for and against rhetoric are used to further an examination of more fundamental concerns such as justice, political leadership, and atonement. Socrates opens the discussion by asking Gorgias and his disciple, Polus, for a definition of rhetoric. Their meaningless replies are unsatisfactory, so Socrates leads the others to a deeper consideration of the nature of rhetoric.

---

11. Bluck, pp. 75, 79; Field, p. 74.

During the process, Socrates utters opinions already expressed in the *Protagoras* and *Meno*. He observes that Gorgias has taught Polus to make speeches but not to answer questions, and as with Protagoras he insists that Gorgias confine himself to brief statements. Gorgias readily agrees, for he conceives the ability to be terse a part of his professional skill (449C).

In the section that follows, Socrates resumes his stance that rhetoric has no subject of its own and he repeats earlier analogies to cobblers, physicians, and artists. But now Socrates does not say that rhetoric is worthy of study, nor does he excuse its faults by assigning apparent defects to substandard practioners. As all know, Socrates defines rhetoric as a practical skill in flattery, something less than an art, an ignoble technique. Rhetoric, says Socrates, is ignoble because it is bad for society and it is not an art because "it cannot give any account of the nature of the things it offers ., . . and so cannot explain the reason why it is offered" (465).

This descriptive, preliminary definition and the long exploration of its ramifications is Plato's strongest condemnation of rhetoric and rhetoricians. Governors, orators, and the courts are all criticized, and rhetoric is the means by which men are led astray. Yet the passage which excoriates rhetoric most harshly also contains hints that Plato has glimpsed the possibility of a "good" rhetoric. This is the change that makes the *Gorgias* more than a lengthy repetition of his previous position.[12]

The groundwork is laid in sections 500-503 in which Socrates demonstrates that many arts have counterparts often mistaken for the arts themselves. Cookery, he says, "is only a practical skill, and not an art at all; whereas medicine [dietetics is the modern speciality] is an art" because the latter must consider "the nature of the patient and the reason for the treatment it gives him" (501). The cook can disregard the effect of food upon the body as long it is flatters the

---

12. Ryle, pp. 206-207, believes that the appearance of a positive position represents an advance in Plato's philosophical journey. "Plato was beginning, for example in the *Gorgias*, to be aware of the differences between arguing against an answerer and arguing against an *impasse*; between trying to rebut an opponent and arguing something out with oneself; between winning a battle of wits and solving a problem. . . . The notion of a valid argument is just beginning to separate itself off from the notion of an unrebutted argument." Plato was now prepared to introduce "systematized argument, that is dialectic, into philosophy." The shift from eristic to dialectic is the subject of Chapter II.

palate. In short, arts benefit society, while similar but lesser techniques only flatter men's desires.

The application of this principle begins with Socrates' assertion that the "true rhetorician" attempts to implant every virtue and remove every vice from men's souls (504E). It is Socrates first use of the phrase, and it implies a "true rhetoric" that might qualify as an art. The acknowledgment comes in 517 where Socrates uses the phrase, "the true art of rhetoric not the flattering form of it."

The requirement that an art must benefit mankind had appeared in earlier dialogues; here the division of rhetoric into a true and a flattering form seems to clear the way for a complete definition that includes all forms of verbal persuasion and indicates the unique subject matter of true rhetoric. The definition was not given, possibly because some perplexities remained in Plato's mind. The former suspicion that a true rhetoric could not be taught had not been removed, and Socrates denies that the true form of rhetoric can be found in society. When Callicles asserts that "there are some public leaders who have a real care of the public in what they say," Socrates replies, "but you have never known such a rhetoric; or if you have, and can point out any rhetorician who is of this stamp, who is he?" (503). Callicles admits that no living orators meet the stipulation, and Socrates refutes his claims for such past orators as Pericles. Thus, the *Gorgias* ends on an uncertain note. Plato's expression of the nature and benefits of rhetoric is still incomplete.

The uncertainty was ended some seventeen years later when Plato wrote the *Phaedrus*.[13] In this dialogue Socrates talks of rhetoric as an art and while doing so he reviews several previous contentions. Lysias' oration and Socrates' first speech justify the charge that orators mislead audiences by clothing errors in charming language or by omitting the definitions necessary as guides along the path toward truth. Ignorant speakers recite popular beliefs as support for their ideas and thereby convince ignorant listeners that they speak truth (260). No rhetorician can express truth until he has learned it himself (259E-260C, 262-262C). The persuasive techniques taught by Sophists as the art of rhetoric are only preliminaries, not the art itself (267-269B).

Having thus reviewed his previous complaint against rhetoric as

---

13. The estimate of Reginald Hackforth, *Plato's Phaedrus: translated with Introduction and Commentary* (London, 1952), pp. 3-7.

conceived and practiced in his day, Plato explains what changes are needed to bring improvement. To become a good (or true) rhetorician, one must have innate ability, knowledge and practice (269D). "All the great arts need supplementing by a study of Nature," Socrates begins, and he continues by once more likening rhetoric to medicine. "In both cases there is a nature that we have to determine, the nature of the body in one, and of the soul in the other, if we mean to be scientific and not content with mere empirical routine when we apply medicine and diet to induce health and strength, or words and rules of conduct to implant such convictions as we desire" (270-270B).[14] Rhetoricians, orators and other persuaders must learn and use dialectics to determine the types of soul, the various ways they are affected, and the type of speech appropriate to each situation, for the function of oratory is to influence men's soul (269D, 270-271D). There is no easier way, but an intelligent man should train himself to please good and noble masters (272-274).

Plato had now revealed all the elements of a true rhetoric. Rhetoric is the art by which leaders who discern the truth guide men toward the good. It is as though Plato at last understood the nature of rhetoric and its place in human affairs and could replace his earlier tentative and inconclusive observations with a coherent statement. Plato did not fully comprehend the nature and function of rhetoric earlier because to examine rhetoric he must first isolate it from such other social activities as government and education, and this was impossible until he had perfected the dialectical method of collection and division.

The *Phaedrus* plainly shows the application of Plato's mature use of dialectic to rhetoric.[15] For the first time Plato collected the observed elements of rhetoric into the general definition (the art of influencing the soul through words in all types of speaking) that is vaguely touched upon in the *Gorgias* (453D-454). He then repeated

---

14. Hackforth's translation.
15. W. C. Hembold and W. S. Holther, *The Unity of the Phaedrus*, Univ. of Cal. Publ. in Classical Philology, vol. 14, no. 9 (Univ. of Cal. Press, 1952), p. 405. Hackforth, p. 9 writes that two purposes for composing the *Phaedrus* were to propose a reformed rhetoric and to demonstrate the dialectical method.
16. Hackforth, p. 11. Ryle, p. 262, hypothesizes that Plato wrote the *Phaedrus* to announce that his academy was going to teach rhetoric in competition with Isocrates' school. The prepatory work would be arduous, but the students would speak and write well once they learned to think.

his division of rhetoric into true and false types. This division allowed Socrates to assign the observed evils to sham rhetoric and to see clearly the benefits of true rhetoric. Having determined the nature of true rhetoric, Plato could describe its unique and useful subject matter (the nature of the soul and the ways of influencing it for the better) and thereby qualify rhetoric as an art akin to dialectic. Instead of merely castigating rhetoric, he was now ready to harness it in the service of philosophy and truth.[16]

The *Phaedrus* is sometimes regarded as a sequel to the *Gorgias* because the *Gorgias* contains some preliminary statements of ideas more fully developed in the *Phaedrus*. It might be better to think of the *Gorgias* as a transition, a bridge, a way station between Plato's earlier, half-puzzled observations and the rounded theory found in the *Phaedrus,* for it is in the *Phaedrus* that the perplexities of twenty years are cleared away. Plato did not vacillate between praise and blame of rhetoric. He unfolded a theory as it developed in his mind.

THE RELATION OF THE *APOLOGY OF SOCRATES* TO GORGIAS' *DEFENSE OF PALAMEDES* AND PLATO'S CRITIQUE OF GORGIANIC RHETORIC*

By James A. Coulter

Τεισίαν δὲ Γοργίαν τε ἐάσομεν εὕδειν, οἳ πρὸ τῶν ἀληθῶν τὰ εἰκότα εἶδον ὡς τιμητέα μᾶλλον ...

(*Phaedrus* 267a)

ῥήτορος δὲ (ἀρετὴ) τἀληθῆ λέγειν.

(*Apology* 18a)

I

The existence of clear verbal parallels discernible in Gorgias' *Defense of Palamedes* and Plato's *Apology of Socrates* raises a problem which has occasioned only little scholarly notice.[1] What is more important,

---

*Reprinted by permission of the publishers from *Harvard Studies in Classical Philology*, 68, Cambridge, Massachusetts: Harvard University Press, © 1964 by the President and Fellows of Harvard College.

The present study is the first chapter, in a much revised form, of my doctoral dissertation, which was written under the direction of Eric A. Havelock. To this scholar I owe a debt of gratitude, both for his help in the initial stages of my research and for his careful reading of this final version. The study has also been read beneficially by Prof. J. H. Finley of Harvard, and by my colleagues at Columbia, William M. Calder III and Charles H. Kahn.

1. I include here a bibliography, chronologically arranged, of all the works known to me in which there is some discussion of this problem.

W. von Christ and W. Schmid, *Geschichte der Griechischen Literatur*[6] (Munich 1912) I 675.

H. Gomperz, *Sophistik und Rhetorik* (Leipzig & Berlin 1912) 9-11.

J. Morr, "Die Entstehung der Platonischen Apologie," *Schriften der Deutschen Wissenschaftlichen Gesellschaft in Reichenberg*, Heft 5 (1929) 29-34.

it has received no really satisfactory interpretation. True, a number of scholars have recognized the imprint, both in matters of phrasing and rhetorical *topoi*, of Gorgias' *Palamedes* on the *Apology of Socrates*.[2] Yet, in spite of the curious implications of this presumed Platonic debt to Gorgias (curious at least in the light of Plato's attitude toward Gorgias and his rhetoric), only three scholars, Joseph Morr, Anton-Hermann Chroust, and Guido Calogero, have sought an explanation for these similarities, which are, I submit, far too precise, and, what is more important, far too pointed, in their implications to be reasonably accounted for by reference to the conventions of dicanic oratory.

In a succinct and important study, Joseph Morr[3] pointed to the verbal echoes in Plato, and concluded that they are conscious allusions to the Gorgianic work; by reminding the reader, Morr argued, of an earlier account of a wise man unjustly condemned, Plato endeavored to set Socrates against the larger backdrop of myth, and to enlarge thereby the meaning of his death. Essentially the same view was held by A. H. Chroust in a later study;[4] this scholar made a special contribution by suggesting that the conception of Palamedes

---

W. Schmid and O. Stählin, *Geschichte der Griechischen Literatur* I,3 (Munich 1940) 74.

K. Freeman, *The Pre-Socratic Philosophers*[3] (Oxford 1953) 363.

A. H. Chroust, *Socrates, Man and Myth* (London 1957) 216-218.

Guido Calogero, "Gorgias and the Socratic Principle *Neomo Sua Sponte Peccat,*" *JHS* 77 (1957) 12-17.

Of these, Chroust, Schmid, and Freeman merely observe that the Platonic *Apology* was influenced by Gorgias' work, without, however, instancing verbal similarities. Gomperz draws up an elaborate list of correspondences, but only in order to establish the priority (and so, he argues, the authenticity) of the *Palamedes*. Morr and Calogero, too, catalogue the similarities, but, in addition, attempt a serious interpretation of the evidence, reaching conclusions which I cannot, however, accept. Chroust also seeks to account for the similarities, but he does not engage in a careful examination of the text of the two works.

2. Since we can date neither the *Palamedes* nor the *Apology* with absolute certainty, the possibility exists that the situation is the reverse of that which has been universally assumed. But Schmid (above, n.1) 74, argues strongly for the influence of the *Palamedes* on Antiphon. This means, of course, that the speech cannot be dated later than 411. Eduard Schwartz, too, detects this influence (see *De Thrasymacho Chalcedonio*, Progr. Rostock [1892] 7-13 = *Gesammelte Schriften* 2 [Berlin 1956] 119-120).

3. Morr (above n. 1) 34.

4. Chroust (above, n.1) 216-218.

as the archetype of the dishonored philosopher was already current and accessible to Plato.[5] For Calogero[6] the parallels suggested that Gorgias was a philosophical mentor of Socrates, and the source of the famous doctrine, *nemo sua sponte peccat.*

A Platonic adaptation of the *Palamedes,* if it can be demonstrated, necessarily involves certain larger implications, which I shall consider

---

5. Chroust (above, n.1) 218-220. See also *hypothesis* of Isocrates *Busiris* in Isocrates *Orationes*[2], ed. F. Blass (Leipzig 1907) II lvii. The author of this hypothesis refers to a tradition that Euripides, in his *Palamedes*, castigated the Athenians for their execution of Socrates, using Palamedes as a mask for the philosopher from a fear of censure. This story is of course impossible on chronological grounds, but it may be based on an authentic tradition. Antisthenes, too, Dümmler argues ("Zum Herakles des Antisthenes," *Philologus* 50 [1890] 295) drew upon this conception in his *Archelaus.*

6. Calogero's study is the most important examination of this problem and demands careful attention. The foundation of Calogero's thesis is an analysis of the techniques of argumentation employed in the *Helen* and the *Palamedes*. From this analysis Calogero concludes that Gorgias has already worked out the ethical point of view which is implied in the Socratic formulation *nemo sua sponte peccat* and which later antiquity attributed to Socrates himself (Calogero, [above, n.1] 12-14). Socrates, however, although taking over this doctrine, sought at the same time to avoid certain immoral consequences to which this theory could lead if it were combined with persuasion indifferently used; his "remedy" was persuasion under the discipline of *dialogos* (p. 16). The many reminiscences in the Platonic *Apology* of the *Palamedes* are evidence for this debt, for Socrates, on the day of his trial, was still under the spell of Gorgias' ethical discovery and therefore worked many allusions to the *Palamedes* into the text of his defense (p. 15). Furthermore, Plato in his *Gorgias* introduces Gorgias into the dialogue, since once he had resolved to portray the philosophical position of his masters Socrates, he could not rightly omit a discussion of the "master of Socrates himself" (pp. 16-17). Lastly, certain indications in Xenophon support the thesis that there was an intimate connection between Socrates and Gorgias (pp. 15-16).

The foundations of Calogero's position in his analysis of the techniques of argument employed in the *Helen* and the *Palamedes*. In this, I think, Calogero has almost certainly overinterpreted the evidence. In the *Palamedes*, all that Gorgias has Palamedes say (and what is, after all, common sense) is that no one incurs all sorts of dangers and risks the possibility of ignominy without the prospect of some considerable advantage. As there were no conceivable advantages for Palamedes, his treachery is therefore unthinkable. That there should be a reward sufficient to offset dangers incurred is a notion easily understandable, even, as Palamedes says (16), to a man of moderate sense. How foolish, then, to deny this understanding to a man of Palamedes' wisdom. (It is therefore perverse to identify, as Calogero does (p. 14), προικα (*Pal.* 13) with εκων of the

at the conclusion of the present study. To this extent, Morr and Chroust were right when they sought some sort of general explanation for the similarities they had observed in the two texts. Nevertheless, Calogero, although his conclusions seem to me unacceptable, was, methodologically at least, on more secure ground when he attempted to relate the parallel elements in the two works to some

Socratic formulation; προικα clearly means here "without profit".) With regard to the *Helen*, it is true that Gorgias attempts to show that Helen did what was wrong because she had been compelled by *logos* to believe that it was right. Yet it seems to me important to keep in mind the chief emphasis of the work. The *Helen* is clearly more a boastful description of the power of rhetoric than a seriously analysis of moral behavior. It is of course possible that Socrates was deeply impressed by the moral implications of the *Helen*, even if these now seem to us secondary.

There are other considerations which make such a reconstruction unlikely. For even if we grant that Calogero's interpretation of the sense of these two works of Gorgias is entirely correct, there are certain chronological difficulties in the view that Gorgias is the source of Socrates' central ethical doctrine. Gorgias, as we know, came to Athens in 427. This consideration would force one to the remarkable conclusion that it was only at some time after 427, rather late in Socrates' life and at a point when he was already internationally known, that he began for the first time to expound the doctrine which was to be associated so intimately with his name and to bring into being that form of enquiry which later writers deemed so characteristically Socratic. This late date for so important a development seems to me most improbable; although, of course, it is not impossible. The evidence, however, of the *Clouds* (423), if evidence it is, suggests that already at a time when Socrates could not have long been acquainted with Gorgias, he was known, and well known, for his interest in dialectic.

Moreover, it is one thing to say that Socrates' defense should show some traces of Gorgias' ethical thought if Socrates had truly been a pupil of the Sophist. But can one believe that Socrates himself worked into his speech such an elaborate web of verbal allusion and adaptation of *topoi* of argument? This surely implies an act of homage ar respect far beyond what one may deem likely. It is odd, too, that Plato in composing the *Gorgias*, the very work which was intended to point to Socrates' debt to Gorgias, should nowhere have portrayed the Sophist as possessing the slightest familiarity with the doctrine which we are to believe is his own discovery. Moreover, and this seems to me conclusive, the clear sense of the whole portion of the dialogue in which Gorgias most prominently figures is that he possesses absolutely no worthwhile knowledge on the subject of right and wrong (*vid.* especially 462b-466a). If Calogero is correct, the *Gorgias* is an extraordinarily perverse bow to "the master of Socrates himself."

Lastly, the evidence of Xenophon is too vague to stand by itself. At any rate,

problem with which the two men had, or could have had, a common intellectual concern. It is this method which I propose to follow. For I shall try to show that the *Apology* embodies a rejection *in detail* of the particular assumptions upon which the *Palamedes* was built. In fact, the polemic relationship between the two works is so intimate that one may justly call the *Apology*, at least on one level of its complex meaning, an *Anti-Palamedes*.

Now, the proposition that the *Apology* represents, at least on one level of its meaning, an effort to subject one of the works of a leading Sophist to a fundamental critique by means of an adaptation with polemic intention is not in itself surprising in view of what we are otherwise familiar with in Plato's literary treatment of his contemporaries and immediate predecessors.[7] Moreover, the work we are discussing, apart from the notion of formal imitation, is marked by clear contrasts which Plato has Socrates draw between his own activities and those of the Sophists and rhetors.

The passage which most explicitly focuses this antithesis is 19d-20c, where Socrates unambiguously distinguishes himself from those teachers who make a claim to wisdom, and who impart this commodity for a fee. There is an ironic implication throughout that the claims to wisdom of Gorgias, Prodicus, and Hippias are more than a little naive and unfounded. In another passage (31d-e) Socrates declares that he purposely avoided an active role in politics because such participation would have involved a serious compromise of his beliefs; the necessary implication is that those who are active in politics continue successful and unscathed only because they gratify the whims of the *demos*. Among these, the rhetors are certainly to be numbered. Moreover, it seems reasonable to assume that

---

the passage in the Xenophontine *Apology* (26) might only mean that Xenophon, had read Plato's *Apology* and added, as his own piece of elaboration, the observation that even in his own time there were many *hβgvi* devoted to the unjust condemnation of Palamedes. Xenophon, moreover, is surely no reliable source for verbatim records of Socrates' remarks on the day his trial.

7. Different aspects of this question will be touched upon throughout the whole of this study. Two classic works, however, which discuss in great detail and often rather audaciously the matter of Plato's literary satire are F. Dümmler *Antisthenika* (Berlin 1882) and G. Teichmüller, *Literarische Fehden im Vierten Jahrhundert*, I (Breslau 1881); II (Breslau 1884).

the rhetors are not the only ones alluded to here, since the Sophists[8] also took an active part in Greek political life.

So unambiguous a position on the part of Socrates toward the activities of the Sophists and rhetors, and what we otherwise know of Plato's estimation of the value of Gorgianic rhetoric, of which the *Palamedes,* as I shall show, is a major exposition, suggest the necessity of rejecting out of hand any hypothesis that Plato used the *Palamedes* for the purpose of imparting dignity and significance to Socrates' death. So sympathetic a use of the Gorgianic work would in fact imply a kind of approbation — a notion which we cannot accept without also assuming a striking lack either of consistency or integrity in Plato's philosophical position. Morr was perhaps aware of his disquieting implication of his thesis, since he took pains to emphasize what is perhaps the only favorable explicit estimate (*Meno* 76c) of Gorgias' intellectual accomplishments in the Platonic corpus — a complimentary account of a theory of color which the Leontine philosopher had worked out.[9]

Nevertheless, despite the fair assumption of the inappropriateness of a sympathetic Platonic reworking of the *Palamedes,* it is still true that the *Apology of Socrates* contains a good number of passages which exhibit surprising and apparently more than accidental similarities to passages in the *Palamedes.* It must first be noted, however, that many of the examples recorded by the scholars whom I mention above are far from convincing, since they can easily be explained by the fact that the two defenses are quite similar in their general character. Among other things, both are delivered by defendants with a reputation for wisdom in reply to accusations which are, in part, attributable to envy. Accordingly, we should not be surprised if we read that both men are called σοφοί (*Pal.* 25 and *Ap.* 18b) and εὐεργέται (*Pal.* 30 and *Ap.* 36c), or that the accusation arises from φθόνος(Pal. 3 and *Ap.* 28a). How else, one asks, could Plato have expressed these notions? Such criticisms aside, there are still a number of verbal correspondences so striking, whether considered

---

8. On the political activities of the Sophists, see Schmid-Stählin (above, n. 1) 41 (Sophists in general and Prodicus); 49 (Hippias); 57 (Gorgias). For rhetors and Sophists as panderers to popular whim, *see Gorgias,* 463e-446a. This passage also illustrates how similar to one another these two activities seemed to Plato to be.

9. Morr (above, n.1) n.129.

separately or, more impressively, *as a group,* that no student of the *Apology* can, in my opinion, afford to ignore them unless he is also willing to forgo the understanding of an important dimension of the work's meaning. Before discussing what I consider to be the significance of these verbal similarities, however, I should like first to catalogue the passages in the two works which seem to me most important in this respect. Furthermore, in order to emphasize the contextual importance which these passages appear often to have, I shall incorporate them into a short analysis of the *Palamedes* and give, in each case, the parallel passage from the *Apology* for the purpose of comparison.

The structure of the *Palamedes* is fortunately straightforward and perspicuous and may easily be represented in summary outline:

I. *Prologue* (1-5) The question here is not death, since all men must die; my honor is at stake. If Odysseus made this charge on the basis either of conjecture or sure knowledge, he is to be commended; but if it was prompted by evil or villainy, he is the most wicked of men. However, I *know* that I didn't commit this crime, and am thus certain that Odysseus is not relying on sure knowledge. He is therefore relying on conjecture, and I shall endeavor to show you that such a conjecture is unreasonable.

II. *Refutation* (6-27)

A. *Argument* (6-21)

1. (6-12) Granted that I did *want* to communicate with the enemy, it would have been *impossible.*

2. (13-21) Granted that it was *possible* to communicate with the enemy, why should I have *wanted* to?

(15) Some will say money prompted me. But this is not applicable to me, since I am not a slave to pleasure and do not need a large fortune.

ὡς δ' ἀληθῆ λέγω, μάρτυρα πιστόν παρέξομαι τὸν παροιχόμενον βίον·

With this Gomperz[10] compares

---

10. Gomperz (above n. 1) 10. Platonic quotation throughout are from Burnet's Oxford Text. Quotations from the *Palamedes* are from Diels, *Frag d Vors*[7], vol. II.

ἱκανὸν γάρ, οἶμαι, ἐγὼ παρέχομαι τὸν μάρτυρα
ὡς ἀληθῆ λέγω, τὴν πενίαν ˙ (*Ap.* 31c)

(20) You can't think that I planned to go over to the barbarian side after my betrayal of the Greeks. What kind of life should I have there?

(21) For a man who has lost his reputation for honesty and trustworthiness (πιστις) cannot live a happy life.

βίος δὲ οὐ βιωτὸς πίστεως ἐστερηνένῳ

Gomperz[11] compares

ὁ δὲ ἀνεξέταστος βίος οὐ βιωτὸς ἀνθρώπῳ ... (*Ap.* 38a)

B. *Interrogation of the Plaintiff* (22-27) The plaintiff is irresponsible. His accusation is self-contradictory.

(26) You accuse me, in effect, of being both wise and foolish at the same time.

οὐκοῦν δὶ ἀμφότερα ἂν εἴης ψευδής.

Gomperz[12] compares,

ὥστε σύ γε κατ' ἀμφότερα ψεύδῃ. (*Ap.* 25e)

III. *Address to the Judges* (28-36) Is it likely that a man such as I could have committed a crime of this nature? I have always tried to help you. I have, in fact, been your benefactor. In other respects, too, I deserve not to suffer at your hands.

(32) οὔθ' ὑπὸ νεωτέρων οὔθ᾽ ὑπὸ πρεσβυτέρων

Morr[13] compares,

εἴτε νεώτερος εἴτε πρεσβύτερος (*Ap.* 33a)

Chroust[14] also compares,

καὶ νεωτέρῳ καὶ πρεσβυτέρῳ (*Ap.* 30a)

and

καὶ νεωτέρους καὶ πρεσβυτέρους (*ibid.*)

(*Ibid.*) I have not harmed the aged, and have helped the young.

τοῖς εὐτυχοῦσιν οὐ φθονερός, τῶν δυστυχούντων οἰκτίρμων˙

11. Gomperz (above, n.1) 10.
12. *Ibid.*
13. Morr (above n.1) 32.
14. Chroust (above, n. 1) 217.

Morr[15] compares,

    καὶ πλουσίῳ καὶ πένητι παρέχω ἐμαυτὸν ἐρωτᾶν, . .(Ap. 33b)

(34) I will not use the customary methods which are designed to arouse pity. You must consider the facts.

    ὑμᾶς δὲ χρὴ ..., μηδὲ τὸν ὀλίγον χρόνον τοῦ πολλοῦ
    σοφώτερον ἡγεῖσθαι κριτήν, μηδὲ τὴν διαβολὴν κτλ.

With this Gomperz[16] compares,

    ἐξελέσθαι τὴν διαβολὴν ἣν ὑμεῖς ἐν πολλῷ χρόνῳ
    ἔσχετε ταύτην ἐν οὕτως ὀλίγῳ χρόνῳ.   (Ap. 19a)

(36) If you kill me unjustly your crime will become known to all.

    καὶ τὴν αἰτίαν φανερὰν ἅπασιν ὑμεις ἕξετε τῆς ἀδικίας ...

Gomperz[17] compares,

    ὄνομα ἕξετε καὶ αἰτίαν ... ὡς Σωκράτη ἀπεκτόνατε ...(Ap. 38c)

IV. *Conclusion* (37) This is my defense. A summary is appropriate only when one is addressing inferior judges. For you, the first men of Greece, this is not needed.

It will be noted first of all that the verbal correspondences in the section devoted to an Address to the Judges are much less striking than those found in the Refutation. Nevertheless, I have decided to include them for two reasons. First, it is precisely this section which contains the most impressive parallels in the matters of arrangement and *topoi* of argument. Accordingly, although the verbal allusions in Plato listed for this section might have little independent significance, the fact that most occur in a section which is in another respect so reminiscent of the corresponding portion of the *Palamedes* will perhaps justify their inclusion. Secondly, the contrast between young and old, rich and poor, which is found in *Palamedes* 32 and paralleled in the *Apology,* is certainly a commonplace. It is striking, however, that both of these antitheses, in the same order and in equally close conjunction, occur in the two works. This consideration is, I think, much less suggestive of the merely accidental.

It should first be pointed out that previous examinations of the

---

15. Morr (above, n. 1) 32.
16. Gomperz (above, n. 1) 9.
17. *Ibid.* 10.

verbal parallels in the *Apology* and the *Palamedes* have been little more than lists such as we have above in which similarities in diction in the two works are confronted. However, the real impressiveness of these similarities has been overlooked because of a failure to examine their relevance to the total meaning of the two works. After a brief discussion of such comparative lists, scholars have drawn the general conclusion that the *Palamedes* was in some way used by Plato in the composition of his *Apology*.[18] But it is surely not enough merely to list verbal similarities, and then straightway offer some hypothesis to explain them. For despite those cases in which passages are strikingly parallel with regard to both diction and special context, the hypothesis of Platonic borrowing cannot easily be confirmed to the satisfaction of a critic of this view. A reasonable and convincing proof must first be given that the *Apology* represents more than a conglomerate of quotations from the *Palamedes,* and there was in fact some very good motive for imitating the work of Gorgias.

II

In the matter of the general outline of the two speeches some remarks should be made. First, if one analyzes these two works, using the traditional terminology for the divisions of the dicanic speech, one is struck by the fact that each work contains a combination of several features which makes it unusual in the body of conventional courtroom oratory, and that, further, this same combination of features is common to both.[19] What impresses one first is the absence of the normal sequence, *Prooimion — (prothesis) — diegesis — pistis — epilogos.* In these two works, after a short *prooimion,* and in the case of Socrates' defense, a *prothesis* necessitated by the dual nature of the accusation, each speaker immediately embarks on his *pistis,* or refutation. In both the *diegesis* of the usual sort is absent.[20]

---

18. Calogero (above, n. 1) is an exception, since he seeks an explanation which takes into account the specific content of the borrowings and not the mere fact of their existence. In this he is unique among the scholars who have studied this problem. See, however, above, n. 6.

19. See Schmid-Stählin (above, n. 1) 74 for similarities in the section devoted to an address to the judges. Schmid does not observe that the similarities in *topoi* extend to the interrogation also. With Schmid's I.a in his tabular analysis of the *Palamedes* cf. *Ap.* 24c-d, 27a; with 2.a cf. 26a.

20. For discussion of early theories of rhetorical *dispositio,* see P. Hamber-

Moreover, the refutation is handled by each speaker in a distinctly similar manner. Palamedes first shows that according to all considerations of probability an accusation of the nature that Odysseus has brought against him is impossible to conceive of; then, in his interrogation of Odysseus, he points out, while casting doubt on Odysseus' honesty, that the indictment contains two elements which are mutually inconsistent. Socrates, in like manner, presents a defense which is bipartite in its structure. In the first portion, Socrates informs the jury of the innocent nature of his pursuits, and draws reasonable inferences about the origins of the widespread prejudices which were the ultimate basis for the accusations of the plaintiff; in the second part, a refutation of the plaintiff, Socrates demonstrates to Meletus and to the jury that the two parts of the accusation,[21] considered logically, cancel each other out, and that Meletus knows this as well as anyone. From a formal point of view, then, each defense has been conceived along similar lines. The difference of *method* discernible in the first portion of the *pistis* is a matter of importance which cannot, however, be discussed now.

The *pistis* is in each case followed by a long and earnest address in which the defendant urges the jury to consider the moral implications of its actions — to consider, in fact, the face they will make in the world for having sentenced to death a wise man and benefactor of their society. In the *Palamedes* the statement that the Greeks will gain an evil name for having voted for the defendant's condemnation occurs before the vote; in the *Apology*, such an unhappy outcome for the good name of the Athenians is the necessary implication of Socrates' frank estimate of the valuable service he has rendered Athens under the inspiration of the god Apollo, although the explicit declaration of this unfortunate prospect cannot occur until the final section of the speech. A further element in the section following the *pistis* which links the two works is the high moral tone with which the defendant rejects the humiliating role of suppliant.[22] Both Palamedes and Socrates rise to the level of a man who is hauled into

---

ger, *Die Lehre von der Disposition in der alten* τέχνη ῥητοτική (Paderborn 1914). Compare Antiphon 1 for a similar deviation from the sequence of *prooimion-diegesis-pistis*.

21. *I.e.*, that Socrates (1) corrupts the young and (2) corrupts them intentionally.

22. Cf. also Isoc. 15.321.

court unjustly and refuses to see the jury in whose hands he is placed belittle themselves by dispensing mercy in such mean circumstances; both assume remarkable responsibility for the scruples of their potential persecutors.

These observations, however, give us a hint of similarities which exist only in the broad outlines of the two speeches. A closer examination of detail will suggest further and more precise relationships. Striking similarities in detail may be discerned in the *erotesis*, or interrogation of the plaintiff; in the *Palamedes* this is contained in sections 22-26, in the *Apology*, 24b-28a. An *erotesis* incorporated into the text, although rare, is nevertheless found in three of the Attic orators.[23] But the interrogations contained in the speeches of Plato and Gorgias are different from these other examples both in their length and in their elaboration. And what is more important, in addition to their special character in contrast to these examples, they also exhibit clear similarities to each other, especially in their use of rhetorical *topoi*.

Both defendants employ an extremely clever *topos* to undermine the claims of the plaintiff to serious consideration: there is the possibility, they suggest, that any accusation which contains so many contradictory elements is the work of a man not entirely to be taken seriously. Palamedes exclaims (25), "How can we have confidence in a man who discussing the same subject with the same man on the same occasion yet makes statements which contradict each other?" Socrates, in a characteristic manner, makes the wry suggestion that Meletus in making an accusation which is so illogical is "really joking with a straight face" (*Ap.* 24c).

There is another *topos* of argument employed by both defendants, in which the conclusions, phrased in a way which would be extraordinarily similar in any case, are in the face of the identical contexts strongly suggestive of conscious borrowing on the part of one of our authors. In the *Palamedes* (25-26), the speaker sums up the accusation and makes his refutation in the following manner: I stand accused, he says, of having tried to betray my fatherland in a manner which necessarily involved a good deal of cleverness (*sophia*). In the terms of your accusation, I may therefore be described as a clever traitor. But, treason is folly (*moria*), so that you are accusing me of possessing two qualities which cannot coexist in the same person,

23. Cf. Dem. 46.10; Lysias 12.25 and 22.5; Andocides 1.14.

viz., cleverness and folly. Therefore, since this combination of qualities is impossible, I either acted in accordance with this cleverness which you attribute to me, and did not attempt to betray Hellas; or, I did attempt treason; but then I could not possess the cleverness which you represent to the jurors. "Therefore, because of either statement (i.e., if either is true) you are proved to be a liar (i.e., in your accusation that I am a clever traitor)." The Greek of the last sentence is,

οὐκοῦν δι' ἀμφότερα ἂν εἴης ψευδής.

In precisely the same manner Socrates endeavors to disprove the accusation that he corrupted the Athenian youth with full knowledge of his actions. After an identical line of argument he concludes (25e): "Either I did not corrupt knowingly; or, if I did, it was done without my desire."

ὥστε σύ γε κατ' ἀμφότερα ψεύδῃ.

III

Further, in the self-portraits which we find in these two works there are three *topoi* which both speakers use in common in their efforts to characterize their lives as altruistic and, above all, innocent. Both defendants first of all emphasize the fact that they are men of wisdom (or, at least in the case of Socrates, so reputed by their contemporaries); secondly, that their wisdom has enabled them to bestow great benefits on society; and, lastly, that their material possessions are rather less ample than most of their fellows.

If we consider first the claims of Palamedes and Socrates to the roles of wise man and benefactor, we observe that, although the *topoi* are identical, as was the case in the sections previously discussed, there is now a clear difference in the manner in which these *topoi* are employed by each speaker. We find that Socrates' characterization of the wisdom which he allows that he possesses, and of the benefits which this wisdom has permitted him to bestow on society, involves more modest pretensions than is the case with Palamedes.

The defendant in Gorgias' speech, in a characteristic argument from probability, points to the absurdity of assuming that he had attempted the betrayal of Greece (or done anything else for that matter) for the sake of gaining honor and esteem. Why should he have? "For I was honored by the most honorable men for the most honorable pursuits – by you, for wisdom." (16). There is no hint here, as there is with Socrates, that there is a disparity between the sense in which he is deemed wise by the multitude and the sense in which he personally accepts this designation. Palamedes' reputation is securely anchored to the popular conception of the wise man as clever and inventive, and it is to this conception that he frankly appeals in the final section (30) of the speech where he recalls the many contributions which he has made to the material and intellectual advances of Greek society.

In contrast to this rather ample catalogue which constitutes the substance of Palamedes' claims to σοφία and εὐερβεσία, Socrates advances the suggestion that he may indeed have a right to that sort of modest wisdom which befits an ordinary mortal, but certainly to nothing more (20d; cf. also 23b). Like Palamedes, Socrates declares that this wisdom has enabled him to bestow important benefits on society. But, unlike Palamedes, who details the many *positive* achievements which have made him illustrious (achievements which we may be sure would have left the Platonic Socrates quite unimpressed), Socrates takes great pains to point out that the good services which he has done the Athenian state are the product of a negative criticism which is merely a necessary preliminary to genuine wisdom. Socrates repeatedly says that his wisdom consists merely in the fact that he knows that this wisdom is worth nothing, or practically nothing. His chief benefit to Athenian society, viewed in this light, is to have shown to those of its members who have a preeminent claim to wisdom that they are really ignorant of those important matters which they profess.

We may now proceed to an examination of the third *topos* which both Socrates and Palamedes employ to fill out the picture they present to the jury of the wise and abstinent man – the *topos* of meager means, of *penia*. Both Palamedes and Socrates see in the modest circumstances of their lives a means of disproving some part of the accusation against which they are defending themselves. For Palamedes, who again bases his argument on considerations of probability, any suggestion that he initiated a plot to betray the Greeks to the barbarians because of a desire for wealth is clearly absurd. He reminds the jury that his means, although moderate, have always been quite sufficient for his desires, which are also moderate.

Furthermore, he has never sought fame and public esteem from a display of wealth. "My life is my witness!"

ὡς δ' ἀληθῆ λέγω, μάρτυρα πιστὸν παρέξομαι τὸν
παροιχόμεον βίον·   (15)

Socrates likewise makes use of his humble means to disprove an implication which the popular conception of him as a Sophist would necessarily involve. The Sophists receive payment for their instruction; Socrates denies emphatically that this has ever been true in his case. Even Meletus has not dared to utilize this element in his slanderous indictment.

ἱκανὸν γάρ, οἶμαι, ἐγὼ παρέχομαι τὸν μάρτυρα
ὡς ἀληθῆ λέγω, τὴν πενίαν.   (31c)

Apart from the unimportant matter of word-order, the phrases are virtually identical. The only difference is the substitution, in two cases, of synonymous, or equivalent, phrases (i.e. ἱκανον for πιστόν, and the specific τὴν πενιαν for τὸν παρόιχομενον βίον).

These substitutions are not without significance. We ought first, however, to observe that, as in the case of the handling of the *topoi* of *sophia* and *euergesia,* an important point of difference can be discerned in the treatment of this *topos* too. The crucial distinction in Palamedes' account is focused in the word μετρια; he is not rich, to be sure, nor has he ever needed wealth to satisfy his modest desires; but he is not, on the other hand, poverty-stricken for

χρήματα μεν μέτρια κέκτημαι.   (15)

With Socrates the case is quite different. In the first section of the *Apology* he also refers to the well-known fact of his poverty; in that instance, however, to show that because of his service to the god he had not only neglected to tend to affairs of the state, a fact for which he had been bitterly reproached; he had also failed to take any care of private matters, to such an extent, indeed, that the only apt description for the state of his life was πενία μυρία (23c).

At this point I suggest that the similarities we have observed are to be accounted for by the assumption that they are the result of a conscious reworking of the *Palamedes* by Plato. But what is Plato's purpose here? Why, indeed, would Plato rework Palamedes' assertion in order to emphasize the differences between Socrates' profession of absolute poverty and Palamedes' rather tepid protestations? The explanation, I submit, lies in the words which make up the last portion of Socrates' statement. "I live in incredible poverty," he says *"because of my service to the god."* With Palamedes, it should be observed, the three *topoi* we have been discussing are used merely as fodder for arguments from probability. In the case of Socrates however, his great poverty, his reputation for wisdom, and his activities as benefactor of Athens, are all viewed primarily as the consequences of the special role to which the oracle of the God of Delphi has led him. "My poverty is great," Socrates is saying, "because I have neglected my own and the city's affairs in order to carry out the god's command in the sense that I understand it. I am the wisest of men because I know that human wisdom, when compared to that of the god's, is worth nothing. I am a benefactor of Athens because in my examinations of her leading citizens — an examination prompted by the god's oracle — I have uncovered their ignorance so that they are now in a position to begin to acquire real wisdom."

IV

In a courtroom defense the essential problem is the refutation of the plaintiff's accusation. In view of this, it is not surprising that the differences which were implied in the treatment of *topoi* in the two speeches should find their clearest expression in the point of view from which each defendant considers the difficulties of his defense. It should be made clear from the start, however, that the manner of refutation which we find in Plato's *Apology* is by no means a mere technical variation of the rhetorical procedures employed in the *Defense of Palamedes*. Rather, as I shall attempt to show, it is a conscious and thoroughgoing criticism of the philosophical outlook which is implied (or which to Plato seemed to be implied) by the rhetorical methods which Palamedes uses in his defense against the charges of Odysseus. But what is this outlook?

I ought perhaps to begin by observing that in the composition of the *Palamedes* only those elements of the myth which have set the trial in motion are alluded to by Gorgias, whereas details which are found in other versions of the story are omitted. Indeed, only two facts are introduced: that Odysseus has charged Palamedes with having attempted to betray his fellow Greeks to the Trojans, and that for this allegation Odysseus has offered no proof whatsoever. This latter state of affairs is effectively under scored by the omission of any reference to the letter, allegedly from Priam, which Odysseus planted in Palamedes' tent.[24] Because of this, Palamedes, in his examination of Odysseus' charge, is forced to offer conjecture in his search for possible explanations for Odysseus' behavior (3). Either Odysseus *knows* (ἐπιστάμενος) that I am guilty of treason, or he has *surmised* (δοξάσζων) it from good evidence. In either case, his accusation can be construed as evidence of patriotism. The other alternative is that he does not have certain knowledge of my betrayal, and that he has no good reason to conjecture such an action on my part. If this alternative is true, the plaintiff has concocted the accusation from motives of envy and villainy. It should be noted that at the very beginning of the defense the familiar and important distinction between *doxa* and *aleitheia* is introduced.[25] This must be emphasized, because, as we shall see, it is precisely in the application of these concepts to the dicanic context that the heart of the difference between Gorgias and Plato lies.

In the fourth chapter of the *Palamedes,* the defendant makes the first of several statements concerning the difficulties and perplexities which must originate from an accusation of the kind which Odysseus has so recklessly instituted. Palamedes' words are important, and should be quoted in full: "Where shall I begin my discussion of these matters? What shall I say first? To what point in my defence shall I turn? For an accusation unsupported by proof causes in me a state of manifest perplexity, and because of this perplexity I must necessarily be at a loss with regard to my defense, unless I learn something from the truth itself and the present necessity, teachers more dangerous than resourceful (i.e. more likely to lead me on a *perilous* course than to provide me with the *means* to safety)."

"The truth itself" means here, of course, "the facts of the matter." But what is "the present necessity"? This surely means the "demands of the present situation," or "the necessity of defending myself at this place and at this time."[26] Compare here the passage (32) where Palamedes apologizes to the jury for indulging in self-

---

24. Although we have only late *testimonia* for its presence in the Palamedes story, this detail may well go back to the fifth century. See *Scholia in Euripidem,* ed. E. Schwartz (Berlin 1887) I *Orestes* 432. The same detail is contained in Hyginus' version (Hyg. 105).
25. See especially *Palamedes* 3,22, and 24; *Helen* 8-14.
26. Cf. Antiphon 6.25 for this phrase in a similar context.

praise: "To be sure, it is not my place to praise myself. *But* the present situation has compelled me to do even this (ὁ δὲ παρὼν καιρὸς ἠνάγκασε καὶ ταῦτα), to defend myself in every way possible now that I stand accused."

More important, however: Why are these two "teachers" more likely to involve Palamedes in danger than to provide him the means with which to extricate himself? And why is it only these two that he mentions? To take the first question, and the phrase αὐτὴ ἡ ἀλήθεια, let us recall the passage in Chapter 33 where Palamedes disclaims all intention of persuading the jurors with tears and lamentations to vote for his acquittal. He adds that he will tell them exactly how it happened (διδάξαντα τἀληθές) – "a procedure in accord with what is most manifestly just." This profession does not mean, however, than in Palamedes' opinion a straightforward narration of the truth will insure an acquittal. For Palamedes is still anxious, and the next two chapters are full of exhortations to the members of the jury. They are urged not to pay more heed to words than to facts, nor to give greater weight to the charges than to the refutation, nor to consider a short space of time a "wiser judge" than a long period of deliberation, nor, finally, to think the accusation more to be believed than their own experience of the matter. In terms of the Gorgianic formulation, the jury should pay more heed to *aleithea* than to *doxa,* especially since by voting for Palamedes' condemnation they will involve themselves in the irreparable ignominy of having executed an innocent man. The point is made even clearer further on (35), when Palamedes advises the jury to prolong their deliberation, and to form a verdict in accordance with the truth of the matter (μετὰ δὲ τῆς ἀληθείας τὴν κρίσιν ποιήσατε).

And so, although Palamedes considers a truthful narration of events the most just procedure in a courtroom defense, he is not for that reason deluded about the uncertainty which attends its use. He has clear awareness of the power of *doxa* in human affairs, and for this reason he anxiously urges the jury to give lengthy consideration to the question before them. It is in this sense, I submit, that "the truth itself" is a "teacher more dangerous than resourceful." As Palamedes says (35), "If it were possible that the facts of this case could become clear and palpable to my audience through my words alone, the verdict would be easy to arrive at (εὔπορος) from what has been said" (with εὔπγρος cf. πόριμος of 4, which was used as the opposite term to ἐπικίνδυνος). A clear presentation of the facts of the matter, however, does *not* insure belief, and so it is one source of Palamedes' apprehension.

We may now inquire why ἡ παροῦσα ἀνάγκη is a risky and difficult "teacher" in Palamedes' perplexity. The text does not offer as full a development of this theme as is the case in the discussion of the dangers implicit in the use of *aletheia*. We may nevertheless form some tentative conclusions in this matter on the strength of several hints in Gorgias' exposition. First, however, there is the commonsense observation that any defendant must of necessity consider as perilous a situation in which he is constrained to defend his life in a short space of time before a body of men who have nothing to base their verdict on save the conflicting claims of the plaintiff and the defendant. To repeat here the more despairing aspects of Palamedes' discussion of the role of αὐτὴ ἡ ἀλήθεια in a defense of one's life: there is always the risk that *doxa* may prevail, unless enough care and circumspection are observed, since the defendant is dealing with a highly volatile part of the human mind. And if, as Palamedes says, he cannot rely on words alone to communicate the true facts of the matter (cf. 35), the consequence is that the defendant is faced, if he is to save his life, with the necessity of producing an *impression* of the truth which will lead to his acquittal. It is a reflection of this necessity, and of the procedures consequent upon it that ἡ παροῦσα ἀνάγκη is to be understood. The term is intended by Gorgias to mirror the compulsion laid upon the defendant to rely on techniques of proof designed to create the impression of truth. And let us remember that arguments based on probability, so abundant in this work (*vid*. 9, εἰκός, where this technique is given its name), are a major species of this type of proof. That this is the sense of the term in the context of the *Palamedes* is made clear, I think, by a passage already quoted above. Palamedes apologizes for having to praise himself with such frankness (32). He has been compelled, however, by the present situation (ὁ δὲ παρὼν καιρὸς ἠνάγκασε). It is clear why he has chosen this particular line of proof. It is intended, with its long catalogue of benefits bestowed upon the Greeks, to make it seem impossible that he could have committed the crime of which he had been accused. His self-praise is to serve, he says, as a sign (σημεῖον, 31), which would point to the impossibility of his guilt.

There is, thus, some reason to believe that the two terms, αὐτὴ ἡ ἀλήθεια and ἡ παροῦσα ἀνάγκη, represent a special application to a dicanic context of the antithesis *aletheia-doxa*. *Ananke,* then, is the special constraint imposed upon the man who must defend his life, and who has not the sure means of representing in objectively convincing terms the fact that the plaintiff's accusation is untrue. Such a man must therefore foster in his listener's mind the subjective impression (*doxa*) that the claim that he makes is true. This is the reason why Palamedes calls ἡ παροῦσα ἀνάγκη a "teacher more dangerous than resourceful."

In summary, a defendant unjustly accused and on trial for his life must take two things into consideration: his personal and certain *knowledge* that he is innocent of the charge, and the *necessity* of convincing the jury that this is so. Now, although Palamedes states that *aletheia* is more conducive to belief than *doxa,* he is at the same time aware that it is not always possible to make the truth of the matter immediately obvious to his listeners. Accordingly, there must be a second "teacher" to direct him in his perplexity, and this "teacher" is the ineluctable necessity of persuading the jury of his innocence, even if this must be done by means of arguments based on *doxa*. And so, although Palamedes concedes the absolute priority of truth (or, at least concedes that it will prevail in due time), he nevertheless grasps the fact that in this contest for his life he is compelled to recognize the unique demands (cf. ἀνήκεστα, 34) of his situation. For, unlike Socrates, Palamedes believes that it lies within the power of the jury to do him real and irreparable harm (cf. 2). Both teachers, then, are dangerous. But why does Palamedes turn to no others but these two? The answer is clearly that there can be no others, for *doxa* and *aletheia,* of which they are but the special manifestations, are, for Gorgias, the only two modes of comprehension available to man.

With regard to the defense, we may say, moreover, that the "teacher" who exercises the more potent influence on Palamedes is ἡ παροῦσα ἀνάγκη. A clear indication of this fact is that Palamedes, for the most part, has not chosen to wait and see if the jury will give their verdict long and thoughtful consideration, and make their decision "in accordance with the truth." He has instead devoted the greater part of his defense to the aim of engendering in the minds of his listeners the *impression* that on all grounds of *probability* it is utterly unlikely that he would have been able in the first place to effect a betrayal; and, granted that he had been able, that he would conceivably have wished to do so. There is, moreover, reflected in the diction of the *Palamedes* a sense of pervasive anxiety. Always mindful of the fact that the one outcome involves an "irreparable" act, Palamedes emphasizes repeatedly the difficulties and uncertainties of the mechanism of persuasion and belief. Indeed, in the ten chapters of the speech where πείθω and words of the same root (πιστίς, etc.) are found, these words occur twenty-three times.[27] Despite a clear apprehension of these difficulties, however, Palamedes is nevertheless compelled to employ, as the chief instrument of his defense, arguments based on probability. For although Palamedes may concede that under certain conditions truth has a greater power than opinion to engender persuasion, he nevertheless shows us by the style of his defense that in the exigencies of the moment the demands of "present necessity" must be the more deferred to.

V

This, if I am correct, is the philosophical position which forms the basis of Gorgianic rhetoric. Plato, in his *Gorgias,* as we know, subjected rhetorical doctrines which he attributed to Gorgias to a detailed criticism. In the following section I shall attempt to show how, in its essential features, the elements of this criticism answer to those which we have found in our analysis of the rhetorical outlook of the *Palamedes.* By thus pointing out an identity with the main features of Gorgianic rhetoric as set forth in the *Palamedes,* I hope to establish beyond reasonable doubt Plato's familiarity with the concrete features of this rhetoric. Although this familiarity may seem an obvious fact, I have chosen to investigate it in order to strengthen the probabilities of my hypothesis that there exists between the *Apology* and *Palamedes* a conscious connection, already suggested by the verbal parallels we have examined above. Moreover, by emphasizing the existence of this *explicit* critique of the rhetoric of Gorgias, I hope to proceed more securely to an exposition of my thesis that the *Apology* is, in one of its aspects, an *implicit* critique of this same rhetoric.

Before turning to the *Gorgias,* however, let us look in passing at

---

27. See 8, 9, 11, 14, 21, 22, 24, 25, 34, 36 for use of πείθω and words of the same root (πιστός, etc.).

the *Phaedrus,* since it contains a passage which is relevant to the present discussion. The long, ironic catalogue (265d-268e) in which Socrates gives the reader a sketch of the "accomplishments" of the students of *techne rhetorike* contains an account (267a) of the theories of Gorgias and Tisias in which are found the lines quoted at the beginning of this study. Socrates says, "And shall we pass over Tisias and Gorgias who considered that the probable was more to be esteemed than the true?" (οἳ πρὸ τῶν ἀληθῶν τὰ εἰκότα εἶδον ὡς τιμητέα μᾶλλον). In the light of our analysis of Gorgias' point of view, as evidenced in the *Palamedes,* this observation is seen to be in large measure correct. Of course, if it is taken in its strict sense, without further qualification, it contains something of a misrepresentation. For we have seen how Palamedes, although he tends in the exigencies of the courtroom to prefer arguments from probability, nevertheless freely grants the primacy of truth in producing persuasion (24). Accordingly, Plato's remark should have been modified by some indication that this preference of Gorgias obtained only in certain conditions. To be just, however, Socrates is talking about theories of rhetoric which were for the most part devised for use in dicanic oratory. Nevertheless, the remark, scornful in character, and just correct enough, should probably be viewed either as a distortion or as the expression of a misunderstanding natural enough in view of the antagonism which Plato felt for this kind of rhetoric.

Let us, however, turn to the *Gorgias* and the more cogent evidence which it contains. The passage which is relevant here is a dialogue of Socrates with Gorgias (454c-461b), containing an elaborate analysis of the art of persuasion, in which Plato introduces philosophical distinctions of great importance for his criticism of Sophistic rhetoric.

In the first section (454c-454e) of his lengthy analysis, Socrates sets up a distinction which is the foundation for his later rejection of Gorgianic persuasion on the grounds that it involves an inferior faculty of the mind. At the very beginning of their discussion, Socrates has Gorgias concede that "to have learned something" (μεμαθηκέναι) and "to have believed something" (πεπιστευκέναι) are two entirely different matters; or, to put in substantial rather than verbal terms, *mathesis* is different from *pistis*. (This distinction implies another, that of *episteme* vs. *doxa,* an implication realized in the case of the latter term shortly afterward.) An important addition to this distinction is made when both speakers agree that, whereas *pistis* may be either true or false, *episteme* is never anything but true. At this point the notion of persuasion is introduced with the observation that it is proper to describe both those who have learned and those who have believed as "persons who have been persuaded." Socrates brings this portion of the argument to a close which an attempt at a formulation which will summarize the conclusions which have been agreed upon up to that point. "Let us posit two forms of rhetoric: one imparts belief which has no basis in certain knowledge; the other imparts knowledge." Socrates then asks Gorgias pointedly to what form of persuasion a rhetoric ought to be assigned which deals with questions of right and wrong in large public gatherings such as, among other things, *law courts*. Gorgias obliges Socrates by indicating that it is a species of that kind of persuasion which produces belief that is without sure knowledge. After this important feature of Gorgianic rhetoric has been agreed upon, the remainder of the discussion is devoted to an examination of the implications of this agreement. In 455a these two εἴδη of persuasion receive their definitive nomenclature: one is called πειθώ πιστευτική, the other πειθώ διδασκαλική. Put in another way, the business of the rhetorically trained speaker is not to instruct members of law courts, or other public gatherings, on matters of right and wrong; he need only implant a certain belief about these matters. He must be πειστικός, not διδασκαλικός.[28]

I should here like to argue that the two forms of persuasion enunciated by Socrates in this discussion bear a very close resemblance to the methods of those two "teachers" whose guidance forms the basis of the rhetorical outlook of the *Palamedes*. That Palamedes in those sections where he relies heavily on arguments from probability is following the procedures of κειθώ πιστευτική is obvious. It may seem at first sight, however, an unjustifiable procedure to connect πειθώ διδασκαλική, which in the *Gorgias* is defined as the form of persuasion which *instructs* law courts and large assemblies on questions of right and wrong, with αὐτή ἡ ἀλήθεια, which simply means in the *Palamedes* "the facts of this particular case." Several considerations, however, may make this connection

---

28. Here we should observe that although πείθω is strictly applicable to both forms of persuasion, this term is nevertheless generally associated, unless it is otherwise indicated, with πειθώ πιστευτική, whereas διδάσκω is the *vox propria* for the activity of πειθώ διδασκαλική.

more likely. First of all, it seems that by large assemblies Plato does chiefly intend the law courts. The law court, at any rate, is the only example of a large assembly singled out for explicit mention (454e and 455a). But this is puzzling, and one may legitimately ask what the function is of instruction on questions of right and wrong in the courtroom, where strictly speaking it is only a matter of determining the responsibility of the defendant for a specific act. Plato, however, surely does not recognize any distinction between the theoretical and the concrete in the sphere of ethics, since for Plato the defendant, although on trial for a specific act, ought nevertheless ideally to lay before the court for judgment, not merely the facts relating to the case, but also his entire moral nature. That this is so we may conclude from two passages in the *Gorgias*. In the first (522c-e), Socrates remarks that the innocent man needs no defense but a life with justice. In the other (480a-d), Socrates lays the paradox before Polus that the best use to which rhetoric can be put is not to enable the guilty man to obtain an acquittal, but to help him persuade the jury that he stands in need of punishment. From the Platonic point of view, then, the narration of the actual facts of the case and the instruction of the jury on matters of right and wrong are only two ways of describing the same fact, since no examination of an individual act can in any case be separated from ethical considerations of a more general nature. The Greek of Plato's $\pi\epsilon\iota\theta\acute{\omega}$ $\delta\iota\delta\alpha\sigma\kappa\alpha\lambda\iota\kappa\acute{\eta}$ makes the transition from the concrete to the general, natural enough in any case to Plato, all the easier, since $\delta\iota\delta\acute{\alpha}\sigma\kappa\epsilon\iota\nu$ means both "to teach" and "to inform about some specific event." Lastly, and perhaps most important, Plato's two forms of persuasion and the two "teachers" of Gorgias correspond in one further important respect, since the two terms reflect in each case Plato's and Gorgias' estimation of the role of *doxa* and *aletheia* in the contest of the law courts.

The abundant use, moreover, of arguments from probability goes a long way in creating the impression that $\pi\epsilon\iota\theta\acute{\omega}$ $\pi\iota\sigma\tau\epsilon\upsilon\tau\iota\kappa\acute{\eta}$ is the form of persuasion which is more favored by Gorgias. (*Pistis* is an important concept in the *Palamedes*, but a full discussion of its meaning in the work, as well as the important place it occupies in Plato's critique of Gorgias, must be reserved for our discussion of the *Apology of Socrates*.) Nevertheless, the bald admission by Gorgias that his rhetoric favors the techniques of $\pi\epsilon\iota\theta\acute{\omega}$ $\pi\iota\sigma\tau\epsilon\upsilon\tau\iota\kappa\acute{\eta}$ and not $\pi\epsilon\iota\theta\acute{\omega}$ $\delta\iota\delta\alpha\sigma\kappa\alpha\lambda\iota\kappa\acute{\eta}$, does somewhat simplify the complex nature of

Gorgias' position. For it seems unlikely that the historical Gorgias would have assented to this conclusion, since it did involve an oversimplification of the position we find in the *Palamedes,* and a consequent misrepresentation of his attitude toward the use of "the truth itself." He did not, in the words of Socrates in the *Phaedrus,* esteem the probable above the true, or *pistis* above *episteme*; at least not in the unqualified sense of Plato's statement. Plato does, however, introduce one consideration which corresponds to Gorgias' ἡ παροῦσα ἀνάγκη, and which serves, as does this factor in the work of Goegias, to mitigate the general omission of a rhetoric which instructs, and the almost complete dependence on the form of persuasion which strives to create a certain *pistis.* In 455a Socrates observes that the rhetor most be πειστικος μόνον." For he would not, I suppose, be able in so short a time to instruct (διδάξαι) so large a group of people on such important matters (*viz.* right and wrong)."

Despite some simplification, then, the major points of the Gorgianic position are enunciated in the dialogue between Socrates and Gorgias.[29] The two "teachers" which serve Palamedes in his perplexity, αὐτὴ ἡ ἀλήθεια and ἡ παροῦσα ἀνάγκη, find their parallels in the two forms of Platonic persuasion, for it is αὐτὴ ἡ ἀλήθεια which the defendant seeks to communicate in his use of πειθώ διδασκαλική, and it is ἡ παροῦσα ἀνάγκη which compels him to employ πειθώ πιστευτική. Moreover, the very two terms (i.e. διδάσκω and πιστεύω) which are chosen by Plato to differentiate the two classes of persuasion are reminiscent of the terms employed by Gorgias to describe the procedures which each "teacher" enjoins upon the defendant, In the matter of πειθώ διδασκαλική, we have already quoted the passage (33) where Palamedes states that he will act in accordance with what is most manifestly just by "teaching the truth of the matter" (διδάξαντα τἀληθές). So far as πειθώ πιστευ τική is concerned, in the long passage (6-21) devoted to the use of

---

29. For parallel elements in the *Helen* and the *Gorgias,* see E. R. Dodds, *Gorgias* (Oxford 1959) on 452e1-8, 456b6, and 456c6. Dodds does not, however, observe the more pervasive parallels, a fact attributable to his skepticism concerning the philosophical positions frequently, and to be sure rather dubiously, assigned to Gorgias (*ibid.* 7-9). Nevertheless, although it may be true that there is no thoroughgoing exposition of a nihilistic philosophy in the works of Gorgias, it does not follow that the author of the *Helen* and the *Palamedes* can justly be accused of a "dazzling insincerity" (*ibid.* 8). For a more sensible position, see R. S. Bluck, *Meno* (Cambridge 1961) on 70b4.

arguments from probability, a form of this persuasion which present necessity compels the defendant to use, it has been pointed out that terms such as πιστός, πιθανός, are extraordinarily frequent. Moreover, as I have argued, there is implied in Gorgias' phrase, ἡ παροῦσα ἀνάγκη, the awareness that the special circumstances of mass persuasion *necessitate* the use of a special kind of rhetoric, and this awareness finds its echo in Plato (455a).

It should be noted, moreover, that Plato, although aware of this mitigating factor, is far from condoning Gorgias' position, as the remainder of this portion of the dialogue makes clear. For, in Plato's eyes, Gorgias is vulnerable on two major counts. First, he has chosen to induce agreement by fostering a subjective opinion that a given notion is true, rather than by convincing the listener of its truth by the slow and dangerous methods of rational instruction. Secondly, although Gorgias (at least the Gorgias of the dialogues) did not disagree that his method was in fact, to create a certain *doxa* in matters involving questions of right and wrong, he nevertheless did maintain, by implication that he possessed the knowledge necessary to discriminate between what was truly right or wrong.

This latter fact emerges quite clearly from Gorgias' reply to a series of questions which Socrates has put to him in an effort to understand the role which a *knowledge of right and wrong* plays in the art of rhetoric (459c-460a). Socrates asks Gorgias whether or not he will be able to impart a knowledge of right and wrong to a student who has come to him for instruction in rhetoric, even though this student does not possess a clear understanding of this subject, so crucial in the court rooms and assemblies. Gorgias' answer is straightforward: "Well, Socrates, I suppose so. If he happens not to know this, he will learn this too from me" (460a). The word which Gorgias uses here is μαθήσεται: the student will gain *mathesis* from me (*episteme* and *aletheia* are equivalent terms; cf. respectively 454d and 459e).

What Plato thinks of this claim of Gorgias is apparent from the long exposition of the thesis that *rhetorike* (in the Gorgianic sense) occupies an analogous place in the realm of the intellect (*psyche*) to that which cooking holds in those activities concerned with the care of the body. The chief point of this analogy is, of course, that rhetoric is no more able to treat the moral questions which arise in the debates of the court room or assembly than is cooking able to heal physical ills. In both cases the real problems are not understood.

Moreover, Plato is not here assailing Gorgias merely for any methodological faults which his rhetoric may happen to contain. We have, rather, a clear attack on the presumption of competence in matters of ethics.

VI

To turn now to Plato's *Apology*: Socrates finds himself in a situation identical to that of Palamedes and, like him, experiences serious perplexity in the face of the necessity of refuting his accusers.[30] Despite this common awareness of present exigency, the consequences, as they are manifested in the spirit of Socrates' defense, are profoundly different. It is the manner of this defense, and the point of view which determines it, that I shall now consider.

As Socrates recognizes, the crucial feature in his defense is the need to give the correct version of the slanderous stories which had centered around his name for many years past. These slanders consisted principally in the suggestion that Socrates was a combination of impious natural philosopher and amoral Sophist. The need to explain the true nature of his activities which had been so prejudicially construed is therefore *primary,* since Meletus is introducing charges which are merely a special expression of the prejudices then current in Athens (19a-b). To give a true and convincing account of his strange behaviour is, in other words, the crux of his defense.

Despite a clear awareness of the importance of this task, which occupies the first portion of the defense (18e-24b), Socrates proceeds in a simple and straightforward fashion. For, unlike Palamedes, to whom the presentation of "the truth of the matter" seems both an inadequate and dangerous procedure, Socrates puts his trust in a simple narration of the incidents which had given rise to the popular image of him as a corrupter of youth and an atheist. He even does this in the face of the possibility that his words may be construed as flippant, and thus prejudice his case (20d). The words which he uses in this section to describe his procedure in presenting the case to the jury are those we associate with calm narration, not anxious persuasion (cf. ἀποδεῖξαι, 20d; διδάξειν, 21b). At the conclusion (24a) of this account he declares: "This is the truth, men of Athens, and in speaking to you I have concealed no matter either great or small, nor

---

30. See 18d (cf. ἀνάγκη), 19a, 24a, 37 a-b.

have I held anything back." We should also note here that the word πείθω, which is the *vox propria* of πειθώ πιστευτική, is *not once employed* in this section, although it would have been natural to do so. To put the matter in terms which Palamedes might have used, Socrates is but little influenced by the demands of ἡ παροῦσα ἀνάγκη.

In contrast to Socrates, the plaintiffs are represented as being eager to implant the *pistis* of Socrates' guilt in the minds of the jury by whatever means possible. "The plaintiffs have spoken very *persuasively*," Socrates says, "although nothing of what they have said is *true*" (17a).[31] In his cross-examination of Meletus, Socrates seeks to discredit the points of Meletus' indictment, and at the end of each argument he taunts Meletus with the suggestion that he has failed to *persuade* anybody (ταῦτα ἐγώ οὐ σοι πείθομαι, 25e; ἄπιστός γ' εἶ, ὦ Μέλητε, 26e; ὅπως δὲ σύ τινα πείθοις ἄν ... οὐδεμία μηχανή ἐστιν. 27e). But not only does Meletus try to implant a false *pistis* in others — he is himself a victim of false *pistis*, since he has enough confidence in the power of the Athenian prejudice about Socrates to base his case on it (19a-b). Indeed, this activity of false persuasion is shown to extend far back into the past (18b-d, where note the characteristic πείθω).

Against this dark background of untruth and false opinion Plato sets the figure of Socrates, the embodiment of truth. This may perhaps seem an unwarranted overinterpretation of a situation in which it is a matter of course for the defendant to represent his own statements as true, and those of the opponent as false. Indeed, the affection of an innocence which is horrified in the face of the unscrupulous allegations of the plaintiff is a natural *topos*. However, a *topos* employed at some point or other in a speech is one thing; another thing is the Socratic defense, whose *whole tendency* is characterized by a calm awareness of innocence, and a disinclination to employ in the account of his mission any methods but those of rational persuasion and simple narration of the truth. Needless to say, it is irrelevant from the point of view of this discussion whether or not we consider the several items of this account, such as, for example, the

---

31. If Riddell had conducted a more careful analysis of the thought of the *Apology*, he might not have been led to the obvious, but wrong, conclusion that the prologue was merely a farrago of rhetorical cliches (*The Apology of Plato*, ed. J. Riddell [Oxford 1877] xxi).

story of the oracle, literally true. What is important here is Plato's ethopoetic intent. The story of Chaerphon's visit to Delphi and the direct dependence of the Socratic mission on this oracle may or may not be true. The veracity of the account does not matter, however, for what we have in the *Apology,* apart from any question of the objective truth of these statements, is a clear striving for a portrait of a man who intends to let the truth speak for itself, and who is determined, for the most part, to avoid arguments based on probability (cf. however, 31c, where Socrates does use the fact of his poverty to convince his auditors of the truth of his assertions). Socrates' behavior in the section of the speech concerned with the *antitimesis* (35e-38b) is a clear indication of this attitude. For who else but a man portrayed as entirely confident of his innocence could make a claim to lifelong support in the prytaneum? And who else but a man portrayed as totally indifferent to the outcome of his trial could risk the reaction which such a claim would surely involve? To explain why he could act this way we must turn to the oracle of the god of Delphi.

In any impasse created by two contradictory claims a solution can be effected by the introduction of an objective and truthful witness. Meletus (like Odysseus in the *Palamedes*) does not do this, a failure which puts him, as plaintiff, in a bad light. Socrates, however, in order to prove the truth of his version of the story, invokes a "worthy" witness, Apollo, the god of Truth (20e).[32]

That Socrates should call upon the god of Delphi is appropriate, since he has in Plato's portrayal spent his life in the service of this divinity. At the god's behest[33] he has devoted his energies to propa-

---

32. Not only is Apollo considered so, popularly, because of his oracular function (cf. also *Ap.* 21b), but for Plato a god who is $\psi\epsilon\upsilon\delta\acute{\eta}\varsigma$ is inconceivable (cf. *Rep.* 2.382e).

33. Hackforth (R. Hackforth, *The Composition of Plato's Apology* [Cambridge 1933] 88-104) sees a problem in reconciling the two stages in Socrates' attitude toward the oracle. Socrates is first, as Hackforth observes, a critic of the oracle; he is then its servant. Is this really so difficult to understand? Must one spend all the time in the discussion of it that Hackforth does? I think not, for Plato gives us a most natural and convincing account of the evolution of Socrates' understanding of the real meaning of the oracle. The turning point occurs when Socrates realizes that the god did not intend him specifically; he was chosen rather to be a *paradeigma* (*Ap.* 23a). After this realization, the interpretation of the oracle as a command, and not a riddle, became inevitable.

gating the modest but important truth that human wisdom, as compared to the god's, is worth nothing, or almost nothing (23a). His first action as an agent of this truth, it should be noted, was to examine the opinions of those citizens who had a reputation for wisdom (τῶν δοκούντων σοφῶν εἶναι, 21b). (Plato here makes full use of the ambiguous δοκεῖν, which can also mean "with a *false* reputation for wisdom.") At the very beginning, then, of Socrates' account of the real nature of the activities which had gained him so evil a name, the antithesis of *doxa* and *aletheia* clearly emerges. And it is this antithesis which occupies a central place in Plato's conception of the benefits which Socrates has bestowed upon Athens.

Socrates' execution of the god's commands is described in many ways. It is called an *examination* (ἐξέτασις, 22e) of Athenian society. Because the god has ordered (cf. n. 30) Socrates to devote his life to propagating the truth, Athens has been granted a *great boon* (30e-31a). In questioning those who are reputed to be wise, and proving them to be the opposite, Socrates is an *ally* of Apollo (23b). Apollo is a *general* whose commands Socrates must follow (28d, 33c). Furthermore, to disobey the commands of the god is to choose ignominy, and to this any form of danger, even death, should be preferred (28b, d-e). There is the hint, moreover, that the dangers which might prompt one to desert the god's service are not to be estimated as true dangers by his servants. When Socrates tells the jury that he will not appeal to their emotions, he says (34c), ἐγὼ δὲ οὐδὲν ἄρα τούτων ποιήσω, καὶ ταῦτα κινδυνεύων ὡς ἂν δόξαιμι, τὸν ἔσχατον κίνδυνον. The same true estimation of the power of earthly dangers is evident in the passage where Socrates declares that he will not change his ways even if he is to die many more times (30b-c).

The reason for these statements is, of course, quite clear: a man who has served the god justly and well is under his protection. As Socrates says, a good man cannot be harmed by the wicked. It is no wonder, then, that Plato makes Socrates say (35d), "I believe in the gods, men of Athens, in a way that none of my accusers does."

Now that the terms in which Plato conceives of Socrates' service to the god have been outlined, we are in a better position to analyze the nature of Socratic "persuasion." First of all, the reasons for Socrates' attitude toward "present necessity" as a factor to be considered in his defense now became explicable. It is clear that Socrates does not hesitate to base his defense on αὐτὴ ἡ ἀλήθεια, and to employ the methods of πειθὼ διδασκαλική for the reason that his actions, the truth concerning which he endeavors to set before the jury, have always been in accord with the command which Plato's Socrates came to see as the latent point of the celebrated oracle. The consequence of this is that what he tells the jury about his conduct is not only true in the sense of the Gorgianic formulation αὐτὴ ἡ ἀλήθεια; *it is also true in a transcendental sense because Socrates' mission, as it is represented by Plato, is the direct consequence of the oracle of Apollo, the god of Truth.* This, I submit, is the reason why Socrates, in his defense, is not governed by his perplexity, and, unlike Palamedes, does not consider αὐτὴ ἡ ἀλήθεια a guide more fraught with danger than safety. The truth which he presents in his defense cannot, in fact, be refuted by the plaintiff, or, indeed, be brought into question by the decision of any earthly court. Socrates does not have to fear the outcome. As he says, "Let the trial turn out in a way pleasing to the god" (19a).

It is no matter for wonder, then, that Socrates should feel a fundamental indifference to the outcome of his trial since the truth of his assertion has been borne witness to by the very god of Truth. Unconcerned with the immediate consequences of his words, Socrates relates the history of his activities with no care for how strange the explanation may appear to the jury. He is aware, however, that this truth will probably not gain immediate credence (19a). His estimation of the power of *doxa* is therefore in this respect similar to Palamedes'; but unlike Palamedes he is not constrained to seek aid from the other guide to which Palamedes must apply in his perplexity. Such are the lineaments of the Socrates drawn for us in the *Apology of Socrates*.

As I have observed, the attitude of Socrates towards his defense is reflected in his choice of words to describe this procedure. One consequence of his rigid preference for terms which are in harmony with the tone of rational instruction in accordance with the truth was that terms associated with the activity of πειθὼ πιστευτική were scrupulously avoided. This obtained, however, only so long as fundamentally ambiguous words such as πειθὼ were still undefined with respect to their sphere of operation. But, we should note that as soon as it has been made clear that Socrates' efforts to disabuse the Athenians of their illusions was a form of persuasion sanctioned by the god, there is no hesitation in introducing terms such as πειθὼ to describe such a pursuit (cf. 30a, 31a-b). Before this time its use might have been misunderstood. Now, however, there could be no question of its being anything but a form of πειθὼ διδασκαλική. We may also compare the passage (35c) in which Socrates describes his intention to persuade, but only after it is indicated to what form of persuasion he is referring (διδάσκειν καὶ πείθειν). The meaning is made even clearer in this passage, since what he intends is in unmistakable contrast to the techniques of emotional pleading.

Apart from this piece of evidence, there are other indications of a quite cogent nature. Early in this study we pointed to several instances in the two works of similarities in phrasing which were all the more striking because they were employed in similar contexts. I shall now turn to what, in my opinion, is the most impressive of the verbal parallels which scholars have discovered in the two works. Palamedes, under the stress of the moment, turned to arguments from probability, as was proper for a man who had little confidence in the power of truth to effect immediate persuasion, and who had no transcendental refuge. The function of the probable is, of course, to create, in the absence of any objective evidence, the impression (*doxa*) of the truth. What is involved here is *pistis* in the double sense of that word. The arguments which Palamedes uses must have *pistis* in the sense that they must have an *aura of credibility* powerful enough to persuade — to produce, in other words, that *subjective impression,* or *conviction, of truth* which the Greeks also called *pistis.*

The diction of the *Palamedes* gives clear evidence (cf. n. 27) of the constraint under which the defendant labors. We may say, without exaggeration, that the *Palamedes* is haunted by the problem which *pistis* brings in its train in a world where truth often comes to light only after it has become useless. In the passage (20) in which Palamedes describes the miseries of exile (on which 37c-d of the *Apology* is perhaps modeled), he raises the hypothetical consideration that since he could not return to the Greeks after his act of treason, he would have to live among the barbarians. But how could he, he says (21), since they more than anyone would know of his treason: "I should not be in a position to be trusted by the barbarians" (οὐ μὴν οὐδὲ παρὰ τοῖς βαρβάροις πιστῶς ἂν διεκείμην). In the same passage he says that when a man has lost his *pistis,* he will never regain it. Prompted by these considerations he exclaims (21), "Life is not worth living for a man who is without *pistis*!"

βίος δὲ οὐ βιωτὸς πίστεως ἐστερημένῳ

The similarity to Socrates' famous dictum is striking and obvious, and, as I have indicated earlier, several scholars have noted it. But what has *not* been noted up to now, in the absence of a comparative analysis of the *Palamedes* and the *Apology of Socrates* is that the Socratic maxim has not only been modeled on Palamedes' despairing utterance; *it is also a challenge and an emendation.* It expresses the awareness of Socrates that he has spent his life in the service of the god of Truth precisely in the same manner that Palamedes' exclamation gives voice to a perplexity which arises from his insight that truth is of so little effect in human life. For Palamedes, if truth is really so tardy in its effects, and if, in addition, a man is deprived of the ability to create an impression of truth in others, *then life is clearly not worth living.*

To turn to Socrates, when he says, ὁ δὲ ἀνεξέταστος βίος οὐ βιωτὸς ἀνθρώπῳ (38a), he means that a life spent without examining himself and others *in the service of the god* is not worth living. That ἐξετάζω means precisely this is clear from two other passages (28e and 29e, especially the latter). Socrates has been a soldier in the army of the god of Delphi, and since he has never deserted the ranks, or disobeyed the god's commands, his life has never lost that divine sanction which makes its truth irrefutable. For Socrates standing on the bedrock of certainty, a loss of *pistis* is not to be reckoned a serious matter. And it is this certainty which gives to his speech its tone of confident objectivity and distinguishes it so effectively from the despair of the *Palamedes*.

We may recall here the climax of the dialogue between Socrates and Callicles (*Gorgias* 522c-e), where Socrates is taunted by Callicles because of the admission that he would be powerless to defend himself before a court on an unjust charge, even though this failure might entail the worst consequences. Callicles asks whether such a man is well off. Socrates replies:

> Yes, Callicles, if he have that defence, which as you have often acknowledged he should have — if he be his own defence, and have never said or done anything wrong, either in respect of gods or men; and this has been repeatedly acknowledged by us to be the best sort of defence. *And if anyone could convict me of inability to defend myself or others after this sort, I should blush for shame, whether I was convicted before many, or before a few, or*

by myself alone; and if I died from want to ability to do so, that would indeed grieve me. But if I died because I have no powers of flattery or rhetoric, I am very sure that you would not find me repining at death (italics mine). For no man who is not an utter fool and coward is afraid of death itself, but he is afraid of doing wrong (tr. Jowett).

VII

With these considerations in mind, I should like to turn to the final portion of the *Apology*. In the valedictory address of Socrates (38c-42a), the first section is addressed to the members of the jury who had voted for his condemnation, the other to those who had voted for his acquittal. By now the implication will be clear that the *Apology* in an entire stratum of meaning has little or no relation to an actual courtroom speech delivered by Socrates on the day of his trial.[34] It seems most improbable that Socrates should have improvised or written a speech which presents a coherent portrait of himself as an exemplar of an anti-Sophistic rhetoric, and then, *in addition*, have reinforced this portrait by clear verbal reminiscences of a Sophistic work to whose hero he considered himself an antipode.

In accordance with this position, I suggest here that the last section of the speech is best interpreted not as a record of Socrates' final remarks to the jury, but, rather, as the words of Plato directed to an audience of some years later, for whom the death of Socrates was still a living issue.[35] In the portion of the speech where Socrates prophesies the emergence of a new generation who will subject Greek society to even more severe criticism than he has done, it is hard not

---

34. The notion has been advanced by two scholars that *in fact* no coherent defense was made by Socrates on the day of his trial. For these two interesting discussions, see H. Gomperz, "Sokrates Haltung vor seinen Richtern," *WS* 54 (1936) 32-43, and W. Oldfather, "Socrates in Court," *CW* 31 (1938) 203-11.

35. It seems most reasonable to view the *Apology* in the context of the renewed debate on the influence of Socrates which scholars have connected with Polycrates' *Kategoria* (ca. 395-390 B.C.). It is also likely that besides the *Apology* we should understand the *Gorgias*, Xenophon's *Memorabilia* and *Apologia*, and Aeschines' *Alcibiades* as like efforts to defend Socrates against the criticism of the restored democracy. For a discussion of Polycrates' work, its probable date, and effects, see P. Treves, "Polykrates," *RE* 42 (1952) 1729-50. For sceptical position of the relation of *Kategoria* to *Gorgias*, see Dodds (above, n. 29) 28-29).

to see a prophecy of Plato made after the fact, since it so accurately describes the appearance of the Socratic schools in the first decade after Socrates' death.

This cannot be proved. But in the second part of this section — that devoted to an address to those who had voted for Socrates' acquittal — there are grounds for thinking that we can detect the voice of Plato, and not Socrates, in these remarks (39e-42a). The words were addressed to those who had confidence in the innocence of Socrates, despite the fact that he had been judged guilty. And although this confidence was unshaken, his followers surely remembered his condemnation with great bitterness. As we have seen, Socrates, in Plato's conception was beyond the harm of evil and unjust men such as Meletus and the other accusers, because his life and his activities had been sanctioned by the god of Delphi. It is this consoling truth which Plato wishes to reveal to those who believed in Socrates' innocence, but who had been aggrieved by the manner of his death. "Since you are my friends, I wish to reveal to you the meaning of what has just now happened to me" (40a).

Toward the end of the speech, in Socrates' description of the other world, there is the celebrated passage (41a-c) in which he looks forward to the possibility of conversing with the famous heroes of the Greek past. Among these there would be some who, like himself, had been unjustly condemned to death; he mentions Palamedes and Ajax. Scholars who have observed the verbal allusions to Gorgias' *Palamedes* have not failed to note that the appearance of Palamedes is no accident.[36] This seems quite reasonable; but, beyond any question, the intention of the passage has been completely misinterpreted by its commentators. The accepted interpretation[37] is that Socrates will be happy to meet Palamedes, because he will find in him a sympathetic fellow-sufferer.

But in the light of our exposition of the great contradictions that exist between the *Apology* and the *Palamedes* such an interpretation seems most unlikely. The suspicion, moreover, that this is not so is confirmed to a large degree by an examination of the diction of the

---

36. Morr and Calogero have observed this; see Morr (above, n. 1) 34 and Calogero (above, n. 1) 15.

37. See, e.g., J. Burnet *ad loc.* (Plato, *Euthyphro, Apology, and Crito*, ed. J. Burnet [Oxford 1924]) for failure to observe the importance of Palamedes' appearance in what is perhaps the best of the commentaries on the *Apology*.

passage. Socrates says that conversing with people like Palamedes will be a marvelous pastime (διατριβή). The advocates of the "sympathetic" hypothesis will be somewhat taken aback if they recall at this point that διατριβή or διατρίβειν has been the characteristic[38] designation for Socrates' divinely appointed mission of refuting pretenders to wisdom. Moreover, that it is this connotation of the word which is intended here is suggested several lines further on in the same passage where Socrates says that he will continue "to examine and to investigate" — ἐξετάζοντα καὶ ἐρευνῶντα. (The significance of ἐξετάζω has been discussed; for ἐρευνῶ, cf. 23b ἐρευνῶ κατὰ τὸν θεόν.) Socrates will discover even in the after-world who is wise, and who is not, all their pretensions to the contrary.

But perhaps this does not apply to Palamedes? I suggest that the phrasing of Socrates' afterthought to his remark concerning Palamedes clearly indicates that it does. He says that he is going to set his experience (*pathe*) against Palamedes'. "It would not be unpleasant" (οὐκ ἂν ἀηδὲς εἴη). Let us recall here the passage (33c) in which Socrates is trying to account for the fact that young people like to associate with him and to hear him refute those who think they are wise but are not so. The young people like this, ἔστι γὰρ οὐκ ἀηδές. It seems most unlikely that a complex of words which have gained such unmistakeable force in the course of the Apology can suggest anything else but that Palamedes, along with the others catalogued here, is a pretender to wisdom whom it will be a pleasure for Socrates to refute.

The connotation of this diction, therefore, and the fact that Socrates in the lineaments of his portrait is conceived of as an antipode to Palamedes, both make it likely that we should *not* interpret, as has usually been done, ἀντιπαραβάλλοντι τὰ ἐμαυτοῦ πάθη πρὸς τὰ ἐκείνων as meaning "comparing my misfortunes (in mutual sympathy) with theirs." Our conclusions all tend to an interpretation something like the following (interpretation, not literal translation; these words are in themselves simple and without overtone): "I set my life, and my death (πάοη), and what they both mean, as a direct challenge to (ἀντιπαραβάλλοντι), and refutation of, the validity of the philosophical position which is at the basis of Palamedes' defense of his life." It should be noted that this interpretation of ἀντιπαραβάλλω is in agreement with the meaning of this word in its

---

38. See 29c, 33e, 37d.

only other occurrence. In *Hippias Major* 369c it is used of two *logoi*, and means there to set one argument against another."

VIII

In this study I have sought to investigate only one level of meaning in Plato's *Apology*. For in this work Plato gives us a deeply complex estimate of Socrates' stature as a man and as a philosopher. I have attempted, more exactly, to elucidate the relationship between this work and Gorgias' *Palamedes*, and to suggest that, when once this is done, a new dimension of the *Apology* is revealed. For in this new dimension we perceive Socrates as the philosophical orator who employs a form of persuasion which rests on truth rather than illusion. Why Plato chose to introduce into the *Apology* this aspect of his total conception of Socrates it is hard to say with certainty. For one thing, since he had already chosen, for whatever reason, to draw a portrait of Socrates on the day of his trial, there was surely no more appropriate moment than this to show what rhetoric could become in the hands of a man who had devoted himself to the problems of philosophy rather than to the gratification of the ignorant mob. Moreover, at the time of the composition of the *Apology* (surely the decade 399-389 B.C. is a fair span), rhetoric had just emerged from its infancy. The 390's saw the production of the mature works of orators like Lysias and Andocides, and Isocrates was just publishing his first efforts in forensic oratory. For such a time rhetoric was an important matter (as it was always to remain in the Greek world), and it is not surprising that Plato should have engaged in the exchange of ideas which must certainly have characterized this period.

Surely, however, these solutions are in themselves inadequate, and it is in another direction that we must seek an explanation for the tone of earnest passion which is manifest in the *Apology*. It will be remembered that earlier in this study I attempted to demonstrate that Plato, in the *Gorgias,* attributes to Gorgias a system of rhetoric very much like the one set forth in the *Defense of Palamedes*. A natural assumption, strengthened by the presence of verbal parallels in the two speeches we have been discussing, is that the *Palamedes* was one of the sources of Plato's knowledge of Gorgias' rhetorical theories, although it is of course quite possible that such ideas were communicated in some other way. Now the *Gorgias,* as we know, is concerned with rhetoric, a fact which provides a link between it and the *Apology*, on the one hand, and between both these Platonic works and the *Palamedes* on the other. In this case, then, the behavior of Socrates in the *Apology* would be, on one level at any rate, an illustration of the rhetorical counter-position implied by Socrates' criticisms in the *Gorgias*; and both together would answer to the *Palamedes*, which, as should be clear by now, is a mixture of concrete forensic situation and theoretical formulation.

The *Gorgias*, however, as is well known, is concerned with more than rhetoric. It is also Plato's classic statement of the two alternative ways of life, the philosophical and the worldly. To this theme rhetoric is, of course, related, for it is precisely this which provides the worldly man with the means to power. In this context, then, Plato's critique of Gorgianic rhetoric, which, as I have suggested, is embedded in the fabric of the *Apology*, is seen to be more than a mere technical disagreement. For Plato, in the *Gorgias*, moves on, after his discussion of rhetoric, to a confrontation of the two ways of life as they are incarnated in the figures of Callicles and Socrates. So too in the *Apology*, which is in one of its aspects a critique of an immoral system of rhetoric, we are shown a man who, by his service to the god and to philosophy, has transcended all need to employ a rhetoric which aims at imparting the semblance rather than the substance of truth.

If this conclusion is true, the connection between the *Gorgias* and the *Apology* is a most intimate one, and one may justly call the former a kind of program for the latter. A corollary to this, in the matter of dating the *Apology*, is that, although we cannot certainly date either the *Apology* or the *Gorgias*, we should probably not date them very far apart. For in both we perceive, if I am correct, the same attitude toward the rhetorical position of Gorgias and in both the same search for a philosophically inspired counter-position to the rhetoric of illusion, or, more important, to the moral world from which it springs. For Plato, Socrates' firm belief in the transcendental rightness of the philosophical life provided the ground from which a new kind of rhetoric could grow, a rhetoric which would not have to take into account the shifting nature of human opinion and the changing relationships of political power.

In conclusion I should like to observe that the manner in which Plato discredited a rhetorical theory whose basis and implications he found unacceptable is a stroke worthy of genius. For by modeling the *Apology of Socrates* on the *Palamedes* of Gorgias he brought it about that the reader who was struck by the profoundly contradictory views of which this work was the expression. If it had been done in another way, the issue might have been ignored by those against whom Plato especially directed the *Apology*. But as it was, Greek readers, who could not fail to observe this source of the portrait of Plato's master, could not for this reason ignore the differences which were so impressively in evidence.

TO MAKE THE WEAKER ARGUMENT DEFEAT THE STRONGER*

ALEXANDER SESONSKE

I

Men often decide questions of importance by argument; hence the lack of surprise, in either Plato's day or ours, that some men should profess the ability to "make the weaker argument defeat the stronger" or "make the worse appear the better cause." That such men should be denounced is equally unremarkable; for the profession acknowledges a distinction of better or worse, weaker or stronger, to be made among causes or arguments, but then purports to settle matters of substance without regard for, or in opposition to, this distinction.

We who read Plato will most likely think first of the Sophists when we hear the phrase "to make the weaker argument defeat the stronger." For, though he does not often state the charge in just these terms, Plato's treatment of Sophists, whether in the sharply etched portrait of Protagoras or the schematic logic of the *Sophist*, seems designed to display this aspect in their activity. Protagoras' preference for "myth" over reasoned argument, like his tendency to disrupt the Socratic dialect by making a speech, is a tactical device in the "battle of words" that he takes his conversation with Socrates to be. Hippias' eagerness to join in the game of interpreting Simonides' poem and Thrasymachus' remark at the end of *Republic I*, "Well, this is a feast day, Socrates; let all this be your share of the entertainment," differ markedly in style from Euthydemus' extravagant claim that he can refute any proposition whether true or false. But the underlying attitude toward argument differs very little. Plato often reveals his view of the enterprise which embodied this attitude, perhaps nowhere no succinctly as in the final "definition" of the

---

*© 1968 by the *Journal of the History of Philosophy*, volume 6, pages 217-231, by permission of the editor and author.

Sophist as a dissembling imitator of appearances, creating a shadow-play of words, the illusion of sound argument, at *Sophist* 268c.

Plainly enough, these dialogues do not merely display, but accuse; an accusation embedded in a portrayal sufficiently brilliant to convict the Sophist for all succeeding ages as one concerned in argument with victory rather than truth, and one who has mastered the arts of persuasion and refutation well enough to achieve victory, regardless of truth, in most ordinary encounters. An exhibition of this verbal skill may be harmless entertainment when it occurs on an idle afternoon in the house of Callias or Callicles or Cephalus. The young men who listen and cheer are not convinced by the "sophistic" arguments and thus led astray — the word-play, not the substance of the talk, evokes their attention and admiration. But just herein lies Plato's deep distrust. For these same young men will pay to learn the verbal skill; will later imitate this sophistic jugglery of words in assembly and court of law, bringing to the most serious business of the city the sophist's zeal for victory in disregard of truth.

If, then, we may just take the phrase "to make the weaker argument defeat the stronger" as a summary of Plato's complaint against the Sophists, it might be useful to state fully the crime which provokes the charge.

When put to the Socratic test, the Sophist, like the poet and the politician, reveals his ignorance. But this cannot be the root of Plato's animus, for in his ignorance the Sophist differs not from any other man. Nor can it be that, though ignorant, he persists in argument — for this too is true of every man, including Socrates. But ignorant men, in the Socratic sense, may seek the truth and *speak* the truth. Though Plato early insists upon and later elaborates the difference between genuine knowledge and opinion of belief, he never limits *truth* to the expression of knowledge. Socrates, who disavows all knowledge, does not hesitate to claim to speak the truth, nor to be able to distinguish truth from falsity. His claim is put most strongly in the *Apology*: "From me you shall hear the whole truth"; "Think only of the truth of my words and give heed to that."[1] The *truths* which Socrates then speaks are predominantly truths about

---

1. In the first speech of the *Apology* there are some thirty passages in which Socrates proclaims either that what he says is true or that what his accusers have said is false. Similar references to truth occur in many dialogues, e.g., *Charmides* 160, 161, 162; *Lysis* 213; *Laches* 194; *Protagoras* 348, 352; *Meno* 75; etc.

events in Athens, the encounters and relations of men. They are, that is, truths about "appearances," about sensible objects in the empirical world, that world of "becoming" which Plato will later identify as the object of "opinion." But this does not, for Plato exclude the possibility that they are true.

Throughout the dialogues, as early as the *Meno* and as late as Book IX of the *Laws,* Plato clearly expresses the view that, however opinion may differ from knowledge, some opinions are true.[2] "True" in this context is neither metaphorical nor imprecise. There may be degrees of truth for Plato[3] but there are not kinds. Plato's theory of knowledge develops, of course, from problems which arise only if some opinions are acknowledged to be true. It is the truth of some opinions, such as that Simmias is taller than Socrates but shorter than Phaedo,[4] which leads Plato to distinguish form sensible object, being from becoming reality from appearance, knowledge from opinion, and to talk of sensible objects "participating" in forms. And when a sensible object does participate in a form, says Simmias in tallness, then the statement expressing the opinion that it (he) does is true – it is a true opinion. Plato is usually clear about this, though his commentators have not always been. We may then say that, at least in the early dialogues, there is for Plato a truth of appearances or opinion as well as that more vital fundamental truth of things "in themselves" – the truth of Forms.[5] And though Plato may later proclaim the existence of a knowledge wholly of truths and a mode of inquiry beyond all appearances, in his earlier dialogues the truths of appearance provide the substance of those arguments that ordinary men, and Socrates, must pursue to gain any deeper knowledge.

---

2. One can have a true opinion, we recall, about the road to Larissa (*Meno* 97ff.). Cf. also *Symposium* 202, *Timaeus* 37, *Theatetus* 187ff. (where the claim that true opinion is knowledge is perhaps refuted, but the claim that there are true opinions is never questioned), *Philebus* 66 and *Laws* 864.
3. Cf. *Republic* 511.
4. Or the opinions that the Greek who remains at his post and fights is courageous but so also is the Scythian who fights flying (*Laches* 190).
5. Henceforth I shall mark the difference by writing "truth$_A$" for "truth of appearance" and "truth$_F$" for "truth of form". My truth$_A$ is meant to correspond to Plato's *doxa*, which includes both the apprehension of sensible particulars and the vague and imperfect grasp of forms characteristic of ordinary men. Cf. *Meno,* ed. R. S. Bluck (Cambridge, Ebg., 1961), pp. 10ff.

There seem at least four types of truths$_A$, apparently accessible to any ordinary man, which serve as starting points of argument, as supplementary premises, and as instruments for testing claims or conclusions occurring in the course of argument. These types, of which numerous examples may be found through the dialogues, are: (1) descriptions and reports of objects, events, actions, or states of affairs, e.g., the son of Themistocles was not a good and wise man in the way that his father was (*Meno* 93e); (2) attributions of some (often moral) characteristic to a type of action, e.g., a man who remains at his post and fights against the enemy is courageous (*Laches* 191a); (3) observational generalizations, e.g., well-bred dogs have a disposition to be gentle with their familiars but the contrary with strangers (*Rep.* 375e); (4) common sense (moral) universal statements, e.g., temperance is noble and good (*Charmides* 159c).

If there is a truth of appearances, there is also a falsity. Hence particular statements of each type may be challenged or refuted without raising a general question of the possibility or actuality of truth$_A$. Such challenge and refutation provides, of course, the dynamic elements from which Socrates constructs his dialectic. But it provides also the logic of the arguments daily undertaken by ordinary men. Hence if there is a distinction to be made between "weaker" and "stronger" in these arguments, it must be that the conclusions of strong arguments are reached or defended by the use of true$_A$ statements which do logically support the true$_A$ conclusion, whereas a weaker argument will be one whose logic is faulty or which proceeds from premises that are not even true$_A$. In these terms weakness and strength are logical properties of arguments, and the relative strength or weakness of arguments is an objective fact about them. To make the weaker argument defeat the stronger is not to make the weaker argument stronger, or the worse cause better, but so to confuse the issue that those who hear the argument will prefer and accept the conclusion of the weaker argument despite its weakness.

Ordinary men can discern truths of appearance; they can also apprehend logical relations between statements and terms. Otherwise the Socratic mission could not have even gotten under way. Hence ordinary men are capable of distinguishing strong and weak in argument. How then can they prefer and accept the weaker argument, allowing the stronger to be defeated? And why should anyone deliberately seek to achieve this perverse result?

Men may pursue, or hear, an argument in three quite different ways. One, the Socratic way, is to enter the argument as an *inquirer* after truth, intent on following each strand of argument to its proper end, willing to accept whatever conclusion arrives, if only it be soundly reached. Another is to enter the argument as a *partisan*, defending a belief one hopes to make prevail, using the argument to establish *this* conclusion rather than its own. The third way is to argue as a *combatant*, neither seeking truth, nor defending a strongly held view, intent rather on refuting or upsetting an opponent than reaching a conclusion, however sound. If one argues as an inquirer, his only interest lies in the logical strength or weakness of the argument, for to make the stronger argument defeat the weaker is the path to truth. But one who argues as a combatant or partisan may find another sort of strength of more concern. This is persuasiveness, the power of the argument to produce belief, a psychological rather than logical strength. Since logical and psychological strength do not always coincide, the partisan or combatant will seek the latter; for if he persuades, his aim in the argument will have been achieved, whether or not truth prevails.

Those arguments undertaken by ordinary men develop in the course of daily events, occurring as attempts to resolve practical questions. The outcome of these arguments is belief and action. Into such arguments most men enter as partisans. Each man, involved in the affairs, sees alternative outcomes as being more or less advantageous for himself, and argues to defend that conclusion which appears best for him. This does not necessarily coincide with truth, but each man tends to accept as true, i.e., believe, what seems to his advantage. This is one factor making for persuasiveness or psychological strength; an argument favoring what one takes to be advantageous has already a degree of persuasiveness, whatever its logical strength. Neither this nor other sources of persuasiveness, e.g., familiarity and emotive tone, provide an index of logical strength. But if logical strength can be obscured, mere persuasiveness may well prevail with ordinary men, being mistaken for truth.

The Sophist enters argument as a combatant. For him an argument is not the occasion for resolving a practical problem, but for exercise of a skill. He will answer any question, respond to any argument, talk on any subject. The content of the conclusion is irrelevant; what matters is that *his* argument should have won. A teacher by profession, largely teaching verbal skill to ordinary men, his advantage seems to lie in impressing others with the power of such skill. Since most men argue as partisans, this can best be done by showing that, whatever cause the Sophist makes his own, it can be rendered more persuasive than opposing views. So the Sophist cultivates those techniques of distraction, digression, exploitation of ambiguity and emotional appeal that still remain the stock in trade of demagogues. In Plato's day, in the infancy of logic, when common speech lacked even the terms to express those logical relations and distinctions intuitively seen, a deliberate attempt to mislead men into accepting bad logic for good might well succeed (as it does now). Even the Sophists, the masters of the game, could be misled, if Plato's dialogues are witness. Though any man can apprehend logical relations, he grasps them firmly only in arguments simple in form and clearly presented, preferably in step-by-step sequence. If the argument be complicated or disordered, embellished by rhetoric or interrupted by digressions, the logical thread is easily lost — persuasion rather than logical strength may seem to offer truth.

In the arena in which the Sophist exhibits his wares, arguments are entertainments and the consequences of argument are slight. The outcome of an argument is victory or defeat; its consequences, cheers or laughter, a slight momentary and local enhancement or decline of prestige. Perhaps a pupil is won or lost; perhaps there are no consequences of the argument at all beyond the victory or defeat. No one's beliefs are changed; no one's actions are influenced. So the Sophist can be magnanimous in victory and gracious in defeat. But when ordinary men inquire and argue, the outcome is belief and action, the consequences will be found in the lives of men and cities, which may be profoundly changed. Having serious results, these arguments should be seriously undertaken.

For Plato, as for Socrates, argument — logically connected discourse — is man's avenue to knowledge as well as his instrument for testing, retaining, and extending truth$_A$. This understood, argument is, we might say, man's hope and his most serious enterprise. Hence Plato's anger at its misuse. Rightly undertaken, an argument is an inquiry — a search for truth. And whatever man's apparent advantage may be, his real advantage lies in finding truth and acting in its light. Hence the only genuine strength an argument has is logical strength, for only logical strength leads to truth. Proper argument is inquiry, with each inquirer committed to believe and act upon the answer reached, persuaded by logical strength, with neither vanity nor fear nor the attraction of apparent advantage allowed to sway the argument from paths of logical strength. Here the weaker argument can defeat the stronger only through error, by men mistaking false premises for true or fallacy for sound logic. Hence the genuine inquirer will state and examine each premise carefully and take each logical step singly — in this manner error may be minimized.

As Plato sees the Sophist, his mode of argument completely fails to conform to this model. He does not argue seriously; he is not committed to believe or act as the argument dictates. He is a performer, not an inquirer, wholly concerned with the manner of his speech and its immediate effect upon an audience. Intent upon the apparent advantage of victory, he knowingly obscures logical strength in order that persuasiveness may prevail. His aim seems indeed to make the weaker argument defeat the stronger, not only in that he wittingly fosters psychological over logical strength, but also in that he treats even strong arguments as weak by denying them their proper role in guiding belief and action. His influence on ordinary men is to encourage partisanship by supplying tricks to enhance any partisan cause and to discourage the pursuit of truth by treating argument as a game in which persuasion takes the prize. Hence the vehemence of Plato's portrayal.

II

Something like this, I believe, is what we tend to understand by the phrase "to make the weaker argument defeat the stronger." As such, it is a philosopher's charge against pretenders to knowledge, and educator's charge against false education. But in the dialogue in which the phrase most frequently occurs, the *Apology*, it has, I think, quite another sense. Here is a complaint made by ordinary men against philosophers and, if the *Apology* may be credited, it is in this form that the phrase was current in ancient Greece. It is worth nothing that in the *Apology* Socrates names five specific charges made against himself by earlier and late accusers. Of the five he answers all but one. The accusation left unanswered, not discussed at all, is, of course, that Socrates "makes the weaker argument defeat the stronger." Thinking of Plato's dialogues, we feel that this complaint, so obviously false, needs no discussion or refutation. Everyone knows that Socrates, more than any other man, was an inquirer who valued truth and scorned persuasion — the complaint is false. The other charges, though perhaps false, may be seriously meant; this one could not be believed by any man. But this is to identify the complaint against Socrates with Plato's accusation of the Sophists. And it is *not* that charge at all! Perhaps this charge by ordinary men cannot be dismissed merely by citing Plato's act of distinguishing Socrates from Sophist. And perhaps Plato knows this too!

I shall contend he does; and that it is a significant fact about the *Apology* that one accusation in five is not discussed. For this accusation, far from being trivial, is *the* important one, the one upon which the verdict of the jury hangs. The other charges can be summarily dismissed; this one cannot. Hence, to see the *Apology* clearly is to see that the whole of Socrates' defense is vitally concerned with this charge. In its entirety his first speech to the jury constitutes paradoxically, both a refutation and a confirmation of the charge, allowing the jury to decide which to heed. Gadfly to the end, here Plato's Socrates has proposed one final test for the Athenians, a test whose prize is his life. A test, alas, which the Athenians fail. But even here one finds a sort of poetic propriety in the failure and its price; for the test is, in a way, a test of Socrates as well. The response of the Athenians to this Socratic test constitutes a measure of the success of Socrates' life in Athens, a measure of the degree to which he has conveyed that great lesson which was his to teach. Hence their failure is also his.

Eric Havelock has recently argued[6] that the great transformation which occurred in Greek culture during the lifetime of Socrates and Plato was transition from a predominantly oral culture to a literate one, from a culture which preserved its store of wisdom in memory and transmitted it from mouth to ear to a community of fluent readers in which knowledge was recorded in the written word and conveyed via the eye rather than the ear. One mark, or condition, of this change is the development of a vocabulary of abstract terms. A critical phase of the transition is the alteration of a vocabulary of abstract terms. A critical phase of the transition is the alteration of modes of thought made possible by this new language of abstractions. In an oral tradition thought and speech tend to poetic form — concrete, rhythmic, formulaic, emotionally charged — a form which

---

6. *Preface to Plato* (Cambridge, Mass., 1963).

fosters identification of the self with the concrete situations and stories described for this is the form that facilitates memory, And education consists largely to developing and stocking the memory, the learner hearing and reciting the rhythmic narrative which embodies the history, technology, social organization and morality of his community[7] until it is memorized, with any portion of it subject to recall. The development of literacy frees the mind from this massive task of memorization. Its energies may now be used to develop and practice other modes of thought, abstract modes in which the object known is distinct from the knower and can be dispassionately viewed – in short, critical inquiry and analysis, the modes of thought which Socrates and Plato pursued in Athens, In a pre-literate community the occurrence of a question is an occasion for the exercise of memory, for searching in the remembered oral record for that portion of the narrative which bears upon the problem now at hand. But with literacy a new technique disputes the propriety of the old; a problem may be met by working out the solution in abstract thought. The full utilization of this technique requires a new form of education, though, with memorization being supplemented or replaced by a method which fosters the understanding of abstract terms and develops the capacity for problem-solving abstract thought – a method which teaches men "to think about what they say, instead of just saying it."[8]

Havelock accords to Plato and Socrates the status of major figures in the Greek transition from oral to literate culture, thus understood. Socrates, perhaps not fully aware of the nature of the change, nevertheless spent his life urging the Athenians to engage in abstract thought. By his persistent questions he demanded that they repeat the things they "knew," thus tending to separate them from the memorized poetic narrative; that they restate them in other words, thus thinking rather than merely saying; that they talk of the "thing itself," thus formulating their awareness in abstract terms. The method of abstraction leads to genuine knowledge – such is the sovereign truth that he proclaims. The ignorance he found engulfing all Athenians consisted in their inability to say what they "knew" in logically-connected, abstract terms. Plato, Havelock contends, knew precisely the nature of the change and his role in it. His great accom-

7. *Ibid.*, p. 198.
8. *Ibid.*, p. 47.

plishment was to formulate and expound once and for all the syntax of the prose of abstract thought and to explore the logic of this language. Consciously opposing tradition, Plato undertook the task of creating "knowledge" as an object and as the content of education. Completed by Aristotle, this effort shaped the dominant mental disciplines of the Western world.[9]

If accepted, Havelock's thesis allows, or perhaps requires, us to read the *Apology* in a rather new light. This reveals, I believe, the accuracy of the claim that the primary charge against which Plato's Socrates constructs his defense is that the "makes the weaker argument defeat the stronger." It also displays the deadly irony of his defense.

The content of this charge as Plato levelled it against the Sophists was sketched above. Here the "stronger" argument is logically strong, with the strength of valid logic connecting true statements, contrasted to the spurious psychological strength of persuasion. We may now recognize that this account of "stronger" is formulated wholly in the language of abstraction which Socrates, then Plato, helped to shape. The truths it bids us seek are the abstract truths so essential for an explicit grasp of logical form. The very formulation is itself a step and an instrument in the struggle to replace the cast of mind characteristic of the oral culture by "thinking" — dispassionate, critical, abstract thought. As such it must contrast with whatever sense of "strong" the populace intend when they raise their charge against philosophers, including Socrates. And Plato, the self-conscious leader of the fight against the old, cannot have confused the two.

We must, then, try to state what "strength" in argument would be for those who accuse Socrates. It will not do to say "persuasiveness," for what men are persuaded by will differ with their modes of thought. Socrates would be persuaded by cool logic.

A strong argument for any man will at least be one he seems to understand, one couched in familiar terms that he can comprehend and proceeding in patterns he recognizes as appropriate to the subject at hand. Assuming that Socrates' accusers were men still close to the oral tradition, we can say what such argument would be for them. Familiar terms would be the concrete, image-making, descriptive terms of the oral record: appropriate patterns of speech, those of

---

9. *Ibid.*, p. 305.

the rhythmic, formulaic, narrative style spoken by the wise men who conveyed to them all the knowledge which the culture treasures and preserves. In an oral culture the wise man earns that name through his powers of memory and speech. He is the man who most completely and readily recalls the poetic narrative within which the tradition is retained. And he is the man who most readily reformulates the new knowledge which the culture needs and gains into the concrete rhythmic patterns which facilitate its retention in memory. Also, of course, he is a man whose arguments are "strong," i.e., a man who should be listened to and heeded when he speaks.

In an oral culture not dominated by a priesthood, as the Greeks were not, we might expect that wise men could be roughly classified into two categories, defined by the area within which their talents are predominantly used. Some will devote their powers to preserving and extending the store of knowledge which is the culture's core, some to applying this knowledge to the problems of contemporary life. The former will be poets, the latter politicians, or rhetoricians, perhaps, if they are more concerned with love than war. Thus in Socrates' statement (*Apology* 23e) that of his three accusers, Meletus speaks for the poets, Anytus for the politicians and Lycon for the rhetoricians, I find some confirmation of the claim that Plato sees Socrates' defense as directed against defenders of the patterns of thought and speech characteristic of the fading oral tradition.

In these terms the claim that someone "makes the weaker argument defeat the stronger" asserts that the accused speaks in terms and forms quite different from those familiar within the tradition, *and yet somehow compels* assent. All of Plato's early dialogues proclaim that this was true of Socrates!

III

In the *Apology* Socrates begins his address to the jury by, in effect, accusing his accusers of seeking to make the weaker argument defeat the stronger. In doing this he strikes two notes which resound throughout the defense. First he insists upon a distinction between truth and persuasiveness; second, he insists that he, Socrates, is different from ordinary men. His accusers have spoken persuasively, but he will speak the truth! Of course, but how are we to understand "persuasion" and "truth" here? The distinction Socrates intends is clear *to us* as that which Plato makes in his attack upon the Sophists, wherein truth follows the logical strength of abstract argument and persuasiveness characterizes any argument which does not proceed in valid logical form and yet calls forth assent. But should we expect that the jury would readily apprehend the distinction in this form? That they would not is implied by the following lines in which Socrates distinguished himself from ordinary men.

At this point the difference Socrates claims for himself is a difference in modes of Speech. He professes amazement that his accusers should undertake to warn the jury against being deceived by his power of speech, for anyone can see that he has no skill in speech at all — unless by power of speech they mean the power of truth, for in that sense he is eloquent. Unlike his accusers he will speak the truth, but not in an oration decked in fine phrases. No, he will continue to speak as he has always spoken — in plain simple speech. For he is a stranger to the courts of law and unfamiliar with the language of the place. Therefore he must be allowed to speak in his own way, and the jury must consider only the *truth* of what he says.

What are we to make of all this? It is not, surely, merely an ironic and disarming opening statement, reminding the jurors of distinctions they all know and accept, cited here simply to place the utterances of his accusers in the proper light. And is it plausible to think that the accusers, in warning against his "power of speech," meant to credit Socrates with either traditional forensic skill or an unusual ability to speak the truth?

Rather, in these opening remarks we find a direct confrontation of the two great cultural forces then at work in Athens, two forces whose difference I have sought to express in two interpretations of the phrase "to make the weaker argument defeat the stronger." Each accuses the other of this crime; yet, as we have seen, the accusations are only verbally alike. The contrast between these two forces is here remarked by Socrates as a difference in patterns of speech — a formulation which, indeed, strikes right to the heart of the affair. His accusers have spoken in a "set oration decked out in fine words and phrases," clearly close to the concrete, rhythmic, formulaic familiar forms of the oral tradition. Such speech is, again it is clear, "the language of this place." But it is a false language which persuades without expressing truth. In contrast Socrates insists upon his right to speak his homely prose, frequently in unfamiliar abstract terms; this is the proper language for conveying truth.

In his defense Socrates does not merely speak in a manner different from that of his accusers, allowing the jury to notice this and make of it what they will. Rather he announces the difference and asserts the superiority of his mode of speech. In this initial claim to speak the truth Socrates thereby declares that his trial must be an open clash of these two linguistic forms, with the jury forced to decide which best expresses truth. To complete his preliminary statement Socrates then urges the necessity of dealing first with the earlier anonymous accusers who said that Socrates, a wise man, speculates about the heavens above and searches into the earth below and can make the weaker argument defeat the stronger. These, he says, are the accusers most to be feared. Here there can be no doubt that the two contesting linguistic forms express the opposition of cultural forces. The accusers are anonymous; their voice is that of the beleaguered oral tradition. The accused are not merely Socrates but rather "philosophers" — wise men — the whole group of intellectuals, including pre-socratics and Sophists, who have promoted a new knowledge and who have developed new abstract forms of thought and speech. The scope of the trial is thus defined and the jurors compelled to weigh the charges in terms of this cultural clash.

Hence Socrates' opening remarks are hardly disarming; they resemble instead a declaration of war. At the least, they proclaim that the trial of Socrates is to be made a test of Athens.

Only in terms of this contest of linguistic forms can the accuser's warning be understood: Do not be deceived by Socrates, who talks in strange unfamiliar ways, difficult to remember and hard to understand, but who still somehow has the power to compel us to agree to what he says.

There are four major "movements" in Socrates' defense: (1) a discussion of the older accusations, (2) an account of those aspects of his life which gave rise to the old charges, (3) a discussion of the current charges, consisting largely in the questioning of Meletus, and (4) an account of Socrates' current beliefs and activities and their relation to the trial. I shall briefly comment on each of these.

1) The old charges, Socrates repeats, are that he searches into things beneath the earth and in the sky, makes the weaker argument defeat the stronger, and teaches these practices to others. To "refute" these charges Socrates first calls upon all present to witness that he has never been heard to propound a physical theory and, second, denies that he has ever offered to teach anyone anything for a fee. About the third charge he says, as I have noted above, nothing.

We may note three things about this refutation: (a) To deny traditional beliefs about the heavens and the underworld may well seem to qualify one as a "searcher" into these areas — for how else could one know that the traditional view is false (or that those who express it "know nothing")? (b) Socrates' replies to the two charges constitute a *logical* refutation of the charges, but only if the charges are given an abstract interpretation. That is, if we define "searching into the earth and sky" as "propounding a physical theory" and "teaching" as "formally accepting students for a fee" then the truth of Socrates' remarks suffices to demonstrate the falsity of the charges. If, however, the charges are understood in looser terms — terms perhaps more appropriate to the oral tradition and probably more familiar to the jury — then these logically strong arguments may seem weak indeed. (c) In replying to these two charges Socrates distinguishes himself from the pre-socratic natural philosophers, who did expound physical theories, and from the Sophists, who did accept pupils for a fee. But in not replying to the third charge he allows himself to remain united to these two groups of "wise men" in their common enterprise of reshaping the language and thought of Greece.

2) Socrates' "mission" is described as an account of the origin of these obviously false charges. For years he has lived in the streets of Athens, examining every man reputed to be wise. First he attempted to refute the oracle and find a man wiser than himself; failing that, he continued in order to show these Athenians that they have only the pretense of knowledge. The mission is completely innocent; knowing nothing, Socrates teaches nothing but only exposes the falsity of others' claims. But if we describe the mission in the terms we have developed here, its innocence may be less apparent. Socrates has questioned all those reputed to be wise, politicians, poets, orators. These are the wise men of the oral tradition; men whose wisdom consists in a superior memory of the preserved wisdom of the tradition and a superior ability to express themselves in its forms. Thus to assert that none of these men are wise is to deny the validity of the whole tradition. We know from Plato's dialogues the character of Socrates' "examination" of these wise men. Its core is the demand that anything truly known be expressed in abstract terms; a failure to comply to this demand demonstrates that one "does not know." Thus conceived, Socrates' mission is to replace the traditional forms

of speech and thought by their new counterparts — to replace reliance on memory by abstract logical thought. Again we note, if "wisdom" is interpreted abstractly, Socrates' claim of innocence is true. But if wisdom means what it has traditionally meant in Athens, his mission is bizarre, perhaps malicious. Bizarre in that Socrates professes to be seeking to determine who is wise, whereas nothing is more easy to discover — everyone in Athens knows. Malicious in that, accosting these wise men, Socrates then "test" their wisdom by insisting that they answer his strange questions — questions no man can answer, and questions quite distinct from any through which wisdom is normally elicited; therefore, questions which cannot by any ordinary standard be admitted as a test of wisdom. In this sense the mission is malicious; its aim is to falsely label wise men fools and to discomfit and embarrass them.

3) The interrogation of Meletus is the once instance in the *Apology* of Socrates' usual procedure. As such it provides the clearest example of the substance of the charge that he "makes the weaker argument defeat the stronger." There are three phases of the interrogation, three arguments in each of which Socrates forces from Meletus an admission that logically refutes some aspect of the charge. In each phase the cogency of the argument depends upon the acceptance of abstract generalizations, e.g., all animals are improved by a specialized trainer but harmed by ordinary men, or, no man intentionally acts in ways harmful to himself. Meletus unwillingly agrees to the steps leading to these conclusions, then is accused by Socrates of being reckless and impudent and not even himself believing the charges he has made.

But consider what Meletus' accusation must have been: a description of this unkempt old man eliciting from Athens' leading citizens those hallowed truths about the gods which are preserved in the oral tradition, then by his verbal tricks bringing them to say that they do not know what piety is. Meanwhile young men look on, imitate the Socratic mode of speech and assert, like Socrates, that the wisest men of Athens know nothing.

And consider what Meletus' view of the world must have been: the view, we assume, transmitted in the oral tradition. In this view Meletus is correct to hesitate to say which person improves the youth — for, as he claims, everyone does. That is, everyone assists in the education of the young by repeating to them segments of the oral narrative, correcting and supplementing their memories when they fail, providing examples of proper ways to act and speak.[10] And only one man corrupts them — the man, like Socrates, who shows them the inadequacy of all traditional wisdom.

Again, only if we define "wisdom" as abstract thought are Socrates' contentions true. For then education *is* a task for the trained specialist, in Plato's Academy perhaps, who can acquaint the student with valid patterns of analytic thought and provide exercises to promote the development of this analytic skill. But how empty the arguments must seem to those still living essentially within the oral tradition — even though they do compel assent. For the propositions refuted have the character of obvious truths within the tradition; the refutation is reached by a series of peculiarly formed questions, not easy to understand, yet each question so formulated that no response other than assent seems possible. So one assents, agrees *to* the propositions. He does not, however, agree *with* it, i.e., allow it to disturb any of his own beliefs. For in its unfamiliar form it falls quite outside the range of propositions to which he accords either belief or disbelief. We would now say that given the abstract conceptions which are Socrates' concern, many of the formulation for which he asks assent are analytic or tautologous. The Athenians questioned could not, of course, say this; if they could they would already have left the oral tradition far behind.

Having assented to three or four Socratic questions, our Athenian suddenly finds that he has contradicted himself and is refuted. But the refutation carries no conviction at all; for, though agreed to, no step along the way has been believed. And yet it cannot be denied! For in their step-by-step procedure Socrates' arguments have a *logical strength* that even the most analytically untrained mind must feel. However, the argument is completely unpersuasive; the conclusion cannot be believed even though it cannot be denied. It wholly lacks the persuasive psychological strength of the traditional wisdom. Hence Meletus' reluctance to answer; hence the shouted interrup-

---

10. Note that in the *Meno,* Anytus, another accuser at the trial, explicitly puts forth this view of education. Asked to whom a young man should go to be taught virtue, Anytus replies, "Why mention any particular individual? Any Athenian gentleman, taken at random, will do him far more good that the Sophists will" (*Meno* 92e).

tions by the crowd; and hence the charge that Socrates makes the weaker argument defeat the stronger.

4) "Enough has been said to answer Meletus' accusation." The remainder of Socrates' defense consists mainly in an assertion of some of his convictions which bear upon the trial: a man worth anything will not be concerned with life and death, but only with right and wrong; the things properly of greatest concern to a man are *thinking* and *truth* and the excellence of the *soul*; no man who consistently strives for right and justice can survive in public life. Heretofore Socrates has been content to state his defense in largely neutral terms, abusing Meletus a bit perhaps, but, apart from his insistence on the propriety of his own mode of speech, saying nothing calculated to outrage the jurors. But now the tone changes considerably; this last segment of the defense bristles with defiance, even arrogance — an arrogance that belittles the jury at every point, proclaiming Socrates' superiority over them. I note here only some of these defiant fusillades:

a) *A worthy man will not fear death, but be concerned only with right and wrong.* This doctrine is put forth in a manner which clearly implies that the jurors do fear death. They are then told that the fear of death is a disgraceful sort of ignorance. Socrates here reminds the jury of his courage on the battlefield and then shows them that he is acting with equal courage now. But it is one thing to act courageously, quite another to call your attention to it as I do. For that rankles, particularly when the hearer is not in a situation equally demanding courageous action. He is made to feel inferior and if he has the power he may well feel tempted to test that claim to courage by drawing the situation to its most extreme conclusion.

b) *If offered acquittal on condition that I cease my usual activities, I shall refuse; for the mission was commanded by God and I believe no greater good has ever befallen the state.* Here Socrates not only declares that he will not reform in any way, whatever the outcome of the trial, but also relates this (stubborn) refusal to a claim to have superior knowledge about the welfare of the state. And in refusing a conditional acquittal before it has been offered he not only eliminates this as a possibility, but also cuts off the possibility that any juror might vote for acquittal in the hope that Socrates will feel chastened by the trial and mend his errant ways. Again, his arrogance tempts the juror to respond: "So! You prefer death to any change in your accustomed ways? Very well!"

c) *If you put me to death you will injure yourselves more than you injure me. So I am arguing for your sakes, not mine. You will not easily find anyone to take my place.* The injury that Socrates contends the jurors will do themselves is dual here; they will have committed an unjust act and they will lose the most valuable member of the community. Even so, who can be pleased at being told by an accused man, "I am only concerned with your welfare here, not my own."

d) *No good man could survive in public life.* Here the implication is that none of the Athenians who engage in politics are consistently concerned with right and justice — as Socrates is.

Are we to lay these remarks to a suicidal urge, or take them as attempts to display Socrates disdain for death? I think not. Rather they are a significant part of the test with which Socrates confronts Athens. In making these arrogant claims Socrates is, as he promised, speaking the truth — if we accept the language of abstraction and the Platonic thesis of the overwhelming importance of developing the tools of abstract thought. This last segment of the defense is replete with the abstract terms which were Socrates' major concern: right, justice, wisdom, goodness, truth, God, thinking and that major Socratic gift to the western world, soul. In their terms Socrates' mission is the greatest good which befell the state and his remarks about death, honor and politics are plausible, at least. But to those still enmeshed in the old tradition the claims must seem quite wild.

Yes, but even if, in this sense, true, why are these remarks couched in such insulting terms? We can answer this question now, I think, by making clear the over-all character of the defense and the nature of the test it poses. The crucial charge to be met, I have claimed, is that of "making the weaker argument defeat the stronger." As the charge is intended, the stronger argument is the familiar formulation of the traditional wisdom; the weaker argument, the abstract, logical Socratic talk which compels assent but carries no conviction. Socrates' response to the charge is, as we have seen, first to define his trial as a confrontation of linguistic forms and to make a counter charge, i.e., the *same* charge, but understood in what I have called Platonic terms. The contest is between truth and persuasion, but the jury must decide which form of speech expresses truth and *then accept this as the basis of belief.* The question with which Plato's Socrates faces Athens is: have you so learned the lesson that I teach that you now recognize the strength of abstract argument and *believe* in its conclusions? Are you ready to respond to and accept genuine strength in argument? For Plato, if not Socrates, knows that this is a test which Athens must pass if the transition from oral to literate culture is to be fully accomplished. The point at which Athens stands, as represented in the *Apology*, is the point at which for many Athenians abstract argument carries truth and thus compels verbal assent, but the familiar formulations of the tradition remain persuasive; they still control belief and action. To achieve a fully literate culture a group must not merely become familiar with abstract terms and patterns of thought, but so accept them that they carry conviction. This now is what Socrates demands of the jury when he claims that the juror's duty is to judge by truth alone.

And so he constructs the test. It will be a genuine test and not an exercise, for the stake is a man's life. And it cannot be evaded; the jury must vote. The question is: can you correctly choose between real truth and mere persuasion. But to be a real test we must, as it were, have both truth and persuasion bare — all truth on one side; all persuasiveness on the other. Thus the test we find in the *Apology* much resembles that which Glaucon proposed to Socrates in the *Republic* when he demanded to be shown that the just man is happy, even though he be shorn of all external rewards. Here the question is, have you been shown that it is only the truth that makes an argument strong, even though it be shorn of all persuasiveness?

All truth on one side: And so it is, if we accept the abstract conceptions of truth and wisdom and forsake the old tradition. For in this light the charges against Socrates are completely false.

All persuasion on the other: In his first words Socrates testifies to the persuasiveness of his accusers. And in his defense he takes great care not to compete with them on this ground. Here we have an explanation for the suicidal tone. Socrates' speech is not devoid of persuasive devices, but all of them are used to weigh the psychological balance against himself. His stance before the jury is: I have told you the truth; I have replied to the charges. Now I shall add to the persuasiveness of my accusers' speech by doing what I can to anger you, to humiliate you, to belittle you. And can you still hold to the truth?

The irony then is that in his defense Socrates does his best to make the weaker argument defeat the stronger. He builds the logically weak case of his accusers to maximum psychological strength, leaves his defense with mere unpersuasive truth to recommend it; then says, "Now judge!"

Had the Athenians, just struggling free of the oral tradition, passed this test, it would have been remarkable indeed. I wonder if we should do as well. Here we can perhaps only agree with Socrates' surprise that so many votes were cast for acquittal.

Given this interpretation of the dialogue, one cannot, of course, believe in the historical accuracy of the *Apology* — if that is any longer in question. The dialogue emerges here not as a description of the actual events of Socrates' trial, but rather as an account of Socrates' life and of a cultural moment of importance in Athens, showing the nature of the test which that life proposed to this culture. It is an account which exposes the cultural conflict for which Socrates' life served as a point of focus, showing both the importance of that life for the community and the reasons for its forcible termination.

GORGIAS*

Paul Friedländer

In the *Gorgias,* Plato returns to the *Thrasymachus,* raising both form and content of the earlier work to a new creative level. The theme in both dialogues is the problem of justice and the struggle against its opponents. In each dialogue, Socrates has three such opponents, and they are progressively farther removed from him. Thus, both dialogues move through three stages with the intensity of the struggle progressively increasing.

Let us at once note the differences. In the *Thrasymachus,* we find, on the first level, old Kephalos, a simple, unphilosophical man representing justice as a natural disposition. Gorgias, however, formally corresponding to Kephalos, bears the stamp of *adikia* even though he is not consistent enough to admit that he belongs to the sphere of the lawless. Thus, the two dialogues differ in their points of departure from which the movement of the whole proceeds to the finale of ruthless exposure. Another difference is connected with this. In the *Thrasymachus,* the problem of justice is presented naked, as it were, in the form of a search for a definition, and this search, in the nature of the early dialogues, must end on a note of *aporia.* Thrasymachos, the sophistic orator, is the extreme spokesman on behalf of injustice. Yet, his profession — his name, "Keen Fighter," would make everybody think of it — is not brought into the dialogue explicitly, so that the connection between sophistic and *adikia* remains obscure. It is precisely this connection that is brought into full

*From *PLATO,* by Paul Friedländer, translated by Hans Meyerhoff, Bollingen Series LIX, vol. II, *The Dialogues . . . First Period* (copyright © 1964 by Bollingen Foundation), reprinted by permission of Princeton University Press: pp. 244-272.

consciousness in the *Gorgias*; for here the figure of the famous orator — Gorgias himself — represents sophistic rhetoric, and the figure of Kallikles represents the kind of immoralism consistent with it. Just as Kallikles, at the beginning, admits to being a follower of Gorgias, so the principles he represents are founded upon sophistic rhetoric. The struggle of Socrates is directed not only against these principles, but against the cultural system itself that is shown to be the breeding ground of this immoralism and must be overthrown intellectually.[1]

In contrast to the two other great antisophistic dialogues, the *Protagoras* and the *Euthydemus,* the *Gorgias* is presented not as a report, but in direct dramatic form. This accounts for the absence of almost all background and symbolism in the spatial setting. The persons of the drama confront each other, directly expressing themselves and their objective differences. The situation at the beginning is similar to the *Hippias Minor*. A famous visitor from abroad has just delivered a polished speech and is still surrounded by a circle of admirers, whom Plato later brings back into the conversation now and then.[2] Gorgias is staying with Kallikles, as Protagoras is staying with Kallias. Socrates, coming from the market place, first meets Kallikles, the host, entering his house. The very first words are spoken by the man who will prove to be the most formidable opponent in the last part of the dialogue; he does not, like Anytos in the *Meno,* burst into the conversation with uncanny abruptness. Thus, the connection between Kallikles and Gorgias, between immoralism and oratory, is

---

1. The answers of antiquity to the question of the σκοπος of the dialogue will be found in Olympiodoros' *Commentary to the "Gorgias,"* ed. Norvin (Leipzig, 1936), Prooem., p. 2: (1) οι μεν γαρ φασιν οτι σκοπος αυτω περι ρητορικης διαλεχθηναι. (2) αλλοι δε φασιν οτι περι δικαιοσυνης και αδικιας διαλεγεται. (3) αλλοι δε λεγουσιν οτι σκοπον εχει περι του δημιουργου διαλεχθηναι (on account of the myth). (4) Olympiodoros censures all these interpretations because they απο μερους τον σκοπον εκλαμβανουσι and says himself: οτι σκοπος αυτω περι των αρχων των ηθικων διαλεχθηναι των φερουσων ημας επι την πολιτικην ευδαιμονιαν.

2. Bonitz, p. 1.

made visible concretely from the outset, as indeed the structure of the whole work is founded upon it.

"War and battle" — it is no accident that these very first words convey the theme of the dialogue. "War and battle," says the proverb playfully quoted by Kallikles, "war and battle should be missed" — as you have just missed the lecture by Gorgias. "In other words, we are arriving late for a feast," Socrates replies in the same tone. Peculiar, dramatic irony: what happened before was really play, the serious struggle is about to come.

It is introduced by a brief squabble between the pupils Chairephon and Polos. The genuinely Socratic question, "What, then, is it (τί ἐστιν, 447C) that this famous man professes and teaches?" immediately touches the heart of the matter. But the callow Chairephon, whom Socrates is using as a kind of advance guard against the enemy, knows as much about the Socratic art of asking questions as Polos, the pupil of Gorgias, knows about the art of his master. Instead of defining the art of rhetoric, Polos, the aspiring orator, delivers a short panegyric upon the subject, ending with a tribute to Gorgias (448C). The conversation lags. Chairephon does not know what to ask next, just as a beginning teacher is thrown off his track when the pupil's reply does not correspond to his preconceived plan. Socrates himself then takes the initiative and draws Gorgias into the discussion. The main dialogue begins. One must be Socrates to conduct a Socratic dialogue.

Let us first note a structural similarity to the beginning of the *Protagoras*.[3] Even as Socrates there tests the young Hippokrates by asking "who" is this revered Protagoras of yours, so here, too, he has Chairephon ask, "who" is Gorgias? In each case, examples drawn from medicine and

---

3. Schleiermacher, II/1, 8: ". . . the opening of the *Protagoras* is resumed here — one might say almost literally . . . . " The coincidences are listed in Pohlenz, pp. 129ff. / Jaeger (II, 127) calls the *Protagoras* and the *Gorgias* "next of kin," which must be considerably qualified by what precedes and follows in Jaeger's own text. Grube, p. 58, also brings "those two great dialogues of Plato's youth" much too close to each other.

the arts of sculpture and painting make it clear that the reply should aim, to begin with, at the nature of the profession to be analyzed critically. The initial comments made by Protagoras in praise of himself and his art (*Protagoras* 318A *et seq.*) correspond to the short eulogy of rhetoric, and of Gorgias as its master, that is delivered here by Polos. In both dialogues, the question about the nature of the art is taken over into the main body of the dialogue; in other words, it is discussed by Socrates with the two great Sophists themselves. For, in each case, the assault aims at the sophistic world itself — envisaged in the *Protagoras* more as a system of education, while here in the *Gorgias* more as the sphere of oratorical and political action. In the *Protagoras*, the discussion subsequently shifts to the question, what is the nature of *arete*? In the *Gorgias*, however, the nature of sophistic oratory remains the primary subject matter.

Once we see these structural similarities between the two dialogues, we also may hear, in the preliminary conversation of the *Gorgias*, echoes that are only meant to reach us as if from afar. Above all, there is the difference between speechmaking and dialogue. Gorgias has just delivered a "great" speech. Kallikles, in addressing Socrates, states the hope that his master will soon give another splendid performance. Socrates, however, immediately pins him down to a "conversation." The speech can wait until later. (". . . Until later," indeed, when the claims of oratory have been defeated, just as in the *Ion* — 530D — Socrates puts off the oration by the rhapsode "until later.") Gorgias can hold his own in a conversation as well. In his case, however, this does not mean that he is moving closer to the Socratic principle of discussion. His conversation is rather another form of rhetorical display, or, in short, a caricature of Socratic dialectics. Here we find echoes of the conflicts that, in the *Protagoras*, are fought through to a point where the conversation threatens to collapse. We are especially reminded of the earlier great dialogue with its characteristic tensions when we hear Georgias announcing the same program as Protagoras. He boasts of being able to give speeches of unparalleled length as well as answers of unsurpassed brevity (*Gorgias* 449BC; *Protagoras* 329B, 334E). These are for the Sophists the two extremes of the same total know-how.

When Polos is asked to define the nature of his master's art and his own, he answers — despite the examples which should serve as guides — that it is "the finest of all arts" (448C). Neither Gorgias nor his pupil sees what is wrong with this definition which, as so frequently, conceals a more serious defect behind the logical flaw; namely, that orators care much less for the subject matter itself than for the formal splendor of their speech and its reflection upon them personally. Thus, Socrates must explain the difference between *describing* an art (ποία τις τέχνη) and *defining* its nature (τίς τέχνη). This is a distinction already formulated in the *Hippias Major* and in the *Euthyphro*, there (*Euthyphor* 11a) even with terminological precision (πάθος—οὐσία), as later in Aristotle.

Socrates turns to Gorgias as the professional representative of the art of rhetoric and asks him what is the object of the knowledge and education on which he prides himself (περὶ τί τῶν ὄντων τυγχάνει οὖσα; *Gorgias* 449D). Gorgias may still think that the question of his fame is of primary concern and, if Socrates had not expressly ruled against it, he might have replied with a panegyric on his art, as Polos did on a smaller scale and as Protagoras does in the dialogue named after him. Gorgias does not suspect that, in submitting to questions by Socrates, he has Socrates' own law imposed upon him, and that sophistic rhetoric now must justify its claims before the bar of philosophy. Gorgias defines the object of his art as "speech" (περὶ λόγους). This is very general and much too broad, again revealing in Gorgias both a lack of logical precision and an exaggerated conception of himself. Socrates helps to clarify matters. He shows that oratory teaches not only how to speak, but how to think and speak (φρονεῖν καὶ λέγειν). Thus he prevents the word from being nothing more than empty sound. Next, he helps — by the method of division — to delimit the field in two aspects. First, he eliminates those arts in which speaking is a relatively minor aspect as compared with doing. But even in those cases where speech is paramount, oratory must be assigned a more definite place as compared with other arts (including mathematics) by clarifying the question, "about what" (περὶ τί)? Gorgias, as if to recapture in strength what his art is losing in scope, defines its subject as "the greatest and the most beautiful" (451D), lapsing back into the error of Polos and, like Polos, betraying both a lack of logical discipline and an abundance of vanity. Yet, this seemingly empty phrase of Gorgias prepares the way for what follows in a peculiarly dramatic irony. For after Socrates has criticized the flaw in the last reply, what now emerges (in a move more wordy than is necessary) is that oratory deals with "persuasion" and, more specifically, with persuasion in public assemblies (ὅστις ἂν πολιτικὸς σύλλογος γίγνηται). The political life comes into view as the characteristic field of rhetoric, and the significance of oratory is heightened inasmuch as it is said to be the source of one's own freedom and of power over others (452DE). We see the main theme of the dialogue emerging briefly. In the concise restatement by Socrates, rhetoric is "productive of persuasion" (πειθοῦς δημιουργός, 453A).[4] Yet, again, this is too broad. And, again, the question is, persuasion "in what"? Gorgias finally defines the subject matter of oratory as right and wrong, or just and unjust (περὶ τούτων ἅ ἐστι δίκαιά τε καὶ ἄδικα, 454B). This makes the claim of rhetoric explicit: it is the highest claim in the Socratic sense. It is much higher than someone like Gorgias realizes, for it is a claim to be made legitimately only by an art altogether different from his own.

Against this claim, Socrates must continue his work of setting logical limits. Together with Gorgias — and, again, by division — he distinguishes between knowledge and be-

---

4. That this is not at all a definition of the real Gorgias but a stage in Plato's strategy is correctly stated by Hermann Mutschmann, *Hermes*, LIII (1918), 440. He also notes that the form occurs previously in the *Charmides* where medicine is defined as ὑγιείας δημιουργός.

lief. Belief may be true or false, but there cannot be false knowledge. It follows that persuasion, or conviction, as practiced by the rhetorician produces belief, or acceptance on faith. It does not produce the certainty of knowledge, if only because it is impossible to teach so large a number of people the truth about matters of such importance in so short a time (455A). Thus, the field of oratory is limited in two respects: first, in scope, for it does not deal with areas of life in which experts are competent; second, in depth for in the area that remains, the just and unjust, rhetoric can make no claim to knowledge. What, then, is left to it?

Yet, at this point when rhetoric seems to have lost so much of its ground and power, the reality of life asserts itself unshaken by dialectics however ingenious — the reality of political and historical life as represented by such names as Themistokles and Perikles, who wrought great things by the power of speech. Goaded on by Socrates, Gorgias once more unfolds the nature of oratory, developing the power (δύναμις, 455D 7, 456A 8, 456C 6, 457A 5) which this art has in the life of the individual and the state, superior to all specialized branches of knowledge such as medicine and the crafts. Along with such power, to be sure, goes the danger of abuse. Gorgias, speaking on behalf of rhetoric but otherwise subscribing to an ordinary code of morality, feels compelled to warn against the possibility of abusing such power. He ascribes the responsibility for such abuse not to rhetoric, but to the individual abusing it, not to the master, but to the pupil.

The contradiction inherent in this view as seen from the perspective of the *logos*, and the danger inherent in it as seen from the perspective of life, are now shown by Socrates. This is his crucial move against the view of Gorgias. As if to heighten the significance of what follows, Socrates first agrees with Gorgias that they are interested only in the matter itself and that personal feeling must not enter into the discussion. Gorgias assents, a little stiffly, and needs some reassurance from the others in the circle to continue with a conversation that is now heading toward his defeat.

From what Gorgias has said about his art, Socrates infers, in a somewhat pointed formulation, that an ignorant person (i.e., the orator) is more convincing than the expert before an ignorant audience (ὁ οὐκ εἰδὼς ἄρα τοῦ εἰδότος ἐν οὐκ εἰδόσι πιθανώτερος ἔσται, 459B). The dubious character of rhetoric cannot be expressed more sharply than in this formulation, to which Gorgias assents, though with some discomfort (τοῦτο ἐνταῦθά γε συμβαίνει). Previously we had learned that the proper subject matter of oratory was "the just and the unjust." Is it the case, then, that the ignorance of the rhetorician — or the fact that he does not even need to know anything — applies to right and wrong, beautiful and ugly, or, in short, to the realities that regulate life? It would be consistent to say that oratory has no factual knowledge in these areas either. Gorgias, who combines the power of the new art with a traditional morality, however, does not go this far. Instead, he asserts — again goaded by Socrates — that it is necessary to have knowledge in the field of justice and injustice. A person trained in oratory (ῥητορικός) *knows* what is just. Thus, he is just, must act justly, and cannot do wrong. Here Socrates shows that Gorgias is caught in a contradiction, for how are these two views compatible with each other: the view that the person trained in oratory cannot do wrong, and the other view according to which not oratory, but the individual abusing it must be blamed?

We might raise some objections to this alleged contradiction. We might cite — with Thrasymachos in the *Republic* (I 340D *et seq.*) — the "orator in the strict sense of the word" (τὸν τῷ ἀκριβεῖ λόγῳ ῥητορικόν) and say that the claim of not being able to do wrong applies to him only, whereas the orator in the general sense — who, strictly speaking, would not then be an "orator" — would be capable of doing wrong. Yet, we would have to ask ourselves again, seriously, on what grounds rhetoric claims to have a knowledge of right and wrong since it disclaims such knowledge in all other fields. It would turn out that rhetoric never can justify this claim. This kind of analysis would lead to a distinction between oratory as represented by Gorgias and the true kind of rhetoric, which — paradoxically — comes into view at the end of the dialogue and is identical with philosophy. That this polarity is inherent in the contradiction here demonstrated by Socrates becomes evident once again, at a more advanced stage of the dialogue (*Gorgias* 508C), when Socrates looking back to the previous discussion, states: "The orator in the strict sense must be just and understand what is right and wrong." The accent is on "strict." It is clear that to resolve the contradiction in this first part of the dialogue, Plato would have had to embark here upon a positive course. But the opponent's position has not yet been developed adequately and, hence, is not yet adequately criticized. Socrates breaks off: "By the dog, it would take a long discussion, Gorgias, to make sufficiently clear to ourselves how these matters really stand."[5] Polos, the pupil of Gorgias, intervenes at this point, and the self-portrait of rhetoric becomes more radical. The dialogue enters upon its second stage.

The portrait of oratory presented by Gorgias was inconsistent in this respect: rhetoric was said to be concerned with appearances only in everything except matters of right and wrong, where a knowledge of the true nature is required. This inconsistency was due to an adherence to traditional commitments, which interfered with a pure statement of the view both in life and in thought. Polos, who is a younger man and does not feel bound by the traditional ties of the older generation (461C 7), now proposes a more radical formulation. By giving up the claim that oratory needs knowledge of right and wrong, Polos puts the emphasis all the more strongly upon the moral problem at stake in the discussion. Thus, when Socrates hails the entrance of Polos on the scene as a welcome move by which youth comes to the aid of an older generation that is faltering, this welcome wavers — as all true irony does — between a yeas and a no.

Again, the difference between Socratic and sophistic

---

5. Following Bonitz, ταυτα οπη ποτε εχει is to be referred as yet unresolved contradiction.

form enters into the discussion. Polos intervenes at this stage of the conversation, in a precipitate, anacoluthic statement.⁶ (He had similarly attracted attention by delivering a brief speech at the beginning of the dialogue itself.) Socrates makes it a condition that Polos submit to the form of dialogue. In this Polos plays the role of the questioner probably because, like Thrasymachos in the *Republic* (I 336C), he thinks it is easier to ask questions than to answer them. An amusing game develops because he does not know how to ask questions in a logical manner and because Socrates guides the questioning, thus putting the questions to himself by way of Polos.⁷ The young man shows clearly that he does not understand the basic principle of a Socratic conversation – logical progression of the argument (τὸ ἑξῆς περαίνεσθαι τὸν λόγον, 454C). For, though he is now the questioner, he makes the same mistake as he did in the preliminary conversation and as Gorgias did later (448E, 451D). And the mistake, again, reveals both a logical and a moral flaw. By asking repeatedly and at the wrong moments whether oratory is not "something beautiful" (462C, 463D), Polos reveals the fact that he cannot distinguish between description (ποῖον) and definition (τί). He also reveals his own vanity; he is more concerned with becoming famous than with gaining insight. As the Sophist lightly adopts the Socratic form of conversation, which is a noble instrument only in the hands of the master and which the Sophist does not know how to use, so Socrates replies by usurping on his own part the sophistic form of delivering a long speech. He justifies this exception explicitly on the grounds that his partner is incapable of conducting a philosophical conversation (465E). It is particularly amusing that the decisive and destructive critique by which rhetoric and sophistic are

6. Cf. Wilamowitz, II, 372f.; L. Reinhard, *Die Anakoluthe bei Platon* (Berlin, 1920), pp. 86f.

7. In 462D 9-11, the distribution of personas as corrected by Hirschig is given in the editions of Schanz (Leipzig, 1880), Sauppe-Gercke (Berlin, 1897), and Theiler (Bern, 1948). Theiler, Appen. crit. 136, has shown it as given in Olympiodoros, p. 67, 27.

included in the system of pseudo-arts is delivered by Socrates in this rhetorical-sophistic manner.

The formal conflict runs through the whole conversation as a mild but continuing skirmish. Socrates criticizes a long speech by Polos as violating their agreement (471D); yet, immediately afterwards, he replies with a long speech of his own. Even some of the questions asked by Polos, it seems, are intended as rhetorical assertions, not as searching questions in the Socratic sense. This is pointed out to Polos, whereupon he tries to give his questions a different character (466A-C). Instead of offering proof, Polos resorts to ridicule and threats (473DE) or he appeals to the judgment of others in the company or of people in general. As Socrates puts it in a jest, Polos wants to bring matters to a vote — an ironic reference to Socrates' own ineptitude in parliamentary procedures and to the fact that such methods are unsuitable in the pursuit of true knowledge (473E, 475E *et seq.*).

One other significant detail of the formal structure should be mentioned. At the point where Polos no longer knows how to help himself in the use of the Socratic method, Gorgias intervenes once more (463D), The conversation continues, for a while, between him and Socrates. Then follows the great speech in which Socrates assigns oratory, at least on a preliminary basis, its proper place — which, if proved true, would defeat it. That Gorgias is drawn anew into the discussion is not only a device to show, all the more insistently, how helpless Polos is. It is also a structural symbol indicating that the level of the first conversation here penetrates the second stage. Thus, for Plato, the two stages of the dialogue are not as distinct from each other as a schematic outline might lead us to believe.[8] The question, What is the nature of oratory? , is deeply rooted in the question of its effect and its relationship to justice.

---

8. Bonitz is certainly right in opposing those who did not distinguish between the Gorgias-stage and the Polos-stage (see, especially, Bonitz, pp. 41ff.). Yet his own over-rigid schema must also be modified.

This question, then, is posed anew. It finds a surprising — though still preliminary — answer in the speech of Socrates where oratory is defined as an art of flattery, or a pseudo-art. This definition emerges within a system of the arts constructed by the method of division, a system distinguishing between those arts that, although counterfeit, claim to benefit body and soul, and those arts that really do benefit body and soul (464B-465D).[9] Thus, oratory appears as a counterfeit of a branch of the true art of politics (πολιτικῆς μόριον εἴδωλον, 463D). This means that it is unreal and fragmentary, and that the serious matters of genuine value — true government, legislation, and jurisprudence — are opposed to it. This is what rhetoric becomes, in the judgment of Socrates, when it is deprived of all necessary connections with "justice." The opponent, however, is not impressed by this critique; after all, it is only asserted, not proved. Thus, it stands here only as a preliminary answer to the question raised on the first level of the dialogue. Also, the principle according to which the system of arts and pseudo-arts is constructed will be developed more clearly in the dialectical struggle conducted on the third level, i.e., the distinction between the good and pleasure (βέλτιστον–ἥδιστον, 464D).

There are two things the opponent regards as indubitably

---

9. The system according to which rhetoric is given a regular place is based upon the diaeretic procedure that largely prevails in the *Sophist* and the *Statesman*. See Lukas, *Einteilung bei Platon* (Halle, 1888), pp. 125ff.; Shorey, *Unity*, p. 51; Stenzel, *Zahl und Gestalt*, pp. 10ff.; Leisegang, cols. 2412ff. Especially akin is *Sophist* 227c *et seq*. The division περι σωμα — περι ψυχην is quite analogous. Even the fourτεχναι are similar. Again, what matters here is the classification of sophistic as there the classification of rhetoric. The word formations in –ικος already play a special role in the *Gorgias*, as noted by Shorey. I add the following motif: there are groups which have no name in common (*Gorgias* 46B ~*Statesman* 260E). Proportion (ωσπερ οι γεωμετραι, *Gorgias* 465B) has its analogy in *Republic* VI 509 *et seq*. See Pierre-Maxime Schuhl, *Etudes sur la fabulation platonicienne* (Paris, 1947), pp. 41ff. ("Mythe et proportion"). / A similar division, only much simpler, is found in Isokrates, Περι αντιδοσεως, 180. / On the concept of the *techne*, see Jaeger, II, 129.

certain: the power of oratory and the fact that it is conducive to happiness. These two theses must be attacked. Their overthrow is the real task of the second level of the dialogue. Since the form of speech was not convincing enough, the refutation must now proceed by means of a dialectical examination.

Let us first note, however, the structural similarity between this second level of the *Gorgias* and the third level of the *Thrasymachus*. There the view that injustice is superior was overthrown in three moves: first, by proving that the nature of injustice is such that it must rank with lack of knowledge and with evil; second, by refuting the claim that injustice is "stronger"; and third, by refuting the claim that it is productive of eudaemonia. On the second level of the *Gorgias,* Socrates conducts a threefold struggle against an oratory devoid of "justice"; first (as we have just seen), by classifying it among the arts of flattery that aim at pleasure; second, by refuting the claim that oratory has power; third, by refuting the claim that it is productive of eudaemonia. The parallelism along general lines is unmistakable. The differences are just as significant. In the first place, the struggle against "injustice," here as elsewhere in this later dialogue, is expanded more explicitly into an attack upon the cultural system itself in which this form of immoralism is embodied – i.e., political oratory. In the second place, we must not overlook the modification in the structural plan. In this dialogue, as we saw, the initial attack upon the nature of injustice is not made in dialectical terms; hence, it is not delivered in full force. Why not? Because this aspect is taken over into the third stage of the dialogue, the conversation with Kallikles, where it is developed independently and with heightened tension. Thus, by dividing the two themes, which in the *Thrasymachus* appear together on the same level, between the second and third levels of the *Gorgias,* Plato drives the decisive struggle over the nature of rhetoric to its highest development.

In the *Thrasymachus* (351A), it was suggested that the claim to power can be refuted by showing that "power" in the true sense of the word would require understanding. This is now demonstrated here in the *Gorgias*. The power of the political orator, it seems, is very great. Polos compares it to that of the tyrants (ὥσπερ οἱ τύραννοι, 466B), and Socrates constantly combines "orators and tyrants" in the same phrase so that the characteristic type of man may be seen as sharply as possible. Then Socrates shows that the reason, or goal, of any action is something good, a "good"; and that this goal is the object of "willing" in the true sense. Thus, he who does something harmful may perhaps act as he "pleases" or do what "appears" (good) to him (ἃ δοκεῖ αὐτῷ) – we note the contrast between appearance and reality – but not "what he wills" (ἃ βούλεται). Hence, he does not have power. This paradox which seems to be splitting hairs is designed to make us see the good as the goal of every genuine, rational act of willing.

The second objective is to refute Polos' claim that oratory is productive of happiness – an oratory devoid of justice and, in fact, virtually identical, during a long stretch of the dialogue, with injustice and tyranny as such. Socrates himself says (472C) that we are approaching the moment of decision where "knowledge is most honorable and ignorance most disgraceful." Thesis and antithesis are sharpened in ever new attempts, until both are clearly formulated and the dialectical refutation begins.

Socrates and Polos present a portrait of the tyrannical man, Socrates using the case of some political orator in the democratic regime of Athens, Polos citing the case of Archelaos, the tyrant of Macedonia. (Plato wants us to see the unmistakable connection between these two types. The tyrant practices what the politician in a democracy rarely can admit to being so openly.) In their judgment, however, the two partners sharply differ. For Socrates the criterion of happiness is based on a standard of right and wrong. Thus, happiness is not success, but consists in the intrinsic nature of the act and the agent. Socrates goes even further by declaring that wrongdoing is the greatest evil and by advancing the famous thesis that, judged from the perspective of happiness, he would rather — if he were called upon to choose — suffer wrong than do wrong. Socrates, the reader should realize, was true to this principle both in life and in death. To Polos, however, all this is incomprehensible; after all, he had just announced that rhetoric has nothing to do with right and wrong. He cannot see what difference right and wrong possibly can make and must regard, with astonishment, the radical Socratic rejection of the "tyrannical ideal" as incredibly paradoxical. He is willing to concede only that success and failure are legitimate criteria beyond the act itself. In this respect, he departs from his original principle. It no longer is the exercise of power as such that is good. "Great power" (τὸ μέγα δύνασθαι) becomes "something bad" or a "small power" if success does not correspond to one's own advantage. These concessions are forced upon him by the dialectics of Socrates, which easily could be extended here into genuine Socratic depths but is used only to expand and sharpen the original statement of Polos by drawing out its consequences.[10]

Socrates conducts the struggle in two dialectical moves leading to the defeat of Polos. He explicitly rejects, at the outset, any appeal to present company or to people in general, so that the *logos* itself may shine forth all the more clearly.

The critical point in the first move is the assertion

---

10. On 470A Bonitz comments justly: "Led to it by Socrates himself, Polos gives his statement a more definite formulation." The sharpness of his dialectic is blunted if one agrees with Saupe (commenting on this passage), Thompson, and Wilamowitz (II,373) is deleting the words το μεγα δυνασθαι in 470A 9 and και μικρον δυνασθαι in 470A 12. (Croiset-Bodin is correct.) Actually, the preserved reading means: "So the great capability seems to you now, in contrast to your former opinion (παλιν αυ), only then to be good when it is to the advantage of him who acts according to his arbitrary will, and hence this is really (εστι) the great capability; in any other case however (it seems to you) something bad and a poor capability." The real point is that by Polos' own admission the previously unrestricted μεγα δυνασθαι becomes under some circumstances a μικρον δυνασθαι.

(agreed to by the opponent) that while wrongdoing might be "uglier" or "more disgraceful" (αἴσχιον), suffering wrong (ἀδικεῖσθαι) is "worse" (κάκιον). The distinction shows that there are no standards to which we can refer (εἰς οὐδὲν ἀποβλέπων, 474D) for judging. The predicate "ugly" or "disgraceful" obviously corresponds to the judgment of the many (ὑπὸ τῶν πολλῶν ἀνθρώπων καὶ ὑπὸ σοῦ, 475D) that Socrates previously had expressly repudiated. (The procedure here is somewhat analogous to the way in which, in the *Hippias Major,* the first serious definition equates the beautiful with the "fitting" or πρέπον.) But the predicate "bad," too, is used in the customary sense (not further clarified) of weakness or cowardice; i.e., "bad" is something harmful to the power of the person who suffers wrong. The radical view later expounded by Kallikles will clarify these matters that here remain in a state of confusion.

For the time being, Socrates attacks the confusion by inquiring into the meaning of beautiful and ugly. Beautiful is what is useful and pleasant; ugly is the opposite. Thus, good in the sense of useful and bad in the sense of harmful are subsumed, as component parts, under the concepts of the beautiful and the ugly. We have overcome the distinction (introduced by Polos) between the good and the beautiful. This way of defining the concept of the beautiful is not without risks from Plato's point of view, as we may infer from the enthusiastic assent expressed by the *Sophist* (475A).[11] He is evidently delighted by the hedonistic and utilitarian overtones of this analysis without suspecting the depths where, as far as Socrates is concerned, pleasure and utility, on the one hand, merge with beauty, goodness, and understanding, on the other.[12] But

---

11. Gomperz (II, 345) considers the "fallacy" to be unintentional. Gomperz' section on the "defects of the Socratic-Platonic conceptual philosophy" in the *Gorgias* is useful even for him who is convinced that Plato knew all about the "logical weaknesses" when he wrote the *Gorgias*.

12. See *Republic* 475B, 580D *et seq.*, and the comment by Apelt, pp. 216f. The proof in the *Gorgias* has a forerunner in the *Alcibiades*, as was shown in ch. XVII, above.

it cannot be denied that at this point in the discussion we might, with a little determination, construct an argument leading to the opposite conclusion. If wrongdoing is "better," or "good," and the good is included in the concept of the beautiful, then wrongdoing would also be "beautiful." Polos, however, does not have such determination; if he did, he would be Kallikles. Nor does Socrates fall back upon his ultimate resources. It is true that the concepts of the good and the beautiful are unified, but this unity is not carried into those depths where Socrates would confront the nature of real being.

Later (482D) Kallikles will criticize this controversy. Polos was not consistent and this logical inconsistency was due to his being afraid. Socrates, Kallikles will say, took advantage of this inconsistency by intentionally confusing the different spheres of *nomos* and *physis,* convention and nature. As a matter of fact, Polos from his own point of view should have kept these two perspectives separate. At the same time, what Socrates concedes, as it were — namely, that wrongdoing is not painful — is also false in a deeper sense, for from the Socratic point of view, what could be a more radical opposite to pleasure than doing wrong? Thus, this dialectical section is peculiar in that it is not conducted, strictly speaking, according to the rules either of Polos or of Socrates. This makes it "sophistic," but it is also seductive in the sense of leading us on to the profoundly Socratic view according to which the conflict between *nomos* and *physis* is resolved through the *Idea* of the *Agathon.*

The first move, then, proved that to do wrong is worse than to suffer it. The second move proves that to escape punishment is worse than to suffer it. We must give attention to something in the meaning of the Greek phrase for "paying the penalty" ($\delta\iota\kappa\eta\nu$ $\delta\iota\delta\acute{o}\nu\alpha\iota$) which is not included in our "being punished": namely, the active element, and the relationship to "justice" and "right." It is "right justice" and, at the same time, "right punishment" ($\delta\iota\kappa\eta$ $\grave{o}\rho\theta\acute{\eta}$), as we read in the *Critias* (106B), "when we lead someone who has gone astray, back to the right path."[13] Thus, in contrast to Polos (*Gorgias* 476B), Socrates does not mean the passive acceptance of punishment; he means that, by our own action, we reinstate the dignity of the law that has been violated. Nevertheless, we must not fail to feel the paradox here advanced as an extreme antithesis to the popular thesis, which Polos defends, that avoiding punishment is preferable to being punished. How far we are moving in a paradoxical world is shown by the conclusion (480C) that we should accuse ourselves and relatives or friends, to uncover their offenses — yet we know how the author of the *Euthyphro* condemned the charge brought by a son against his father when this actually happened before a court in Athens.

The paradox is carried to grotesque dimensions. If we wish to harm a criminal we must protect him against being punished; immortality would be the worst fate for him; to live as long as possible, the next worse. To Polos this sounds strange, but logical. When Kallikles interrupts expressing his astonishment, Chairephon confirms that Socrates is completely earnest. And so he is despite the paradox. For he is here hinting at a completely different system of language, opposed to the prevailing system of sophistic rhetoric which makes might triumph and then protects the victory. This different language would be a system in the service of the good as practiced by Plato's Socrates. It is a system alluded to, at the end of the *Gorgias* (517A), by the iridescent name of a "genuine art of rhetoric." It is elaborated, in the second part of the *Phaedrus*, into a philosophical rhetoric, and, according to the *Statesman* (304A), it is a "rhetoric allied with the royal art of government."

The various steps of the argument are as follows. The first assumption is that "what is just is beautiful" (476B). Polos immediately agrees, despite a warning by Socrates. As before, he obviously means "beautiful" as it is commonly understood. Justice, if it takes the form of punish-

---

13. In *Laws* 728B, δικη and τιμωρια are expressly distinguished. On the problem of punishment, see Apelt, pp. 189ff.

ment, would not commonly be called "beautiful." He does not suspect —as the reader should — how correct his agreement is in a deeper sense.

The second assumption deals with the invariant correspondence between activity and passivity. The way in which the agent acts determines the way in which the object suffers (οἷον ἂν ποιῇ τὸ ποιοῦν, τοιοῦτον τὸ πάσχον πάσχειν, 476D). Perhaps we might object to this general formulation on the basis of experience[14] — but even then, only those cases would be excluded where it is a matter of subjective impressions so that the question, "For whom?" would be justified. In the case of justice, however, as an objective state of affairs in the sense of Socrates, this question would be meaningless. Thus — in a sublime balance — punishing justly and suffering just punishment correspond to each other. According to the foregoing, therefore, both alike are "beautiful" and hence "good." The person who is punished or "pays the penalty" experiences something good (477A).

Finally, there is a brief discussion — we know the subject from the *Alcibiades Major* (see ch. XVII, III 2) — about the ordered structure of the self or the soul, what belongs to the soul and what belongs to the body, what is part of the soul and what are goods and possessions of the body. Each sphere has its own badness or defect (πονηρία) that is worse in proportion to the values of each sphere and, therefore, worst in the case of the soul. For each sphere there is a corresponding art or power that delivers it from its badness. In the case of the soul, this is right or justice. These analogies lead to a scale of happiness depending upon whether there is no evil in the soul, whether the soul is delivered from the evil present in it, or whether it is not so delivered. We are reminded of the *Thrasymachus* in its concluding part, to which we referred earlier as being similar to the second level of the *Gorgias*. There we learn about the "proper excellence" (οἰκεία ἀρετή, *Republic* I 353C) of each thing and, ultimately, of

---

14. Cf. Gomperz, II, 346f., who, however, does not get beyond these subjective objections.

the soul. Justice is its intrinsic excellence and happiness is the condition of the soul in which his proper excellence is exercised. The *Gorgias* provides, despite a more negative twist, a richer development of the same thought, in the end leading the moral problem back to a discussion of the nature of oratory from which it arose. We see how the two problems are connected. Rhetoric in the ordinary sense fails to develop the proper *arete* of the soul; a different art of rhetoric, therefore, is needed to develop it.

The result we have gained so far must withstand the most severe attack that is now launched by a consistent immoralism, or, to put it differently, by the arrogant thesis that might makes right. Both speakers indicate that the moment of decision has come. Kallikles says at the outset: "If you are serious and if what you say is true, then the life of people like us is turned upside down" (481C). Socrates replies in a tone of serious playfulness. Kallikles is dealing not just with some individual, but with a power transcending the individual — i.e., philosophy. If he cannot refute this power, he always will be in conflict with himself, and that is the worst thing for any human being. Later (487A *et seq.*), after Kallikles has delivered his great programmatic speech, Socrates commends him on three counts: understanding, good will, and candor (παρρησία). Thus, if Kallikles should come to agree with him, then the subject they are discussing will have had its most thorough test.[15] It cannot be stated more clearly than this is the moment of decision.

In between these comments by Socrates, there is the great speech of Kallikles.[16] It begins with a critique of the halfheartedness displayed by Gorgias and Polos, both of whom were trapped into subscribing to the prevailing morality, and with a critique of Socrates who exploited their confusion in order to refute them. Kallikles distinguishes sharply between *physis* and *nomos,* nature and convention, as two separate levels between which the other

---

15. G. Bornkamm, "ΟΜΟΛΟΓΙΑ" [XIII.7], pp. 377ff.

16. "The most eloquent statement of the immoralist's case in European literature is put into his mouth": Shorey, p. 154.

speakers wavered in their judgment and discussion. There is a morality by nature, genuine, original, and founded upon true being — a morality of powerful men to whom suffering wrong is not only worse, but also more disgraceful, than doing wrong. A genealogy of morals shows that the many, who are weak, have introduced the prevailing, counterfeit system of moral rules into law and language.[17] Yet, it takes but a man sufficiently endowed by "nature" and "inner strength" to let the law of nature (τὸ τῆς φύσεως δίκαιον) shine forth again.

Thrasymachos had talked in the same spirit of the strong man or tyrant. What is new in this statement by Kallikles is the contrast between nature and convention. This makes the argument sharper and also more seductive. For Thrasymachos still admitted that the will-to-power was unjust and merely characterized this injustice by giving it another prefix, as it were; Kallikles, however, calls this will-to-power "justice according to nature," which bestows a higher rank upon it and makes it still more attractive. As its mythical prototype, he cites Herakles who ran off with the cattle of the giant Geryon. Moreover, in a bold move, he converts a saying of Pindar dealing with this myth into its opposite. Pindar said: "Law makes right out of might" (νόμος δικαιῶν τὸ βιαιότατον), which was new and bold enough. Kallikles says: "Law disposes with might over what is right" (νόμος βιαιῶν τὸ δικαιότατον).[18]

The other difference from the *Thrasymachus,* as we have emphasized before, is that the earlier dialogue deals with a conflict of moral principles. In the *Gorgias*, these principles are presented as different ways of life (βίοι). Kallikles adopts the distinction (introduced by Socrates)

---

17. Aristotle, *De sophisticis elenchis* 173ᵃ 13 : ην δε το μεν κατα φυσιν αυτοις το αληθες, το δε κατα νομον το τοις πολλοις δοκουν. / See F. Heinimann, *Nomos und Physis* [I¹⁷], pp. 101ff.; W. Kranz, "Das Gesetz des Herzens" [1¹⁷]' *pp.* 222ff.

18. Cf. Wilamowitz, I, 218 = I² 221; II, 95ff. The only improbability is that Plato's reversal of Pindar's words is "a failure of memory." Surely he twisted them around very sarcastically (*"consulto"* A. Turyn, *Pindari Carmina* [Cracoviae, 1948], p. 351), the more so since "βιαιων is by no means a usual word."

between the political man and the philosopher, expanding it into a distinction between the practical and theoretical types of men. This is depicted, on the level of myth, in the debate between the twin brothers, Amphion and Zethos, in the *Antiope* of Euripides.[19] The contrast between these two types of men is the concrete expression of the clash between two different systems. Kallikles, to be sure, does not completely do away with philosophy. He does not recognize it as a way of life, but he does grant that it has a place in the education of the young. This indicates a certain concession on his part, as does the fact that he consents to talk with Socrates at all. Men who really are in actual life what Kallikles would like to be would and should not do this; for by entering into a discussion, they acknowledge the validity of a law that must, ultimately, cause their downfall. Kallikles, however, is well disposed toward Socrates in other respects and would like to win Socrates over to his own side by an argument *ad hominem*: if you are attacked, you will not be able to defend yourself. Thus, the trial of Socrates emerges as the crucial test in the background of this controversy. We realize that Kallikles' speech confronts us with a matter of life and death. Three separate issues converge upon a single focus — the struggle between immoralism and justice, the struggle between practical politics and philosophy, and the struggle between the Athenians and Socrates.

The decisive attack, as usual, is preceded by a clarification and amplification of the enemy's position, and some light skirmishes. What, then, does it mean to say that we have justice in the true sense of nature when the superior person has more than the inferior and rules over him? Are better (βελτίων), stronger (κρείττων), and more powerful (ἰσχυρότερος) all synonymous? Kallikles says yes, thus using the concept of "good" in its primitive, unclear state where it may mean any kind of superiority or distinction. Socrates sets out to clarify this concept. In the *Thrasy-*

---

19. See B. Snell, *Die Entdeckung des Geistes*³ [ΣΙΙ⁸], pp. 405f.; H. von Arnim, *Supplementum Euripideum* (Bonn, 1913), pp. 11ff.

machus, we find that Socrates replies to the definition that justice is the same as the advantage of the stronger with a malicious interpretation that compels the Sophist to make his meaning more specific. Here we find something similar, only in more pointed form. If we define superiority or power in numerical terms exercised by a majority, so that the individual would be the weaker as against a large number of people, then the law of the stronger would be identical with the slave morality of the many. This kind of sophistry shows that the concept is still quite vague.

Finally, the two men agree, or seem to agree, that the superior should mean the "more intelligent" (489E *et seq.*). But what does "intelligent" mean, and what is the meaning of such expressions as "wanting to have more" and "wanting to be superior"? These phrases can be misunderstood amusingly if we take the case of specialized branches of knowledge and the specific advantages enjoyed by the specialist in each of them. Kallikles, however, means by "intelligent" to be "knowledgeable in political affairs," and he adds — evidently lest knowledge be misunderstood as nothing but passive "theory" — the characteristic of "brave" (ἀνδρεῖοι), which he connects with "ruling" and "having more." These additions make us suspect Kallikles' formula about the rule of the intelligent, which as such is quite close to the Socratic view. To elicit the full meaning of the other's view, Socrates asks the decisive question: Must the ruler also be capable of "ruling himself" (σώφρων)? This is the criterion of judging the words "intelligence" and "courage" in the Socratic sense, rather than intelligence as practiced in a specific field or courage as a natural disposition. Now we see that for Kallikles, ultimately, the life of pleasure has the highest value. Self-mastery and justice are but restrictions imposed upon the pleasure principle, and courage and intelligence are only means to satisfy this principle. Socrates aims at unifying the virtues in one single virtue. (Again, we recognize the significance of the main problem in the *Protagoras.*) Kallikles, however, chooses among the virtues according to the standard of pleasure. "What pleases is permissible," he might say with Goethe's Tasso.

What is at stake is a decision on "how one should live." These are Socrates' words to open the real struggle itself. But even here the means by which this struggle is conducted are subject to improvement. The first thrust does not score. It cites the analogy, derived from Orphic-Pythagorean sources, comparing the life of the pleasure seeker to a leaky vessel and the life of the rational man to a pitcher without holes. This analogy does indeed express clearly, although in a symbolic context, the difference between the two types of lives that will be elaborated in the subsequent demonstration, but the comparison is no substitute for proof. Socrates himself does not ascribe such power to it. Precisely because these images fail to convince the opponent, they make clear what dialectics can and must do and where myth has its place in Plato's thought.[20] On the other hand, they bring out the opponent's resistance all the more forcefully; for Kallikles, the life of self-discipline is that of the stone or the dead. Finally, these similes are significant for the work as a whole, if only because they prepare, at an early state, what will later enter into the dialogue with intensified power in the great myth at the end.[21]

Myths are not a sharp weapon, only dialectic is. Socrates sets out to make the representative of the pleasure principle acknowledge that shameful pleasures are shameful. He does not hesitate to cite the case of the man who scratches himself because of an itch, or the sexual tickle of the catamite. We feel that Kallikles would like to exclude these pleasures as base; nevertheless, he sticks to this thesis so as "not to contradict himself" (495A), although he does not quite subscribe to it any longer. To put it differently, the hedonist, in order to be consistent, cannot admit that

20. See *Plato* 1, ch. IX. / See Frank, pp. 90f., 298ff.; Ivan Mortimer Linforth, "Soul and Sieve in Plato's *Gorgias*," *University of California Publications in Classical Philology*, XII, no. 17 (1944), 295ff.; E.R. Dodds, *The Greeks and the Irrational* [I[24]], pp. 209, 225.

21. See Schleiermacher, II/1, 11: "The experiments which Socrates conducts with Kallikles may easily be the most skillful part of this work." Cf. also the sentences which follow.

there are qualitative differences among pleasures and he must thus accept even the basest pleasures as being of equal value. Otherwise he would acknowledge a standard of value beyond pleasure. Moreover, itching and scratching are a mixture of pleasure and plain (*Philebus* 46D). It could be shown, therefore, that what is desired here is not pleasure at all, but a mixture — which reminds us of the first words of Socrates in the *Phaedo*.

Thus, the assault, though repulsed, has shaken the enemy's position. Now follows the decisive attack. Plato shows that we are approaching a decision because, as it is imminent, Kallikles tries in vain to wriggle out from under the force of the argument (497A *et seq.*).

To begin with, the views of Kallikles are restated. He holds that "good" and "pleasure" are the same. (We may add that he already had indicated that he would distinguish between pleasures that are "better" and those that are "worse." His position is here stated in its extreme form. If this is overthrown, it will be easy to deal with the qualified version as well.) Yet, Kallikles admits that "knowledge" and "courage" are different from each other and that both, in turn, are different from pleasure and the good. (For him, different concepts of value may run side by side and against each other, whereas for Socrates they all find their common center in the *Idea* of the Good.)

Two skillfully constructed proofs refute Kallikles' position. First (495E), well-being and misfortune, good and evil, happiness and unhappiness are opposites that exclude each other. Pleasure and pain, however, may be mixed. Moreover, not only may pain change into pleasure as happiness may change into unhappiness, but in the act of quenching one's thirst, both the pain of being thirsty and the pleasure of quenching one's thirst disappear at the same time. It follows that good and pleasure must be different. What is unchanging and fixed is opposed to what is constantly changing.

Second (497E), someone is good if the "presence of good" (ἀγαθῶν παρουσίᾳ) is in him. If good and pleasure were really the same, then we would be good because of the presence of pleasure. Yet, Socrates and Kallikles had agreed earlier that the intelligent and courageous man is good, the cowardly and stupid man bad. Even though the two men did not quite mean the same thing, Kallikles did commit himself through his definition to a standard of the good different from pleasure. Thus, Socrates can now easily refute him by a *reductio ad absurdum.* Since the good (i.e., the intelligent and brave man) can experience as much pleasure or pain as the bad (i.e., the cowardly and stupid man), or since the good may, in fact, experience more pain than the bad and the bad more pleasure than the good, we have reached the absurd consequence that the good may be evil and the bad good, or the good man may, in fact, be worse than the bad and the bad man better than the good.

These consequences are as absurd as the view that good and pleasure are the same. The two concepts are quite different, and the good is by no means included in the concept of pleasure. (It is immaterial, for the moment, whether Socrates does not also regard the good and pleasure as in some sense converging upon each other.) This conclusion is reinforced when we realize that the "presence" of goodness by virtue of which someone is good only *seems* to be identical with the "presence" of pleasure or pain by virtue of which someone enjoys himself or suffers. If someone is either good or bad, but if both the good and the bad man may experience pleasure or pain, it is clear that the "presence of goodness or of evil" refers to objective realities, not interchangeable and never changing, whereas the "presence of pleasure or of pain" refers to changing conditions which, like the shadows of a cloud, fall upon and blur the absolute opposites of good and evil.[22]

22. The commentators disagree as to whether the "theory of *Ideas*" is meant here or not. Those who say yes are surprised that Plato says "inexactly" $\alpha\gamma\alpha\theta\omega\nu$ instead of $\alpha\gamma\alpha\theta o\nu$ (thus Sauppe-Gercke's commentary). That is a dogmatic quarrel over words. $\alpha\gamma\alpha\theta\omega\nu$ is a somewhat looser form of expression. The strict form, in which the *Agathon* is not capable of pluralization, is not chosen because the discussion remains in the area of the provisional. But

Let us consider a few details that show how often one would have to reply differently from Kallikles. Socrates asks (496D): "Shall I go on with further questions or do you agree that every state of want and desire is painful?" Kallikles replies, "I agree"; yet, through this ready assent, Plato gives the reader a hint pointing in a different direction. For is there not a great difference between the painful desire of a man dying of thirst, on the one hand, and, on the other, the "desire of the whole" (*Symposium* 192DE), the "desire for the most beautiful life" (*Letter VII* 327D), or the desire aiming at perfect knowledge which is both "a desire and a joy" (*Republic* I 328D)? Later in the *Gorgias* (497B), Socrates asks Kallikles whether it is not true that in the case of a thirsty or a hungry man, satisfaction of the desire causes a cessation both of pleasure and of pain. Kallikles finally says yes, after first protesting strongly against such unworthy questions. Does not this resistance again convey some hint of a joy that does not cease, as pleasure does after drinking, but may increase — even to the happiness of the highest knowledge?

Kallikles has talked himself into a radical position that he does not, in fact, hold. He already had acknowledged, at least as a matter of feeling, that there is a difference between pleasures that are better and those that are worse (see III 2b above). Now he says explicitly that no one would deny this difference, and that he did not mean to say that good and pleasure·are the same. This is more true than he suspects; yet, he fails to see that after the radical thesis has been defeated, the more moderate version cannot be maintained either. If pleasures may be both good and bad, it is clear that we must desire those that are good. Once we know the difference between good and pleasure, there can be no doubt as to which should rule.

---

it seems very doubtful to say (with Ueberweg-Praechter, p. 243) that the choice of the plural is the point of departure for an intentional paralogism. Could this proof, or rather, this *reductio ad absurdum*, not be carried through as well?

Thus, it is enough for Socrates to refer back to what has been agreed upon in the conversation with Polos (468B), that actions invariably aim at the good. Moreover, it is no accident that, while previously the sphere of the good often had been referred to in the plural (τὰ ἀγαθά), it is now put into the singular as a sign of the uniqueness and identity of its nature determining the course of human action.

We have pointed out repeatedly that the discussion in the *Gorgias* moves on two levels — a discussion of moral principles and a discussion of different ways of life. Kallikles, too, at first played political oratory off against philosophy. Then the struggle shifted from this human conflict in everyday reality to the level of conceptual analysis. On this level, the incompatibility of modes of being is translated into the form of a logical contradiction. The practical way of life represented by Kallikles as an aspiring politician of the market place is not yet overthrown by this refutation of its conceptual foundations. Hence, there follows a struggle over what is the proper vocation or way of life. It is introduced by Socrates at the point where he secures the admission that if the good is the measure of all things, it cannot be anybody's business to decide what is good. It must be a matter for the expert (τεχνικός).[23]

In this last struggle here beginning, there will be no turning back for Kallikles. He has committed himself too far to the kind of life he has chosen. As a matter of fact, he concedes (513C) that there is something in what Socrates is saying when the latter demonstrates the superiority of the just life even at the risk of death. But Kallikles cannot appropriate this conclusion for his own life, and Socrates knows why: love of the demos (ὁ δήμου ἔρως)

---

23. Bonitz, pp. 13f., considers our second part as belonging to what follows. Our disposition agrees with Sauppe-Gercke [XVIII[7]], p. xxiv. One must realize that this section moves over into the third. By still representing the hedonistic thesis without reference to a specific *bios*, it belongs to what precedes. But by representing this thesis in a form that permits Socrates to call for the τεχνικος, the transition to what follows is made at the same time.

lures him, counteracting the influence of Socrates. Here, in condensed form, is the portrait of a typical fate — which, with greater human intensity, is developed in the *Alcibiades Major*. Kallikles has just begun to embark upon the career in public life which Alkibiades is still planning (*Gorgias* 515A; *Alcibiades* 106C). Both wish to rule or govern (510A; 106C). Both are told that they should first learn something themselves (514AB; 109D). As for the *Gorgias,* Socrates, at the end, is resigned to Kallikles' love of the demos; in the other dialogue, however, he expresses a deep concern lest Alkibiades be weaned away from him by the same love (δημεραστὴς γενόμενος).[24]

The debate over the right way of life is conducted in three great movements which, though not sharply separated from each other, may be distinguished clearly by the behavior of the antagonist. In the first section, the resistance of Kallikles grows to the point where he openly withdraws from the conversation. In the second section, Socrates is virtually alone once more, outlining the principles on which he acts. This continues until the major principle that to suffer wrong innocently is better than to do wrong successfully has emerged as a conclusion "bound fast by a chain of arguments as strong as iron and steel." In the last section, then, we witness the victory of the Socratic form of life as the right way of life for the individual in the state. Socrates makes it clear at the outset, with great seriousness (500CD), that the decisive and most important question is at stake. Which of the two ways of life should a man choose?

Socrates recalls the distinction between genuine arts and pseudo-arts of flattery that he had introduced previously in the conversation with Polos (463A *etseq.*). At that time, the classification of rhetoric alongside of cooking and cosmetics struck a blow which did not penetrate, because we did not as yet have a principle for the classification. Now we do have a twofold principle, in the distinction between "good" and "pleasure," by means of which we

---

24. The motif is prepared for by 481D *et seq.(* γυῆνς and Δημου will likewise be understood in 513c.

can construct the two systems of classification. Thus, the difference in value is unshakably fixed, and we can add a number of other arts to the system of pleasure or pseudo-arts — contemporary instrumental music, dithyrambic poetry, and tragedy. Looking ahead to the *Republic* where this blueprint of the *Gorgias* is expanded, we can see that in order to construct a state in the image of the good, as against a state based on the principle of pleasure, Plato must purge the former of the pseudo-arts of flattery. He will be able to do this because he is conscious of creating a dramatic and dithyrambic poetry entirely different from the old forms.

In the *Gorgias*, however, the subject is oratory, which shares with these pseudo-arts the aim of providing pleasure to the public. This is the kind of rhetoric that is actually practiced. Perhaps there is still another kind, an educational rhetoric, we might say, because its aim is "to make the citizens as good as possible" (502E). This kind of oratory — to the astonishment of Kallikles and the shock of the reader (he is supposed to be shocked!) — was not practiced even by the great statesmen of Athens, for they, too, aimed at satisfying their own desires or those of the public. He who practices the genuine art of oratory will not talk just at random (οὐκ εἰκῇ ἐρεῖ) but will "look at something definite" to give his speech a form, just as a craftsman keeps his eye on a definite form to give his work a specific "shape" and to make a well-wrought object (τεταγμένον τε καὶ κεκοσμημένον πρᾶγμα). Thus, the "something definite" must be a shape or a well-ordered form.[25] Again, we are reminded of the *Republic* (VI 500C) where the philosopher keeps his eye on something well-ordered (τεταγμένα) and unchanging, or of the carpenter in the *Cratylus* (389A *et seq.*) who looks toward the prototype of the weaver's shuttle. After the model of

---

25. The anacoluthic sentence ωσπερ και οι αλλοι . . . (503DE) is correctly printed in Croiset-Bodin. On this, cf. L. Reinhard, *Observationes criticae in Platonem* (Berlin diss., 1916), pp. 51ff.; *Die Anakoluthe bei Platon* [XVIII⁶], p. 146. αυτων is more probable than άυτου.

any good handicraft, therefore, a good art of oratory must remove "injustice" or excess (ἀκολασία) from the soul and must produce order, i.e., *arete* in the soul, by imposing moderation (κολάζει). What emerged as a paradox at the end of the conversation with Polos is now given a secure conceptual foundation because the *Eidos,* the *Agathon,* has become the guiding principle. And we suspect that Socrates is the only representative of this true art of oratory. At this moment, then, when lack of discipline is overcome by the *Idea* of the Good, and the prevailing pseudo-art of rhetoric is confronted by the true art, Kallikles withdraws from the commitment to conduct a conversation. By this act he reveals the same lack of discipline in matters of the *logos* that his theory proclaims to be valid in life (οὐχ ὑπομένει ... κολαζόμενος, 505C 3).

The second movement begins once more "at the beginning." It starts with the distinction between "good" and "pleasure"; it makes clear again that the true aim of every action is the good; and then it shows that "virtue" is the realization of the good in man and that, in concrete terms, virtue refers to an order in the soul. This order goes with the unity of the virtues. We recall that Kallikles earlier (III 1 above) had advocated arbitrary distinctions among them. In the *Protagoras,* Socrates defends this unity of the virtues against the Sophists. In the aporetic dialogues in search of a definition, he shows how the virtues converge toward such a unifying concept. In the *Republic*, this unified system becomes the cornerstone for the education of the individual as well as for the structure of the state. The good man does good things only; hence — in Greek this correlation is shown by using the same verbal expression — he is well off or "does well" (εὖ τε καὶ καλῶς πράττει, 507C 3); in short, he is "eudaemonic" or happy. The bad man does evil things; hence, he does not "do well," but is miserable.

We may recall that a similar scale is set up in the *Charmides* (172A) and in the *Alcibiades Major* (133E *et seq.*).[26] Here in the *Gorgias,* the conclusion is that we

---

26. On the apparent double meaning of ευ (κακως) πραττειν,

must practice *sophrosyne* or self-discipline and that we must avoid the lack of discipline so highly extolled by Kallikles. The value gained through this "taming" by means of self-discipline shines forth once again. The cosmos, or the universe as an ordered structure, becomes the comprehensive model for the "cosmos" or order of the soul. The greed-for-more or will-to-power reveals an ignorance of geometric proportion, a neglect of the study of geometry. (This is an ironic, paradoxical reference to the educational principle of Plato's *Republic* and of the Academy.) Then we return to some matters carried over from earlier parts of the dialogue where they were left as paradoxes, or remained incomplete and controversial; e.g., the statement, in the conversation with Polos, that oratory is designed to punish wrong and that to suffer wrong innocently is better than to do wrong; or the statement, in the conversation with Gorgias, that the true orator (ὀρθῶς ῥητορικός) must possess the knowledge of justice. Even the argument *ad hominem* by which Kallikles, at the end of his first great speech, tried to frighten Socrates (464A *et seq.*) is brought up again that it may be rejected solemnly and decisively (508D *et seq.*). "Bound fast by a chain of arguments as strong as iron and steel" — so Socrates describes the conclusions reached. Yet, even such a conclusion is not meant as a dogma, but as something that, in true Socratic spirit, he would submit to genuine critical examination.

The discussion of moral principles, then, has turned again into a struggle of two opposing ways of life. This struggle is now fought through, for the last time, on the firm basis of the conclusions reached so far. Kallikles still holds fast to the following convictions: that, for the sake of one's own protection, one must be either a ruler himself (ἄρχειν ἢ καὶ τυραννεῖν) or a friend of the ruling regime

---

see *DGrA*, II, 20f. πραττειν means to live actively. See Aristotle, *Nicomachean Ethics* 1098[b] 15-22. Our "multilingual age" (J. Bernays, *Die Dialoge des Aristotles* [Berlin, 1863], p. 80) finds it difficult to accept such an argument as shown by Grote II, 126f., n.9 ("equivocal," "fallacious").

(510A); moreover, that the great statesmen of Athens, though they did not aim at the education of the citizens in the Socratic sense, nevertheless increased the power of the *Polis (515CD)*; *that it is a disgrace if a man cannot defend himself (522C)*; and that Socrates, for the sake of his own safety, should adapt himself to the powers that be and protect himself against possible dangers (511A, 521AB).

Socrates, however, draws his conclusions from his own system of moral values unshakably founded upon the *Agathon*. He shows once more that it is more important to avoid wrongdoing than to protect oneself against the wrongdoing of others. He transposes the clash of moral principles into the new dimension of political realities and the two competing ways of life. Thus, he defeats the claim made by a political oratory that avoids suffering wrong but, in doing so, commits wrongs, and, ultimately, rests upon an exaggerated estimate of the value of mere living as compared with the value of leading the good life ($ε\grave{υ}$ $ζ\tilde{η}ν$, 510A-512E). He defeats the claim made by the politicians — most clearly expressed in the extreme case of the four greatest statesmen of Athens — that they increased the power of the state since, in truth, their actions only produced a state swollen and festering, and since the fate they suffered refutes them in that it would not have happened to them had they, in fact, improved the citizens (515C-519C).[27] Finally, he defeats the claim made by sophistic, the sister-art of rhetoric, with regard to education of the young; for this claim is voided by the mere fact that the Sophist takes money for his services and

---

27. The attack upon the great statesmen of Athens is not to be understood polemically as an answer to the polemic treatise of Polykrates (thus Gomperz, II, 343f.). With Plato, polemic is probably never an adequate explanation; besides, Polykrates' treatise is most likely later than the *Gorgias* (Wilamowitz, II, 98f.). A biographic interpretation — "renunciation of the world" (Wilamowitz, I, 230ff. =I², 233ff.) — is not convincing either. The *Gorgias* could at most be a renunciation in the thoroughly ambivalent sense in which, according to Festugière, pp. 381ff., the wise man withdraws into contemplation; but *"telle vie contemplative est essentiellement politique."*

even complains about recalcitrant clients' refusing to pay, whereas, if his claim were justified, he should have awakened in his pupil a desire to do good in return for the benefits received (519C-520E).

In this struggle there emerges as the proper function of the political man the task of rendering a true service to his fellow men; i.e., to make them as good as possible (513E). There emerges the demand that he who wants to be a ruler must first have learned something — from whom, we may wonder? — and that he must show proof of his ability to "improve" matters on a small scale so as not "to learn pottery by first trying his hand on a wine jar" (514A-515B). As against the counterfeit product, there emerges the "true art of oratory" (ἀληθινὴ ῥητορική, 517A 5). Finally, in a proud paradox, Socrates proclaims that he is "one of the few Athenians — not to say the only one — who is studying the true art of politics and the only man now living who is practicing it" (521D). According to the charge of Meletos in the *Apology* (25A), Socrates is the only man who is corrupting the Athenians. The paradoxical claim made here in the *Gorgias* is the most radical reply to this charge.

Thus, the struggle with Kallikles culminates in Socrates' bearing witness to his life's work or his "existence." Philosophy is a matter of life and death. Socrates is so completely clear about the fate awaiting him in his own city that he predicts, in almost the exact words, the charges that will be brought against him (521E *et seq.*). But he has no doubts that the aim of his speech and his education must be the good, not pleasure. He takes his place beside the physician and the architect, not beside the cook. Therefore, as he predicts, his defense appealing to the cause of "justice" he has served will be of no avail to him. For this is the kind of service the others in the city do not want and do not understand; yet, for Socrates it is precisely this question of justice that renders worthless any concern over possible dangers to his life. The decision as to worth or unworth is made on the grounds not *whether* he can "defend" himself, but *how* he can. The question, whether life or death, recedes before the question, whether a just or unjust life. The commitment to the *Agathon* decides his calling — or has decided it long ago.

We see at the end, then, these several strands gathered together: the struggle between pleasure and the good; the struggle between a false sophistic rhetoric and true philosophy (which, at the same time, is the true art of rhetoric and the true art of government); and finally, the struggle between the Athenians and Socrates. The *Agathon,* philosophy, and Socrates are victorious, but they do not prevail in the sense that the struggle is won forever. On the contrary, this struggle is always alive. It is, indeed, necessary for the cause of the *Agathon* itself on whose behalf even Kallikles — especially Kallikles — fights as a rebel against a legal system grown rigid and feeble.[28]

In the concluding myth of the dialogue, the trial of Socrates is reviewed before the tribunal of eternity and the results of the dialectical arguments are consecrated in a world beyond.[29] Here we have, for the first time in the works of Plato, a Socratic myth. And here Socrates says, for the first time, that "the *logos* stands firm" (527B), a goal that was, in the *Euthyphro* (11D), still but a wish. For the first time, the dialogue not only leads the way; it also gathers up, as in a book of laws, what we have discovered on this way and, filtered through a myth, puts the stamp of the eternal upon it.[30] Yet even these firm foundations

---

28. One may ask whether K. Schilling, *Platon* (Wurzach, 1948), pp. 92f., is right in saying that Kallikles is "incurably wicked." Cf. *Plato* 1, pp. 166f.

29. On this myth, see *Plato* 1, pp. 184ff.

30. The new form of speech in the last part of the *Gorgias* ("Confession") is discussed by F. Solmsen, *Die Entwicklung der aristotelischen Logik und Rhetorik* (Berlin, 1929), pp. 266f. / The "consistently positive attitude" of the *Gorgias*, as Natorp (p. 41) puts it, has often been emphasized in contrast to the aporetic dialogues. All the same, the view with which E. Hoffmann begins his *Platonismus und Mittelalter* [XVII[15]] is surely erroneous. There he calls our dialogue the first of Plato's writings "which aims at expounding a philosophical doctrine of its own and no longer merely portraying Socrates." Even the aporetic dialogues aimed

are not meant as dogma, but would be subject, at any time, to further critical inquiry in a dialectical conversation. For now, however, this is the *logos* that has come to light. According to it one must live — and die, we must say, remembering Socrates.

at something more than this. Cf. also Hoffmann, *Platon*, (Zurich, 1950), ch. 11. / When Taylor (p. 103) ascribes to the *Protagoras* "a riper mastery of dramatic art" and calls the *Gorgias* "an early work and probably a work dating not many years after the death of Socrates," he confuses two things: the *Protagoras* has a greater abundance of characters, more varied colors in its happenings, more animation in its dialogical course. The *Gorgias* is much more economical in its means; it is, however, incomparably more tense, profound, closer to tragedy, advancing toward the *epekeina*.

Gorgias

RECENT EDITIONS AND TRANSLATIONS: A. Croiset-L. Bodin, *Platon Budé*, III (1923); W.R.M. Lamb, Loeb V (1925); K. Preisendanz (Jena, 1925); C.O. Zurretti (Palermo, 1927); E. Martini (Turin, 1929); B. Stumpo (Palermo, 1931); G. Modugno (Florence, 1936); L. Cooper (London, New York, 1938); W. Theiler (Bern, 1943); J.C. Bruyn (Amsterdam, 1944); R. van Pottelbergh (Antwerp, 1948); R. Rufener and G. Krüger (Zurich, 1948); J. Calonge Ruiz (Madrid, 1951); W.C. Helmbold (New York, 1952); W.D. Woodhead and G.C. Field (Edinburgh, 1953); O. Apelt, PhB 148 (4th edn., 1955); N. Sabbatucci (3d edn., Bari, 1956); J.B. Bergua (4th ed., Madrid,

RECENT INTERPRETATIONS: J. Geffcken, "Studien zu Platons *Gorgias*," *Hermes*, LXV (1930), 14ff.; J. Humbert, *Polycratès: L'accusation de Socrate et le "Gorgias"* (Paris, 1930); Hildebrandt, pp. 121ff.; W. Schneidewin, *Das sittliche Bewusstsein. Eine Gorgiasanalyse* (Paderborn, 1937); J. Duchemin, "Remarques sur la construction du Gorgias," *RevEtGr*, LVI (1943), 265ff.; I.M. Linforth "Soul and Sieve in Plato's *Gorgias*," *Univ. Calif. Publ. Class. Philology*, XII (1944), 295ff.; A. Rivier, *Les Horizons métaphysiques du Gorgias de Platon* (Lausanne, 1948); E. Voegelin, "The Philosophy of Existence: Plato's *Gorgias*," *Review of Politics*, XI (1949), 477ff.; G. Rudberg, "*Protagoras-Gorgias-Menon*: eine platonische bergangszeit," *SO*, XXX (1953), 30ff.; Gauss, II/1, 24ff.; F. Zucker, "Der Stil des *Gorgias* nach seiner inneren Form," *SBBerl*, 1956; M. Vanhoutte, *La Notion de liberté dans le "Gorgias' de Platon* (Leopoldville, Congo, 1957); H. Reiner, "Unrechttun ist schlimmer als Unrechtleiden," *ZphF*, XI (1957), 548ff.

ADDITIONAL BIBLIOGRAPHY: Shorey, p. 501; Geffcken, Notes, p. 65; Rosenmeyer, p. 180; Cherniss, *Lustrum*, pp. 97ff.

THE SELF-REFERENCE OF THE GORGIAS*

Adele Spitzer

In this paper I shall argue that the *Gorgias* is self-referential: that it not only explicates the nature and defects of rhetoric through argument, but also demonstrates the nature and defects of rhetoric through the words and actions of the characters; that it not only evaluates rhetoric by explicitly comparing it with an ideal art of speech, but itself demonstrates the contest between the two arts — or rather, between the one art and its shadowy imitator; and in demonstrating the contest, it dramatizes its outcome, the triumph of the true art.

I shall contend that the three protagonists — Gorgias, the teacher, and his students, Polus and Callicles, represent the three facets of rhetoric as it emerged and developed in fifth century Athens: rhetoric as an art form, a set of literary techniques and devices, not tied to any particular end or ends (Gorgias), rhetoric as a self-conscious study aware of its power to gain wealth and position for its practioners (Polus), and rhetoric as politics, the actual practice of gaining those ends (Callicles). I argue that a far clearer picture of the nature of rhetoric emerges when these characterizations of the protagonists are taken into account than when the discourses alone are considered. I am contending, furthermore, that rhetoric is far more thoroughly routed when the dramatic defeat of the three orators is taken into account than when the arguments alone are considered. I shall argue, finally that a conclusion climaxes the *Gorgias* that is never explicitly mentioned in the discourse: that is, that philosophy is the true art of justice, that Socrates is its representative, and that in his dramatic triumph over the three orators, Socrates' art is shown to be the only true statesmanship or politics; he is the philosopher-king.

---

*Reprinted with permission of *Philosophy and Rhetoric,* 8 (1975), 1-22, and the author.

I. There is a general assumption behind what I have been saying to the effect that the details of character in the Gorgias are deliberate, purposive, and integral to the dialogue's message of mission. This assumption is perhaps ultimately justified pragmatically — by being shown to work in the dialogue. And a display of how the characterizations in fact operate will be a major part of this paper. But more obvious justifications for treating the dramatic details seriously are both possible and necessary. The first consideration on behalf of the assumption is theoretical: the evidence of Plato's statements in several different dialogues that dramatic or literary creations must have a philosophical purport in order to be acceptable; the second consideration or set of considerations are a number of clues in the texts of the *Gorgias* itself making it really quite clear that, in the *Gorgias* at least, the characters do represent concepts.

As for the first and more general consideration: Plato had much to say about criteria in the arts, particularly the verbal arts, and I think it unlikely that he would have written the dialogues without attending to his own structures. Organic unity is the essential characteristic of the art that Plato approves (*Phaedrus* 264C): a unity signifying continuity of function in all parts of the whole, an integration of parts in the service of the purpose defining the thing. Obviously, a work so unified cannot contain inessentials. Assuming that Plato's practice is consistent with his theory, the literary details of each dialogue must be esssential to the dialogue, and integrally related to the philosophy expressed in the dialogue's explicit arguments.

Books II and III of the *Republic* lead to the same conclusion: the aim of creating virtue and knowledge in the souls of the literary audience must control what is said and how it is said in a work of art. That is, the work must praise justice, temperance, generosity, etc., and show the deficiency of their opposites (400A). The style can and must follow from the content, the rhythm and harmony from the style, in such a way that the style follows from and conforms to the right disposition of the soul (400D). Clearly it is a philosophical purpose and philosophical knowledge that must inform a work of art. Book X of the *Republic* reinforces this conclusion in a negative way: art that fails to embody truth and lead to virtue is condemned and eliminated from the ideal state.

Plato assumes in all of this that it is possible and desirable for art, both in its form and more articulately, to imitate and resemble the good soul. Justice and temperance are as pertinent to aesthetics as to ethics despite the fact that these qualities are more fully and clearly expressed in the spiritual realm (*Republic* 400B-401A). Here, as in the Divided Line simile, the lower levels of knowledge and reality are what they are by virtue of their formal participation in the higher. Art is "true" and acceptable inasmuch as it serves philosophical ends.

But Plato in his dialogues depicts ignorance and vice as well as virtue. Can characters who are less than virtuous be depicted so that their effects are ultimately beneficial and the requisites of a true *techne* are met? My analysis of the three rhetoricians in the *Gorgias* will provide an example of how Plato meets the problem. This much can be said in anticipation: images of vicious or defective characters must provoke the reader to reject those characters and impel him toward the images of virtue present in the work of art, and the images of virtue should eventually impel the reader beyond images altogether toward truth and virtue in their full and spiritual reality (*viz. Phaedrus* 275A, D and *Epistle VII,* 344C).

We read these dramatizations, then, assuming that the images "mean," that they are germane to the philosophical message of the dialogue. The *dramatis personae* represent concepts or ideas; their interplay resembles and represents the development of a position. By attracting or repelling the reader, or by bringing him from the one feeling to the other, the images create friendship or enmity for the ideas they represent. Thus the literary form of the dialogue prepares the soil for the argument; it creates a receptive frame of mind in the reader, so that "when reason comes he will recognize and greet her as a friend with whom he is long familiar" (*Republic* 402A).

II. I should now like to set forth the explicit evidence from the text of the *Gorgias* that the characters in the dialogue represent versions of the ideas or concepts that the dialogue is about, along with the evidence that the interchange between Socrates and the three orators represents the contest between rhetoric and dialectic (i.e., Socratic art, which I identify with the true art of justice).

That the three protagonists *were* intended to represent their art against Socratic rhetoric is abundantly clear: there are numerous signals in the text pointing to this conclusion. The evidence is as follows: The first sentence of the dialogue is, "To join in a fight or a fray, as the saying is, Socrates, you have chosen your time well enough" (447A). Of the conversation with Gorgias, more than half is talk about talk, or demonstrations of talk, that contribute nothing to the discursive argument: in this short bout Socrates draws attention to the Gorgian mode of answering no less than five times (448C; 449B; 449D; 451A. 451D), and he makes five references to his own methods of speaking and the fact that he is demonstrating them (451A-C; 452A-D; 453C; 453E-454B; 454B-C). It is equally clear that the talk with Polus is a demonstration, this time of the two rhetorics encountering one another in active argument. Between 471 and 476 Socrates refers four times to the kinds of argument that Polus is using, twice to his own methods of debate, and twice more to the fact that they are comparing two modes of refutation. Then, by allowing Polus to take a turn at asking the question (after which, as Socrates says, they will proceed by his own method), Plato leaves no doubt that the demonstration is intended.

Signals in the text indicate that Gorgian rhetoric is not only represented as art by the conversation of these men; it is also tested for its ethical implications by the success of these men in polemic against Socrates. Thus Socrates tells Gorgias that he is:

> ... One of those who would be glad to be refuted if I say anything untrue, and glad to refute anyone else who might speak untruly; but just as glad, mind you, to be refuted as to refute, since I regard the former as the greater benefit just as it is the greater benefit for oneself to be delivered from the greater evil than to deliver someone else. For I consider that a man cannot suffer any evil so great as a false opinion on the subjects of our actual argument (458A).

Thus it is the rhetorician's *knowledge* that is to be tested by the strength of Gorgias' arguments. Should he fail to prove knowledgeable enough to withstand Socrates' polemic, he shows himself to be unhappy in the greatest degree because it is justice that he does not know.

Then to Polus, Socrates says,

> ... If you are going to leave me unrefuted, the orators who do what they think fit in their cities, and the despots, will find they have got no good in doing that, if indeed power is, as you say, a good ... (467A).

and again,

> How then can the orators or despots have great power in their cities unless Socrates is refuted by Polus, and admits that they do what they wish? (467A).

Thus it is the rhetorician's *power* that is tested through Polus, if Polus' arguments prevail, they demonstrate the rhetorician's ability to secure his will, his happiness. If, on the other hand, his arguments should fail to persuade, Polus will serve as a living example of the impotence of Gorgian rhetoric.

Finally, Socrates warns Callicles that he

> ... must either refute her (philosophy) ... or, if you leave her unrefuted, by the Dog, god of the Egyptians, there will be no agreement between you, Callicles, and Iorgias, but you will be in discord with him all your life. And yet I ... should rather choose to have my lyre, or some chorus that I might provide for the public, out of tune and discordant, or to have any number of people disagreeing with me and contradicting me, than that I should have internal discord and contradiction in my own single self. (482C).

Since "internal discord and contradiction in my own single self" is exactly what Socrates calls injustice, it is the rhetorician's *justice* that is tried in the outcome of the debate with Callicles.

In sum: the evidence shows that the *Gorgias* is an account of rhetoric conceived as the several dimensions of an art of words; the conversation with Gorgias exhibits rhetoric as discourse, the conversation with Polus exhibits rhetoric as polemic, the conversation with Callicles exhibits rhetoric as political speaking. Then some further hints inform us that the dialogue is at the same time a demonstration of rhetoric on the ethical level. If the three rhetoricians are refuted, it means (1) through Gorgias, that rhetoric lacks the true knowledge needed to prevent the greatest wretchedness; (2) through Polus, that rhetoric cannot help a man attain his advantage and consequently leaves him with no means to happiness; (3) through Callicles, that the rhetorician is not just himself and cannot make others just.

There are two further quotations that deserve notice. To Polus, Socrates says: "Resign yourself into the healing hand of the argument as to a physician without shrinking, answer yes or no and no harm will come to you." (475D). But it is the art of justice that is said to be for the soul what medicine is for the body. (464B/C). Thus Socratic argument is being identified with the art of justice through the analogy of physicianship, and Callicles, after he refuses time and again to be corrected in argument, Socrates says: "You are an example of what our talk is about, an unjust man who refuses to be chastised." (505C). But if contradicting oneself and refusing correction is the same as injustice unwilling to be treated, then Socratic *therapeia* is the art of justice that endeavors to heal an unjust soul.

This, then, is the articulate evidence, both general and specific, to the effect that the protagonists of the *Gorgias* represent aspects and deficiencies of the rhetoric they practice, that Socrates is the true rhetorician and statesman, and that Socrates is engaged with the rhetoricians in a contest whose outcome is of considerable moment. (*viz.* 458A and 500C). I shall attempt, next, a close examination of the way that the characterizations in the *Gorgias* actually function — what the portraits contain and how they behave in the dialogue. This, as I suggested earlier, will be perhaps the ultimate evidence of the thesis I have set out to demonstrate.

The *Gorgias* demands and affords some incredibly complex machinery for the interpretation of its dramatizations. By way of a preliminary example: the dialogue is about rhetoric, hence the speaking style of each of the characters is automatically data for conclusions about the types of rhetoric they represent. Rhetoric is also polemic or debate; therefore their modes of argument and their success or lack of it against Socrates are further evidence of the nature of their rhetorics; finally, rhetoric is politics, which means that the way in which each character handles the others he confronts should be evidence of rhetoric's potentiality as an instrument for adjudicating and administering the common weal.

At the same time, the dialogue is about the ethical concepts that rhetoric implies. That being so, the ways in which the characters behave as persons will be further data. And because we are told that there are cross-implications between the art of speaking (and arguing and politicing) and the value-concepts that ground it (pleasure, power, justice), we can expect to find evidence of the ethical condition of each character in the way he speaks, argues, and responds to arguments as well as in his personal mannerisms. Then the same procedure obtains on the third level, the level of political ideas, and the characters offer data on each of the other two levels that make them pertinent representatives on this new plane. There are further considerations that make the structure for interpretation even more complex, but fortunately, as has already been suggested, each protagonist is especially representative of one idea and explicitly designated as its surrogate. Moreover, each represents his idea on one level rather more than on the others: Gorgias represents the aesthetical level, the rhetorician's knowledge, and he does so especially through his speech; Polus represents the ethical level, the rhetorician's power, and he does so especially through his techniques for arguing; Callicles represents the political level, the rhetoricians' justice, and he does so especially through the manner of his response to Socrates. Socrates, of course, represents the true rhetorician's knowledge (i.e. *techne*), power, and justice, and he does so in all of the possible ways (i.e., speech, argument, and manner toward others).

GORGIAS

Perhaps because defeating a caricature of the enemy gains no converts away from the enemy in his full force and appeal, Plato sees to it that the three orators — and so the values they represent — are at first look attractive. Gorgias, for example, is encountered at the height of his career, on the occasion of a triumphant display, surrounded by worshipful students and audience, apparently gentle and accommodating, yet confident and proud. For he can answer any question and as briefly or as lengthily as you please. He is, indeed, an expert at pleasing — the able host at a banquet of verbal pleasures. Socrates, by contrast, makes a rather poor impression: he arrives barefoot and ragged with the ludicrous and quite unpromising Chaerephon by his side and he arrives too late for the speech, for he has talked too long at the agora. (447A-B). But Plato makes certain that the reader is not drawn to Gorgias for long; Gorgias' foolish boasting is offputting and soon suggests a new perspective on his character in general. Much about Gorgias that might at first have seemed positive or at least neutral takes on a different coloring at second look. Indeed, the boasting seems to be only the most obvious symptom of a pervasive and overweening concern for appearances. Gorgias is gentle because of his fear of offending, of losing the approval of his audience; he refuses to associate himself or his art with the illicit use young people make of it (475B) in order to appear upright, to keep face with his public: He wants to please because people want to be pleased (or think they do) and gratifying others is the condition of gaining their good opinion. All of these are nothing more or less than signs of an over-mastering concern with "image", with the impression one is making on others.

Gorgias' mode of speech tells the same tale in another way. Ignoring the function of words to convey meaning and reflect truth, Gorgias makes symphonies of his sentences through alliteration, assonance, consonance, and other available devices. His dialogue is a solo instrument to display his virtuosity: brief only to show how briefly he can speak; lengthy to exhibit verbal prowess. But according to the standards set by the content of the discussion, the size and shape of Gorgias's speeches are irrelevant caprice. When Gorgias decides to speak briefly, twenty additional questions are required, four Stephanus pages passed through (449-453), before even the beginning of an answer appears.

Not surprisingly, it is this over-mastering concern with "image" or appearance that causes Gorgias' defeat — first of all because he has cared more for appearance than for learning and knowing (i.e. being proficient enough to win in dialectic and in dialectical discussions of justice); secondly because, not really knowing justice, he asserts that he teaches it to his students. He makes the boast in order to maintain appearances with the audience. But the boast is fatal by Socrates' standards and by his own as well. For, coupled with his disclaimer of responsibility for his students' unjust use of his art (and the admission that knowing justice implies being just and acting justly), it leads him to contradiction. Self-contradiction, however, is the outward and visible sign of injustice in the soul (482C). Thus it is his being immersed in concern for appearances that makes Gorgias an example of injustice. It makes him, moreover, *appear* the fool. The special irony that the images work on themselves is that as a result of their failure to meet the high standards established by Socrates' definitions, they fail to achieve their own abortive aims as well. At the end, Socrates, caring only to know and not at all interested in appearances, appears attractive and persuasive at Gorgias's side.

Socrates introduces the first conversation by telling Callicles that "I want to find out from the man what is the function of his art" (447C). And as the man is, so is his art: flattering and illusory, without substance or center. The lessons one learns from the character of Gorgias are general: overweening concern with appearances is injustice (its aesthetic face, artlessness, or the failure to have a rational method determined by true knowledge of one's subject matter), and such concern fails even to attain the appearance that it seeks. But the lessons are also particular; they are about the art of rhetoric. In fact Socrates does find out from the man what is the nature of his art, for in the conversation with Gorgias Socrates maintains that he does not know what rhetoric is, while even in the very early parts of the conversation with Polus Socrates finds himself able to state that rhetoric is a branch of the knack of flattery and a sleazy imitation of the true *techne,* without subject or substance.

How likely that that conclusion is a result of the encounter with Gorgias and of a shrewd analysis of the man. Thus it is through the dramatization of Gorgias that Plato teaches us the specific features of the aesthetic face of injustice and identifies the latter with the modes of speech of the rhetorician. Furthermore, as we have seen, it is the philosophical deficiencies of the concept behind the image that are behind the dramatic defeat of the image in the mind of the reader. Thus the image is acceptable as art because it serves a philosophical purpose by representing a deficient position *as* deficient and so moving us on to the more sufficient images of virtue apparent in Socrates.

POLUS

The image or images of Polus work in very much the same way. Polus, at first blush, appears an accomplished intellectual and eager for discussion. Although not more than about twenty years of age, he has written a book so widely read that Socrates has seen it in Athens (462C). In the dialogue itself it is made quite clear that Polus is a master of alliteration, assonance, consonance, and hyperbole as well as the Gorgian techniques for winning arguments and persuading vast audiences. Socrates, on the other hand, speaks in plain words and is always saying the same things in the same way (*Symposium* 221E) and using the same simple-minded examples and analogies. He does not seek to persuade or influence and he does not claim to know. At times, indeed, it seems that he has nothing to offer but questions, that he is avoid only to feed off the opinions of others (*viz.* Thrasymachus' accusation, *Republic* 336C-D, 337A). The contrast is clearly not favorable to Socrates.

But Polus is too impertinent, too disrespectful to retain the reader's favor for long (*viz.* 461C, D, 462D, and throughout the first half of his participation). Things that seemed at first to show enthusiasm for argument — as, for example, when Polus twice interrupted the discussion between Socrates and Gorgias — begin to appear to be signs of impatient self-importance and lack of discipline. His seeming "quickness" and eagerness are in fact an inability to attend to the matter in question. We notice how his mind runs at full speed round the question and away from it, taking off after the *quale* when asked for the *quid,* assembling irrelevant arguments, returning again and again to affirm points that he has already agreed to deny, balking at each conclusion, unable and unwilling to contain himself within the necessary structures of thought and argument. The devices he uses in argument add up to the same thing: he laughs when his opponent is serious (473E); he "raises hobgoblins" in order to terrify Socrates into acquiescence (473C); he "calls witnesses" (472D) so that Socrates may be humbled by the threat of ostracism (not literally, of course. Threats on that scale are saved for Callicles). Nowhere among these devices can one discern any concern for the truth about the question at issue or for the well-being of the man who asks it. Polus is concerned to conquer, to overwhelm, and nothing more.

Clearly power must be unbridled force if Polus is its exemplar. "Colt by name and colt by nature", Polus is, as we have seen, impertinent in character, uncontained in speech, undisciplined in logic and irrelevant in argument. In every aspect of his behavior, verbal and non-verbal, we find Polus knocking down fences and overleaping boundaries. He represents the refusal to allow that power can be channeled or defined by knowledge and responsibility. To be, or to express oneself, means for Polus brooking no obstacles, acknowledging no limits, obeying no orders. If this boundlessness is what the rhetorician means by power, it is clear once again that this idea is diametrically opposed to that of Socrates'; according to Socrates power involves a just order and it is only by reflection of that just order that polemic derives its articulate aim and structure, its ability to secure the speaker's advantage and, not incidentally, its capacity to prevail.

Again it is not the logical defect of the notion, its failure to meet Socrates' standards, that makes a drama of its defeat; but rather that Polus, concerned above all to prevail, emerges dazed and confused from his encounter with a power that aims to teach and not to overwhelm. The forceful Polus must yield quietly to the "bonds of steel and adamant" with which Socrates secures their joint hypotheses. It is Socrates who prevails. Thus it is through the dramatization of Polus that Plato illustrates the ethical face of injustice, sketches in its features, and attributes those features to the rhetorician's notion of power. Since it is agreed that power is the ability to get one's true advantage, which is justice for the soul, the rhetorician's power is impotence and injustice, for it is because of Polus' practice of Gorgian rhetoric that he contradicts himself in argument and evinces, thereby injustice in the soul. And, as we have seen, the defeat is double-edged. Polus is defeated not only by Socrates' standards, but by his own.

Let me point out in conclusion, what may already be clear, that the drama of the reader's participation in the character of Polus is the drama of the demise of a defective concept, i.e., the notion of power that rhetoric espouses and claims to enable its practioners to purchase. Thus, once again, Plato's *techne* meets his requisites.

CALLICLES

Callicles is a more complicated character than Gorgias or Polus. He is, in fact, so much more real and more attractive than they that some have taken him — rather than Socrates — to be the hero of the dialogue. That move, as I shall make apparent, is patently unjustified. I think that Callicles is made as compelling as he is in order that the strongest claim rhetoric has to offer can be laid to rest. He is, though, compelling. Callicles is everything that Socrates is not and everything that Socrates has been most frequently criticized for not being. Suave, debonair, eloquent, an aristocrat by station and education, Callicles is successful by almost any standards, an obvious candidate for political office. With his native shrewdness and subtlety and the advantages of wealth and position, he should have little trouble gaining favor in the eyes of the many-headed beast of state. He is, in sum, worldly and efficient; able to cope with events and turn them his way, obviously able to provide for his own welfare and the well-being of those dear to him; a likely leader of men.

Socrates himself compliments Callicles on his intelligence, candor, and goodwill, saying that these qualities make of him a touchstone, a worthy opponent, the one at last against whom Socrates' own mettle can be tried. So worthy, in fact, does Callicles at first appear, that Socrates' whole life is called into question by the comparison. Son of a stonecutter and a stonecutter himself, poor by birth and uneducated, Socrates has not tried to compensate for his deficiencies. He has always been — and still is — unmindful of the harsh realities that living presses upon us. Oblivious of the need for material goods, careless about the sustenance of his wife and sons, uninterested in serving the state, Socrates has spent his days in irresponsible (and often disrespectful) conversation with his betters. And in so doing he has allowed himself to remain untutored in the ways of the world and the ways of gaining the favor of those in power. He has learned nothing of practical importance, hence is unable to provide for his own safety and that of his family and friends. By Callicles' standards, a more hapless example of a man cannot be imaged (*viz.* 484C-486D). But even those who do not completely accept the standards of success and power that Callicles represents must be somewhat impressed by the contrast.

In the long run, however, Callicles puts us off just as much as the other protagonist do. He does so finally in a number of ways, but the way in which Plato meant him to do so first and most is by now, I am afraid, a matter of conjecture. Callicles does not exist in written history. We have records of Gorgias and Polus and the other persons mentioned in the dialogue, but about Callicles, nothing whatever. It is not likely that Plato would place an invented character alongside real people and events. More likely Callicles was a real person contemporary with the others assembled in the dialogue, and his absence from written history has historical reasons. Dodds[1] offers an explanation of why "such a vigorous and richly endowed personality" should have left no mark on the history of his time. His clue is an allusion in the *Gorgias* itself: Socrates warns Callicles that in return for his political service, the citizens "may perhaps lay their hands on you . . . and on my friend Alcibiades" (519B). Alcibiades *did* suffer at the hands of the citizens between the dramatic date of the *Gorgias* and the time it was actually written. Therefore the statement is a prophecy *post-eventum* about Alcibiades. And what Dodds suggests is that linking the names of Callicles and Alcibiades in this *post-eventum* warning is a way of alluding to their linked destinies. He speculates that in the last years of the Peloponnesian War or in the ensuing revolutions a man as ambitious as Callicles may well have come to a calamitous end. Thus Dodds is suggesting that Callicles died too young to be remembered. I would like to add my suffrage to Dodds'. By the time he wrote the Gorgias, Plato must have known what had become of Callicles, and the linking of his name with that of Alcibiades could have no other purpose in the dialogue than that of indicating to the reader that Callicles, too, came to a bad end. Plato's planting of the clue perhaps more than Callicles' absence from written history makes it quite likely that the conjecture is fact.

But what is the significance of the fact? The issue between Callicles and Socrates is nothing less than the way life should be lived, the most serious of all questions, as both Socrates and Callicles affirm (500C); Socrates' counsel is to preserve the inner man at all costs;

1. E. R. Dodds, *Plato: Gorgias* (Oxford: Clarendon Press), p. 13.

Callicles' answer is, nourish the outer man, for material reality is the ground of everything and life is the condition of the good. Callicles is thoroughly materialistic: the good is a long life, art is the capacity to survive, and power is the power to get. It is a life devoted entirely to petting and courting the many-headed beast of state in order to have "more" of life and its tangible rewards. That such a man should be killed or ostracized for political reasons is the ultimate irony. It means that the power that he seeks with all his soul cannot be had. There *is* no power sufficient to guarantee these ends; a life spent trying to acquire them is wasted.

We remember Cimon, Pericles, and Themistocles who also spent their lives courting and flattering the *demos* and ended by suffering at its hands (515Cff). And Archelaus, too, the tyrant Polus praised and envied who was killed in the same year Socrates was executed. *What* art of survival, we may well ask. Callicles and Socrates were both victims of the city in spite of the fact that Callicles spent all of his effort mastering techniques that were designed to prevent just this. Callicles turns out to have been a shrewd businessman indeed, sealing a bargain in which he ended by paying on both sides of the counter and receiving on neither. The price is too high no matter what it is, and we are ready to question the wisdom of anyone willing to pay it. Such a man could not, in any case, have thought very deeply about the alternatives before him.

And that, the superficiality of judgment, the deciding of crucial matters on the basis of gratification, and not even of long-range gratification at that, is Callicles. It is what makes him the man he is and what colors all of his characteristics: it is what Socrates finally shows us at the center of the traits he attributed to Callicles earlier: his intelligence, his candor, and goodwill. Note, for example, about Callicles' intelligence: his statement of the crucial distinction on which his argument is based, the distinction between natural and conventional law, is superficial and "appetitively" grounded. He is unclear about what he means by the "better" according to nature; he allows that he means the stronger, then is caught unaware when Socrates points out the contradiction involved in trying to maintain this equation and affirm at the same time that doing injustice is less disgraceful than suffering it according to the law of nature. For the many believe that doing injustice is more disgraceful than suffering it, and since the many are stronger than the few, they are the "better" and their judgments and enactments are true law. Then according to Callicles' careless equation of "better" and stronger, doing injustice is more disgraceful than suffering it by nature as well as by law. And it is, of course, Callicles' appetitiveness that obstructs his intelligence in this instance, for as a democratic leader Callicles is caught between his own self-centered will to power, his image of himself as *Übermensch*, and the necessity of catering to the masses in order to gratify that will. The conflicting desires of an appetitive man lead to contradition in argument. Again and again Callicles involves himself in contradictions like this one because his thinking is forced to subserve his divided interests.

His "candor" suffers from the same deficiency. Callicles is willing enough to say aloud "what most men think and fear to say" (492B). But he is not at all willing to say what he himself thinks when that thinking is at odds with the thinking of the multitude. Real candor involves real courage; it involves the willingness to be one's own man. But Callicles is willing to be his own man only as long as that being does not conflict with what the multitude desires. Note, for example, how upset Callicles is when forced to acknowledge a part within him that assents to Socrates' not very popular doctrines (513Cff. after which he becomes more contentious than ever).

It is impossible that a person as intent as Callicles is on stifling his inner self could be a real friend to anyone. Socrates points out that self-knowledge, one-ness with oneself, is the condition of friendship, one-ness with others (507E-508A). And Callicles neither knows nor wants to know his ignorance or his truth. Socrates himself makes the connection between Callicles' responses and his "good-will." After conversing with Callicles for some time, noticing his many evasions and obvious unwillingness to have his convictions tested (495A, 501C, 505C) or to acknowledge his confusion, (495A, 497A, 498C, 499B, 505C) Socrates gives up the idea that Callicles is his friend:

> I thought I would not have to fear any intentional deception on your part, you being my friend; but now I find I was mistaken, and it seems I must . . . make the best of what I have got and accept just anything you offer. (499C).

Thus the admirable qualities of Callicles turn out to be the appearances of an incorrigibly appetitive man. Choosing the great instead of the lesser evil and refusing to "submit to the healing hand of the argument" (475D) when he is caught in contradiction, Callicles demonstrates the truth behind the appearance of justice that rhetoric offers. Its appearance of justice is in fact incorrigible vice. It is illness so severe that the cure is more painful than the canker and the physician is more feared than death itself. In his present condition, which is an image of the city's discord, Callicles can hardly be expected to cater to the citizens' best interests. (514D-E). Vice feeds on vice: to maintain the lie in his own soul (as he obviously means to do), Callicles would nourish the lie in theirs; to be mighty in his own eyes, Callicles would have the citizens dependent upon him; he would bloat them and keep them submerged in the flux of wanting and getting so that they continue to need him the way a suckling needs its mother. The "justice" he offers is food for the wound and not for the soul that is wounded. We learn from the characterizations of Callicles, then, that the rhetorician's justice is dominion by desire, rule by the many heads of passion whose conflicting voices drown each other out and leave no head, no order, no self. We learn that incorrigible appetitiveness is the political face of rhetoric and we learn from Callicles its features in a man's manner and in his modes of argument. Because Callicles, even so, is the best that rhetoric has to offer, we may conclude that rhetoric has failed in its claim to provide a head of state. It provides a body, a *demos*, the perennial swarm (see *Republic* 560ff. — the description of the democratic man and state on their way to tyranny), but for a head, we must now look to philosophy and to the anticipation in the *Gorgias* of the *Republic*'s philosopher-king.

The Philosopher-Statesman

Just as Plato's portraits of the three rhetoricians follow from deficient concepts of art, power, and justice, so his portrait of Socrates in this dialogue follows from the adequate concepts of art, power, and justice. In order to show that this is the case, I have constructed the following character study by *inferring* the hero's features from the concept of justice applied to the art of rhetoric. It will be seen, not surprisingly, that the features inferred parallel the actual characteristics Socrates manifests in the *Gorgias*. This portrait, then, shall be the final step in my argument that the *Gorgias* is self-referential, demonstrating in *erga* what it argues in discourse — and a little more besides.

I said that the Socrates of the *Gorgias* is Plato's portrait of the just rhetorician or statesman. I also said that his characteristics are inferred and inferrable from the adequate concepts of art and power, as well as justice. It seems advisable, before beginning to analyse that portrait, to show how the concepts of art and power are related to the concept of justice, making the portrait of a just man at the same time necessarily a portrait of the true artist and the truly powerful person. The dialogue's arguments make these connections and a summary of their thrust will therefore serve as a suitable preface to the portrait of the just rhetorician.

With Gorgias, Socrates discusses the question of the nature of rhetoric, what kind of an art it is. From what Gorgias says, Socrates concludes (in conversing with Polus) that rhetoric is no art at all. In coming to this conclusion, Socrates develops the criteria by which an activity qualifies as an art. A true art defines itself by its subject matter; it is the nature of the subject matter that determines the procedures of the art. But then an art requires knowledge; for unless the nature of the subject matter were known and known truly, methods and responses could not be determined in the right way. Since Polus has argued that a rhetor need not know justice and injustice, and since it is clear that neither he nor Gorgias does know the truth about these matters, it follows that rhetoric is not an art. It is a sham, a mere appearance of an art standing to the true rhetoric as cookery stands to medicine or cosmetics to exercise (465C).

But what power can be purchased by a pseudo-art? If power is the ability to do what one wills, the knack of rhetoric is not helpful in gaining it. For the most universal object of will is the good or best; that is, all men want or will their true advantage. But they may have different ideas about what that advantage is and what steps should be taken to gain it. Therefore a distinction can be made between what one wills and what one thinks best (467Aff.); if a man is mistaken about his own best interests, what he thinks good will not coincide with what he wills. And such mistakes are frequently made.

The distinction between "what one wills" and "what one thinks best" is based on a prior distinction between good and pleasant. What men take for their advantage is what seems most pleasant or comfortable, but if the pursuit of pleasure can confound a man's true advantage, it must be that the good transcends the pleasant and cannot be measured by it.

Power, then, if it is the ability to do what one wills, must involve a knowledge of what is good and not merely of what is pleasant. But the good for anything is always a function of its nature; it is the particular order or balance that indicates the health of the thing. The good for man involves an order in which reason legislates for the whole soul, controlling the appetites and enlisting the energies in its causes. Each part of the soul performs its proper function with the result that there is balance and harmony overall (cf. *Republic* IV, 442-443). Justice is the name for this balanced condition of the soul, its nature and its health (*Gorgias,* 504).

But the false rhetoric proceeds without justice and knowledge of justice (i.e., of the good for man) and so procures a power that can deprive a man of his true advantage and of the name and nature that is his as Man. Without justice and the knowledge of justice there can be no talk of art and power. For a man's happiness depends on the just order of his soul (507). Since power is the ability to gain one's weal, it is power only if it aims at justice. Aiming at justice involves knowing justice and knowing that it is distinct from pleasure. Therefore a practice that bases itself on the equation of goodness and pleasure can be neither an art nor a means to power. It misconstrues the good of man and as a result invites the greatest wretchedness for persuader and persuaded both.

A true art of rhetoric would be based on the knowledge of justice and the knowledge that justice is the nature of man. Justice would determine the methods of the art that "endeavours . . . to make the citizens' souls as good as possible . . . to say what is best, whether it prove more or less pleasant to one's hearers" (503A). In sum, talk has a subject matter and a function: the human soul is its subject; its function is to provoke the soul to recall itself to its proper state. "Talk" is an art only when it is based upon knowledge of the soul's well-being. And only an art can purchase power, one's true advantage, for they both presuppose the same knowledge: that one's true advantage is a just soul. Thus the concepts of art, power, and justice are related in such a way that art and power both presuppose justice and the knowledge of justice, and, on the other hand, art and power follow from justice in the soul.

Then the true rhetorician, is a man who allows the good of the other to determine his mode of speech and techniques of argument. And since the human soul is the "other" to which the words are aimed, it is the soul's specific order (i.e., justice) that guides the rhetorician and informs his art.

> . . . it is this that our orator, the man of art or virtue, will have in view, when he applies to our souls the words that he speaks, and also in all his actions,

and in giving any gift he will give it, and in taking anything away he will take it, with this thought always before his mind: how justice may be engendered in the souls of his fellow citizens, and how injustice may be removed. how temperance may be bred in them and licentiousness cut off; and how virtue as a whole may be produced and vice expelled (504B).

We can expect to see, then, in the way that a true rhetorician speaks, in his manner of arguing, and in his behavior toward those with whom he discusses, the marks and characteristics of a just man's knowledge, self-accord, and concern for the well-being of others. For these, (i.e., speaking, arguing, and acting) are the aspects of rhetoric, and these are the three levels of concern (i.e., aesthetic, ethical, and political) of an art of justice.

What follows is an analysis of Plato's portrait of the true speaker-statesman, structured according to these three parts of rhetoric and these three levels of being. There follows, first, a characterization of the just man independently of his being a rhetorician, with regard to his own psychic condition and, second, with regard to his relationships with others. After that, I consider the implications of justice when applied to his vocation as orator: first, to his speaking style, its appearance, its content, its purposes or consequences; second, to his mode of arguing, its "shape", its substance, its purpose; third, to his manner or behavior, and especially its aim of humbling, restraining, and tempering the opponents with whom he deals.

I. The just man as such:

(1) Because he measures himself by the truth and not by appearances, a just man cares to know the good rather than to appear good to others. (2) Because he measures his welfare by the harmony of his own soul, a just man is courageous rather than rude or overbearing (515C). (3) Because his service is the administration of order, the just man is a paradigm of temperance and moderation.

II. The just man as such in relation to others:

(1) Aesthetic: A just man tells his friends the truth; he does not flatter them. This is because a man who flatters is concerned above all with the impression people have of him. (His *esse* is *percipi*). Others are nothing to him except media of his own appearances. The fact that they are pleased with him is important because it confirms

his existence; but what they are in themselves he does not know or care about.

(2) Ethical: Nor is the just man forceful. The man who relates to people in too forceful a way is controlled by the idea that he must prevail over others in order to affirm his own being. This means that he measures his own existence by their non-existence. But a just man is powerful by being self-sufficient; therefore he treats his friends in terms of their intrinsic value and not in terms of some pernicious need of his own.

(3) Political: So a person whose friend is just can expect to become more knowing and more whole because of that relationship. A man who is led by his appetites inevitably abuses his friends; for passion erases the boundary between self and other, evaluating all things by the pleasure or pain they provoke. But a man whose passions are disciplined sees the true nature of people and things and responds to them accordingly. It follows, then, simply from the definition of justice as the self-sufficient order of the soul, that the just man will be modest (i.e., not have the conceit of wisdom) courageous, and temperate, and will not flatter, force, or abuse the men around him, but will act in all things for the best.

III. The just man as rhetorician:

Then if this "all things" includes a public or political aspect — if the just man must also be a true politician — we shall expect his public faces to reflect the just contours of his private self. The speeches, debates, and political activities of the true rhetorician are determined in every particular by knowledge, virtue, (which, applied to man, is the power-to-be of a just soul) and concern with the virtue of others.

(1) Speech, appearance: Because the true rhetorician is not concerned with the superficial pleasure of the hearer, he will undoubtedly choose "always to be using the same terms for the same things" (*Symposium*, 221E). He will attend to the substance of his talk and dispense with those rhetorical devices that make words ornaments and deprive them of their natural function. He chooses the words that make his meanings clear. (*Gorgias*, 517D-E).

Content: In the first place, his speeches are neither too brief to answer the question (*viz*. Gorgias) nor too lengthy for relevance (*viz*. Polus). The fitness that reveals the rationality of an art demands that a man determine the length and scope of his speeches by the objective variables of the situation and not capriciously or autistically, as by his wish to impress. Thus a just rhetorician speaks lengthily when his opponent's answers are too brief to allow the argument to go forward (466A, 519C), briefly when the other confuses the issue with an abundance of words.

Purpose and consequences: Justice and the aim of engendering justice in the souls of others make his speeches orderly: he "arranges everything according to a certain order, and forces one part to suit and fit with another, until he has combined the whole into a regular and well-ordered production" (504A). His speeches are coherent and orderly by being suited to the question asked, the requirements of the particular soul to which the speech is directed, the specific subject matter of the speech or question, and, finally, by the logic and method that the soul in its rationality dictates.

It should be clear that this description of the true rhetorician's speaking style represents the implications of justice applied to the aesthetic face of rhetoric: rhetoric as speech. Examining what justice implies with regard to a rhetorician's modes of *arguing* puts us on the ethical level. Here the just rhetorician must aim at an encounter where respect for his own self-hood and for the self-hood of his protagonist are the chief marks. Concern for justice will mean, then, aiming at (1) teaching his opponent the truth rather than cajoling him into belief; (2) withstanding the opposition rather than conquering him; (3) correcting the opponent's weakness rather than taking advantage of it. To wit:

(2) Argument; "shape": Because the true rhetorician aims to secure and teach the truth rather than to amaze or cajole his audience, the accord of the audience is no test of his success (474A). Only one man's suffrage is important to him – that of his opponent, whose acquiescence is his own triumph because it means that he has given up the lie in his soul.

Substance: Since the opponent must be respected as a rational being, our speaker avoids the kind of argument that makes a young man fitful. He does not, for instance, confuse his friend by laughing when the talk has been serious (473E) or frighten him by telling ghost stories (473C). Arguments like these arouse the passions; they persuade the man by dazing him and leading him away from the point. This is the way to overcome an enemy, not the way to instruct a friend. Therefore the man who knows and speaks always with a view to the best lets his arguments flow from the logic and truth of his position. His opponent is refuted because his assertions are not true, because force becomes power only when it is disciplined by logic and grounded in truth. For only the arguments that truth carves out are secured "with bonds of steel and adamant" and remain standing when the opposition, having built a fortress on infirm ground, finds himself unprotected in the midst of the fray.

And if Socrates is truly just, he does not contradict himself, however long or tortuous the argument. For, as we have seen, inconsistency in discourse is the outward sign of discord in the soul (482B-C). The justice that gives the soul its harmony and makes a man one instead of many, informs and unifies his speeches as well; as the man just rules with one head, so he speaks with one voice.

Purpose: The true statesman must use his polemic to help his subjects avoid and correct contradiction. For the inward chaos reflected in inconsistent speech is the greatest evil a man can suffer (482B,C; 509C,D; 522E) and it is the statesman's task to try to help his people escape the greatest evil (504D,E). To the end, then, of the health and harmony of the city, the true statesman will seek to expose and remedy the confusions of the citizens — by refuting their false arguments to temper their vigor with foresight and purpose, to chasten their appetites, to direct them to a better way.

Evidence of justice on the third and final level, the level of political efficacy, should be sought particularly in the rhetorician's manner and behavior toward others. The tone he adopts toward his listeners should indicate an adequate appraisal of their intellectual and moral deficiencies and the concern to "cure" them, if cure is possible.

(3) Manner: The politician's aim, if he is a practioner of the true art, will be to make his opponents humble (i.e., wise without the conceit of wisdom), courageous, and temperate, these being the character-traits of a just man. Accordingly, his tone will be calculated to chasten arrogance, restrain force, and temper passion. And the physician's medicine will be bitter in direct proportion to the extent of the patient's vice.

(1) Where an opponent is old, not pervasively vicious, yet not amenable to change, our speaker is himself courteous and patient. If he is convinced that the older man cannot be taught, perhaps this rhetorican can use the conversation as an example and refute his respondent in a kindly way simply in order to discourage young men

in the audience who would follow him. (2) If, on the other hand, our speaker is opposed by a rude, vigorous youth, respect for the truth would make him ironic and insistent rather than courteous. And if the youth seems at all likely to benefit from instruction, the most likely tactic would be to cast him down for his impertinence and self-importance, for these stand in the way of knowledge and the real power and courage that follow from it. (3) Against a contentious, accomplished, clever politician, our techer would employ still another tone and technique: because his own appetites do not obscure his responses, he is angry, but only for his patient's sake: If he shouts it is because one sometimes must in order to be heard above the din of desires that contend for the soul of an unjust man.

Conclusion

The man who exhibits these characteristics is the only man who can honestly say:

> ... I am one of few, not to say the only one, in Athens who attempts the true art of statesmanship, and the only man of the present time who manages affairs of state: hence, as the speeches that I make from time to time are not aimed at gratification, but at what is best instead of what is most pleasant ... (521E).

— And it is Socrates who says it.

The *Gorgias* does not conclude explicitly that the true rhetoric is philosophy and that the philosopher has the knowledge and virtue required to rule a state properly. But Socrates begins his argument with Callicles by identifying himself with philosophy, explaining that it is philosophy who "speaks what you hear me saying now" (482A) and concludes it — as though the conclusion were somehow established in the interim — with this assertion that he, Socrates, is the only true statesman. The *Republic* does make the connection between philosophy and statesmanship explicit and accomplishes this by elaborating a discursive portrait of the philosopher-king (*Republic* 475-485) that incorporates all of the characteristics that I have inferred here from the idea of a just rhetorician.

From this schematism, and from the fact that Socrates fits the portrait in every particular, I conclude that Plato intended the *Gorgias* as a demonstration in *erga* of the argument that the *Republic* takes up on a more articulate level: the argument that the philosopher is the just man and proper ruler of the state. The *Republic*'s assertion follows negatively as well as positively from the images in the *Gorgias*. Socrates claims not merely to be a true statesman but, after talking with three of the supposedly ablest men in Athens, to be *the only* Athenian who can manage affairs of state. By the time the dialogue concludes, three candidates have been tested for the position and found wanting. Socrates alone has been found to have the qualifications for ruling the state.

PLATO AND CONJURING*

Jacqueline de Romilly

Rhetoric was bound to meet strong opposition from Plato, and everything in Gorgias' *Helen* about the power of speech seemed to call for that opposition. Speech, Gorgias had said, could be used in different ways — good or bad — just as there are poisonous drugs, and others that heal. Fairly enough, Plato, in his *Gorgias,* remembered that distinction; for his Gorgias says that rhetoric can be used for right or wrong purposes, just as the art of fighting can turn out to be either beneficial or mischievous, according to the use made of it (456Cff). Yet this very neutrality could seem rather dangerous to a moralist like Plato.[1]

But there was something worse. Gorgias had also admitted in the *Helen* that the very principle of the art of speech was to stir passions, and thereby to deceive. It was ἀπάτη. He had established this power of speech on the frailty and uncertainty of human opinion, δόξα.[2] Now nothing was so averse to Plato's passion for accurate knowledge than such an attitude. Indeed, he was severe enough against poets for not being always truthful; he could not approve of rhetoric, when its avowed aim, ἀπάτη, was to falsify truth. Gorgias' reference to poetry, therefore, could not help. On the contrary, it looks very much as if each of these arts inherited, in Plato's eyes, the dangers and shortcomings of the other.[3]

---

*Reprinted by permission of the author and publishers from *Magic and Rhetoric in Ancient Greece* by Jacqueline de Romilly, Cambridge, Massachusetts: Harvard University Press, Copyright © by the President and fellows of Harvard College.

1. Rostagni, *Studi it. fil. class.* 22 (1922) 155-156, compares this neutrality with the attitude of Antisthenes and with an old Pythagorean saying, quoted by Diog. Laert. 8.32. But this does not imply any influence in any way; what we have is only a plain statement of fact, in each case.

2. See also B3, about the fact that what is, is irreducible to thought or speech.

3. See the different passages quoted p. 7 and note 13. One could add the fact that poetry stirs the part of our soul that is turned toward passion and

The dangers of rhetoric were even greater, not only because its very principle was deception but because of the direct influence it could have in practical life; the part played by rhetoric in politics during the last thirty years of the fifth century made that danger both obvious and terrifying. Now, the very definition given of rhetoric in Plato's *Gorgias* calls our attention to this political function; for it says that rhetoric deals with the power of persuading the judges in court, the councilors in the Council, and the people in the assembly (452D). And the whole point of the dialogue is to prove that it is better, in the courts of justice, to be punished for one's own faults than to escape punishment and that it is better, in politics, to go against the people's wishes rather than agree with them so as to get their approval. It will even be noticed that the last person to take part in the dialogue — last, but not least — is Callicles, a man whom we do not know and who perhaps never existed, the only thing we can say about him is that he is an ambitious man, who wants, with the help of rhetoric, to grasp power for himself. This is indicative enough of the practical danger of rhetoric. It explains why the notion of tyranny has such an important place in the dialogue (as we see in 466B-E, 470C-471D, which is the part about Archelaus, or 510A-511C, where the aim pursued by Callicles is discussed, not to speak of the fact that in the myth all tyrants are, with Archelaus, condemned to perpetual penance). It also explains why the great men of Athens, known for their skill and success, also fall under criticism; the examples of Pericles. Cimon, Miltiades, and Themistocles are introduced to show that even they pursued the wrong ends: they succeeded in producing ships and walls and power, whereas they should have taught the city not to wish for such unhealthy swelling (517B, 518E). The aim of rhetoric is wrong, not only because it is deceptive but because it has an evil influence.[4]

Plato's attack will develop along very different lines from those of Gorgias' own account of rhetoric. Yet in fact throughout his whole battle with the sophists, Plato turned against them the very analogues on which Gorgias had built his praise of speech. The analogue of

---

irritation (*Rep.* 605B); this actual effect of poetry is the very aim and purpose of rhetoric. Thus Plato can speak, shortly afterward, of the ancient opposition between poetry and philosophy (607B).

4. Once more, and in a very surprising way, this criticism is extended to poets, who, in the *Republic*, are described as supporting tyranny (568C).

poetry had turned out to be dangerous. The analogue of magic turned out to be disastrous; and Plato, with malicious insistence, kept returning to it.

'Απάτη, or illusion, is the aim of rhetoric. It is also the aim of magic, when the magician calls up phantoms and makes people believe in things that do not exist. That this is the very principle of rhetoric is obvious. An antilogy, where one speech opposes another, shows that it is possible to see in the same reality now one aspect and now another. Protagoras himself was proud of making the weak thesis strong, and the strong thesis weak. And we all know (thanks to Plutarch, *Pericles* 8) what Thucydides, the son of Melesias, told Archidamus when the Spartan king asked him who was the better fighter, he or Pericles: "When I have knocked him down in a fight," he said, "he argues he didn't fall and wins the fight by persuading the people." That is illusion. To call it also the very nature of magic requires a word of explanation; for such a view can only take place in a general context where magic has been separated from religion. Perhaps there had been too much religious criticism to leave room for sacred magic, and there was too much uncertainty about life not to leave room for tricky witchcraft;[5] credulity generally outlives devotion. Indeed, in the fourth century, we hear no more about trials for impiety, but we do hear about trials for witchcraft, drugs, poison, incantations, and irregular meetings of immoral cults.[6] And it is a fact that the so-called magician could be an object of prosecution.[7] This degradation of what we have called sacred magic is made clear by Walter Burkert's study of the word γόης.[8] It explains why the very notion of magic came to be used with an unfavorable meaning and applied to anything that was deceptive. This meaning already

---

5. Already in Gorgias, witchcraft was turned into a τέχνη, which means it has become an effort to gather superhuman powers for one's self. The difference is well explained in Philostratus' *Life of Apollonius of Tyana* 1.2.

6. See the cases of Ninus, Theoris, Phryne.

7. See the passage of the *Meno* quoted below, p. 33, where the γόης is taken to prison. There was, of course, a δίκη φαρμάκων for the use of poison. For the contempt of magicians and conjurers in Plato, see *Laws* 649A, quoted below, n. 15, and 909A-D, which is very severe against such practices.

8. "ΓΟΗΣ: zum griechischen Schamanismus," *Rheinisches Museum* 105 (1962) 36-55. The author believes the *polis* to be the cause of such an evolution. It seems difficult to accept this explanation, considering that the change occurs in the fourth century, precisely when the *polis* was in a state of crisis and decay.

appears in the Hippocratic treatise *On the Sacred Disease* (2), where magic is opposed to religion and piety. It becomes frequent in the fourth century. Callicles, in the *Gorgias,* speaks of the laws of the city, which try to stop the legitimate ambitions of the strongest, calling them γράμματα καὶ μαγγανεύματα καὶ ἐπῳδάς (written formulas and trickeries and spells, 484A). Similarly, when Achilles is condemned as a liar, in the *Hippias Minor,* he is called γόης καὶ ἐπίβουλος (a treacherous imposter, 371A). And Demosthenes is attacked by his rival as being an impostor, a γόης.[9] The new magicians are impostors.

Now Plato, of all people, would be the very last to approve of such practices. His religion was much too pure and ideal for that, and so was his love of reason — hence his joy in using against rhetoric or sophistic the analogue first offered by Gorgias. Indeed, he returns to it over and over again, in order to cast discredit on the ways of the sophists. It may be a general criticism; it is also sometimes a precise one. Such is the case when he hints at their manner of discussing or at their way of beguiling listeners, these two notions being illustrated by the names of two famous magicians of old: Proteus and Orpheus.

Proteus is the symbol of elusive transformation; for, instead of fighting in a direct and honest way, he used to change himself into a number of deceptive forms and shift from one to the other. Now, in a discussion, such a way of behaving is no doubt dishonest, but very effective. And in almost all the dialogues, Socrates keeps complaining that his adversaries shift from one thesis to another in that same shrewd fashion. This is Proteus' trick — or the trick of the sophists.

In the *Republic,* such magic is mentioned in a very interesting context: it is presented as unworthy of the gods and is brought into connection with the two notions normally used for rhetoric — namely, "deceiving" (ἀπατᾶν) and playing on "false impressions" (δοκεῖν). The passage, indeed, deals with the fact that, according to the poets, gods can take different aspects and thus beguile mortals; and it says, at the very start: "Do you believe God to be a magician (γόητα), appearing[10] as it were on purpose in different forms, now being himself present but changing his figure into different shapes, and now deceiving us and making us believe in such false impres-

---

9. See Aeschines 3.137, Demosthenes 18.276 and 19.109.
10. The word for "appearing" is φαντάζεσθαι, which suggests phantoms, and it recurs in other similar passages.

sions? Or do you consider him to be simple and never to leave his own form?" (380D). The answer is, of course, that God could not change in that way, for he hates lies. And by and by, after having mentioned the name of Proteus, Plato insists on the conclusion that gods are not to be thought of "as γόητας practicing metamorphosis, nor as leading us astray by lies, whether in words or in deeds" (383A).

Gods do not act so, or should not. But the sophist whose very aim is to deceive and make us believe and lead us astray by lies, will do just that. In the *Euthydemus,* the two sophists offer an exceptionally sophistic discussion (in the modern meaning of the word *sophistic*). Each thesis is destroyed, one after the other; then one of the assistants, Ctesippus, gets into a rage, but Socrates pacifies the situation by celebrating the astounding skill of the two sophists (θαυμασία σοφία) and suggesting that they were not in earnest: "They were imitating the Egyptian sophist Proteus and using witchcraft (γοητεύοντε ἡμᾶς);[11] so we must imitate Menelaus, and not loose hold of these men before they make an appearance where they are themselves in earnest" (288B-C). That Proteus is called the Egyptian sophist add to the closeness of the assimilation between him and the sophists; this is a common device in many Platonic similes, where each of the two elements to be compared borrows some of the words belonging to the other.[12]

In other cases, the sophists, or rhetoricians, may not be engaged in a discussion, but in delivering speeches and pouring out words, which have a magical and seductive influence on the audience; here is magic again, only it takes not after Proteus but after Orpheus. Now, in the very beginning of the *Protagoras,* Plato mentions the great number of young foreigners whom Protagoras drags from the cities he has been visiting: he does it by "charming them with his voice, like Orpheus; and they follow him, obeying the charm of his voice" (315A). The fact that the verb κηλεῖν is used twice in two lines is just as revealing as the double assimilation in the *Euthydemus,* and the irony against the

---

11. One should perhaps note that these two "magicians" came from the same western countries as Gorgias. (But their connection with Pythagorean politics, suggested by Rostagni, pp. 178-179, does not seem to me very convincing.)

12. Cf. *Rep.* 556E, where the body στασιάζει αὐτὸ αὐτῷ while the city νοσεῖ.

sophists is the same. In most cases, however, no specific magician is named, nor is the simile made to bear on such specific habits; Plato just says the sophist is a γόης — and that is enough.

Anything that is irrational and deprives you of lucidity is witchcraft, γοητεια. Anything that suggests an erroneous impression is γοητεία too. This can be shown from two passages in the *Republic*, both of which deal with pleasure. The first deals with pleasure as a spell that deceives man. Plato says (413B-D) that good and sound principles can be taken away from men by theft or charm or violence. This charm, which he mentions with insistence (cumulating the words γοητευθέντες, γοητευθέντας, γοητείας, δυσγοήτευτος), is connected with the notion of being deceived (we find also ἐξαπατῷτο and δυσεξαπάτητον). Let us beware of such "charms"! Plato was deeply conscious of their danger; for, in the *Phaedo* too, he says the soul is beguilded (the word is γοητεύειν) by the body and its pleasures (81B). Now we must not forget that rhetoric also could be accused of leading people astray by aiming at pleasure.

As for the second passage in the *Republic*, it does not deal with the spell of pleasure, but with its relativity. Coming after pain, absence of pain. It is therefore nothing real, only an appearance and a phantasm, γοητεία τις (584A).[13] Again, we are confronted with illusion and reminded that the same argument, thanks to rhetoric, could appear now weaker and now stronger.

These two passages, though they do not deal with rhetoric, show how the simile of magic could be used by Plato against the sophists or orators. Sould we be surprised? All arts of illusion are γοητεία. In the *Republic,* so are ἡ σκιαγραφία and ἡ θαυματοποιία, scene-painting and conjuring.[14] Sophists and orators are no better, and their treatment is just as severe. In fact, the condemnation, in their case, is often made clearer and stronger by the addition of other catchwords — some suggesting phantoms, such as εἴδωλα or φαντάσματα, while others introduce a sort of nonfigurative explanation of the simile (among which are μιμητής and μίμησις).

In the *Menexenus,* the authors of funeral orations (a type of eloquence marked, no doubt, by the influence of Gorgias) make Socrates feel himself under a spell: γοητεύουσιν ἡμῶν τὰς ψυχάς (235A).

---

13. See, in the passage, οὐκ ἔστιν ἄρα τοῦτο,' εχλ ῭ε]ξ[' τουτων των φαντασματων.

14. 602D: γοητείας οὐδὲν ἀπολείπει.

He remains listening, taken by a charm (κηλούμενος). The influence of the speech is the result of its sound and of its flattering appeal, which is just as magical as was Protagoras' voice; for Socrates says the words and sounds "ring in my ears and penetrate me so well that only after three or four days can I recover consciousness and find out where on earth I actually am." The simile of magic is used with splendid irony.

In the *Republic*, Socrates speaks of an art in general as being an imitation; and he says that whoever pretends he possesses all the practical skills is only deceiving people just as "a magician and imitator" could do (598D: γόητί τινι καὶ μιμητῇ). Here, the word ἀπατᾶσθαι is used twice (598B and D), and the word φάντασμα is also added (598D), so that the condemnation is extremely emphatic.

In the *Sophist*, it is conceded that there may be an art of speech by which the young can be persuaded. And how? Their ears are bound by a charm (234C: γοητεύειν), and they are presented with fake images (εἴδωλα). A long time will then be required to undo their faith in these phantoms (φαντάσματα). The conclusion is that the sophist is a magician (253A: τῶν γοήτων ... τις) who merely imitates reality. He therefore can be counted among the conjurers (235B: θαυματοποιῶν). Again, later in the same dialogue, his art is connected with all the creators of illusions and wizards (241B: ψευδουργῶν καὶ γοήτων).[15] Even Plato's theory of imitation could gain in clarity by being brought into relation with his hate of conjurers.

However, in the *Politicus*, the man who deals with politics without possessing political knowledge is "the greatest magician of all sophists" (291C: τὸν πάντων τῶν σοφιστῶν μέγιστον γόητα). Such people are to be cast off as being the producers of the greatest phantoms (εἰδώλων), as being "imitators and magicians more than anybody else, and sophists more than any sophist" (303C).

All these examples prove that the three notions of magic, sophistic, and imitation are used by Plato as being almost synony-

---

15. It could be added that in *Laws* 649A, when Plato mentions wine as providing sudden confidence, he says that among the founders of the new city there is no drug to produce fear; God has not given any nor has one been found out: "for the magicians (γόητας) are not members of our feats." Now rhetoric had boasted it could use words as φάρμακα to produce fear; an allusion to rhetoric is not unlikely here. The hostility to magicians is anyhow made clear.

mous. We can therefore feel no surprise when we read in the *Symposium* that love is "a magician and a sophist" (203D: δεινὸς γόης καὶ φαρμακεὺς καὶ σοφιστής) or when we find in the *Laws,* as members of the same group, people who deal with magic, tyrants, orators, leaders, and sophists (908D: μαγγανείαν ... τύραννοι, δημηγόροι, στρατδγοί ... σοφιστῶν μηχαναί).

The sophists, as is shown by the example of Gorgias, had claimed the wonderful power of magic; they are confuted as practicing the irrational and deceitful art of conjurers.[16] Their very pretense was, for Plato, the key to their undoing.

Yet things are not quite so simple. We are here confronted with two baffling circumstances: the first is that the quality of the magician, in Plato, is given not only to the sophists but to Socrates himself; the second is that it is not mentioned at all in the *Gorgias* or in relation to Gorgias himself.

That Socrates is presented as a magician is a well-known fact, and he is so presented in some quite famous similes. Two of them, at least, are loci classici.

In the *Meno,* Socrates is compared by Meno to the torpedo or electric fish. This does not sound like magic, but the context is well worth looking at: "Now, it seems to me, you behave with me like a magician, like a wizard, using drugs, and you really beguile me by your incantations, so as to make me feel at a loss" (80A). The three words are γοητεύεις, φαρμάττεις, κατεπᾴδεις; and the cumulative effect is remarkable. Then Meno goes on to explain how surprising his own bewilderment is. And he concludes: "You are wise, I think, not to sail away from here or go abroad, for, if you behaved like that, being an alien in a foreign country, you would soon get put into jail as a magician" (80B: ὡς γόης). This passage confirms that witchcraft was already regarded with distrust and contempt. It also proves that the simile was not just an accident; it is indeed so insistent that, even if it were isolated, it would leave us with a problem.

But it is far from being isolated. In the *Symposium,* Alcibiades draws a well-known comparison between Socrates and Marsyas.

---

16. I did not use the fact that, in the beginning of the *Protagoras,* the discovery of the various sophists is a close imitation of Homer's style in the νέκυια; this may be just a nice game of learned allusion. Still, the atmosphere is **remarkable.**

Marsyas was as ugly as Socrates; he was a flute player, not a magician, but the context once more brings us back to magic. Marsyas' music used to cast a spell on his listeners: it charmed them (215C: ἐκήλει), so that they were, so to speak, possessed (κατέχεσθαι). And Alcibiades' view is that Socrates does the same by his mere speech: everybody feels startled and possessed (ἐκπεπληγένοι ἐσμὲν καὶ κατεχόμεθα). Alcibiades even confesses that on such occasions he feels a sort of corybantic ecstasy: his heart beats quickly, he weeps, and his soul is all upset, while nothing of the kind happens when he hears even the best orators. Socrates' influence on his listeners is magical. Alcibiades, as if he wanted to leave us in no doubt about it, adds another simile to the first one. He says the only way to escape is to stop one's ears and run away "as from the Sirens" (216A: ὥσπερ ἀπὸ τῶν Σειρήνων). This brings us back to the very first appearance of the magic arising from music and voice, as we might find it in Homer.

To these famous examples could be added some others. For instance, in the *Republic* (358D), Glaucon thinks Thrasymachus has given in too easily; he has been charmed by Socrates like a serpent under the spell of music: ὥσπερ ὄφις κηληθῆναι. Just as we had the shrewd magic of the sophists, who were conjurers, we have the seductive magic of Socrates, with its mystery. And the parallel goes further. Just as there is a magic charm in pleasure, which beguiles us, there is a magic spell in noble speeches, which act upon the soul so as to cure it. This is said in the *Charmides* (157A), where the word *incantation* (ἐπῳδή) is used four times in succession and is connected, as it was in Gorgias, with the word φάρμακον. Similarly, in the *Republic*, whereas the magic spell of poetry is acknowledged and its danger described by the word κηλεῖσθαι (607D), the necessity of resisting this charm is put forward, and the very *logos* that will help resist it is called an incantation (608A: ἐπᾴδοντες τοῦτον τὸν λόγον καὶ ταύτην τὴν ἐπῳδήν).[17]

We could add to these passages the different texts where the *logos*, or the text of the laws, is called a φάρμακον. Is that magic, or medicine? Who could tell? It may depend on cases. And we must remember that, in the *Helen*, we had already seen, toward the end, a

---

17. The interpretation in the Bude translation rests on an impossible construction; the translator shrank from the idea that the *logos* could be an ἐπῳδή!

curious hesitation between both, with the distinction between good drugs, which could cure, and bad drugs, intended to kill. After all, this very ambiguity is rooted in the empiric (and magical) nature of early medicine.[18] For Plato, of course, there is a great difference. In the *Laws* (933C), he speaks of the danger of giving drugs (φαρμάττειν) without a real knowledge of medicine, or of using magic charms without being a seer. However, we do find a good φάρμακον in the dialogues. Sometimes, to make things clearer, Plato calls it ἀλεξιφάρμακον,[19] as in *Alcibiades I* 132B and *Laws* 957C-958A. In other cases, the context is clear because the φάρμακον is actually given by a doctor (so in *Charmides* 115D). But the meaning is obviously the same wherever virtuous advice or a sound argument is said to act as a φάρμακον, capable of curing evil and breeding wisdom (so, particularly, in *Politicus* 310A and in the *Charmides*).

One can, of course, deal with such passages by considering that they do not imply any sort of magic, but only good and sound medicine. The ambivalent meaning of the word allows such an interpretation. Scholars may even try to elicit a theory about the ambivalent nature of the φάρμακον. Jacques Derrida has built an original theory, according to which the bad φάρμακον is writing, whereas *logos* is the antidote.[20] However that may be, we can get rid of the passages about φάρμακον. But then, what about the ἐπῳδή?

Naturally, if we want to get rid of the ἐπῳδή, we can. The metaphor, in the context of the two passages quoted, is made much easier by the presence either of an actual medical treatment, such as the treatment of headache in the *Charmides*, or of an actual spell, such as the spell of poetry in the *Republic*. This could account for

---

18. See the double meaning of the word in tragedy: the φάρμακον can be a poison (*Medea Ion* 845, 1221), or a drug producing certain feelings (*Andr.* 157) or making people disappear (*Or.* 1497); it may also have an honest, medical meaning (so *Prom.* 249, 475; Sophocles frs. 514.4, 733; Eur. *Hipp.* 389, 516, 699, fr. 292).

19. Yet, in *Politicus* 280E, the art of antidotes (ἀλεξιφάρμακα) is given as the object of magic (μαγευτικήν).

20. "La pharmacie de Platon," *Tel Quel* 32 (1968) 3-48, and 33 (1968) 18-58. According to him, the magic or poisonous φάρμακον is writing, whereas the medical and profitable φάρμακον, which can be used as antidote, is the *logos*. This is not wholly convincing, and the article does not deal with Plato's actual direct meaning, which is what we are trying to grasp.

the metaphor and suggest that is just occasional. Still, it is a little annoying to have to get rid of too many things. And after such dubious efforts we should still have the magician himself: we should still have Socrates. So we must face the problem: how can the passages about him be reconciled with the deprecatory use made of the same simile against the sophists? What does this double application mean?

I think the problem might be clarified by a closer examination of Socrates' magic — which, in fact, is something quite different from the magic of the sophists. It rests, obviously, on the combination of two very different qualities that Socrates combined. First, how could we forget that Socrates had a sort of divine quality about him? What he calls the demonic voice is, indeed, inspiration of some sort; and is not wholly different from the obscure certainty that the chorus in the *Agamemnon* experiences about the impending disaster. It is perhaps less mysterious, less irrational, and closer to moral intuition. Yet, it is not moral intuition only; for it implies piety and constant devotion and direct dependence on the will of God. It is indeed a sort of irrational power, but a power that arises from a close contact with the divine. This inspiration may therefore resemble a magician's gift, except that it has nothing to do with the sophists' magic.

But, practically, what puzzles people about Socrates is not this mysterious inspiration; it is the way he discusses, clinging to reason and truth, and trying to do away with all fake appearances, all unsound arguments or definitions. Those who complain that they cannot resist him, or cannot see where they stand after having discussed with him, are merely bewildered by the power of thorough analysis. They do not understand what happens to them, but we do: they are just confronted with unyielding logic. Whereas the magic of the sophists aimed at producing illusion, Socrates' magic rests on the obstinate destruction of all illusions. It is the magic of implacable truth; and certainly it is not just by chance that those who describe that magic spell of Socrates are young men or laymen, not used to thorough reasoning, men such as Meno and Alcibiades.

It is therefore one magic against another, the one taking the former's place, but with opposite aims and means. This very parallelism between the two series of texts thus becomes illuminating. It shows clearly enough that in Greece rational and irrational were often combined; so they were in Gorgias, so they were in Socrates, so they were in Plato, who could use so well the magic seduction of style and imagery. But, what is even more important, it shows how deeply these Greeks of the fifth century were, at all levels, enthralled by the power of speech. Gorgias represented the deceiving power of style, or of the choice and arrangement of arguments, which could create at will any kind of emotion. Socrates represents the stimulating power of reasoning and discussion, when devoted to the search for truth. But in both cases this power was bewildering, amazing, magical. The Greeks were lost in wonder at the marvel of the instrument they were learning to master.

This external similarity explains, in a way, how Socrates could be mistaken for one of the sophists; but it also brings to light the radical opposition between his aim and theirs, between his means and theirs. The new magic was the answer to the first one, and Plato was perfectly coherent when, after laughing at the sophists as conjurers, he drew his splendid portrait of his wonderful and disturbing master.

Once we are free of this first difficulty, we can also understand, I hope, the other puzzling circumstance that I have mentioned, namely, that Plato never used the simile of magic while discussing Gorgias.[21] Magic and all the tricks of the sophists or stylists could be made fun of. But Gorgias' personal case was different. If only he had been but a conjurer! In fact, what made him dangerous was that he had turned this magic into something that could be taught and could deceive people in all sorts of situations, mainly in the field of justice and politics. He had succeeded, and the change in Athenian politics was his doing, not because he himself was a conjurer but because he had claimed that this rhetoric of him was something serious, a $τέχνη$, and because everybody had followed him. Plato resented not the magic, but the offensive pretense of turning it into science.

Now this had been Gorgias' boast. In § 10 of the *Helen,* the word $τέχνη$ appears in the same sentence that deals with magic: he says that two $τέχναι$ have been found for magic, the one resting on the soul's being in error, the other on the deception of judgment ($ψυχῆς$

---

21. It has been suggested by F. Dümmler, *Akademika* (Giessen, 1889), p. 22, that the mention of magic in connection with an *epitaphios,* in the beginning of the *Menexenus* (see above, p. 31), was a direct allusion to Gorgias. I doubt very much that the allusion can be so precise, especially since the voice is mentioned **and Gorgias could not actually have delivered his *epitaphios.***

ἁμαρτήματα καὶ δόξης ἀπατήματα, another play on words!). Further along in the same passage (§ 13), he alludes to a speech τέχνῃ γραφείς, written with art.[22] Finally, in a passage already mentioned, he speaks of φάρμακα developing one humor or another in the body, that is to say, of the art of medicine.[23] The art of speech is not only magic but something technical, and even scientific. That was Gorgias' orginality. That was the discovery of rhetoric, ἡ ῥητορικὴ τέχνη. And that was what Plato could not condone.

The choice of characters and the order in which they appear in the *Gorgias* dramatize in an illuminating way the danger implied in rhetoric and the consequences it could have. The first part of the dialogue is a discussion between Socrates and Gorgias himself, showing that rhetoric does not aim at truth. The second part is a discussion between Socrates and Polus. Gorgias' disciple, showing that therefore rhetoric is not a τέχνη but a low practice aiming at flattery and pursuing an advantage that is, in fact, an evil. The third part is a discussion between Socrates and Callicles, a figure who represents the ambitious young statesmen who used Gorgias' rhetoric in order to fulfill their own longing for power; this part shows that the very aim of fulfilling such an ambition is a wrong aim, which should never be entertained, for it ruins the only desirable end, which is justice.

The very movement of the dialogue, therefore, shows with what skill Plato could shift a problem from one level to another. Gorgias has only to acknowledge that he does not teach truth or justice; the implications and consequences of such a position are then searched through other people, less and less close to Gorgias, and considered from a wider and wider point of view. The danger is not rhetoric but the philosophy implied by the pursuit of rhetoric.

It is not less illuminating to observe that, throughout this development, the notion of τέχνη is prominent; it is treated from different angles, so that the discussion seems to reach higher and higher, leaving rhetoric well behind. In the first section, it bears only on the nature of the τέχνη that Gorgias teaches and on its proper field;[24]

22. γραφείς, as opposed to ἀληθείᾳ λεχθείς. The choice of words shows that Gorgias is thinking about written prose, which was to be so important in Isocrates' activity.

23. The relation between rhetoric and medicine is on an utterly different level from the relation between emotion and physical madness, studied in Flashar's article in *Hermes* 84 (1956) 12-48.

24. This is the very question that Socrates came to ask (447C: βούλομαι γὰρ

the conclusion is embarrassing, for rhetoric deals with justice but does not teach justice; or does it? The very embarrassment suggests that rhetoric has no proper field of real knowledge. In the second section, Socrates goes further and boldly states that rhetoric is not a τέχνη at all (462B: οὐδεμία ἔμοιγε δοκεῖ). It is practical skill, similar to cooking, and it is, like cooking, some low kind of flattery, but no τέχνη (463A: τεχνικὸν μὲν οὔ; 465: τέχνην δὲ αὐτὴν οὔ φημι εἶναι). In the discussion with Callicles, the same idea is repeated (500B, E, 501B, 503A, D); but it is also extended to the realm of politics. Rhetoric is the means of the common statesman, but Socrates is one of the rare men, or perhaps the only man, to practice true πολιτκὴ τέχνη (521D).

Socrates' argument is an insistent rejection, an obstinate defense against Gorgias' dangerous success. Plato made a similar attack upon rhapsodes and poets, in the little dialogue called the *Ion,* where he says that they may well act under divine inspiration but certainly have no lucid knowledge, or τέχνη.[25] Rhetoric and poetry are once more treated alike. But what is an innocent teasing in the case of poetry is an unrelenting attack in the case of rhetoric, for rhetoric had higher pretentions and presented much greater danger.

The dangerousness of rhetoric accounts not only for the structure of the dialogue but for the choice of the image that seems to command the whole discussion. The image is not magic but medicine, which also occurred in Gorgias' *Helen,* where he suggested toward the end of the passage mentioned above that rhetoric was, in a way, similar to medicine.

Such a parallel, of course, may have been natural, in view of the parallelism of soul and body, which plays an important part in the opening of the *Protagoras* (312Bff). But it was also something that must have appealed to Gorgias. It offered him a place for his magic, since medicine had started in close union with magic. It offered him also a stimulating catchword, since medicine was at that time the great field of scientific progress. It had a special meaning for him personally too, since his brother was a doctor. But precisely because it revealed his ambition, the assimilation of rhetoric to medicine was

πυθέσθαι παρ' αὐτο τίς ἡ δύναμις τῆς τέχνης τοῦ ἀνδρός); it is repeated over and over again (see 448E: τίνος Ιοργίας ἐπιστήμων, and cf. 449C, 450C).

25. The date of this dialogue places it in the same period as the *Gorgias,* whatever the exact year of the latter's composition.

to prove unfortunate, and even more so than the witchcraft simile. Plato seems unable to refrain from returning over and over again to the idea that rhetoric has nothing to do with medicine; his dialogue can be read as an obstinate and passionate refusal of such a parallelism.

The very first question he asks about the nature of rhetoric is framed around a contrast with medicine, and an allusion is made to the fact that Gorgias' brother was a doctor (448B). Then, when it has been admitted that rhetoric deals with speeches, Socrates asks what particular speeches, again introducing a contrast with medicine (450A).[26] Then, when Gorgias boasts that the speeches he deals with bear on the greatest and best things in human life, the discussion suggests that this could be said of medicine (452A). And, when Gorgias wants to explain how wonderful rhetoric is, he boldly asserts that, were he, with his brother, by the side of a patient, the patient would listen to him, not to his brother the doctor (456B). All that, of course, leads us to understand, progressively, that rhetoric does not rest on actual knowledge. Indeed, toward the end of the first section, Gorgias admits that the man who has learned rhetoric could persuade an audience, about any matter, better than the specialist – among whom the doctor is again the first to be mentioned – and this although the rhetorician knows nothing of technical matters (459A-B). Medicine rests on knowledge, rhetoric does not.

It is no surprise, therefore, to see that, in the second section, when Plato wants to classify the real arts and the fake ones, he once more starts with medicine as a real art (464A) and draws a strong opposition between such arts and rhetoric. The contrast with medicine recurs a number of times in this second section (476C, 477C-478A). It also assumes a new meaning, for Socrates insists that rhetoric does not provide a real good, whereas medicine does. Doctor's treatments are not agreeable, but they are useful (478B-C). Therefore, one should pity the man who does not go to see a doctor and suffer what the doctor wants him to suffer in order to be cured (478D-480D). By such an argument Socrates progressively puts forward his great rule of life, which is the undoing of rhetoric, and of its very aim: I mean the idea that it is better, when one is at fault, to be punished and

---

26. He adds the contrast with gymnastic, which prepares the reader for the description of the real arts, given in 464ff. On this presence of gymnastic, see below, pp. 48 and 56.

cured than to escape punishment and remain with an evil soul or a sick one. The action of medicine is good; the action of rhetoric is not. And the example of medicine, which Gorgias wanted to emulate, is used to refute his claim.

Now it would seem that in the last section, which is less technical and less oriented toward definitions, this continued contrast should fade away; but it does not. It is often recalled as an important part of Socrates' doctrine (490B, 501A, 504C, 505A, 514D). What is more remarkable still, now that the interest turns toward politics and ambition, the contrast between rhetoric and medicine again provides the key to the new discussion: rhetoric and its use in politics only produce an unhealthy swelling (518E-519A), whereas doctors always act for the good of the people (517D-518A). Even Socrates' condemnation, which is foreshadowed in the dialogue, is explained by the fact that those who will accuse or judge him have no real knowledge of what is good in politics: he is like a doctor, attacked by a cook and judged by a court of children (521D-522C). The accusers of Socrates were, of course, people trained in rhetoric. So here we reach the ultimate contrast between rhetoric, which ruins political life, and an art like medicine (we can call it πολιτικὴ τέχνη), which alone could save it. Finally, even in the myth, the same contrast is present; for the whole point of the punishments in hell is that they can cure people of their sins, or, in the worst cases, help others to recover moral health and sanity.

Rhetoric, therefore, is always treated — whether one considers its subject matter or its aim or its use in politics — as contrary to medicine. To be a conjurer could be condoned; to be a conjurer acting as a doctor and treated as one was intolerable. That this criticism of Plato's was paving the way for the foundation both of dialectic as a search of truth, and of political science as an ideal, is obvious; it is important also to see that, in launching these ideas, the direct controversy with Gorgias had been of so much help and influence.

But this controversy was only the opening of a wide discussion, which was to go on for the whole century and even longer. Severe as it had been, the *Gorgias* was in no way the ruin of rhetoric. There were answers, rectifications, arguments of all sorts. Now, although I have insisted on the contrast with medicine, I have not considered in detail the classification of the four arts and the four fake arts that is put forward in the middle part of the dialogue (464ff). I have not done so because the discussion of that matter has been particularly precise and continuous and provides a good example of the manner in which the Greeks held a sort of perpetual dialogue, where each author answers his predecessor with precision and subtlety. This we shall see in the next chapter. But now we must prepare for a short parting with one of our two themes — the theme of magic. Plato had laughed at the conjurers, offered the example of another, greater magic, and attacked rhetoric as being no τέχνη. In order to save rhetoric as a τεχναι, one had to ignore all connection with magic. The great argument of Plato, finally, could be put into these simple terms: "You can't be both." Perhaps he was right. But he weighed heavily, not only on the status of rhetoric but on its development, and on literary taste itself, which was more serious. It is his fault that we have to say, for a while, farewell to the magicians.

PLATO'S VIEW OF RHETORIC*

EDWIN BLACK

Whether Plato had a consistent view of rhetoric and, if he did, what that view was have been subjects of considerable debate among commentators and critics of the dialogues. The interpretive controversy of twenty-three centuries has so encrusted his ideas that, though we seldom seem to see them in the same way, it must be even more seldom that we really see them at all. Of course, Plato is difficult to understand. He is complicated, variegated, audacious, and sometimes paradoxical. The apparent elusiveness of his view of rhetoric, alone, has engendered a vast accumulation of commentary, with few of the commentators in substantial agreement on the defining characteristics of that view. Indeed, the only uniformity which crystallizes from this diversity of interpretation is the judgment that Plato disapproved of rhetoric, and was, in fact, rhetoric's most effective historical opponent.[1]

Fortunately, we still have the dialogues, their durability so manifestly established that they could not be hurt by one more fresh look. The objective of the present investigation is to attempt that fresh look.

It is inevitable that any expositor will approach a work from a certain point of view. His frame of reference may be subconscious and unsystematized, but it will assuredly be present, shaping the bias of his interpretation by influencing the direction of his attention, selectively sharpening some and dulling others of his sensibilities, and molding the nuances of his judgment in a thousand imperceptible ways. The critical presuppositions of this study can be simply and dogmatically put. They are that Plato was both a subtle and dis-

---

*Reprinted by permission of the Speech Communication Association, from the *Quarterly Journal of Speech,* 44 (December, 1958), 361-74.

1. See e.g., Everett Lee Hunt, "Plato and Aristotle on Rhetoric and Rhetoricians," *Studies in Rhetoric and Public Speaking in Honor of James Albert Winans* (New York, 1925), esp. pp. 18-42.

ciplined thinker and a subtle and disciplined writer, that he would not have allowed patent inconsistency or contradiction into the constantly revised body of his work,[2] and that the dialogues, as speculative inquiries, must explain and justify themselves independent of any circumstances impinging on their composition.[3]

Such are the premises from which the present examination of Plato's view of rhetoric will proceed. The dialogues in which the view itself receives its most elaborate and methodical treatment are the *Gorgias* and the *Phaedrus*. Plato's treatment of rhetoric is not confined exclusively to these two dialogues; on the contrary, his consideration of rhetoric bears relations with philosophical subjects treated throughout his extant writings. But these relations will develop and clarify as we explore the main body of Platonic rhetoric expounded in the *Gorgias* and the *Phaedrus*. The former is generally considered to have been the earlier written of the two and hence invites our scrutiny first.

The diversity of interpretations which have been placed on the *Gorgias* amply evidences its perplexity for Plato's literary interpreters.[4] It is curious that these interpreters, all excellently equipped

---

2. If the dialogues themselves are not evidence enough of a systematic perfection of literary and philosophical technique, we have also the testimony of Dionysius of Halicarnassus that Plato "curried and combed the locks of his dialogues" to the end of his days.

3. Some commentators undertake to "understand" the dialogues in terms of events which are thought to have affected Plato. See: Theodor Gomperz, *Greek Thinkers. A History of Ancient Philosophy,* trans. Laurie Magnus, II (New York, 1901); George Grote, *Plato and the Other Companions of Sokrates,* II (London, 1867); William Hepworth Thompson, *The Gorgias of Plato* (London, 1894), esp. pp. xiv-xviii. Such psychologizing is fascinating to read, but of limited utility in the interpretation of the dialogues. Likewise, Richard Weaver's "reading" of the *Phaedrus* in "The Phaedrus and the Nature of Rhetoric," *The Ethics of Rhetoric* (Chicago, 1953), is an interesting performance, but is so deficient in evidence as to be irrelevant to the study of Plato.

4. Thompson, after quoting Olympiodorus approvingly, paraphrases him: "The aim of the Gorgias is to discuss the principles which conduce to political well-being. It [the preceding paraphrastic sentence] explains, at least to a considerable extent, the later as well as the earlier discussions; whereas if we assume that the main end of the dialogue is to bring the art of rhetoric and its professors into discredit, we can assign no significant motive for the importance assigned to a character like Callicles, who heartily despises the profession of a Sophist and hates the schools and their pedantry." Pp. xii-xiii.

Thompson asserts that the *Gorgias* was "the public vindication" of the confor study in classical philology, and all having reference to exactly the same document, cannot agree on its meaning. The cause of the confusion does not seem to lie in any obscurity of statement in the dialogue. Rather, we discover what troubles the commentators the moment we compare the *Gorgias* with the *Phaedrus*: the former, satirical, contentious, and refutative, the latter emerging with a constructive, affirmative judgment clothed in the most majestic poetry. The contrast is both striking and discomforting. Have we here irreconcilably contradictory views of rhetoric expressed by the same author? The dilemma solicits resolution, and the commentators have responded by maintaining either that Plato changed his mind or that Plato did not mean by "rhetoric" in the *Gorgias* what he meant by "rhetoric" in the *Phaedrus*. The first position tacitly assumes that

viction, held by a Plato disillusioned by the execution of Socrates, that "it was hopeless to amend the laws and practices of the Greek communities by any of the ordinary and constitutional means." P. xxx.

Herman Bonitz's interpretation of the *Gorgias* is summed up in the statement, "Schwerlich kann dann noch ein Zweifel sein, dass die mit Kallikles verhandelte Frage: 'ist Philosophie im Platonische Sinne, oder ist politische Rhetorik in ihrem damaligen thatssächlichen Zustande eine würdige Lebensaufgabe? den Kern und Zweck des ganzen Dialogs bezeichnet." *Platonische Studien* (Vienna, 1858), p. 33.

Bonitz's position is, in its general characteristics, shared by E. M. Cope, *Plato's Gorgias,* 2nd ed. (London, 1883). See esp. Cope's introduction; and Werner Jaeger, *Paideia: The Ideals of Greek Culture,* trans. Gilbert Highet, III (Oxford, 1954), p. 50. Both Cope and Jaeger take the references to "rhetoric" in the *Gorgias* to refer to all the activities of Athenian society associated with oratory, especially the practices of the courts, the aspirations of the young, and the popular systems of education.

Gomperz interprets the *Gorgias* as a literary counterattack against Polycrates, who was supposed to have written a lampoon of Socrates after the latter's execution. II, p. 343.

Eduard Zeller interprets the *Gorgias* as containing a wholesale condemnation of rhetoric as an instrument of Sophistical ethics. *Plato and the Older Academy,* trans. Sarah Frances Alleyne and Alfred Goodwin (London, 1876). p. 190. This condemnation is unqualified in Zeller's view, although when, in the same book Zeller deals with the treatment of rhetoric in the *Phaedrus* (p. 515), he does not seem even to recognize a logical difficulty in his interpretation, nor does he attempt to resolve the question of how Plato can be read as unqualifiedly condemning rhetoric in one place and writing of it constructively in another.

Walter Pater argues that Plato opposed rhetoric, and opposed it because it represented to him the abhorrent Heraclitean metaphysics *Plato and Platonism* (London, 1920), esp. chap. 4.

our author admitted a patent and obvious contradiction into his literature; the second position tacitly assumes that our author was inconsistent or, at the least, careless about his use of language. Since I hold that one should not adopt either of these assumptions in interpreting Plato except only as a last resort, after every more generous alternative has been vainly tested, I shall tentatively reject these possibilities.

One other difficulty besides the apparent difference in the moral attitude toward rhetoric expressed in the *Gorgias* and in the *Phaedrus* plagues the commentators. This other difficulty relates to the internal structure of each of the two dialogues, and presents itself to us in the form of two questions: What is the theme of the *Gorgias*? and What is the theme of the *Phaedrus*? If the *Gorgias* is concerned with ethics, why is so sizeable a portion of it devoted to the subject of rhetoric? If the *Phaedrus* is concerned with rhetoric, why is so much of the dialogue taken up with a consideration of love? Of course, these questions and those who ask them presuppose, without proof, that a literary work must have a single theme. One might reply to these questions by denying the assumption and asserting that in the *Gorgias* and the *Phaedrus* we have two dialogues with multiple themes. I shall not adopt this position at this stage of the analysis. The search for a single theme in a literary work can provide fruitful insights into the work. But the point is worth making that, after all, there is no binding fiat of literary activity nor any logical necessity demanding that a piece of writing, even a great piece of writing, and especially a dialectical inquiry, must have one and only one paraphrasable theme. The suggestion, once made, need not be pursued. It is enough to note for the present that determining the themes of the two dialogues is one of the major difficulties which commentators have found.

All major modern commentators on Plato's view of rhetoric, with the exceptions of Walter Pater, Paul Shorey, and possibly Werner Jaeger, design their interpretations of the *Gorgias* or the *Phaedrus* to deal with one or both of the difficulties mentioned. Troubled by the apparent inconsistency of the *Gorgias* and *Phaedrus,* they infer a change of heart and mind, and a concomitant modification of doctrine, by Plato. Or, troubled by an inability to assign a single theme to one or both of the dialogues, they redefine and expand the meanings of key terms to make the work fit themes which they wish to assign to it. Now, it follows that if these two difficulties can be resolved with more parsimony of assumption and with stricter adherence to the texts of the dialogues than has heretofore been the case, then the interpretations of the commentators will have been circumvented, for the problems which these interpretations were designed to resolve will have evaporated. Further, if these two difficulties are to be resolved, their resolution would involve a clear and accurate explication of Plato's view of rhetoric, which is the object of this inquiry. With these observations before us, we might begin the investigation of the *Gorgias* by determining what the term "rhetoric" means there.

2.

The crucial passages in the *Gorgias* which deal directly with the definition of "rhetoric" occur in what might be called the first act, i.e., the conversation between Socrates and Gorgias. Pressed for a definition of "rhetoric," Gorgias defines the term as meaning the art of that kind of persuasion which is exercised before public assemblies and is concerned with the just and the unjust. Having elicited this definition, Socrates goes on to force from Gorgias the admission that sometimes rhetoric is used for unjust purposes. Since Gorgias contends that the rhetorician has knowledge of the just and unjust, or, at least, must have such knowledge before Gorgias will call him a "rhetorician," Socrates claims to have discerned a contradiction in Gorgias's position It has been alleged by some commentators, Cope and Shorey among them,[5] that Socrates is made to argue sophistically in this portion of the dialogue. The main objection is that Socrates is incorrect in assuming that if a person knew the just and unjust, then he could not act but justly. As a matter of fact, there are strong reasons which Plato might have adduced to support this contention.[6]

Suppose the case of a man who enjoyed committing murder and who committed murder at every opportunity; yet, every time someone asked the man if he knew that murder was wrong, he said

---

5. Cope, pp. xlii-xliii; Paul Shorey, "The Unity of Plato's Thought," *The Decennial Publications of the University of Chicago,* First Series, VI (Chicago, 1904), p. 23.

6. The assumption was evidently considered too obvious to require explanation. Cf. the concept of *phronesis* in Aristotle's *Nicomachean Ethics,* esp. Book VI, chap. 12.

that he did. Suppose further that this man made no claims of acting under duress or compulsion, but chose to commit murder freely and soberly. Should we not conclude, in the presence of such evidence, that he did not really "believe" or "know" that murder was wrong? In assuming, as he did, that the rhetorician who knows the nature of justice and injustice will actually be just, Plato took the position that to understand a moral rule necessarily involves obeying it, since part of understanding the rule would be understanding its obligatory quality, i.e., understanding that it is a *rule.*

To dismiss the exchange between Gorgias and Socrates as a "conscious dialectical sport," as does Shorey,[7] is to ignore an important moral insight which Plato presented. Put in simpler terms, Plato's analysis of the Gorgian definition of "rhetoric" might run as follows:

If a person (the rhetorician) claims knowledge of the just, then it follows *as a necessary condition of having such knowledge* that the person will be just. What if Gorgias had refused to concede the point, and had instead contended that the rhetorician does not necessarily know the just? In that case, Socrates could contend that such a person could not possibly use rhetoric because, since part of the definition of rhetoric is that it is persuasion about the just and unjust, such a person could not know what rhetoric was and hence could not use it. So, Gorgias is obliged to concede that according to his definition of rhetoric, the rhetorician must have knowledge of the just and unjust. As a result of the arguments in the dialogue, we can see that Gorgias's definition implicatively claimed a moral feature for rhetoric which in fact rhetoric does not have. A logical consequence of the Gorgian definition is that there can be no such thing as morally bad rhetoric, or rhetoric which is unjust. Plato knew, as we know, that there is morally bad and unjust rhetorical discourse. It therefore follows that the Gorgian definition is false.

We must bear in mind that the definitions which Plato sought by the dialectical process were neither stipulative nor lexicographical definitions. They were what Richard Robinson calls "real definitions."[8] That is to say, when Plato sought a definition, he was not satisfied with a stipulation about how a term was to be used or with a report about how it was generally used; he sought, rather, a description of the nature of the thing designated by the term. Looked at in

---

7. *Loc. cit.*
8. Richard Robinson, *Definition* (Oxford, 1950), pp. 7, 8, 161, 162.

this way, we can understand how Plato could call a definition "false" in the sense that the definiendum was inaccurately described, while a lexicographical definition might be false only in an entirely different sense, and a stipulative definition could not be false at all.

It will assist our consideration of the *Gorgias* to amplify a bit more Plato's dialectical procedure. It is a procedure which is described in the *Phaedrus, Philebus, Cratylus, Sophist, Politicus,* and *Laws.*[9] Cornford gives the following account:

> The expert in Dialectic will guide and control the course of philosophical discussion by his knowledge of how to "divide by Kinds," not confusing one Form with another. He will discern clearly the hierarchy of Forms which constitutes reality and make out its articulate structure, with which the texture of philosophic discourse must correspond, if it is to express truth. The method is that method of Collection and Division which was announced in the *Phaedrus* and has been illustrated in the *Sophist*. Finally, to discern this structure clearly is the same thing as "to know how to distinguish in what ways the several Kinds can or can not combine." In other words, the science will yield the knowledge needed to guide us to true affirmative and negative statements about the Forms, of which the whole texture of philosophic discourse should consist . . . .[10]

> The meanings of common names and verbs are the Forms. Statements are not propositional forms but actual significant statements, existing while we utter them. The science of Dialectic does not study formal symbolic patterns to which our statements conform, nor yet these statements themselves, Nor does it study our thoughts or ways of reasoning, apart from the objects we think about. It is not "Logic" if Logic means the science either of *logoi* or *logismoi*. What it does study is the structure of the real world of Forms. Its technique of Collection and Division operates on that structure.[11]

> . . . Dialectic is not Formal Logic, but the study of the structure of reality — in fact Ontology, for the Forms are the realities.[12]

> The goal of Dialectic is not to establish propositions ascribing a predicate to all the individuals in a class. The objective is the definition of indivisible species — a Form — by genus and specific differences. What we define is not "all men" but the unique Form "Man."[13]

These cullings from Cornford's exposition should serve to clarify not only Plato's *modus operandi* in all the dialogues, but as well the

---

9. *Phaedrus,* (section nos.) 265, 266, 270D; *Philebus* 16-18; *Cratylus* 424C; *Sophist,* 226C, 235C, 253ff.; *Politicus,* 285Aff; *Laws,* 894AA, 936D, 965C.

10. Francis Macdonald Cornford, *Plato's Theory of Knowledge* (London, 1935), pp. 263-264.

11. *Ibid.,* p. 265.

12. *Ibid.,* p. 266

13. *Ibid.,* p. 269

way in which he deals with the Gorgian definition of rhetoric, When Plato sought the meaning of "rhetoric," he was seeking a series of true propositions about an existential class.

What does all of this imply for our analysis of the *Gorgias*? Primarily that all we have a right to infer from the first conversation between Socrates and Gorgias is that Gorgias's description of "rhetoric" has been overthrown. *Rhetoric in general has not been attacked.* Indeed, up to this point in the dialogue,[14] Plato has not written a single line about rhetoric, the Form. Plato's concern has been with Gorgias's description of rhetoric, and nothing else. Why has Plato given so much space to overthrowing a definition which he has put into the mouth of Gorgias? Of course, we cannot be certain of all his reasons, though we can be reasonably sure that they are not reducible to "conscious dialectical sport." The probability, suggested in somewhat different contexts by Cope, Bonitz, and Jaeger,[15] is that what Plato represents as Gorgias's view of rhetoric was widely held by influential and respected Sophists; it was a view with sufficient currency and respectability to seem to Plato to merit careful examination.

It is in the portion of the dialogue with Polus that Socrates is made to formulate the famous argument that rhetoric is not an art but is merely a knack like cookery, a counterfeit of a part of politics. This passage, like the one discussed above, has been widely interpreted as a wholesale condemnation of rhetoric. Such an interpretation is unwarranted by the text. We have, for example, within the passage itself clear indications that the "rhetoric" being dismissed as a knack is not *all* rhetoric. We find Socrates hesitating about making accusations against rhetoric with the comment, "I fear it may be somewhat rude to say the truth; for on Gorgias' account I am reluctant to speak out for fear he should suppose that I am satirizing his professional pursuits. At the same time whether this *is* the kind of rhetoric that Gorgias practices, I really don't know."[16] It is perfectly clear that Plato conceives of a rhetoric that is not open to this analysis since he suggests here that Gorgias might practice another kind of rhetoric. Later in the same dialogue, in the conversation

---

14. *Gorgias*, 461.
15. *Loc. cit.*
16. *Gorgias*, 462D. Unless otherwise indicated all quotations are from Cope's translation.

between Socrates and Callicles, Socrates says, "So then it is to this [justice] that the genuine orator,[17] the man of science and virtue will have regard in applying to men's souls whatever words he addresses to them, and will conform all his actions; and if he give any gift he will give it, or if he take aught away he will take it, with his mind always fixed upon this, how to implant justice in the souls of his citizens and eradicate injustice, to engender self-control and extirpate self-indulgence, to engender all other virtue and remove all vice."[18]

It is impossible to maintain that Plato intended the *Gorgias* to be a total condemnation of all rhetoric as a "knack" and a "counterfeit of politics" when, in that very dialogue, he already sketches out some of the conditions of a rhetoric which would deserve the name of art. Obviously, the passage in which rhetoric is called a knack has been misinterpreted. The "rhetoric" referred to in the passage must be that which Gorgias has attempted to define. Plato's attack is limited only to a particular practice of rhetoric, and it is clear enough from the *Gorgias* alone that the attack was legitimate, deserved, and, given the Platonic theory of Forms, logically valid.

When we add to the evidence already adduced from the *Gorgias* the passage in the *Laws*[19] in which Plato, with a clear opportunity to condemn rhetoric as unscientific, waives the question of whether rhetoric is an art or a knack, and the passages in the *Phaedrus*[20] which lay down the conditions for rhetoric to be an art, we are bound to the conclusions that Plato did not intend his condemnation to apply to *all* rhetoric. At the risk of being repetitious, I shall reiterate that all we have a right to infer from the text of the *Gorgias* is that Plato opposed only a particular view of rhetoric unsuccessfully defended in the dialogue by Gorgias, Polus, and Callicles, and probably actually defended by leading Sophists and rhetoricians of Plato's time.

At this point the question might arise, if Plato wished to oppose the Gorgian view of rhetoric, why did he attack its definition rather than its practice? The answer to this question must be, as previously indicated, stated in terms of the objectives and methods of dialectic.

17. The phrase is rendered, "true and scientific rhetor," by Paul Shorey, *What Plato Said* (Chicago, 1933), p. 503.
18. *Gorgias,* 504C.
19. *Laws,* 938A.
20. E.g., *Phaedrus,* 263B.

Plato sought to know the true Form. In the *Gorgias* and the *Phaedrus* he was seeking the Form of rhetoric. That was his objective. His method, too, has been mentioned, as Ross has described it: "Plato has in the *Phaedrus* described dialectic as consisting in a joint use of collections and division. Of these operations, the first seems to be merely preliminary to the second. In the attempt to reach the definition of a specific term the first stage — the 'collection' — is the tentative choice of a wide genus under which the term to be defined seems to fall."[21]

With the dialectical procedure in mind we can understand why Plato approaches the subject of rhetoric in quite the way that he does in the *Gorgias* and also why that dialogue is a unified literary work with a single theme. Plato's attack was on the Gorgian view of rhetoric (which was probably a general Sophistical view of rhetoric). The attack focussed on the Gorgian definition, though "definition" in the distinctively Platonic sense. This definition could be expected to have two parts: the collection and the division. The *Gorgias* is a refutation of both parts of the Gorgian definition. We find in the first two parts of the dialogue, where Gorgias and then Polus are Socrates's prime antagonists, that Socrates aims to overthrow the "collective" definition. The burden of Socrates's argument in these sections is to establish that rhetoric does not belong to the genus. art-concerned-with-justice. The introduction of Callicles does not represent a change in theme; rather, it represents a shift in focus to the "divisive" definition. Against Callicles, Socrates might describe his own position thus:

"But even if we grant for the sake of argument this 'collective' definition which I have just refuted, I shall now demonstrate that even your 'divisive' definition is false."

This is what Socrates proceeds to do. The animus of the argument against Callicles is that Callicles' analysis of justice is wrong. Why did Plato trouble to refute a definition represented by Callicles in the dialogue? While the question is not central to the present study. the probability is that Callicles's views were widely and influentially held in Plato's time, just as we know them to be held in our own time. We can further infer that, if the present view of the thematic unity of the *Gorgias* is correct, the opinions represented by Gorgias, Polus,

---

21. W. David Ross, *Plato's Theory of Ideas* (Oxford, 1951), pp. 116-117.

and Callicles were probably held as a coherent theory by the people whom Plato intended to refute when he wrote the *Gorgias*.[22]

Before proceeding to a consideration of the *Phaedrus*, it might be well briefly to review. I have attempted to demonstrate the following points:

1. The *Gorgias* is a thematically unified dialogue having for its single main theme the refutation of the Gorgian definition of rhetoric.

2. The *Gorgias* is concerned with ethical questions because the definition being subjected to dialectical inquiry claims a moral characteristic for the definiendum; however, there are no issues raised in the *Gorgias* which are not demonstrably pertinent to the definition of "rhetoric" presented by Gorgias early in the dialogue.

3. The *Gorgias* is fundamentally a refutative rather than a constructive dialogue, as are other of the "Socratic" dialogues, i.e., dialogues written early in Plato's career, as the *Gorgias* evidently was.

4. Plato cannot be interpreted as having pronounced a general condemnation of rhetoric.

3.

With these points clear, I shall proceed to propose that the *Phaedrus* is the constructive complement of the *Gorgias* and that the two dialogues taken together constitute a consistent view of rhetoric. A. E. Taylor pronounces the judgment with which my proposal is consistent:

> In taking leave of the *Phaedrus*, we may note that while it supplements the *Gorgias* in its conclusions about the value of "style," it modifies nothing that was said in the earlier dialogue. The moral condemnation pronounced on the use of eloquent speech to pervert facts and produce false impressions remains the same. So does the verdict that the sort of thing professional teachers from Tisias to Thrasymachus profess to expound is not a science but a mere "trick" or "knack" (and therefore cannot be conveyed, as they profess to convey it, by "lessons"). In adding that a thorough knowledge of a subject-matter and a sound knowledge of the psychology of the public addressed furnished a really scientific basis for a worthy and effective style, Plato is saying nothing inconsistent with the results of the *Gorgias*. There is thus no sufficient ground for thinking that the

---

22. The important thing is that we not strain credulity by attributing to a philosophical genius reasons that are ill-defined, trivial, or plain silly.

teaching of the *Phaedrus* represents a later "development" from the more "Socratic" position of the *Gorgias*.²³

Since there is considerably less disagreement among students of Plato and among expert commentators about the interpretation of the *Phaedrus,* there is no need for a detailed examination of that dialogue here. Plato turns the collective and divisive resources of dialectic on "real" rhetoric, and his examination is clearly reported in the *Phaedrus*. The collective definition is: "Must not the art of rhetoric, taken as a whole, be a kind of influencing of the mind by means of words, not only in courts of law and other public gatherings, but in private places also? "²⁴ And further on: "The function of oratory is in fact to influence men's souls."²⁵

Plato's divisive definition is explicated by his setting forth the conditions necessary to make speech-writing an art:

> The conditions to be fulfilled are these: first, you must know the truth about the subject that you speak or write about: that is to say, you must be able to isolate it in definition, and having so defined it you must next understand how to divide it into kinds, until you reach the limit of division; secondly, you must have a corresponding discernment of the nature of the soul, discover the type of speech appropriate to each nature, and order and arrange your discourse accordingly, addressing a variegated soul in a variegated style that ranges over the whole gamut of tones, and a simple soul in a simple style. All this must be done if you are to become competent, within human limits, as a scientific practitioner of speech, whether you propose to expound or to persuade.²⁶

In sum, Plato conceived a true art of rhetoric to be a consolidation of dialectic with *psychogogia* — applicable to all discourse, public and private,²⁷ persuasive and expository, which aims to influence men's souls. Dialectic was Plato's general scientific method; rhetoric is a special psychological application of it.²⁸ This definition of rhetoric is in one sense narrower, in another broader than the definition

---

23. A. B. Taylor, *Plato, the Man and his Work* (New York, 1929), p. 319.
24. *Phaedrus,* 261A. Unless otherwise indicated, all quotations from the *Phaedrus* will be from R. Hackforth, *Plato's Phaedrus* (Cambridge, England, 1952).
25. *Phaedrus,* 271C. The more famous rendering of this passage, "Oratory is the art of enchanting the soul..." is by Benjamin Jowett, *The Dialogues of Plato* (New York, 1937), I.
26. *Phaedrus,* 277BC.
27. Cf. *Sophist,* 222C.
28. See Shorey, *What Plato Said,* p. 52.

which Plato overthrew in the *Gorgias*. It is narrower in the sense that he does not admit the nature of justice and injustice to be a part of the "art" of rhetoric, but places it rather in the "art" of statesmanship. It is a broader definition in that Plato does assign to the art of rhetoric a specific province of its own, and a province which is not, as with the earlier Sophists, confined to forensic and deliberative oratory, but extends to all discourse which influences men. Plato's position here is fully consonant with that of the *Gorgias*; indeed, the treatments of rhetoric in the two dialogues supplement one another.

The question of the thematic unity of the *Phaedrus* too has puzzled commentators. It is evident from the dialogue itself that its main subject is rhetoric; on this point, there is virtually unanimous agreement. But the three speeches on love in the dialogue, occupying as they do such a large proportion of space and reaching, in the third speech, such a luminous intensity of poetic eloquence and philosophical insight, have suggested to some readers a formal defect in the dialogue's structure.[29] The speeches fasten the reader's attention on themselves; Socrates's second speech is the climax of the drama: all converse in the dialogue builds up to and then down from that section. How can we account for the unity of the dialogue? I believe that we can account for the speeches by observing that they operate on at least seven different levels of meaning, at least five of which are directly and clearly pertinent to a consideration of rhetoric. By my reference to "levels of meaning," I indicate only that there are at least seven different ways in which these speeches might legitimately be understood by a reader:

1. The three speeches are investigations of love, and are intended to convey Plato's ideas on that subject. As such, they are not directly and clearly pertinent to a consideration of rhetoric, though they still have great value taken exclusively in this non-rhetorical sense.

2. The speeches, culminating in Socrates's second speech, are intended to express Plato's counterpart of Sophistical education. It is clear that Socrates's second speech focuses on and advocates the development of the intellectual and moral qualities of the beloved by the lover. It would not be inaccurate to characterize Plato's ideal lover as a philosophical tutor; certainly he is given a primarily educative function with respect to the beloved. Since, in the *Gorgias*, Plato attacked some of the pretensions of rhetorical education as

---

29. See, e.g. Shorey, p. 198.

conducted by the Sophists, we might expect a more constructive treatment of education in the *Phaedrus*.[30] Even so, the speeches, read in this way, cannot be said to have an unqualifiedly clear and direct relevance to the subject of rhetoric. The remaining five "readings," however, do have such relevance.

3. The three speeches can be taken as specimens of rhetoric. In this way they serve a function to the theme of the dialogue so obvious that few commentators have even troubled to remark it directly. The speeches represent different kinds of persuasion, each superior to its predecessor, and the third represents the apogee of rhetorical discourse. The first speech, besides being subject to all the criticisms which Socrates makes of it, appeals exclusively to the prudential self-interest of the auditor. It is devoid of dialectic, and its disorder is evidence of its lack of adaptability to any possible person.[31] The second speech argues from grounds of definition and moral self-interest. It is better than the first because at least it is a kind of dialectic, though it is not "true" dialectic, as Socrates's later critique of it observes. The third speech is the perfection of the technique: the consummate amalgam of dialectic and *psychogogia*.

In exemplifying dialectic in a speech, Plato would not encounter any unusual literary problems. All of his dialogues illustrate dialectic in one way or another. But the exemplification of psychogogia certainly must have been a unique literary problem to Plato, a problem which he brilliantly resolved by choosing love as the subject of the speeches. Plato could not very well have exemplified the psychogogic aspect of rhetoric *only* by having Socrates's speeches adapted to Phaedrus. If Plato had done only that, his exemplification might not have been clearly made, and he uncharacteristically would have limited the applicability of his paradigm to the dramatic situation created in the dialogue. Plato's resolution of the problem is to have Socrates discourse directly on the soul, which the subject of love enables him to do. Since the theory of the soul presented in the speech is itself the product of dialectic, the speech becomes an explicit consolidation of dialectic and psychogogia and, as such, a

30. This interpretation is obliquely suggested by W. C. Helmbold and W. B. Holther, "The Unity of the Phaedrus," *University of California Publications in Classical Philology*, XIV, No. 9 (Berkeley and Los Angeles, 1952).

31. Plato insisted that principles of organization be based on human psychology. See *Phaedrus* 277C.

paradigm of Platonic rhetoric in a philosophical as well as a literary sense.

4. The three speeches can be taken as considerations of a particular type of rhetoric: courtship. As such, the speeches can be interpreted as dealing with the objectives of the suitor and, implicatively, with the objectives available to rhetors in general. Plato rejects personal pleasure and reciprocal pleasure as worthy objectives, finally endorsing the love of wisdom as the aim worthy of fulfillment. Considered in this way, the third speech can be taken as a poetic restatement of the doctrine developed in the *Gorgias* that the true orator and statesman aims at the moral improvement of his audience. This reading would reveal that the speeches in the *Phaedrus* contain paradigms within paradigms, i.e., the speeches *qua* speeches are paradigms of artistic form, and their contents are also paradigmatic.

5. The three speeches can be taken as Plato's advice to audiences. In a view of rhetoric so concerned as Plato's with the sorts of things rhetors ought to say, we should rather expect a concomitant treatment of what audiences ought to attend to. The speeches of the *Phaedrus* can be read as functioning in that way. We must not neglect the care with which the character of Phaedrus is drawn in the dialogue. He is neither a witless foil for Socrates's ironies nor the representative of an antagonistic philosophical idea. Phaedrus is a lover of discourse, a young man who is impressionable, an auditor. Several times in the dialogue Socrates insinuates that the Lysian speech was composed to influence Phaedrus and that Socrates' own speeches have the same objective.[32] The three speeches, taken together, constitute a symposium on the subject of whether one ought to yield to the lover or the non-lover. Since, as was observed in the fourth "reading" above, the wooing of the lover would be a type of rhetoric in Plato's schematism, we might suppose him to have wished his readers to generalize from the particular case, wooing, to the general Form, rhetoric. Since these speeches are directed to Phaedrus, we might be expected to take him as the paradigm of audiences. Once the generalization is made, it becomes evident that the speeches deal with what sorts of arguments one should be influenced by, and to what sorts of speakers one ought to listen. In this light too, the speeches would be taken as a restatement of the *Gorgias's* doctrine

---

32. E.g., *Phaedrus,* 237B, 257.

about the proper objective of oratory, with the emphasis falling on the moral implications which this doctrine has for audiences.

6. The speeches can be taken as poetic discussion of the moral attitude which the speaker takes toward his speech. More than once in the dialogue Socrates describes Phaedrus and himself as "lovers of discourse." They would therefore belong to the genus "lover" according to the prescriptions of Platonic dialectic, and whatever is true of that genus would be true also of them with respect to discourse. Accordingly, the third speech would be read as saying that the true lover of discourse will strive to enhance the moral quality of the object of his love: his discourse.

It may seem odd to the modern reader to encounter the concept of a "love" of discourse, but we know from Plato's writings and from a multitude of other sources in antiquity that the Greeks did take a deep and critical pleasure in rhetorical discourse, Plato, then, was setting down the conditions for the expression of that love, holding, in effect, that the lover of discourse will imbue his discourse with moral elevation.

7. The three speeches can be taken as a consideration of benign and malign forms of "madness" or inspiration, with the third speech exemplifying poetic inspiration in form and erotic inspiration in content. Plato recognized the existence of four types of benign madness, two of which are discussed and exemplified in these speeches.[33] The relationship between poetic madness and Platonic rhetoric will be briefly examined below.

These seven readings of the speeches may well not exhaust the possibilities, but the levels of possible interpretation are numerous enough to reveal the plurality of function of the speeches. Since Plato was a conscious literary artist, I believe that we must take this ambiguity as deliberate. Considering the fact that this ambiguity enables Plato to write on one level about an apparently disparate subject while, at other levels, still to maintain a unitary theme in the dialogue, we must judge that his ambiguity is actually a glorious tour de force. I hope at least to have established that the speeches in the *Phaedrus* represent a violation of the dialogue's thematic unity only when they are read in only one of several possible ways. The general

---

33. For a fuller discussion of this subject see: Ivan M. Linforth, "Telestic Madness in Plato," *University of California Publications in Classical Philology*, XIII (Berkely and Los Angeles, 1950).

inference which can be drawn is that there is no lack of thematic unity on either the *Gorgias* or the *Phaedrus,* nor are the positions taken in those two dialogues anything but fully consistent and logically complementary to one another.

4.

Plato is not so directly concerned with rhetoric in dialogues other than the two we have been considering, but even so, some of the darker corners of Platonic rhetoric are illuminated by his insights in other areas; This is especially true of his seminal contributions in the area of epistemology.

One recurrent distinction which Plato makes between knowledge or intelligence and true belief is particularly noteworthy for its implicative relevance to rhetorical theory. The pertinent section in the *Timaeus* is:

> If intelligence and true belief are two different kinds, then these things — Forms that we cannot perceive but only think of — certainly exist in themselves; but if, as some hold, true belief in no way differs from intelligence, then all things we perceive through the bodily senses must be taken as the most certain reality. Now we must affirm that they are two different things, for they are distinct in origin and unlike in nature. The one is produced in us by instruction, the other by persuasion; the one can always give a true account of itself, the other can give none; the one cannot be shaken by persuasion, whereas the other can be won over; and true belief, we must allow, is shared by all mankind, intelligence only by the gods and a small number of men.[34]

We find a restatement of this position in the *Theaetetus,*[35] and though the context in that dialogue is different, the important point is that Plato did draw a distinction between knowledge and conviction, and based this distinction on the method by which each was attained. Plato looked upon knowledge, the object of instruction, as accompanied by an unshakeable certitude which conviction, the object of persuasion, lacked. This deficiency of certitude was not affected by the truth-value of the conviction. "True belief," by which Plato meant a state of having been persuaded to accept a proposition that was in fact true, was still, despite its truth, more

---

34. *Timaeus,* 51 DE. Translation from Francis Macdonald Cornford, *Plato's Cosmology* (London, 1937).
35. *Theatetus,* 201 A.

tenuously held than knowledge (*episteme*) or intelligence (*noesis*), i.e., rational intuition.[36]

To Plato, belief or conviction (*pistis* was one of four possible states of mind in an hierarchy of mental states.[37] The lowest of these states of mind is imagining (*eikasia*), which Cornford describes as, "the wholly unenligthened state of mind which takes sensible appearances and current moral notions at their face value — the condition of the unreleased prisoners in the Cave allegory ... who see only images of images."[38]

Above imagining is belief which, when true, is a sufficient guide to action, but which can be shaken by persuasion and is the objective of persuasion. Higher on the scale is thinking (*dianoia*) characteristic of mathematical procedure. It is reasoning from premise to conclusion in which the premises are taken axiomately. The highest state of mind is intelligence or knowledge, in which the premises themselves are examined and the ultimate principle on which they depend is apprehended.

In the third speech of the *Phaedrus* and in the *Meno*,[39] Plato discussed an unusual mental phenomenon which he called "madness" or inspiration, by which one, possessing only true belief, utters profound truth. It is clear in these passages that Plato did not consider the profoundest insights to be exclusively the product of intelligence or knowledge. The poet, the statesman, and the orator might have moments of vivid revelation by which audiences can be inspired, but the source of this revelation is not in any state of mind. Rather, it is divinely inspired.[40] Its capacity to persuade is due to the epidemic quality of divine madness. Such inspirations have nothing to do with art. They are the gifts of God, and cannot be further explained.[41]

In these considerations we have perhaps the only instance in the formal history of rhetorical theory of an investigation of the episte-

---

36. Cornford, *The Republic of Plato* (Oxford, 1941), p. 223.
37. *Republic*, 6.509ff.
38. Cornford, *Republic*, p. 222.
39. *Meno*, 98Bff.
40. This notion is developed in the *Ion*.
41. See Hackforth, pp. 60-62.

mological character of rhetoric, and the relative strength with which any persuasively induced belief will be sustained measured against a broad psychological scale. Plato's conclusion was that no matter how fervent our conviction that a proposition is true, that conviction will always be less secure than the knowledge even of a more trivial proposition. The method by which a belief has come to be held makes all the difference.

Given the observation that belief or conviction is inferior to knowledge in certitude and persistence, and given also Plato's deep commitment to the pursuit and cultivation of knowledge, the question arises: What place, if any, would rhetorical persuasion have in Plato's doctrine of politics? What place could rhetoric have when the state itself is designed to serve philosophical ends, when its leaders are carefully selected and arduously trained philosophers, and its economy, educational system, family pattern, artistic enterprise — all of its institutions, including even the most personal and intimate — are arranged to serve the interests of abstract Justice? Where is there room for the flexibility of argument, the contingency of decision, and the inconstancy of commitment, all so characteristic of rhetorical activity, when the fabric of society is woven after the pattern of certain, immutable, universal Truth? Plato answers these questions, and defines with precision the place of rhetoric in the Platonic commonwealth.

In considering the social utility of rhetoric, Plato's emphasis falls on the function of persuasion as a means of social control. As such, its utility to the state is obvious, and Plato has not neglected it. Despite the ideological differences between the *Republic* and the *Laws,* a congruous view of the function of rhetoric is maintained. Its place is defined in the *Politicus,* where rhetoric is made subordinate to the art of statesmanship; but even though in a subordinated capacity, rhetorical persuasion is considered by Plato as the only means of social control besides coercion which the statesman can exercise.[42]

In the *Republic*, Plato not only states that rhetoric should be used by the Guardians, but explicitly condones the use even of willful deception in the best interests of the community.[43] The state is to

---

42. *Politicus,* 304.
43. *Republic,* 3.388, 413, 459.

be organized and governed after metaphysical principles, yet metaphysical knowledge cannot be apprehended by unmetaphysical minds. Hence, it is justifiable to simplify complex truths and to present them appealingly.

In the "second best state," rhetoric occupies the same place and discharges the same function as in the *Republic*. Here too, it is a means of social control to be used by the Legislator,[44] who may use even a benevolent lie to persuade.[45] Since Plato considered freedom of expression inimical to the best interests of the community, his condoning of deception is not general, but is always confined to the governing class. The *Laws* explicity bans unrestricted forensic advocacy and shyster lawyers from the state,[46] but nowhere in his political writings do we find a general banishment of rhetoric.

In addition to social control, Plato attributes an educational value to rhetoric. Moral and metaphysical truths are to be rhetorically disseminated, not alone for the maintenance of political order, but so that they will be believed for their own sakes as well.[47] Young men who are without philosophy, and so are not yet equipped to attain true knowledge, would be attracted to the study of philosophy by "persuasion."[48]

5.

It may now be apparent that Plato did not despise rhetoric, but only the excesses of the Sophists. He was far from blind to the practical need for social order and to the limitations of the popular mind, and he gave to rhetoric some functions for which, even today, no apologies need be offered. Certainly Plato was repelled by the Gorgian view of rhetoric: by the pretensions of its claims, the flaccidity of its formulation, and the easy virtue of its practice. But he was far too good a writer and clear a thinker to overstate his case or to extend it unreasonably.

It is undeniable that Plato's preoccupation with the moral character of rhetoric in his critique colored his positive formulations of rhetorical theory, so that he gives us not an account of rhetoric, but

---

44. *Laws*, 4.720-722; 10.885D.
45. *Laws*, 2.663ff.
46. *Laws*, 11.937E.
47. *Laws*, 2.664.
48. *Euthydemus*, 274ff.

an account of a "true art" of rhetoric, not an account of the general social functions of rhetoric, but an account of its utility to the Ideal State. That there were actually theories and practices of rhetoric which did not fit his mold, no author has observed more brilliantly than he. But these other theories and practices were not "true" arts of rhetoric; they were "false" arts, knacks only. Plato did not deny their reality; what he denied was their moral efficacy.

From our perspective in history, we are able to perceive the irony that Plato, the arch-enemy of the Sophists, was actually closer to them in his rhetorical theory than was his successor, Aristotle. Plato's repudiation of Sophistical rhetoric was neither so complete nor so thorough as his student's, for though Plato rejected and refuted with finality the particular moral interpretation of rhetoric which the Sophists propounded, he did not reject the attempt to suffuse an investigation of rhetoric with a moral concern. It is on this very point that his great disciple departed from him.

Still, we must regard it as an open question whether Aristotle surpassed him by that particular departure. Can it be denied that so fearsomely potent a force as rhetoric participates in moral values? Is it the case that any instrument which affects human life is not subject to moral assessment? Aristotle affirmed the moral neutrality of rhetoric; Plato's answer to both these questions was an emphatic negative. When, in recent history, we find the clamorous spirit of fanaticism at large in the world, sustained by rhetorical discourse; when we contemplate the undiminished and undiminishing potentiality for savagery latent in all men, waiting to be triggered by suasive language; and when we observe the Sophists of our time, rationally discredited but thriving still, we may begin to suspect that, after all, Plato was even wiser than we had thought.

THE UNITY OF THE PHAEDRUS*

PAUL PLASS

In the first part of the *Phaedrus* Socrates listens to a speech on love read to him by Phaedrus and written by Lysias. He responds with two speeches, the first patterned on Lysias, the second a highly charged presentation of his own views. All of this takes place in a dramatic setting itself set at a high pitch. Phaedrus is intensely excited at Lysias' speech, and Socrates for his part professes to be inspired by the local nymphs. The second part of the dialogue is then given over to a detailed discussion of rhetoric in a notably cooler manner. The problem of coherence created by the shift in subject and mood has caused as much discussion as the similar problem of structure in Sophoclean tragedies which seem to fall into two distinct parts.[1]

Posed in purely literary terms the problem of coherence is apt to become somewhat unreal, since it is difficult to see what canon of artistic unity could be applied to the dialogues. As a literary form the dialogue is bound only to the broad probabilities of the conversations which it depicts, and if in this respect a dialogue does not grossly offend by a lack of unity, it has effective unity. From this point of view there is no serious difficulty in several lengthy statements about love in various rhetorical styles being followed by a discussion of rhetoric. And even if the literary form is less successfully adjusted to the philosophic idea than it is in many dialogues, the *Phaedrus* is at least no weaker in this respect than the *Republic*, where the discussion becomes improbably long and covers a very wide range of subjects to accommodate Plato's desire to make a comprehensive philosophic statement. As for the conflict between Socrates' inspiration in the first part and the subsequent analytic

---

*Reprinted with permission of Universitetsforlaget, Oslo, from *Symbolae Osloenses*, 43 (1968), 7-38.

1. For a brief discussion of the question see R. Hackforth, *Plato's Phaedrus* (Cambridge 1952), 8f; below, note 24.

discussion, since inspiration and love are precisely the sort of things which unaccountably come and go, the pronounced change in mood is natural enough, or only as unnatural as inspiration itself is. As a medium for philosophy, however, we can expect the dialogue form to contain a much more definite unity of thought, even when Plato is writing in the mood of a 'glücklicher Sommertag,'[2] and much of the difficulty that has been felt about the unity of the *Phaedrus* arises in the first instance from the extraordinary complexity of the ideas which it brings together.

Plato's new synthesis of love and rhetoric is affected from the start by a factor which is characteristic of his thought in general. He often seems to be talking about everything at once — notably in the *Republic* — as he moves with the greatest of ease from one subject to another. Discussion, as Socrates repeatedly says, must be allowed to go where it will. Whatever the logical dangers of moving freely among ethics, ontology, politics and epistemology, the free flow of thought itself helps underscore the philosopher's persistent search for unity behind the variety of experience, and the fact of that unity is a matter of prime and substantial significance. Plato's attachment to the dialogue form may in part be motivated by his awareness that its flexibility lends itself particularly well to tracing the interplay of different areas of experience. The *Phaedrus'* lack of unity is in part only a superficial incoherence that points to the necessity of discovering a principle which can connect things disconnected, organize disorganized energies and direct them toward their proper goal. Plato himself touches on the problem of unity when he makes Phaedrus wonder about the unusual broadness of Socrates' concept of rhetoric (261B). Since the areas into which Socrates extends rhetoric are those private areas in which Eros can be active, Phaedrus is implicitly wondering how rhetoric is relevant to love.

The most natural place to look for connections between love and rhetoric is in cross references between the two parts of the dialogue. Whenever Socrates talks about *logoi* in his speech he is fact foreshadowing much of what he says later about rhetoric. But passages in the later portion which echo things he has just said about love reflect the unity of the dialogue more clearly, and we shall consider some of these.

His criticism of rhetoric begins with a use of words far removed

---

2. The title of Wilamowitz's chapter on the *Phaedrus*.

from love. Lysias has been sneered at for being a writer of speeches for others (a *logographos*), and Phaedrus fears that he might give up writing (257Cf). Socrates starts to expand 'rhetoric' by including in his discussion of 'written works' not only forensic speeches but bills (which he calls *logoi*) introduced at meetings of the council as well as the more comprehensive legislation of lawgivers. Though the reference to bills has a witty *tu quoque* touch — all active politicians are authors and vain ones at that — at least the allusion to lawgivers as authors is seriously meant, for law-giving is a highly important form of persuasion. Later he again talks about political writings in connection with law-giving and mentions Solon as one who 'wrote compositions calling them laws' (278C, 277Df; cf. *Symposium* 209D). He then goes on to a further extension of rhetoric: it must be obvious to everyone that 'the mere act of writing speeches is not bad (αἰσχρόν)'; what *is* bad is 'speaking and writing not well (καλῶς) but badly (αἰσχρῶς τε καὶ κακῶς) . . . whether public or private compositions in meter or in prose' (258D). The point at issue is 'how one speaks and writes well or badly' (259E). From this point of view the written word too can have considerable value. In fact the passage is indirectly a defence of the dialogues, and it has been supposed that Plato is responding to someone who had raised the Socratic problem.[3] If this is so, 'good' and 'bad' would refer to the truth or falsity of what is written and 'truth' would be fidelity to Socrates' philosophic intention rather than to historical accuracy.

But the fact that Socrates talks of both writing and *speaking* and actually criticizes Lysias on grounds of rhetorical technique shows that in the first instance at least Plato is not thinking of his own written work. The use of αἰσχρῶς and καλῶς reflects primarily his concern with the philosophic and ethical value of what is written or spoken. Moreover, though the pairing of 'written and spoken' here and elsewhere (261B, 271B,C) may be simply a formal 'polar' expression including every possibility, it is more likely that Plato has at least vaguely in mind his theory of true rhetoric, which does center around the peculiar effectiveness of spoken words in forming character. In explaining the role of spoken words later (277Df) Socrates

---

3. F. Ast (*Platonis Opera*, Leipzig 1829, X, *ad* 275B) suggested that Socrates' criticism of those concerned about *who* said something rather than about whether it is true also touches on the issue of whether Plato's picture of Socrates is entirely accurate.

refers back to 258D. In any case, the passage at 258D prepares for 277Df by expanding the discussion of rhetoric to include all forms of verbal communication. We can see now how all men are in effect rhetoricians. Persuasion can have many different objects (271D6, 272A3); rhetoric taken in its full range is a 'craft of leading souls through words, not only in courts and other public assemblies but also in private meetings (σύλλογοι, 261A).' And such an extension takes rhetoric in the direction of eros. The second members of each alternative mentioned in 258D — written/spoken, public/private, meter/prose — make up a form of rhetoric directly relevant to love. *Syllogoi* are the small intellectual meetings whose more or less erotic character is obvious in many dialogues as well as in Phaedrus' present encounters with Lysias and Socrates.[4] Such *syllogoi* are naturally also tied to the spoken word and therefore to philosophic dialogue.

The 'writtenness' of Lysias' speech is a serious point against it, as the 'writtenness' of dialogues is a point against them (*Epistle VII*. 341C). Conventional rhetoric certainly appreciated the power of spoken words and knew the value of spontaneity.[5] But it was often tied to set written passages or text books of a sort,[6] and so when he places it next to live philosophic dialogue Plato feels in it the dead hand of the merely clever writer who has nothing better than the written words which he has 'spent a long time turning up and down'

---

4. The difference between fruitful and futile meetings is described in *Republic* 499A: 'They have not been sufficiently involved in fine and free discussions of the sort devoted to searching out the truth intently (συντεταμένως; cf. *Phaedrus* 253A1) for the sake of knowledge. They have been involved too much in discussions devoted to showiness (κβυψά; cf. *Phaedrus* 227C7) and cleverness (ἐριστικά), discussions which strive only for appearance (δόξαν; *Phaedrus* 260C) whether in law courts or in private gatherings.' Though Plato says nothing about eros here, there are many points of contact with issues raised in the *Phaedrus*; Lysias' performance is nicely described in the second sentence.

5. Alcidamas (*On the Sophists* 9) urged independence from written speeches without reference, of course, to the sort of inspiration that Plato uses to reinforce his concept of spontaneity which is linked to the theory of reminiscence. Cf. Isocrates, *Against the Sophists* 12f; A. Gercke, 'Die Alte ΤΕΧΝΗ ΡΗΤΟΡΙΚΗ und ihre Gegner,' *Hermes*, XXXII (1897), 361f.

6. On early rhetorical theory see A. Gercke (above, note 5), 351f; K. Mras, 'Platos Phaedrus und die Rhetorik,' *Wiener Studien*, XXXVI (1914), 295f; XXXVII (1915), 88f; S. Wilcox, 'The Scope of Early Rhetorical Instruction,' *Harvard Studies in Classical Philology*, LIII (1942); G. Kennedy, *The Art of Persuasion in Greece* (Princeton 1963), 52f.

(278D). The dramatic play about Phaedrus' effort to hide his copy of Lysias' speech reinforces the point; he seems vaguely embarrassed at being caught having it in his hand and memorizing it. When Lysias 'speaks' his speech, when Phaedrus 'speaks' it again to Socrates, they are reading or reciting and not really speaking. They do not recognize the two marks of rhetoric at its best: the truly fruitful spoken word and knowledge.

> ... unless a man is able to discriminate among the natures [or souls] of those who will hear him, unless he is able to arrange things by class and embrace each in an idea, he will never reach the limit of a human being's skill with words. He will never attain this skill without much work — work which the disciplined man (σώφρονα) must undertake not for the sake of speaking and acting (λέγειν, πράττειν) with men in view (πρὸς ἀνθρώπους) but with a view to saying things pleasing to the gods (θεοῖς κεχαρισμένα) and doing (πράττειν) things in a way that will please them as far as possible (273Df).

Socrates here caps his outline of true rhetoric by revealing its most startling and unorthodox application. Not only does rhetoric embrace every conceivable use of words; its real audience turns out to be not human but divine. Conventional rhetoric is now outflanked on both sides, or rather it is absorbed from independent existence on both sides by true rhetoric, which on the one side is directed beyond the world of men to the gods, on the other especially to small circles of those seeking knowledge.[7] True rhetoric typically exercises a deep personal influence with no regard for the 'standards of the many' (δόξας πλήθους, 260C) and with all regard for divine standards. Socrates' insistence that the rhetorician should know how to place things under an appropriate class or form (εἶδος, ἰδέα, 273E) echoes an earlier passage which describes dialectic technique in similar terms (265Df). These passages themselves take us back to the speech on love and tie the dialogue together, for in 249Bf Socrates had spoken of man's ability to 'understand according to form (κατ' εἶδος)' in connection with eros. But we are concerned not so much with the link between dialectic techniques and eros as with the link between rhetoric on the one hand, eros and inspiration on the other. To this his striking advice about 'saying and doing things pleasing to the gods' is especially relevant; 'the gods' are a major vehicle for Plato's conception of inspired talk and love.

---

7. For conventional τέχνη and the new, true τέχνη see R. Hall, *Plato and the Individual* (The Hague 1963), 80.

The *Phaedrus* as a whole and Socrates' second speech in particular are examples of the style which the true rhetorician is capable of using. In addition to the usual Socratic dialogue there are substantial passages written in the styles of high poetry and sophisticated rhetoric as well as a brief but prominent passage of austere apodeictic. If, as seems most probable, Plato himself is the author of Lysias' speech he has attained with it a supreme kind of parody: an imitation so skillful that it has often been taken as quotation. And Socrates' second speech is an equal tour-de-force, for its 'unwonted flow' (238C) has often been taken as parody. The play with literary style is in fact one of the most effective forms taken by irony in the dialogue.

Socrates frequently employs the maneuver of attributing an idea to someone else, especially a religious idea to venerable religious or poetic figures. The attribution usually indicates that he is seriously borrowing from tradition something which can be made philosophically useful. In the *Meno*, for example, he takes the doctrine of reincarnation from 'priests, priestesses, Pindar and other divine poets' (81Af). In the *Phaedrus* he takes the poetic style itself. The use of words commits a man to a style, and the style in which his attitude toward eros in particular expresses itself becomes in the *Phaedrus* symptomatic of his ethical style. The sharp contrast between Socrates' inspired style and Lysias' frigid rhetoric creates in the first place an aesthetic impression. And since good taste and sensitivity to what is truly beautiful are important features of love, style easily becomes an aspect of eros, i.e. Socrates' inspiration becomes a natural expression of erotic *mania* and stands against the mere calculated smartness of Lysias' view of love.

Moreover, the contrast between the two styles, verbal and ethical, helps establish the link between rhetoric and love as Plato sees it. Conventional eros too was tied to *paideia*, and since *paideia* is inseparable from the use of words, rhetoric is at least in a general way tied to love. It takes no special philosophic insight to see these connections; they were implicit in the use of words, the eros and *paideia* familiar to Plato's public. In fact, from Socrates' point of view Lysias is all too aware of the erotic uses to which rhetoric could be put.[8]

---

8. Because of the highly practical ethical problem which it faces, the *Phaedrus* is particularly concerned with the consequences of using the art of words. Speaking improperly is a serious matter because it means inducing people

Speeches on love like his were set as exercises in schools of rhetoric, but it is improbable that they remained purely formal exercises with no relation to the actual erotic attachments that were part of contemporary *paideia*. The fascination which rhetoric held for impressionable young men and the persuasive techniques it provided could hardly have failed to be exploited for actual persuasion. Pausanias seems to have this in mind when he offers an ingenious sociological

to 'do evil instead of good' (260C); speaking properly induces them to respond to 'lawful ways of life and lawful words' (λόγους τε καὶ ἐπιτηδεύσεις νομίμους, 270B; cf. Gorgias, νομίμων ἐρώτων [Diels, B6]; *Republic 479D. This applies all the more to love. A lover's evil nature tries to force his better self to approach a youth 'for the purpose of words' (ἐπὶ λόγους, 154D). 'Words' here are clearly not theoretical; the approach is part of the 'approach to a beautiful body' (238C, cf. 237Ef) caused by lust. Alcibiades had such words in mind when he expected that Socrates 'would say the things lovers usually say' (*Symposium* 217B); Lysias is himself using them in a highly sophisticated form. On the other hand, when a man has brought his evil nature under control, a youth can safely accept his 'conversation and company' (λόγον καὶ ὁμιλίαν, 255B). *Homilia* is vague enough to include all aspects of the relationship, and the continuing interplay of word with erotic deed also in the highest forms of love is made clear by the following lines in which Socrates speaks of the true lover 'touching' the youth when they are together in gymnasia and other places. Before he enters into such decent conversation with his lover the youth has been warned by friends to avoid him because it is shameful to approach a lover (255A). For διαλέγεσθαι and eros see *Symposium* 183C, 213D. *Charmides* 154E; Xenophon, *Lacedaemonian Constitution* II.12. The entire passage at 255Af is one of the many responsions between Socrates' second speech and Lysias' speech. It was Lysias who had said that a lover's behavior is shameful and who had noted that when men see a lover and a youth talking together (διαλεγομενοι) they suspect the worst (232Af). Lysias had repeatedly alluded to the specifically erotic *praxis* that is the aim of his rhetoric; Socrates dealt with the same kind of *praxis* in some respects even more openly. When he introduces his remarks on the spoken word with a reference to the 'pleasing deeds' that go with words 'pleasing to the gods' (cf. πράττων ἢ λέγων, 274B, 273E), true rhetoric is tied in with the moral problem raised by pederasty. The force of πράττειν in this context arises from the dramatic situation of the dialogue as a whole, i.e., from the efforts of Socrates and Lysias to persuade a youth. The connection of word and deed (without special reference to eros) is again no more exclusively a philosophic insight than is the importance of the spoken word. Rhetoric was important precisely because of its practical uses: *Protagoras* 318E; Aristophanes, *Clouds* 419 (νικᾶν πράττων). Again in Isocrates' theory of rhetoric, word and deed go together (e.g., *Antidosis* 274f); cf. W. Steidle, 'Redekunst und Bildung bei Isokrates,' *Hermes*, LXXX (1952), 265f.

explanation of the connection between rhetoric and eros in the *Symposium* (182B):

> In Elis and Boeotia and wherever there is no skill in speech the law simply states that it is a good thing to indulge lovers, and neither young nor old would say that it is shameful. The law is designed to get around the trouble of trying to persuade young men, for men [in those states] cannot speak well.

Pausanias' own speech is full of the rhetorical techniques which would be an important part of the effective persuasion that lovers in Athens must be able to exercise. And Lysias' proposition about indulging the non-lover is an example of how the art of speaking well could be used to defend paradoxes cleverly and to make the worst argument seem better specifically in matters of love.[9] But Plato's emphasis upon the erotic *mania* embodied in Socrates' strangely inspired rhetorical style by way of contrast to the sterile eros embodied in Lysias' style points to what *is* a peculiarly philosophic insight: that true love and a true art of words arouse all of the soul's powers. And in this we recognize a key idea advanced in the second part of the dialogue, a speaker must have insight into soul types (271Dff). Valid psychology is possible only in light of the analysis of the soul outlined in Socrates' speech on love, and the analysis there makes clear that truly to know the nature of any soul involves knowing the nature of the passion aroused in all souls by remembrance of true being. Such passion is not necessarily erotic; nothing is said in the *Phaedrus* to indicate that the true rhetorician must be a lover. But the classification of soul types offered by Socrates (252Cf) is in fact a classification of lovers according to the gods they follow, and the sample of rhetoric he offers is an ἐρωτικὸς λόγος.

Plato makes as much play with the motif of 'the divine' in the *Phaedrus* as he does with inspired style. The link between love and the art of words is directly established by the presence of Eros on the one hand, inspiring deities like the Muses and nymphs on the other.

---

9. For love as a subject of school exercises see W. Jaeger, *Paideia,* trans. G. Highet (New York 1944), III, 186; on the genre of ἐρωτικοὶ λόγοι see F. Lasserre, 'Erotikoi Logoi,' *Museum Helveticum* I (1944), 169f and F. Wilhelm, 'Zu Achilles Tatius,' *Rheinisches Museum,* LVII (1902), 55f. The occasional connection in Aristophanes between pederasty and rhetoricians (*Ecclesiazusae* 112; *Clouds* 1089 with Leeuwen's note) is simply a sneer at the character of politicians ('rhetoricians'); cf. V. Ehrenberg, *The People of Aristophanes*, 2nd ed. (Oxford 1951), 353 and S. Wilcox, (above, note 6), 129f.

The manifestations of the divine range from 'primitive' immediately present figures like nymphs or Pan, to remote celestial gods who feed upon true being and direct the cosmos. Eros in a special way spans the entire spectrum of the divine; he is both a brute emotional experience and man's divine capacity to see Beauty itself. Plato's emphasis upon the truly divine nature of Eros and upon the irresistible power of deities of inspiration associated with him points in the same direction as does the highly poetic style of Socrates's speech. The wide spectrum of the divine answers to the widely different levels of soul and to the many forms through which it expresses itself; Eros, nymphs, Muses, celestial gods are from one point of view 'projections' of powers within the soul. Whatever Plato's precise attitutude toward their status as objective deities may have been, their overwhelming presence reinforces the central idea that true love or true rhetoric involves exercising influence on the complex 'whole' (270Cf) which makes up human nature and which includes especially a divine part.[10] The 'gods' whom the true rhetorician should address, then, are a great deal more than unctuous symbols for, say, fidelity to truth. For one thing, although Plato treats true rhetoric as a tool which can be effective also in ordinary politics, its *divine* audience reflects his continuing recognition that the philosopher is inept when measured by the human standards of popular rhetoric. Socrates in the *Apology* (41A) had hoped that he would find better judges in Hades.[11] More important, the gods help convey the greatness of the 'whole' of human nature. We see its dimensions in literally spatial terms through the picture of the soul's activity in the cosmos. With

---

10. The 'whole' strictly is the whole soul, i.e., its rational and irrational parts: 'Do you think one can really understand the nature of soul without [knowledge of] the nature of the whole? ... The true rhetorician will demonstrate accurately the essence of the nature of that to which he applies his words — and that is soul' (270C, E). But the context favors a reference to the whole universe; Plato may have had both in mind. On the meaning of 'whole' here see L. Edelstein, Περὶ ἀέρων und die Sammlung der hippokratischen Schriften, Problemata, No. 4 (Berlin 1931), 117f; R. Joly, 'La Question Hippocratique et le Témoignage du *Phèdre,'* Revue des Etudes Grecques, LXXIV (1961), 69f; P. Vicaire, *Platon Critique Litteraire* (Paris 1960), 356f. In *Charmides* 156E the knowledge which the physician must have is knowledge of the whole *man*; in *Theaetetus* 174A the philosopher searches out 'the whole nature of the things that are.'

11. For the philosopher's ineptness cf. *Theatetus* 174Bf; *Gorgias* 486Af.

its portrayal of the celestial world and the soul's share in the gods' life the eschatological myth in Socrates' second speech reveals the full significance of his conviction that popular rhetoric does not know how important it really is to please one's audience

The paradoxical notion of a rhetoric which aims to please the gods rather than men thus takes us back to the motif of inspired words (Socrates delivers his inspired speech to Eros, 257A) as well as to the theology which sustains the theory of love (Eros is a god or god-like, 242E). The superficiality of the love represented by Lysias' speech is marked by the complete lack of any such sense of the divine. By the same token Lysias has an incomplete grasp of human nature. For him 'eros' is merely an immanent, physical impulse, and when he does consider its wider effects he cannot go beyond the world of appearances. Plato had made the same point against rhetoric in the *Gorgias*. He approaches the arts of rhetoric and love as he approaches many arts — the essential things are, first, to be aware that skills are put to uses which have far-reaching results and, second, that the results can be measured only by the measure of human nature. Because the specifically erotic *praxis* in which speaker and hearer alike engage is commonly part of the complex relationship sustained by the use of words, a true craft of words becomes of great ethical importance. In the *Phaedrus* as elsewhere Plato insists that the discovery of a truly good goal is the only way in which the power of arts can be directed to proper ends, and so true love as well as true rhetoric depend upon the discovery of right goals. In the first part of the dialogue Socrates has found a divine goal as well as a divine source of love. The lover must 'look to god' (253A), he must 'look to the youth as to a god' (251A). If he does, as he is drawn toward the youth's physical beauty his memory will be 'carried toward' (254B) the impersonal Beauty fused with *Sōphrosynē* which he saw in heaven. At the end of his speech Socrates prays that Eros turn Lysias 'toward philosophy' and that Lysias' lover (Phraedus) 'live a life directed toward Eros accompanied by philosophic conversations' (257B). We are then told in 273E that the *sōphrōn* will take care to say and do things pleasing not to men but to the gods. Lysias' speech and the 'non-love' it urges are good examples of rhetoric attuned entirely to human opinion and to spurious *sōphrosynē*. Though the principle of 'doing and saying things pleasing to the gods (rather than to human *doxa*) applies to rhetoric of any sort, it more specifically echoes Socrates' earlier speech about how true love is aware of a divine presence and works through a correct use of words. And the echo of this moral issue is reinforced by Socrates' mention in 273E of τὸν σώφρονα. We might expect a word like 'wise' or 'skillful.' But in the earlier part of the dialogue σωφροσύνη had a specifically erotic meaning, for a major theme of Socrates' speech was that the true lover exercises self-control as he persuades the young.

The gods, then, for whom the true rhetorician speaks, carry rich erotic associations from the earlier speeches. The passage at 273Df sums up the discussion of rhetoric and, at the same time, it sums up the discussion of love. The dialogue, however, is not quite over. Socrates goes on to insist upon the advantages of spoken over written words, and he makes his point by using a sustained image of 'sowing living seeds in your souls' (276Bf); such words 'must be spoken of as one's legitimate sons' (278A). The sexual imagery of the passage (cf. τόκος ἐν καλῷ in the *Symposium*) again makes explicit the erotic aspect of rhetoric.[12] The lover's search for the right kind of youth to use persuasive words on (ἀνευρίσκων ... φύσιν, 252E) is a specific case of the general principle that the true rhetorician must choose a suitable kind of soul with the help of dialectic insight (276E) and must search for the kind of speech proper to each soul (φύσει ... ἀνευρίσκων, 277C). The educational nature of the use of words (278A) and the knowledge which they must contain (276A,E) recall other familiar aspects of love. The dialogue has come full circle.

The erotic significance of rhetoric comes close to the surface in several other places. Socrates extends rhetoric to private *syllogoi* in order to bring it into connection with philosophic dialogue. In 271Df he says that after the rhetorician learns what kinds of speeches persuade what kinds of souls he must observe his knowledge in action. By recognizing the actual presence of a certain kind of soul to which a certain kind of speech must be offered if one wants to bring about persuasion, he develops the ability to follow such things in action (ἐν ταῖς πράξεσιν ὄντα τε καὶ πραττόμενα) with sharp perception (ὀξέως τῇ αἰσθήσει) and to perceive clearly (διαισθ ανόμενος) what sort of person he has in front of him (παραγιγνόμενον). Socrates has in mind the general rule that rhetoric requires knowledge, innate ability and practice (269D).[13] The last two prerequisites

---

12. The comparison of education to planting is again a sophistic commonplace: W. Jaeger, *Paideia,* trans. G. Highet (New York 1943), I, 309f.
13. Cf. Isocrates, *Against the Sophists* 17f; *Protagoras* B3, 10 (Diels).

mean essentially the same thing for true and for conventional rhetoric; the first is a peculiarly philosophic requirement. In these terms 'sharp perception' of actual situations would be a part of practice: one must be sure that what is learned from books or teachers does not remain mere theory. The rule of practical training has a very general application; intelligent sensitivity to the particular nature and moods of people is, for example, highly useful in political situations. Socrates often states the principles of true rhetoric in such a way as to show their applicability to areas in which conventional rhetoric functions. True rhetoric, however, is most applicable to that kind of communication from which knowledge springs, i.e., from the intimate dialogue which often includes an erotic dimension of persuasion. This is touched upon when the audience which the rhetorician must 'perceive sharply' is said to be one person ($παραγιγνόμενον$). Feeling for character, a perceptive response to a whole situation through knowledge of the whole human nature which is present are precisely what Socrates displays in his tete-a-tete with Phaedrus (243E):

> Now where is the boy to whom I was speaking? I want him to hear this too so that he does not out of ignorance first go and give his favors to the non-lover.
> He is here always very close beside you (πάρεστιν)

In the same way the knowledge of souls which the rhetorician is supposed to employ has special erotic use. Like all true rhetoric Socrates' speech is based upon the rhetorical principle of abstract, neuter Beauty and the soul's relation to it. However important the manner of speaking may be, however fascinating erotic overtones of *syllogoi* may be, the impersonal truth lying behind the manner is of greater importance. At the end of his speech Socrates remarks that he was *forced* to use a poetic style for Phaedrus' sake. He might have used another style in a different situation for a different audience; the philosophic direction would have been substantially the same. But the speech is also about personal, physical beauty and it works most persuasively upon a παῖς καλός [14] By framing his speech with

---

14. For the interplay of neuter and masculine beauty cf. the ambivalent gender of καλοῦ in 252A; this phrase is surrounded by two phrases which point to its ambivalence: τὸν ἔχοντα τὸ κάλλος (251E) and τὸν τὸ κάλλος ἔχοντα (252A). 'It is fated that evil never be friend of the evil (κακὸν κακῷ φίλον) and that good always be friend of the good' (οὐδ' ἀγαθὸν μὴ φίλον ἀγαθῷ, 255B).

erotic vocatives (ὦ καί καλέ, 243E, 252B, 256E; cf. καλλίπαιδα, 261A), Socrates keeps in view the level of direct personal dialogue and thereby makes true rhetoric an erotically persuasive *act* in which true knowledge of the soul works through an 'art of love' in many respects quite conventional. That is what the speech envisages too in its portrayal of love as a physical and emotional as well as intellectual relationship.

The interplay of words, love and gods is touched on also in the pleasant little story of the locusts and Muses (259Bf). Socrates returns here for a moment to the free play of fantasy in his speech. He starts from the tradition that the Muses have a special relationship to the poet, that they are his tutelary deities (*Odyssey* VIII. 63,481; *Theogony* 94). He imagines that the locusts in the branches of the tree under which he and Phaedrus are sitting report to Terpsichore the names of those interested in the dance, to Erato the names of those interested in love. Their reports, he says, help 'increase friendship' between men and the Muses whom the men 'honor." Calliope, eldest of the Muses, and Urania make the most beautiful music because they are concerned with 'heaven and with words (*logoi*) human and divine.' To them the locusts report the activity of men interested in philosophy, i.e., men who 'honor' *their* art.

When attention is focused upon the forms in which poetic inspiration issues (e.g., *Ion* 536A), the various Muses are symbols of literary *genres*. Plato has this tradition in mind when he *distinguishes* Erato from Calliope-Urania,[15] and he uses it to make a point much like that made by Socrates' claim that he was 'forced' to use a poetic style: philosophy (Calliope-Urania) is inspired by and concerned with far more than erotic experience (Erato), just as its style is not necessarily poetic. The distinction between Calliope-Urania and Erato parallels the distinction in the *Symposium* between Uranian and Pandemian Aphrodite, though Plato does not stress the gross side of what Erato represents because he is in the *Phaedrus* intent on fusing conventional love with philosophy. Such fusion is helped by the fact that the distinction among various Muses tends to disappear

---

Taken as masculines the adjectives say something about human relationships, as neuters they state a general principle which guides relationships. Cf. I. M. Crombie, *An Examination of Plato's Doctrines* (London 1962), I, 184.

15. Cf. Hesiod, *Theogony* 77f for Calliope, Urania and Erato; Calliope is 'chief of the Muses.'

when a poet writes about love or a lover turns to poetry. Then poetic inspiration coincides with erotic inspiration.[16] Though poetry deals with a wide variety of subjects, its special affinity to love is most obvious in the case of the poetic lover. Love 'makes everyone a poet' *Symposium* (196E). Sappho and Anacreaon, who are vaguely associated with Socrates' inspiration, are examples of the lover-poet. Socrates is himself an example of the more common poetic lover. His speech is a nymph-inspired hymn to Eros; erotic and poetic emotion shade into each other throughout. In light of this the later *distinction* between Erato and Calliope-Urania is also an aspect of the larger *interplay* between eros and rhetoric which is the theme of the dialogue. That interplay is touched on when Socrates says that Calliope-Urania preside over 'heaven and words human and divine.' The imagery takes on special force from his contention in the second speech that Eros and other divine patrons can help guide the soul through earthly love and human logoi to its celestial destiny. The

---

16. So in the *Symposium* 'Uranian' Aphrodite suggests the Muse Urania. In commenting on the linking of μουσικός and ἐρωτικός in *Phaedrus* 248D Hermeias (98.8, Couvreur) remarks upon the 'interweaving of various forms of *enthousiasmos.*' Hesiod's description of the Muses (*Theogony* 1f) makes clear that different forms of beauty — physical and poetic — are components of the creative vitality embodied in the Muses, whose connection with groves and springs brings them close to the nymphs. The Muses not only sing and inspire song; 'they dance on soft feet around the blue spring and the altar of the great son of Cronus, and when they have washed their tender bodies ... they make their lovely, beguiling dances.' A lyric fragment pictures girls dancing around an altar in much the same way: 'Cretan girls dancing with tender feet around a lovely altar and pressing the soft, smooth flowers of the grass' (E. Lobel and D. Page, *Poetarum Lesbiorum Fragmenta,* Oxford 1955, 294). Cf. Sappho's 'Come hither, soft Graces and lovely-tressed Muses' (Lobel and Page, 92). For the connection of Muses and Nymphs see F. Krafft, *Vergleichende Untersuchungen zu Homer und Hesiod* (Göttingen 1963), 145. The cult of the Muses at times involved prostitution: J. S. Morrison, 'Pythagoras of Samos,' *Classical Quarterly,* L (1956), 145. On their simplest level, responses to physical and poetic beauty come close together. On the physical basis of poetry's effect see E. Havelock, *Preface to Plato* (Oxford 1963), 145f; M. Lasky, *Ecstasy* (Bloomington 1961), 77t, 197f; E. Kris, *Psychoanalytic Explorations in Art* (New York 1952), 300f; A. B. Lord, 'Homer and Other Epic Poetry,' in *A Companion to Homer,* ed. A. Wace, F. Stubbings (London 1963), 179f; below, notes 19, 31. In *Symposium* 196f Agathon plays sophistically with the idea of a basic *poesis* embracing many different creative impulses as well as the erotically creative impulse which he regards as primary.

idea that human activities are under appropriate Muses recalls his contention that different kinds of lovers are under various gods (252f; Calliope-Urania would correspond to Zeus). The word play on καλλίπαις (261A) a few pages later has a similar point. Phaedrus is both 'καλὸς παῖς' and 'father of beautiful words' (cf. Calliope, 'Beautiful-voice'). The former touches on the earthly, erotic occasion for words, the latter on their philosophic dimension.[17] At the same time the bond of friendship between gods and men established by the 'honor' which philosophers show to their Muse answers to the rhetorical principle of saying and doing things pleasing to the gods. And this, as we have seen, is itself relevant to love; in true love the bonds of friendship are drawn tight as the man 'honors' (252E) his youth 'as though he were a god.' The influence exerted by a true rhetorician is often erotic, and awareness of a divine presence is useful in helping to guarantee the sanctity of the relationship. By placing the craft of words directly under the Muses' locust 'spies', Socrates clothes his serious moral warning in a charming fancy.[18] In his treatment of the delicate problem posed by pederasty Plato typically uses a free play of imagination about love as a vehicle for insistence upon self-control.

17. Phaedrus is again 'father of the speeches' in the *Symposium* (177D); cf. the words which are 'legitimate sons' (*Phaedrus* 278A). Calliope embodies eloquence and beauty, Urania embodies astronomy: Van Camp and P. Canart, *Le Sens du Mot θεῖος chez Platon* (Louvain 1956), 121. Cf. Plutarch, *Eroticus* 758C on Eros, the Muses, Aphrodite and the Graces. On the universal power of Urania: *La Notion du Divin,* Entretiens sur l'Antiquite Classique, I (Vandoeuvres-Geneve 1954), 121. The archetypal contrast of up (superior, divine) and down (inferior, human), which is fundamental to the kind of stellar theology that appears in Platonic myth, goes back to old religious attitudes and is a common image in poetry; the poet has power to exalt himself and others above the destructive flow of time and above vulgar values into an eternal sphere of fame (e.g., Horace, *Odes* I.1, sublimi feriam sidera vertice). For a transposition of this into philosophic inspiration cf. Lucretius, *De Rerum Natura* I.72f: Ergo vivida vis animi pervicit et extra/ Processit longe flammantia moenia mundi/ Atque omne immensum peragravit mente animoque . . . nos exaequat victoria caelo. The wing is the primary image of this in the *Phaedrus.*

18. Socrates uses what appears to be an astrological motif in his speech: lovers are arranged in classes, each under a god who embodies the characteristics of his class (252Cf). The idea is primarily part of Plato's astral theology, but it is also relevant to the conduct of eros on earth, for lovers' awareness that their love is under the sign of a god naturally makes that god into a kind of chaperon.

The interweaving of philosophy and love comes out even more clearly in the discussion of madness. Socrates again makes a point of distinguishing various kinds of madness. He separates poetic from erotic madness (265B); the former comes from the Muses, the latter from Eros. However, the verbal inspiration granted by the Muses is in many ways not really distinguishable from the inspiration granted by Eros. Socrates is seized by nymphs, and he proceeds to link erotic inspiration to philosophy, which depends upon the use of words. In fact, the source of inspiration which underlies true rhetoric goes deep enough to include even more than Eros and the Muses, for though Socrates also distinguishes the inspiration (granted by Dionysus) derived from initiation, this distinction too tends to break down in his use of erotic imagery (249C) drawn from the mysteries. All of this is another example of the free molding of the protean ideas of 'the divine' and of inspiration embodied in the daemonic figures who appear in the dialogue. In Plato's reinterpretation of *mania* not only eros but also poetic and religious inspiration are drawn into a stream which flows from one source — the vision of true being — and finds its most authentic outlet in philosophic *mania*.[19]

Because of his particular interest in philosophic logoi and in eros Plato draws special attention to his extension of rhetoric to cover that kind of logos characteristic of intimate dialogue. In response to the question whether he had ever heard that rhetoric could be used in private as well as in public gatherings Phaedrus says that he had heard only of judicial and deliberative rhetoric (261B). Several pages later (268A) he still speaks of rhetoric's great power 'at least in public gatherings.' In the second passage he may be expressing some doubt that rhetoric is *effective* in private gatherings rather than sur-

---

19. The convergence in Eros of the various kinds of inspiration mentioned by Plato in 244f and 265B (Muses, Apollo, Dionysus, Eros) is, according to Furtwängler (quoted in Pauly-Wissowa *sub* 'Eros,' 502), parallel to developments in fourth-century art: [In the fourth-century] wandte sich die Kunst den jugendlich anmutigen Gottheiten zu, zumal dem apollinisch-dionysisch-aphrodisischen Kreis. "Die neue Richtung der Kunst auf den Ausdruck des Innern, des Seelenlebens liess ein Wesen wie Eros, den Repräsentanten eines Gefühls, in den Vordergrund des künstlerischen Interesses treten; dazu kam die zunehmende Verehrung weicher Frauenliebe und Schönheit, deren Vertreter wiederum Eros war" (Furtwängler).' Cf. column 508: 'Auf Vasen ist ja Eros überaus häufig als Begleiter und Diener des Dionysos, direct als Erreger bakchischer Lust.'

prise that it can be used there,[20] but in any case Plato treats private rhetoric as something new because of the new and special uses to which he puts it. When Socrates asks (261B) whether he has heard only of the rhetorical textbooks written by Nestor and Odysseus but has not heard of Palamedes' craft, Phaedrus supposes that Nestor is Gorgias, Odysseus is Thrasymachus and Theodorus. The scholastic notes that Nestor is comparable with Gorgias in respect to old age, Thrasymachus or Theodorus with Odysseus in respect to 'forcefulness.' Nestor was also a notably wise old man, Odysseus a notably clever man, but Plato does not seem to be using them as representatives specifically of deliberative and judicial rhetoric. He is primarily interested in that aspect of rhetoric which is pertinent to the use of words on small audiences, and he goes on to throw his net wide enough to include Palamedes', i.e. Zeno's, 'anti-logical' technique of inferring contradictory propositions from the same premise. It applies, he says, not only to deliberative and judicial rhetoric but to all spoken things (261E; cf. *Sophist* 232Bf, especially E). Here, as elsewhere, Plato regards Zeno's logic as something all too easily used for eristic play.[21] It is relevant to rhetoric and to love because it provides a man with a weapon to 'prove' that his aims, however dubious they may be, are reasonable and sophisticated. Zeno is brought into the discussion partly to connect misguided persuasion and action with confused but apparently clever arguments, partly to show that even conventional rhetoric cannot do without techniques which involve a certain amount of disciplined thinking. Once this is recognized, the role that dialectic plays in true rhetoric and true love will seem less strange, Socrates himself in a way uses 'antilogic' in his successive speeches against and for Eros (263C). In this case, however, the contradiction is not merely clever. Eros and *mania* are truly ambivalent things, human diseases as well as divine visitations, and dialectic finds its way through the maze for philosophically respectable purposes.

Epideictic, the third main branch of rhetoric, in some ways comes

20. Alcidamas (*On the Sophists* 4) talks about 'those who address the people, who speak in court, and who engage in *private discussion.*' Cf. Isocrates, *Antidosis* 276; M. Pohlenz, *Aus Platos Werdezeit* (Berlin 1913), 344; Wilcox (above, note 6), 147, note 60.

21. Cf. F. Cornford, *Plato's Theory of Knowledge* (New York 1935), 169. For *antilogikon* cf. *Sophist* 225B.

closest to a rhetoric that may be used especially on small audiences. Phaedrus has just heard an example of it in the speech which Lysias delivered to a more or less private gathering at a house in Athens.[22] The speech purports to be a non-lover's appeal to a young man. Since Phaedrus is the 'youth' to whom the speech is really directed by Lysias, who is really the 'non-lover,' Plato is providing an example of how conventional rhetoric can itself be used in personal relationships.[23] Nevertheless, Phaedrus' surprise at Socrates' extension of rhetoric to private gatherings indicates that Plato is treating the use of rhetoric on a small audience as something unusual and does so because the private uses he has in mind are specifically philosophical.

By extending the scope of rhetoric in these directions during the course of the second half of the *Phaedrus,* Plato moves from an artificial rhetoric linked to writing, as much deceived as deceiving and directed especially to public uses, through the use of such rhetoric on smaller audiences, to true rhetoric. When true rhetoric is put to public uses it will be based upon knowledge and therefore highly effective. But because it is based upon knowledge, it works best on the smallest of audiences — a youth seeking education — as well as on the most important of audiences — the gods.

In a dialogue like the *Republic* politics, ontology, psychology, epistemology interlock with ethics because each reflects the pattern of the One and the Many. The world of multiplicity is in its various aspects to be interpreted in light of its relationship to the world of unity and true being. Love and rhetoric interlock in the same way and for much the same reason in the *Phaedrus*. Both are to be judged in accordance with their relationship to truth. To show their common ground Plato emphasizes the way in which rhetoric can extend into areas where it touches love; in influencing each other through words men may be at once rhetoricians and lovers. Love and rhetoric are aspects of an underlying power of persuasion, which can be used only when it reflects valid epistemology, psychology and ontology. In his second speech, which provides such a basis for true

---

22. The efforts of the sophists to persuade a young man in the *Euthydemus* (274D), of the Just and Unjust Logoi in the *Clouds* to persuade Pheidippides (934, 950), and of the non-lover to persuade the youth (*Phaedrus* 235A), are all *epideixeis*. But the distinction among the various kinds of rhetoric is not rigid and Lysias' speech can just as well be classified as deliberative.

23. Above, p. 14 and below p. 32.

rhetoric, Socrates in effect defines man as that creature which has had a vision of true being (249B,E). Phaedrus unconsciously confirms Socrates' conviction that all men have it in them to respond to truth when he somewhat extravagantly says that he virtually 'lives' for intellectual pleasures (258E). In so far as Forms in general are objects of knowledge the vision expresses itself in the rational use of words. Forms may also be grasped intuitively, and in so far as Form like Beauty is 'seen' the vision expresses itself in irrational *mania* and a 'wealth of words' (*Symposium* 209B).

Since love and rhetoric are specifically human modes of intercourse, particular importance attaches to an understanding of human nature. Gorgias had already given attention to the psychology of rhetoric and apparently had brought it into close connection with a theory of knowledge. For Plato too, rhetoric rests upon knowledge of the whole of human nature and upon comprehensive philosophic insight into the true nature of things. Truly fruitful communication with another person reflects the complex nature of man, that is, it reflects the primary fact that man possesses a rational as well as irrational soul. Plato's aim accordingly is to penetrate below both conventional rhetoric and conventional love to a deeper level of communication which more effectively deals with the whole of human nature. It is that underlying art of communication which holds the answer to the problem of coherence in the *Phaedrus*, whether it is posed as a problem of unity or as a problem of subject (is the dialogue about love or about rhetoric?).[24] True rhetoric requires in the first place appreciation of the power of words to communicate on many levels, a power which answers to the com-

---

24. For similar approaches to the unity of the *Phaedrus* cf. M. Pohlenz, (above, note 20), 354f; F. Horn, *Platonstudien* (Wien 1893), 223f, 234; L. Cooper, *Plato Phaedrus, etc.* (Oxford 1938), XXXII, 4f; J. B. Bury, 'Questions Connected with Plato's Phaedrus,' *Journal of Philology*, XV (1886), 80f; O. Regenbogen, *Kleine Schriften* (Munich 1961), 266f. P. Händel, (*Formen und Darstellungsweisen in der aristophanischen Komödie,* Heidelberg 1963, 272) sees in Socrates' contention (*Symposium* 223D) that the same man should write comedy and tragedy an effort to find a deeper level at which categories of art converge: 'Was Sokrates damit will, ist wohl dies: eine über den getrennten Gattungen der Realität stehende Dichtkunst aufweisen, die ihre Gesetze habe, ohne Rücksicht darauf, ob es um Tragödie, um Komödie gehe.' Cf. von Fritz Wehrli, 'Der erhabene und der schlichte Stil,' in *Phyllobolia für Peter von der Mühl* (Basel 1946), 15f, 21.

plexity of each whole human soul as well as to the many different kinds of souls. In the myth the class of lovers is itself divided into various subclasses according to the god each follows, and Socrates' later remarks about 'classes of soul' (271Df) include every kind of soul. The already considerable power possessed by the conventional art of rhetoric is further expanded by emphasis upon live dialogue and poetry, both of which are prominent in Socrates' true rhetoric. Rhetoric is now in a position to understand and direct a wide range of responses — intellectual and emotional. In the case of love it deals even with a physical response, since the passion for physical beauty goes hand in hand with the passion for rational Beauty articulated in discourse. To indicate how deeply into the nature of things and of man true rhetoric can cut, Plato repeatedly uses the language of religious experience in his portrayal of the effect which philosophic words can have. At this point rhetoric and love come together with special clarity, for Eros *is* a god emboyding both the powerful physical or emotional impulses that were part of education and the divine, i.e., rational energy at work in words. The elaborate psychology in Socrates' second speech is designed to reveal the complexity of human nature; the vivid portrayal of love's course is, in accordance with that psychology, designed to illustrate the complexity of the art of words properly understood.

We can now return to our examination of echoes between the two parts of the *Phaedrus* and consider the interplay of love and rhetoric in '$\pi\epsilon\iota\vartheta\text{o}\iota$' ('persuasion'). Since the middle of the fifth century 'persuasion' had been a rhetorical catchword; rhetoric was the 'craftsman of persuasion.'[25] Because of its application to politics rhetorical persuasion meant in particular influencing people in large numbers. It is at this point that all of Plato's reservations about masses of people and about what is necessary to deal with them come into play. In the *Republic* his alternative to contemporary society and the values which it dictates is a tightly knit, relatively

For the view that rhetoric is the main subject: H. Bonitz, *Platonische Studien* (Berlin 1886), 277; W. Jaeger, (above, note 12), III, 186. For the view that the *Phaedrus* is in fact badly constructed: Bonitz, 290; H. Raeder, *Platons Philosophische Entwickelung* (Leipzig 1905), 267.

25. The definition is often attributed to Corax or Tisias, but see Wilcox (above, note 6, 138; cf. the note on Gorgias A28, Diels) for the possibility that Plato coined the phrase in *Gorgias* 453A.

small society controlled by an even more tightly knit group whose values are developed from within through an education which becomes progressively exclusive. Looked at politically, this is the group which should rule society and whose public rhetoric would be controlled by knowledge. Looked at philosophically, the same group is the community of philosophers whose private rhetoric is aimed at mutual persuasion in the search for truth.

In the *Republic* Plato makes the highly rhetorical suggestion that philosophers should persuade those whom they rule to believe such falsehood as may be convenient. After provocative allusions to the idea of deliberate deception (382D, 389B) Socrates finally explains what such a useful lie might be (414Bf): the citizens are to be persuaded about the truth of an old Phoenician tale which says that they are earth-born. In this case 'persuasion' has little to do with rhetoric; since Socrates wants to persuade the rulers too, the story would be a part of the educational system as a whole. In 389B he comes a step closer to a conventionally rhetorical use of falsehood: the rulers will be allowed to use lies if the city benefits politically or militarily from them. The reference to military matters picks up the earlier passage (382Cf) in which Socrates had argued that a lie is permissible whence one deals with an enemy or with a friend who is insane. Such useful lies which benefit the city might well be publicized in a speech using falsehood to sustain optimism in war or to counter some undesirable domestic development (cf. *Phaedrus* 261Ef for deliberate falsehood). But Plato does not develop the idea in the *Republic,* and in the *Politicus'* (304D) passing mention of an acceptable rhetoric serving the art of enlightened politics, little is made of judicious untruth. Nor does the *Republic* develop the idea that 'persuasion' (as a complement of dialectic) plays a role in the rulers' own philosophic activity. Nevertheless, while the early stages of their education (gymnastics, μουσική) point ahead to the study of dialectic, by themselves they work especially upon the affective, irrational side of human nature. The relationship of these early stages to dialectic is in this respect parallel to dialectic is in this respect parallel to the relationship of eros or persuasion to reason. Persuasion is the handmaid of dialectic; eros is the best helper for the attainment of virtue (*Symposium* 212B). In any case, persuasion guided by knowledge, responsive to the emotional life and capable of enriching philosophic loyalties with sentimental loyalties, is something that might well be used among the rulers of an ideal state. There is initially a rough parallel between the *Republic's* concept of men naturally fit to be rulers and the *Phaedrus'* concept of the philosophic type, attached by nature to 'Zeus the leader' (246E) and naturally inclined to talk with and love its own kind. In the *Phaedrus* where Plato is concerned not so much with the relationship of philosopher or highminded lover to another kindred soul, persuasion — rhetorical and erotic — comes into its own.

'Persuasion' in an erotic sense had long been embodied in Peitho, who, like Eros, is a frequent companion of Aphrodite and represents old religious ideas about the workings of love through words.[26] Again like Eros, Peitho is both a divine person and the human capacity to exercise and experience persuasion. Although Peitho apparently enjoyed a more vigorous life in cult than did Eros, in poetry she was less prominent than Eros or Aphrodite. She represents the gentler, civilized aspects of love, and her connection with 'love-talk' made the transition to non-erotic, rhetorical persuasion in the fifth century more easy.[27] Rhetorical persuasion was a human skill to be manipulated rather than a divine being to be seriously invoked. It is this attitude that Plato combats in the *Phaedrus,* not by treating Peitho as a deity but by emphasizing the divinity of Eros who is to a large extent simply another embodiment of Peitho's seductive power.

Since persuasion epitomizes both love and rhetoric in this way, it effectively mirrors the unity of the dialogue. Plato had already shown in the *Symposium* that pederasty has both a physical and an intellectual side and that its proper or improper handling depends upon which side dominates. To the division of eros in the *Sym-*

---

26. Pauly-Wissowa *sub* 'Peitho'; Krafft (above, note 16), 102f. For *peithein* = 'seduce' see, e.g., *Laws* 836D. 'Euryalus, son of the sweet Graces ... darling of the fair-tressed [Horae?], Aphrodite and the tender-eyed Peitho nourished you amid the roses' (Ibycus fg. 7,D. Page, *Poetae Melici Graeci,* Oxford 1962). In origin Peitho was a goddess of love and marriage closely related to Eros, Pothos, Himeros, the Horae and Graces. For her connection with Aphrodite Pandemus see Pausanias I.22.3. Pausanias also mentions statues of Aphrodite, Peitho and Paregoros together (I.43.6). Paregoros is the goddess who helps a man persuade a woman. Fc. D. Grene, *Man in His Pride* (Chicago 1950), 142. In a commentary on an Orphic theogony dated to about 350 B.C. Peitho appears with Aphrodite, Harmonia and Zeus: Gnomon XXXV (1963), 222f.

27. Peitho is *opposed* to eros when eros degenerates into sheer force (βία). Cf. Gorgias, *Helen* (6ff) on persuasion, necessity and force; *Philebus* 58Af.

posium into philosophic and vulgar he adds in the *Phaedrus* the division of persuasion into public and private. But what he emphasizes is not the difference between spheres of persuasion so much as the psychological processes which underlie the persuasive power of words.

The extreme language which he often uses to portray the effect of philosophic discussion reveals the powerful forces aroused by 'persuasion.' Since the response to physical attractiveness was the primary cause of eros, the erotically colored excitement aroused by Socrates had a great deal to do with what he said. The standing connection between pederasty and *paideia* is here given a special turn which provides the starting point for reinterpretation of both. In a society sensitive to masculine beauty Socrates' power over young men was a new and strange eros which could be an eminently suitable starting point for a relationship in which grossly erotic persuasion is subordinated to the non-erotic persuasion which philosophy takes over from rhetoric and redirects to higher ends. Socrates has such a persuasive power of words in mind when he says that the lover's words 'strike' (ἐκπλήττει, 255B) the youth who hears them.[28]

The *Phaedrus* opens with some elaborate play on the theme of the 'striking' power of words. Socrates confesses to a sick passion for hearing logoi and supposes that Phaedrus will be pleased to recite Lysias' speech to him because he can then have Socrates as a 'fellow Coryband' (228Bf). It appears from the subsequent discussion that Phaedrus' Corybantic frenzy is for the most part merely a matter of delight at Lysias' technical cleverness. What is more objectionable, Lysias has exercised a persuasive influence over him on an ethical level too, and here erotic as well as rhetorical persuasion comes into the picture. In view of the subject of the speech and the nature of contemporary *paideia*, it appears that Lysias himself is speaking through the non-lover. In such a context Phaedrus' own intense excitement shades into an erotic response, however diffuse it may be. The insidious thing about persuasive rhetoric of this sort is that it distracts attention from the ethical content of the words. The smooth style and show of reasonableness in Lysias' 'non-love' are aimed ultimately at *praxis*, and Phaedrus has at least been attracted if

---

28. For ἐκπλήττειν in connection with the impact of love: Xenophon, *Cyropaideia* I.IV.27, *Symposium* IV.23; *Phaedrus* 250A, *Philebus* 47A. Cf. Democritus B32 (Diels).

not persuaded. In a passage which stronly suggests that Phaedrus and the youth in Lysias' speech are the same person Socrates feels the need to warn the *pais* about granting the non-lover favors before hearing a defense of love. It is Phaedrus who hears the defense and who responds to the warning (243E). But like the Lysian persuasion to which he responds, Phaedrus is not yet capable of anything so deep and genuine that it can seriously be spoken of as a religious response. Socrates' phrase about Corybantic seizure is comic hyperbole as it applies to Phaedrus. Applied to himself it is not hyperbole; his own love of words will shortly lead to a divine seizure which is to be taken much more seriously and which also in context involves a certain measure of erotic exhilaration. 'Seizure,' 'sickness' and 'passion' are taken over from the popular psychology of love and foreshadow its connection with rhetoric.

We can see the Corybantic effect with Socrates' own persuasion has on others in the *Symposium* (215Df). Alcibiades' speech displays Plato's interest in the psychological effect of logoi and highlights the verbal as well as the erotic side of persuasion:

> Whenever someone hears you or hears someone else repeating your words, even if the speaker is not very good — whether the hearer is a woman or man or boy — we are struck (ἐκπεπληγμένοι) and possessed (κατεχόμεθα). At any rate, gentlemen, if I wouldn't seem simply to be drunk, I would have told you under oath what sort of things I have myself suffered and still now suffer through his words. For whenever I hear his words, I experience a leaping of my heart and a flow of tears more intensely than those in a Corybantic seizure, and I see very many others experiencing the same things. When I heard Pericles and other good orators, I always thought that they spoke well but never experienced such a thing. My soul was never disturbed nor was it distressed at being in a slave-like condition, but I have often been made to feel by this Marsyas that my present way of life was not liveable . . . Of all mortals he alone can make me feel what one would think I could never feel: shame . . . Often I would gladly see him dead, and yet if that happened I know I would be much more distressed, so that I don't know what to make of the man. Both I and many others have experienced such things through the piping of this satyr, Hear from me how like he is to the Sileni with which I compare him and how wonderful a power he has. For you must understand that none of you really knows him . . . You see that Socrates is erotically disposed to handsome young men and is always about them and is struck (ἐκπέπληκται) by them. At the same time he is ignorant of everything and knows nothing. He is really much like the Sileni. For he has thrown his manner around himself just like a carved Silenus, nut inside when he is opening he is brimming with σωφροσύνη, fellow drinkers . . . I do not know whether anyone else has seen the images within, which appear when he is

opened and becomes serious. But I once saw them and they seemed to be so divine, golden, beautiful and wonderful that I had to do at once what he said. Supposing that he was eager for my beauty, I thought it to be a bit of wonderful luck that I could hear everything he knew by offering him my favors. For I had a very high estimate of my beauty. With this in mind I sent away the companion who had always been with me in his presence and I was repeatedly with him alone ... and I thought that he would immediately talk to me about those things that a lover usually talks about when he is alone with his youth. But nothing like this ever happened. He would spend the day with me talking as usual and then go off.

When Alcibiades specifically compares the effect of conventional rhetoric with the effect of Socrates' conversation, he is touching upon the complex power of words which is the theme of the *Phaedrus*. Meno also remarks on Socrates' power to 'bewitch' (*Meno* 80A), and in the *Phaedrus* Socrates for his part concedes the power of a conventional rhetorician like Thrasymachus to rouse emotions and then to soothe them with incantations (267Cf, cf. *Protagoras* 328D). None of this, of course, need have anything to do with love. Socrates' words arouse a general feeling of inner dissatisfaction, and they have that effect upon practically everyone, though there is some drunken exaggeration in Alcibiades' assertion that anyone — including women — who hears his words even at second hand will fall under his spell. Alcibiades is speaking in the first instance of the same sort of experience that Socrates speaks of in the *Apology* when he mentions the stinging, gad-fly effect of his words upon Athens. Even the confession that sometimes he wishes Socrates to be dead, but then realizes that he would be still more distressed if he were, may be intended to suggest a general attitude.[29] But the remark, like the Silenus imagery, also has a peculiar morbid intensity about it which indicates that Alcibiades is revealing something intimate. His claim that he understands Socrates as no one else does and the frank portrayal of his attempted seduction of Socrates point in the same direction. Rhetoric and eros go hand in hand. The expectation that Socrates would 'talk about (διαλέξεσθαι) those things that a lover usually talks about when he is alone with his youth recalls Lysias' remark about the suspicions aroused by a lover and a youth talking together (διαλεγόμενοι, 232A). The conversation which Socrates as usual actually did engage in is, then, an example of the true rhetoric

29. The idea reappears in the tradition about Athens' regret at its execution of Socrates: Diogenes Laertius II.43.

envisaged in the *Phaedrus*. Although in the *Symposium* Plato is concerned to emphasize the self-control necessary in such situations, Alcibiades' feelings make it clear how large a part eros can have in dialogue. And Socrates too is often 'erotically disposed' to those with whom he speaks (cf. *Protagoras* 309Af); that is a natural part of his 'passion for words' and is clear enough from his willingness to be in such a situation. His erotici disposition is touched on again when Alcibiades compares him with Sileni.

What Alcibiades alone has come to understand is that self-control can hold itself in 'ironic' balance with eros even in the most intimate situations. And it does so through Socrates' 'usual talk.' The two sides of Socrates' logoi are caught in Alcibiades' imagery: in coming to know the Silenus-like Socrates intimately, one discovers within him also 'divine images' and 'σωφροσύνη.' So again in the *Phaedrus* the lover's physical passion is balanced by intellectual discovery of things within as he is 'carried away to the divine [image of] Beauty on a pedestal with Σωφροσύνη' (254B) which he once had seen in heaven. Alcibiades is thus responding to philosophic words on an erotic (*Symposium* 222C) as well as a religious and intellectual level — the same levels of experience which come together in the *Phaedrus*. Rhetoric can be more than a technique that works only upon the surface of human nature, when it comes to appreciate the full potential of words to reach into and release the store of forgotten knowledge. And since the release of knowledge often goes hand in hand with a release of strong erotic feeling, if not of the desire to 'know' physically, the art of words and philosophy are profoundly relevant to each other.

In Lysias' speech πειθώ is mere 'seduction.' It is aimed for the most part at physical love and has nothing of the aura surrounding Eros. The speaker was 'soliciting' (αἰτῶν)[30] the youth and attempting to 'seduce' (ἔπειθεν, 237B; cf. 233A, B; *Symposium* 182B) him. When Socrates says in his second speech that lovers 'persuade their παιδικά (253B) to follow a divine pattern, persuasion appears in a different light. The divine patterns which youths must be persuaded to follow are high ambitions for the best, stimulated by love. In the case of the philosophic type the pattern is a life of

---

30. Αἰτεῖν: Menander, *Dyscolos* 752; Athenaeus 553E. Προσαιτεῖν ('beg') is used in an erotic context in Xenophon, *Symposium* VIII.23; the image of 'Eros the beggar' in Plato's *Symposium* (203Bf) may play on this usage.

reason, for the philosopher 'persuades' in accordance with the highest of patterns — that of Zeus himself. But the presence of divine patterns which determine persuasion does not exclude all of the erotic overtones of 'persuasion.' As we have seen, the gods are not simply symbols of rational activity; they also suggest several erotic motifs — Eros the god or god-like power, the lover's 'holy' service to the παῖς καλός as to a god. Plato uses the idea of divine patterns to explain *all* kinds of love excepting only the most gross, and in the case of lovers who follow gods other than Zeus 'persuasion' retains much of its regular meaning in such situations. Hence in so far as following a divine pattern is tied to the behavior of lovers, also in the case of philosophic love *'persuading* a youth' to follow a divine pattern retains erotic overtones.

In the second part of the dialogue rhetorical persuasion naturally comes to the fore. However, since the theory of true rhetoric grows out of the psychology which Socrates has elaborated for his theory of love, 'persuasion' often can have an erotic application as well. Imagine two men, says Socrates, neither of whom knows what a horse is. It would be merely funny if one of them were actually talking about an ass as he tries to persuade the other to use a horse for warfare. But it is a serious matter when a rhetorician, not knowing good or evil and paying attention only to popular opinion, takes a city that is similarly ignorant and persuades it to do evil instead of good. From such a 'sowing' rhetoric can reap only evil fruit (260Bf). The reference to a city which the rhetorician might try to persuade makes clear that Socrates is thinking of political persuasion, but the entire discussion also runs parallel to things which he has said about love. The erotic counterpart to ignorant political persuasion attuned to public opinion is Lysias' vulgar love which persuades to evil instead of good *praxis,* because it is preoccupied with reputation. The counterpart to political 'sowing' is the seed capable of bearing good fruit sown by the philosopher in individual souls (276E). Having made the point that knowledge is a prerequisite for proper persuasion, Socrates freely admits that a man who knows the truth will not necessarily be able to persuade someone else about it (260Df). This establishes the usefulness of persuasion and helps motivate the detailed discussion of conventional rhetorical techniques that follows. Rhetoric's claim to be a craft of persuasion, Socrates thinks, may be supported by the discussion they are about to hold, but there are other arguments which contend that rhetoric is a mere 'knack' and not a craft. In any case, he calls upon the discussion to 'persuade' Phaedrus, the καλλίπαις, to philosophize (260Ef). Καλλίπαις echoes the 'καλὸς παῖς' vocatives addressed to Phaedrus in the course of Socrates' second speech and reminds us in passing that the true art of persuasion may have an erotic side.

Phaedrus admires and Socrates concedes the great power of rhetoric (268A). In light of the foregoing theory of love his concession is not simply a grudging tribute to conventional rhetoric, for we have come to see how rhetoric can play a part in developing the soul's philosophic power. Exactly how it can be integrated into philosophy is shown by Socrates' second speech, which he hopes is 'perhaps not entirely unpersuasive' (265B), and again the dramatic situation in which the speech has been delivered gives an erotic color to the phrase. With knowledge of the soul's nature one can 'apply lawful *logoi* and lawful acitivities' to the soul; one can 'pass on the persuasion and virtue which one wants' (270B). Such knowledge enables a man to fit his *logos* to the type of soul he is dealing with and to say which soul will 'necessarily be persuaded,' which will not (271B). 'Necessary persuasion' has a slightly paradoxical ring, and Plato may be playing upon the commonplace antithesis between necessity and persuasion, an antithesis which often appears in connection which eros. With its insight into human nature true rhetoric does provide a man with a means of working his good will most effectively, if not irresistibly, and yet doing so in a most persuasive way. In 270B the erotic dimension of persuasion is very close to the surface, for socrates is speaking of persuasion exercised more in an intimate relationship than in public.

The dialogue, then, is held together by the movement of Plato's thought toward progressively greater insight into what is really involved in persuasion. We begin from the familiar persuasion exercised on the soul by love and rhetoric. We go on to the nature of soul itself and of the logos which truly answers to its complexity. At this stage to convey the wide scope of persuasion Plato allows religious, poetic and erotic *mania* to run together. Rhetoric is a magic 'conjuring' with souls (ψυχαγωία. 261A). At last we are brought to see everything in the perspective of the soul's cosmic and metaphysical life, where *mania* in all its forms is transmuted into rational activity. The power of the logos is no peculiarly philosophic discovery. It is one of the more prominent features of Greek culture, and the *Phaedrus* gives every indication, especially in its strange dramatic setting and vivid evocation of erotic *mania*, that Plato is quite aware of how old, deep and complex is the power he is dealing with.[31]

31. 'The logos is a great master who with the smallest and most insignificant means produces the most divine results' (Gorgias, *Helen* 8). Cf. C. P. Segal, 'Gorgias and the Psychology of the Logos,' *Harvard Studies in Classical Philology*, LXVI (1962), 99f, 116f. Gorgias later compares the persuasive effect of the word to the effect of medicine (14) and emphasizes the *interplay* of body and mind, of reason and enchantment which also underlies Plato's use of poetry, rhetoric and love (which is also a 'master,' e.g., *Phaedrus* 265C). On the magic power of words: Segal, note 73; Wilcox (above, note 6), 142; G. Morrow, 'Plato's Conception of Persuasion,' *Philosophical Review*, LXII (1953), 238. For the connection of magic words and medicine see Segal, notes 40, 41.

THE NON-LOVER IN PLATO'S *PHAEDRUS**

by Stanley Rosen**

1

In this paper, I offer an interpretation of the most neglected portion of the *Phaedrus*: the beginning. My immediate purpose is to cast light upon the philosophical function of that much and unjustly maligned character, the non-lover. In a secondary sense, my paper is intended as evidence of a thesis on how to read a Platonic dialogue. Since I have defended this thesis at length elsewhere, I shall restrict myself in the present context to a detailed application of the method I favor, rather than engage in polemical justifications of that method. Only one preliminary comment: the method is simplicity itself; it amounts to the careful and reflective consideration of every aspect of the dialogue under study. As is especially appropriate in the study of a dialogue devoted to the perfect writing, I assume nothing more than that Plato knew what he was doing, and that all portions of his written text are meant to convey their meaning to the careful reader. In this way Plato, rather than the interpreter, or contemporary academic fashion, becomes the standard for what is important in a Platonic dialogue; namely, everything.

The beginning of the *Phaedrus* is an invitation to return to the beginning of the *Symposium*. Phaedrus, we recall, is the "father of the logos" at Agathon's banquet; the dialectical ascent in the *Symposium* begins dramatically from the fact that he is the beloved of the physician Eryximachus. Eryximachus, himself a moderate drinker, turns the banquet from drinking to a praise of Eros, in response to Phaedrus' complaint that the god has been neglected by poets and other encomiasts. Despite the atmosphere of celebration, excitement, and hybristic self-exaltation, the *Symposium* begins in a sober

*Reprinted by permission of the author and publisher of *Man and World*, 2 (1969), 423-37.
**This paper was delivered at the Society for Ancient Greek Philosophy in Washington, D.C. in December, 1968.

mixture of medicine and utilitarianism. This note of sobriety is never absent from the banquet, even during the presence of the drunken Alcibiades, who reveals to us the sober interior of Socrates' erotic hybris. Socrates' nocturnal behavior toward the young Alcibiades is thus a reflection of the at least initial sobriety of the nocturnal guests of Agathon. The sobriety of Socrates would seem to be the "erotic" peak or fulfilment of the apparently base sobriety of Phaedrus.

This inner connection between Socrates and Phaedrus is reinforced by the dramatically later dialogue bearing Phaedrus' name. This time, however, instead of being obscured by the darkness of the night, the presence of other speakers, and the peculiar indirectness of a recollection of a recollection, Socrates and Phaedrus are isolated in the light of high noon, and presented directly to the reader without any dramatic mediation. We are not in the home of the elegant tragedian Agathon, but outside the city wall. In the *Symposium*, Socrates takes the unusual step of wearing shoes; in the *Phaedrus*, he is unshod, but is portrayed for the only time in the Platonic corpus as walking in the countryside. The sunlight, the dramatic immediacy, the isolation of Socrates and Phaedrus, the simplicity of their surroundings, all suggest a much more sober, and to that extent visible, setting for a dialogue on love than is apparent in the *Symposium*. The setting of the *Phaedrus* is in a way the inverse of the setting of the *Symposium*, but there are certain features common to both. The first is the emphasis on something unusual concerning Socrates; the second is Socrates' interest, for whatever reason, in speeches, especially in those delivered by sophists or students of sophists. This interest in speeches, of course, provides us with the initial explanation for the link between Socrates and Phaedrus. Both are more interested in talking than in doing; differently stated, both prefer the sobriety of speeches about Eros to the madness of erotic possession.

Socrates insulates himself from the dangerous erotic currents of the banquet by wearing shoes; he counters the excessive sobriety of Phaedrus by meeting him in a beautiful country location with a specially erotic mythological significance; the rape of Oreithuia. However, let us note that, even in responding to the erotic defect of Phaedrus, Socrates has recourse to speech — in this case, a myth — rather than to deed. One might almost say that, in the *Symposium*, Socrates employs corporeal protection (a bath and special clothing) whereas in the *Phaedrus*, he employs psychic protection (myth and the praise of madness). Despite the praise of madness in the *Phaedrus,* which incidentally is absent from the *Symposium* (where only Alcibiades links philosophy to mania), it is already evident that the greater sobriety of the *Phaedrus* turns upon a more radical abstraction or ascent from the body than is true of the *Symposium.* The *Phaedrus* deals with the psyche and the vision of Ideas in a purer form than the *Symposium.* The purity of this form is not contradicted but underlined by the praise of madness. The almost complete silence about divine madness in the *Symposium* is a sign of the defective nature of the discussion of Eros there portrayed. That is, the silence about madness is a kind of silence about the divine; for example, Socrates, following Diotima, calls Eros a daimon in the *Symposium,* whereas in the *Phaedrus* (242D9 ff.), he is said to be the son of Aphrodite, and a god. In the *Phaedrus,* philosophy or madness is a "divine portion" or gift; in the *Symposium,* the erotic ascent is entrusted to exclusively human supervision. As we see from the polymorphous natures of the speakers at the banquet, Eros unassisted by the divine is scarcely likely to transcend itself in philosophy. Whatever we may say about the peculiar nature of Socrates as portrayed in the *Symposium,* it is clear that this speech does nothing to convert his auditors to philosophy, and that he has failed completely in the case of the one man (among the figures in the dialogues) who interested him most: Alcibiades. Something is missing in the *Symposium.* We might call it the sobriety of madness, with greater preparation for a phrase which, in itself, seems too cryptic. Let us say simply that, by writing the *Phaedrus,* Plato tells us that the *Symposium* is a necessary but insufficient step in understanding the nature of Eros. We have to start again, and we start once more with Phaedrus.

The name "Phaedrus" designates a human being rather than something inanimate. It does not name an abstraction, like "The Republic," an event, like "The Symposium," or a human type, like "The Sophist." Furthermore, "Phaedrus" is the name of a historical person, not a mythical one like "Minos." The person is an approximate contemporary of Socrates, unlike "Parmenides," and someone to whom Socrates is clearly superior, as is not apparent in the case of "Timaeus." This superiority does not preclude regular association; Socrates may not be a friend of Phaedrus in the strict sense of the term, but he is a companion of Phaedrus, as he is not of "Protagoras." This companionship is a kind of imitation of friendship, as is not true of Socrates' relations with "Gorgias," "Meno," or "Hippias." Phaedrus is not a young boy whom Socrates meets for the first time, and whose nature he tests, like "Charmides" or "Theaetetus." He is not silent like "Philebus," not a fanatic like "Euthyphro," not an old and sober friend like "Crito," not a disciple like "Phaedo." So far we seem to be proceeding entirely by negation. Even if this were so, the results would be instructive, since a negative description, as we know from theology, is perhaps the only way to define a unique entity. But we can now be rather more positive. The connection between Socrates and Phaedrus turns upon Eros. However, Socrates does not claim to be in love with Phaedrus, as he does with "Alcibiades"; nor is it ever suggested that Phaedrus loves Socrates. The point is that Socrates and Phaedrus share a love for speeches. The love of speeches is more sober than the love of bodies; Socrates and Phaedrus are united by the sobriety of their Eros. However, Phaedrus' sobriety is base, because directed primarily to the care of his body; whereas Socrates' sobriety is noble, because directed primarily to the care of his psyche. Phaedrus and Socrates represent the two poles of erotic sobriety. The difference between them is suggested in the *Phaedrus* by their different attitudes toward myth. Phaedrus may well be an atheist; Socrates may well not be. Put less obliquely, Phaedrus represents the degenerate nature of merely human or corporeally centered sobriety, whereas Socrates' sobriety, as psychic or divine, is transformed into, or indistinguishable from, the divine madness. The peak of sobriety is at once the peak of madness; the distinguishing mark, I may add, of Plato's conception of philosophy.

The *Phaedrus* is not simply about Eros, as one might perhaps say of the *Symposium*. It is also about speeches or rhetoric, and it culminates in a discussion of writing. In the *Symposium,* speeches are delivered as a consequence of Eros; in the *Phaedrus,* we are given a discussion about the writing of speeches to Eros. Similarly, the *Symposium* culminates in cryptic reference to a conversation between the sober Socrates and the drunken poets Aristophanes and Agathon about writing. In the *Phaedrus,* the discussion culminates in a technical conversation between the sober and non-poetic Socrates and Phaedrus about writing. The greater sobriety of the *Phaedrus,* in comparison to the *Symposium,* is shown by its movement from Eros to the *techne* of writing, and thus to the mention of dialectic. The link between Eros and writing is the psyche: more specifically, the myth of the varieties of psychic madness, and primarily, of the divine or philosophical madness. Thus we see again that, implicit in the sobriety of the *Phaedrus* is madness. To this extent, at least, the dialogue would seem to be appropriately named: Socrates describes the perfect writing as a living being, and Phaedrus is a living being who loves speeches. In less playful, or more sober, terms, the ascent to the divine madness, as a necessary completion to the teaching of the *Symposium*, requires first a criticism of the teaching of the *Symposium*. And this requires another look at the principle or progenitor of the earlier discussion: Phaedrus. We require another look at sobriety before we are ready to move on to madness (and I add parenthetically that this is an excellent recipe for philosophy: two parts of sobriety to one part of madness).

Although the sober Phaedrus and Socrates both claim to be erotic about speeches, neither is a writer. Poetry and sexual generation are both associated with madness; the sobriety of the Eros of Phaedrus and Socrates has an explicitly passive inflection. Neither Phaedrus nor Socrates generates speeches of his own. Of course, both "speak," but in the crucial instances, they either speak the speeches of others, like actors (hypocrites), or else, in the case of Socrates at least, they test the speeches generated by others. However, both may be regarded as indirect generators of speech. According to Socrates, Phaedrus has inspired more speeches than anyone except Simmias. According to the Platonic dialogues, Socrates goads or stimulates men into making speeches, thanks to a process which he calls "midwifery," but which is perhaps more frankly portrayed in the *Apology* as a kind of disagreeableness or ungentlemanliness. Phaedrus is a "father" of logoi because of his beauty, whereas Socrates seems to cause others to generate speeches because of his ugliness. Phaedrus' physical beauty seems to prevent his lovers from ascending to the love of his not so beautiful psyche. Socrates' "ugly" behavior, together with the manifest ugliness of his body, seems to pose no insurmountable obstacle to the love of his unusually beautiful psyche: no obstacle, that is, for those with eyes to see. In terms of the erotic ascent described by Diotima in the *Symposium*, the transition from corporeal to psychic Eros requires a "guide." Diotima does not explain how this "guide" leads to the lover to prefer the extremely beautiful psyche of an ugly body to the not so beautiful psyche of a beautiful body.[1] A genuine understanding of the difference between love for Phaedrus and love for Socrates is not visible in the *Symposium*. Thus Alcibiades is laughable to the other guests because of his obvious if incoherent erotic attraction toward Socrates. Love of Socrates ceases to be laughable when we understand the divine portion or fate by which madness is transformed into sobriety, and sobriety into madness, or by which the beautiful becomes ugly and the ugly beautiful.

Let me approach this point in a slightly different way. Phaedrus espouses the cause of the non-lover, both in the *Symposium* and in the dialogue bearing his name. Socrates, although he defends the lover in the *Phaedrus,* does so by developing a myth of the psyche, attributed to the poet Stesichorus, the highest function of which consists in guiding us to the essentially passive enterprise of looking at the Ideas. In the *Symposium,* Socrates presents himself as a student of the prophetess Diotima, that is, as a young man who is defective in his erotic understanding, and who is taught that the peak of erotic activity is, again, a kind of passive looking. Prophetess and poet agree that the highest erotic man is, if not non-erotic, a divine voyeur. What does this mean so far as the three main themes of the *Phaedrus* are concerned? Eros is first criticized and then praised by two passive or "sterile" erotics, who nevertheless paradoxically stimulate others to generate; this praise, having been prepared by criticism, culminates in a speech about the psyche, according to which human perfection, paradoxically called a species of divine madness, is identified as the passive-erotic vision of non-erotic Ideas. And discussion of the themes introduced in the first two parts of the dialogue leads to the technical discussion of the *techne* of writing: a technical discussion between two amateurs or non-practioners of the art in question.

One might well be tempted to conclude that the *Phaedrus* is a comedy, on the basis of the observations just made. If so, however, we must append that it is a "divine comedy," and hence not lacking in tragic overtones. The praise of passivity is inseparable from the Platonic conception of human perfection as a transcendence of the corporeal Eros; the sobriety of the non-lover has therefore something essential in common with the madness of the philosopher. The steri-

1. Cf. my *Plato's Symposium* (New Haven: 1968), pp. 265 ff. and *Symposium* 210A4ff.

lity of the passive erotic is similar to the anti-poetic vision of the eternal Ideas; even further, the attenuation or cessation of the corporeal Eros, although accompanied by a flowering of the psychic Eros, leads, precisely if the latter is successful, to the suppression of one's human individuality. Wisdom as the fulfillment of philosophy, at least if wisdom is perfect vision of perfection, amounts to the transformation of man into a god – or rather, into a noetic Idea. Only in this case, one may suggest, would the meaning of the otherwise mysterious saying of Parmenides becomes perspicuous: τὸ γὰρ αὐτὸ νοεῖν ἐστιν τε καὶ εἶναι.

II

Socrates encounters Phaedrus on the way from Lysias, son of Cephalus, who was Socrates' host in the *Republic*. Phaedrus is walking in the country for reasons of health, in accord with the advice of Acumenus, the physician, and father of Eryximachus. He no doubt needs the exercise in order to recuperate from what Socrates calls the "banquet" of speeches offered by Lysias (227A1-B7). Phaedrus allows medicine to tend his body and rhetoric to tend his psyche. The defect of rhetoric as psychic medicine is suggested by the fact that it kacks moderation; as a consequence, the lover of rhetoric seems actually to be ruled by the corporeal physician. In any case, Phaedrus has no trouble in interesting Socrates in the topic discussed at this new banquet: lysias has written that a beautiful youth "ought to gratify the non-lover rather than the lover" (227B8-C8).[2] Phaedrus refers to Lysias' speech as "refined"; Socrates points out that, with some expansion, its elegance would be properly called "useful to the demos," with whom he ironically associates himself (227C7-D2). Let us bear in mind the conjunction of the non-lover, the demos, and utility. Meanwhile, we observe that Phaedrus regards Lysias as the most talented writer of the day, and would rather be able to memorize his speeches than come into a fortune (228A-4). Phaedrus imitates the philosopher in valuing speeches and memory beyond money; unlike the philosopher, he admires "democratic" rather than "aristocratic" speeches. Pre-

---

2. Socrates quotes Pindar, *Isthmian* I, lines 1-2, in such a way as to compare Phaedrus to my mother Thebes." Pindar places the glory of his polis beyond everything else. For Socrates, the love of speeches transcends the polis; this is related to the location of the dialogue outside the city-wall.

sumably he believes that rhetoric is more useful than money, although in view of his tastes, this may be an error on his part. The most charitable, as well as the most cautious, interpretation is probably that Phaedrus loves speeches or rhetoric for selfish reasons, but transcends his selfishness by virtue of his love for speeches. And this love is passive or imitates the non-lover whose praise he admires: Phaedrus wishes that he could memorize Lysias' speeches, not that he could write his own.

Socrates has a "disease for listening to speeches" (228B6) which, he implies, can be ameliorated by Phaedrus. Phaedrus' "medicine" will be shared by doctor and patient alike; the repetition of Lysias' speech will induce a mutual corybantic enthusiasm that replaces the atmosphere of intoxication in the *Symposium* (228B7). To anticipate Socrates' remark upon the conclusion of the speech, Phaedrus is transformed by rhetoric into a Dionysian reveler, an appropriately feminine condition in which Socrates claims to share (234D1-6). How different this is from Phaedrus' characteristic passivity, we may easily infer from his conversation with Socrates about the myth of Boreas and Oreithuia. Phaedrus is vague on the geographical details, and obviously does not believe in the truth of the story.[3] As Socrates implies, Phaedrus interprets myths in terms of physics, like Anaxagoras and Metrodorus. Socrates finds this kind of demythologizing "charming" — that is, it indeed charms men away from the more important task of understanding themselves, and hence amounts to a "kind of boorish wisdom" (229C6-230A6). Socrates must devote his time to investigating his own puzzling nature, which he compares to mythical beasts. It is not clear to him whether he is more complex and puffed up that Typhon, or whether he has a more divine and less vain nature; as we might say, Socrates has not yet understood the nature of his own hybris. He does not therefore deny the possibility of giving physical interpretation to myths, but rather its utility. A proper study of the prodigious nature of man requires acquiesence in conventional religious views (230A1 ff.). Despite the Bacchic susceptibilities, Phaedrus does not share this respect for nomos. His enthusiasm for rhetoric is selfish rather than political; Socrates indicates that this selfishness leads to self-neglect and ignorance. There is a sobriety in Socrates' madness, but a "madness" in Phaedrus'

---

3. 220C4: I take his oath to show exasperation with those who believe such tales; this is certainly how Socrates responds to Phaedrus' question.

sobriety. Although Phaedrus is accustomed to walk in the countryside, whereas Socrates is not, he is ignorant of the topography and associated myths, which Socrates knows. The countryside and trees do not wish to teach Socrates, but he has learned from men their human significance (230D3). This love of learning, interestingly enough, permits Socrates to appreciate the natural beauty of the locale in a "most unusual" manner — as though he were a stranger seeing it for the first time. Socrates suggests that this is indeed the case, and that he has been lured into the country by his hunger for speeches (230D5ff.). Whether this is true or not, Socrates is not "drugged" (230D6) by the prospect of a feast, so as to be unable to make an intense and articulate response to the environment. Phaedrus, on the contrary, is aware of almost nothing but Lysias' speech and his desire — quickly divined by the mantic Socrates (228D7) — to recite it to Socrates.

We are now approaching high noon, the hottest part of the day and in the hottest season of the year. The two companions have "turned aside" from their walk to sit down beneath a plane tree, with bare feet — normal for Socrates, unusual for Phaedrus — for wading in the stream. The location is marked by grace, purity, and clarity; as Socrates says, it is a good place for maidens to play (but not perhaps for Bacchic maidens). Light and shade, heat and coolness, reclining humans and a flowing stream, feminine nature and masculine logos: the setting takes on the character of a harmony of opposites (229A1-C3). This is especially appropriate for the demonstration of the identity between the divine forms of sobriety, and madness. Phaedrus, mad with love for Lysias' apparently non-erotic speech, has been prevented by Socrates' prophetic sobriety from testing his memory, and will read to Socrates from the copy he had concealed beneath his cloak.

III

Lysias, author of the demotic and utilitarian praise of the non-lover, is a rhetorician and *logographos,* especially famous for his courtroom speeches. He appears at the beginning of the *Republic,* in the home of his father, Cephalus. The members of this family are there portrayed as conceiving of justice in terms of utility. The ascent in the *Phaedrus* from the non-lover to the lover is parallel to the ascent in the *Republic* from a utilitarian interpretation of justice to the virtual identification of justice with moderation and its subordination to philosophy. In the *Symposium,* which emphasizes the hybristic nature of Eros, justice is not mentioned as one of his attributes. The one man who seems seriously concerned with justice is Alcibiades, whose intoxicated appearance at the banquet transforms it into a trial of Socrates for hybris, with himself as the plaintiff. Alcibiades' speech soon reveals, however, that even though he may be correct in his perception of Socrates' nature, his own complaint against Socrates is unjust and rooted in immoderateness. I suggest that the *Phaedrus* begins with Lysias' speech in order to indicate something about the defective or incomplete nature of the *Symposium.* Eros and justice, as the *Republic* makes explicit, are, if not simply incompatible, opposites which need a "third" element to bind them into harmony. The sobriety of the non-lover is more like moderation than is the madness of the lover. An immoderate criticism of the passive Eros is no more just than a praise of Eros that is silent about justice. In the *Phaedrus,* the ascent from sobriety to madness is not an "abstraction" but rather a sublation, just as, in the *Republic*, the notion of utility is not discarded but sublated into the final interpretation of justice.

In the *Symposium,* Phaedrus is the father of the logos; in the *Phaedrus*, it is Lysias who serves this purpose. The speech of Lysias both criticizes the end of the *Symposium* and returns us to the theme of the beginning. Our new start is an improvement on the beginning of the *Symposium* in two ways. First, it is the speech of a professional rhetorician or generator of discourses, and not simply of a lover of discourses. Second, the professionalism of the author renders his speech free from contradictory or obscuring effects that might arise from the enthusiasm of the speaker. Lysias' mastery of the rhetorical *techne* permits him to give a "disinterested" or just presentation of the merits of the non-lover. His speech imitates philosophy to this extent: it combines technical skill with praise for the utility of sobriety; Lysias is a sober, rather than a mad or inspired, poet. On the other hand, this latter fact represents the defective nature of Lysias' speech; it inspires Phaedrus, but for the wrong reasons, because it is not itself inspired.

Let us now turn to the main points of Lysias' speech. As is befitting its sober message, the speech begins (and indeed continues throughout; see Hackforth's outraged commentary[4]) with no rhetorical flourish; its rhetoric, one might almost say, is anti-rhetorical. The boy knows the situation, and the non-lover has already spoken of their "joint interest" (230E7): there is to be an exchange of goods, or a wholesale rather than a retail business contract. Lovers confer benefits freely only while their desire lasts; the cessation of the erotic desire thereby endangers, perhaps terminates, the advantages enjoyed by the beloved. The non-lover, on the contrary, because he acts from freedom rather than necessity, in a sober and business-like manner, which does not interfere with an efficient and technically accurate calculation of profits and losses, nor lead him to quarrel with relatives over the distribution of property, may devote his energies to the benefit of the beloved (231A1-B7). The non-lover's case rests upon a distinction between "what I need" ($\tilde{\omega}\nu\ \delta\acute{e}o\mu\alpha\iota$) and the desire ($\dot{e}\pi\iota\theta\upsilon\mu\acute{\iota}\alpha$) of Eros. Is this defensible? At least in this sense: according to the non-lover, he desires gratification, as an "objectified" commodity, independent of the personality of the boy, who is to him not a beloved but a reified unit in the free-market economy, whose wares are subject to the laws of supply and demand. The non-lover agrees in part with Marx's analysis of capitalism, but approves of the results. Objectively grounded in a technically competent selfishness is preferable for buyer and seller to the authentic, human esteem praised by Marxists and existentialists.

Like the modern exemplar of the Protestant ethic, the non-lover prides himself upon his autonomy and industrious efficiency; like the philosopher, he is a sober master of the *techne* of division and collection (i.e. of profits and losses). He acts in accordance with his own capacity, both toward himself and his family as well as toward reified youths; whereas the lover is carried beyond his capacity, with consequent injustice to all concerned, by the transcendence of madness. In sum, he combines the qualities of hedonism, utilitarianism and technicism in such a way as to abstract from such human qualities as the beautiful and ugly or the noble and the base. Like the philosopher, he disregards human individuality in his pursuit of the general or steadfast. But the manner in which he does so leads to a transformation in the meaning of the true and the false; by beginning from the lowest or common denominator of animal passion, the non-lover

---

4. R. Hackforth, *Plato's Phaedrus* (Cambridge: 1852; LLA reprint).

terminates in the advanced sciences of cost-accounting, game theory, and, in an anticipatory sense, of computer-based psychology. The origin of this line of development is in the distinction between erotic and non-erotic desire; the former turns upon the personality or humaneness of the beloved, and the latter upon the common physiological structure of buyer and seller. The lover is presented as faithful, not to the beloved, but to his desire for the beloved as beloved, whereas the non-lover is uninterested in the loveableness of the boy, but is faithful exclusively to the possibilities for gratification, considered physiologically or in terms of the body in virtual disregard for the psyche — probably even for certain bodily qualities, although nothing is said on this point. The non-lover minimizes the connection between his position and desire; however, reflection shows that his more serious claim is not to eliminate desire but to make it autonomous. His own autonomy is not from desire but from the ἀνάγκη of Eros, or the trans-human, i.e. what we call the *divine*. The non-lover is a "humanist" as well as a hedonist, utilitarian and technicist. But his humanism is inseparable from, or rather identical with, a debasement of the human to the physiological. In slightly different terms, the successful application of the quasi-mathematical version of division and collection to human affairs depends upon the debasement of Eros by physiology.[5]

Eros is an illness leading to immoderateness or the inability to master oneself (231D2ff.); the combination of rhetoric and medicine represented by Lysias and Phaedrus cures the illness, or makes self-mastery possible thanks to a new and lower interpretation of the self. There are very few lovers, or at least few excellent lovers, whereas there are many candidates for the title of "extremely useful"; as Socrates initially observed, the non-lover is a democrat in addition to being a humanist, hedonist, utilitarian and technicist (231D6-E2). Since "desire" means "physiological gratification," the non-lover brings us egalitarianism or freedom from the subjectivity of value-judgments. Strictly speaking, it should even be irrelevant whether non-lovers and non-beloveds are physically beautiful, young, or in any other corporeally oriented sense (even perhaps their sex) pre-eminent. But now the defect in Lysias' exoteric or obvious teaching becomes manifest. In a democratic business society of the kind sketched by the non-lover, there is a contradiction between physio-

---

5. Cf. *Sophist* 227A7ff.

logical difference between the non-lover and the object of his "non-erotic" desire. The non-lover takes it for granted throughout his speech that the boy is not himself motivated by erotic but by financial considerations, or at least by concern for his reputation: for "keeping up appearances" (231E-232E2). Thus he regularly refers to his relationship with the boy as one of φιλία rather than ἔρως, of "gratification" rather than of "desire".[6] The pederastic relationship is regularly contrasted to the relation of friendship (cf. 231C1, 233C6 *et passim*) or said to interfere with it. But "friendship," as we know, means "advantage," and since "advantage" is essentially economic, while certainly not erotic, it would seem to be most advantageous for the youth to gratify only the wealthiest non-lovers. Even further, his best interest may lie in the sober plundering of wealthy lovers whose technical vision is blinded by the madness of erotic passion. This continues to hold true even if the youth is also motivated by the non-erotic or physiological need for gratification. Where all other factors are irrelevant, a rich "friend" must be preferable to a poor one.

It is not clear that the non-lover sees this defect in his position. For example, he observes that lovers must fear rivals possessing greater wealth or intelligence (232C4-8). Apparently the non-lover does not share these fears because he has achieved what he needs δι ἀρετήν (232D4-5); i.e. through his own efficient management of the joint advantage of himself and the boy in question – through his intelligence or *techne*. We have to realize, furthermore, that only a man of a certain degree of wealth or business acumen could profitably avail himself of the argument of the non-lover. The non-lover clearly assumes that, although others may be richer than he, he is rich enough, if others are more intelligent, he is intelligent enough. Indeed, if he loses one boy to a superior rival, there are surely many others, just as there are many non-lovers. His teaching, like many another *techne*, is a substitute for personal excellence, and its very persuasiveness is a better protection for his own interests than the advantages traditionally predicated of a lover. Nevertheless, in the last analysis, the teaching of the non-lover turns upon the difference between rich and poor; it is oligarchical rather than democratic.

What of the tacit assumption that the boy is either non-erotic or

---

6. E.g. 231E1-2, 232B4 (where φιλία is equated with ἡδονή), 232D4, 232E1, 232E6.

prefers money to the higher considerations? According to the non-lover, friendship comes from intelligence rather than from Eros, again, incidentally, an imitation of the philosophical teaching. That is: in the erotic relation, physical desire for a specific individual precedes, and is the condition for, friendship. In the case of the non-lover, who is disinterestedly interested in physical gratification, and objective toward, or disinterested in, the personal or lovable attributes of the person, friendship — i.e. a rational relationship based upon mutual advantage — precedes physical gratification (232E3-233A5). This means that the non-lover, thanks to the impersonal, and hence sober or less compelling, nature of his physical desire, can guarantee the financial advantage of the boy prior to gratification. It is the vulgarity or bestiality of the non-lover's position, and not his freedom from desire, that makes his suite more advantageous. In fact, the non-lover *is* moved by Eros, but by a very low form of Eros. The success of his argument then turns upon the possession of wealth, and the capacity to corrupt the young by employing the *techne* of rhetoric to excite greed rather than lust. The non-lover is in fact a concealed lover, however base a lover.

Before we rebel against the baseness of the non-lover, let us remember the results of the earlier stage of our investigation. It is perfectly reasonable to claim that passion interferes with friendship, as well as with the pursuit of the useful, the just, and the true. Furthermore, the non-lover praises moderation, intelligence, and a prudent concern for the future (233B6ff.). He is eager to improve the condition of his friend, to free his perception of pleasure from the pain accompanying Eros, to teach him self-mastery, and to balance justice with mercy. I have pointed out that this whole argument is, among other things, a legitimate criticism of the general teaching of the *Symposium*. This is made clear in an amusing way. The erotic man (as the *Symposium* asserts) is the most needy man. If one must gratify the most needy, then one must gratify the worst rather than the best. In philosophical language, if we love what we do not have, must not the lover of goodness be bad? Those men who strive most assiduously for perfection must themselves be worthless (233D5ff.). In other words, the erotic mania, if it is not regulated by a divine fate, or a prophetic synopsis, is extraordinarily dangerous, and more likely even in the rarest cases to produce an Alcibiades than a Socrates. We must first have what we desire, thanks to divine madness, precisely in order to desire it soberly. Thus the non-lover warns us that, to follow Diotima's advice, would mean inviting beggars rather than friends to our "private banquets" (233E1). He suggests, in effect, that this is the mistake made by Agathon; and, appropriately enough, at this point his speech sounds more like that of Pausanias (Agathon's lover) than like that of Phaedrus, or like a mixture of the speeches of Pausanias and Phaedrus. One should gratify those moderate, sober, stable, clever lovers (who are best able to show their gratitude. In exotic terms, one should gratify those on whose pensions (οὐσία) one can rely; in esoteric terms, one should gratify those who already possess the good or ουσια in the ontological sense (233E6-234C5). In sum: the baseness of Lysias' speech contains a serious teaching, or rather two serious teachings, in however ironical a form. As always in Plato, the low prefigures the high; the philosopher must learn to understand dirt and other low things if he is to understand the psyche and, finally, the cosmos. The difference between the philosopher and the gentleman leads the latter to recoil from vulgarity, whereas the philosopher has inured himself to practice his ἀκριβολογία even upon a "tedious piece of rhetoric" which, in Hackforth's words, "deserves little comment,"[7] The non-lover, then, teaches us something about human baseness, but he also has something to say about the nature of philosophy.

---

7. Hackforth, *op. cit.*, p. 31.

THE MIDDLE SPEECH OF PLATO'S *PHAEDRUS**

Malcolm Brown & James Coulter

In the present paper we offer a contribution to the solution of two problems in the interpretation of the *Phaedrus*.[1] The first is the question of how we are to "read" the middle speech. Is it, as some have suggested,[2] a generally well intentioned half-way stage on the way to Plato's own position as expressed in the Great Speech? Or should we rather conclude, as others have done,[3] that the speech is faulty in every vital respect, and that it is repudiated by Plato *in toto*? The thesis of the middle speech, that the nonlover is to be preferred to the lover, is clearly rejected. But, are there nonetheless beningly placed anticipations of the full truth to come? The second problem is the much debated one about the unity of the *Phaedrus*. We deal with this in only a general way, although we believe our interpretation of the middle speech implies a clear answer to at least one part of the problem, i.e., "is there an *inherent* connection between the two themes of the dialogue, eros and rhetoric? " The question about how to interpret the middle speech is the central one of the paper and has been treated in far greater detail.

Our main argument aims at the conclusion that in the middle

---

*Copyright 1968 by the *Journal of the History of Philosophy,* volume 6, pages 217-231, by permission of the Editor and Authors.

1. The "we" of this paper is not an editorial fiction. The two authors have written the piece in close cooperation and neither of us disclaims responsibility for any part of it or for its organization as a whole. Nonetheless it is true that Brown is principally responsible for the writing of the first half, Coulter the second.

2. E.G. Hackforth, Plato's *Phaedrus* (Cambridge, 1952), p. 40, who goes so far as to see in the middle speech "a glimpse of the *erastes par excellence,* Socrates himself." Hackforth is anticipated, at least in the general view that the middle speech is congenial to Platonism, by Hermias (*In Platonis Phaedrum Scholia,* ed. P. Couvreur [Paris, 1901], 50, 2-14).

3. The notable example of this is P. Friedländer, *Plato* III (Princeton, 1969), pp. 222-226.

speech Plato is sketching a certain type of rhetorical sophist whose philosophy (or more accurately "philodoxy") is totally unPlatonic. We go a step further when we venture to identify the mentality represented with that of Isocrates. Whether or not the stronger thesis is true, the thought of Isocrates, representing as it does at least the *type* of rhetorical sophistic culture we have in mind, can be used as a touchstone of that culture in the study of the middle speech.

I

Let us first review the speech to bring out some of its more obvious features. It is delivered by a dissembling lover, in blame of love. Before the speaker gets to the blame, he executes a definition of his subject. Moreover, he insists upon the general point that such 'theoretical preambles' ought to introduce any properly constructed speech. The definition itself is formed on a strained etymology linking the word *eros* to *rhome,* or force, and implies that love can only be of bodies and pleasure from them (238C). The speaker supports the definition with an argument about the human soul: it has two parts, and two only, namely *epithymia* and *doxa*. In the well ordered soul, *doxa* is in the lead position.

The preliminaries methodically taken care of, the speaker proceeds to the substance of the attack on love. He premises it on the assumption that love can be judged only in terms of utility, pleasure, and the trust which joins the lovers. The form of the attack is as follows: (1) when somatic love is measured against the standard of utility (subdivided into psychic, somatic and financial), it is found positively harmful, (2) it fares no better when measured against the pleasure standard, and (3) lovers are untrustworthy: they are unlikely to remain in love. The speaker's emphasis falls on love's effects on the soul and its education, especially what he calls its 'philosophical' education. The injury love does to 'divine philosophy' is cited in the first part of the attack; in the summing up at the end it is "the soul's education" that tops the list of goods jeopardized by love. Education is the holiest and most honored thing either among men or gods, either now or even, he says.

The speech as a whole occupies a middle position between those of Lysias and Plato conceptually as well as in the structure of the dialogue. There is a semblance of Plato's concern for virtue and education, and also a semblance of Plato's method of definition. It is a middle conceptually, then, because it is like Lysias' speech in its conception of love, but unlike it in method, whereas it is like Plato's in method, but unlike it in the conception of love.

Who is the speaker, or what is his mentality? Let us hypothesize, on the basis of his review of the speech, an educator whose medium is rhetoric, and whose "philosophy" is really a "philodoxy" in sheep's clothing — a fact suggested by his two-part psychology headed by *doxa*, his distorted ('demotic') conception of the virtues (as will become clear in the sequel), and a sharp eye for utility or pleasure conjoined with a blindness to Ideal Beauty. We may note a correspondingly debased conception of education, and of love. More specifically we hypothesize an educator whose technique of speech-making places him in a middle position between the merely rhetorical style of the mindless phrase-turner Lysias and the purely philosophical rhetoric of Plato. Could it be the same one to whom Socrates is to bear the message about rhetoric which Phaedrus is later instructed to bear to Lysias (cf. 278E), the educator Isocrates?

A caveat is in order. We do not mean to say that Plato aims at Isocrates as a person only, but always at least as a representative of a species of rhetorical-sophistic culture. Nonetheless it is worthwhile to distinguish a weaker and a stronger version of our thesis, and to argue them in series. The weaker says only that the doctrines and method of the middle speech characterize a mentality that fits Isocrates quite accurately, even if it may also fit others as well; thus it implies that Isocrates must be included, and included as a leading representative, in any group Plato is sketching in the middle speech. The stronger form says that, just as in the epilogue to the *Euthydemus* (306A-C, where Isocrates is almost certainly the one ridiculed),[4] so in the *Phaedrus* Plato's sketch aims at Isocrates himself. Plato's criticism conceives of Isocrates as somehow in the middle position between rhetoric and philosophy, a position in which the anonymous figure comes off worse than either extreme in trying to combine both activities into one. From the philosopher's point of view the 'bit of

---

4. Rosamond Sprague (*Euthydemus* [Library of Liberal Arts, 1965], p. 63) notes but does not concur in Bluck's skepticism about identifying the anonymous target here with Isocrates. We concur in the principle that one ought not find Isocrates (or Antisthenes) under every Platonic stone. But this does not prevent their being found under some. There are definite and further reasons, adduced by Coulter ("*Phaedrus* 279A: The Praise of Isocrates," *Greek Roman and Byzantine Studies,* 8 [1967], pp. 230-232) for discovering Isocrates in the *Euthydemus* passage, and these are not unconnected with the *Phaedrus*.

philosophy' incorporated into the speech in the middle is worse than none at all; by refusing to subordinate persuasion to truth, the middle speaker compromises his philosophy hopelessly. From the point of view of purely rhetorical effect on the other hand – a point of view Socrates expresses willingness to take as he reviews Lysias' speech (235A) – again the middle position is inferior. The charm of wordings and phrasings must not be compromised just to save the truth or to satisfy the demand for method, says the mere rhetorician.

II

We proceed to support the first of our theses on the basis of a detailed study of the speech, its method and its thought. The thesis is that the particulars of the speech fit together into a pattern congruent to the mind of Isocrates, even if not to the exclusion of all others. The speech begins with what may be called a theoretical preamble (237C-238C). Now the idea of having such a preamble, in which a definition is offered, either of the topic to be discussed or of the method, is surely a worthy idea in Plato's eyes. In *Phaedrus* itself Socrates asks if he had (in his raving) remembered to define love first (263C). Many of the other dialogues attest, albeit indirectly, to this. For want of a leading definition, discussions of rhetoric or virtue or love are seen to go astray. The speaker here in *Phaedrus* puts the point so forcefully, in fact, that Sextus Empiricus picks it up, with only a slight change, as a formula for clarifying one of Democritus' three "criteria of genuine knowledge." "Concerning everything, son," Sextus has Democritus say, "the one principal thing is to know what the inquiry is about" (*Adv. Math.* VII, 140). A recent critic has emphasized the principle of definition for a different reason. K. Ries[5] takes the speaker's rule as an expression of Plato's own fundamental requirement for rhetoric to become philosophical.

But not just any theory can be advanced in this lead position. To satisfy the full-fledged Platonic requirement, it has to be *the true theory*. Thus it is perfectly possible for someone Plato represents to be half-right in this matter: rightly seeing the need for a definition, but failing to see the right definition. Indeed there is an important example of just such a success in principle which turns into a failure in execution. Plato represents Agathon in such a "middle" position

---

5. Klaus Ries, *Isokrates und Platon im Ringen um die Philosophie* (Diss., Munich 1959), p. 114.

between mere rhetoric and ultimate philosophical truth in his speech in the *Symposium*. Not surprisingly in the case of a fellow descendant of Gorgias, many congruences in points of detail can be listed between Agathon's speech and the one we judge to be Isocratean. In the first place the topic of both is *Eros*. each speaker attends first to the matter of defining his topic.[6] Thirdly, the speaker calls attention to the special value of such preambles, and claims superiority over rival speakers on this point of method. Fourthly, the speech itself, while it exhibits much refinement of diction (including a play on *eros-rhome*), treats its subject shallowly, being restricted by the shallow theory of love which it is premised on. Fifthly, Plato treats the achievement of the speech ironically. He had Socrates praise the worthy aim of putting theory first, but then condemn the faulty execution: the theory is false. Sixthly, Plato then proceeds to exhibit the (Platonic) truth of the matter, to complete the refutation of the speech.

Now in Isocrates' own speeches one frequently finds him driving home this very point of method. He boasts at the beginning of the *Helen* that his speech will be superior to that of his rival (presumably Gorgias) in that he will define correctly the natures of *encomia* and *apologiai,* and avoid confusing the genres. He uses this requirement as a weapon of sarcasm when he makes the same point at the beginning of the *Busiris*. In the *To Nicocles* the parallel to the middle speech of *Phaedrus* is still closer:[7] Isocrates tells his young (roal) disciple that before discoursing on how to rule, he must first define 'kingcraft'.

What details of the *Phaedrus* speech show that its effort at definition is an unsuccessful one? Love is defined as that sort of irrational desire for enjoyment of beauty which characterizes a soul newly taken over by desire. The usurper is reinforced and made wanton by other comparable physical appetites. Hackforth has noted that the

---

6. Buchheit (*Untersuchungen zur Theorie des Genos Epideiktikon* [Munich,1960], pp. 54-64; 38-40) shows that theoretical preambles were important in Gorgias himself; thus the trait is present in the Father. Gorgias defines his genre, however, not his subject of praise. Isocrates does the same in his earlier speeches (*Helen, Busiris*), but in a probably later one (*To Nicocles*) he is Socratic in that he defines the topic instead.

7. R. L. Howland, "The Attack on Isocrates in the *Phaedrus,*" *CQ,* XXI (1937, pp. 151-159, finds two references to the *To Nicocles* in the *Phaedrus*. We will have reason to return to this "handbook for rulers," to show the importance of its political content as well as its rhetorical form in relation to *Phaedrus*.

definition leaves an ambiguity about the *summum genus*: is the genus of love desire or wantonness? If it is desire, then the speaker mislocates love when he finds it within wantonness, which is not part of desire, but rather a special state resulting from its rule. If it is wantonness, then the speaker has taken for *summum genus* what is plainly only an inferior one. From Plato's criticisms later in the dialogue one can draw other objections to the definition. What of the speaker's assumption that beauty provokes only wantonness and unrestraint? On the contrary, in the Great Speech, when the soul's charioteer is reminded of *to kalon*, he is restrained from bodily excesses (254B). Nor is beauty exclusively, or even primarily, bodily, as the speaker assumes. In sum, the speaker takes lefthanded love for the whole, failing as he does to discriminate love's two sides.[8]

It has already been pointed out that the technique of theoretical preambles exhibited here has parallels in Isocrates' speechwriting. The parallel between the middle speech and the *To Nicocles* extends further, however, than just to this formal similarity. The subject Isocrates is defining there is kingcraft, and the content of his definition would be bound to have struck Plato as perverse. Isocrates defines it as "on the one hand minimizing public misfortunes, on the other hand maximizing public fortunes, and in general making a lot out of a little" (*To Nicocles*, 9). In the companion piece composed some few years later, Isocrates represents his young king boasting of his own kingly justice in that he avoided exiling or killing anyone, but nonetheless built up the royal treasury (*Nicocles*, 32). One is reminded of the defense Isocrates offers, out of the mouth of this same king, of the concept of "*pleonexia* with virtue" (*Nicocles*, 2); Isocrates is defending this against those who attack rhetoric for its

---

8. As confirmation, we may note that the style mirrors these faults of theory. Plato expresses scorn for the resulting definition by the disparity he contrives between the earnestness of the method itself and the frivolous net result of it. It all ends up in an etymology of a most fanciful sort: *eros* is derived from *rhome* (cf. *Helen*, 55). The defining formula is also introduced by a banal remark. The speaker contrives a balanced antithesis for his sentence, but only at the cost of having to compare, in point of clarity, what is said with what is *not said*. Hackforth follows Burnet's text here, which rejects the readings of B and T, and thus removes the foolishness of the antithesis. On our interpretation, the foolishness present in the best MSS has its point. Our speaker has put in some "padding" to fill out his antithesis. Isocrates' habit of doing this was noted by Dionysius of Halicarnassus (*De Demosthene* [Usener-Rademacher, I.], p. 168).

service of *pleonexia* and who assume that there could be no such thing as combining it with virtue. This concept of kingly virtue, in other words, is squarely opposed to Plato's depreciation of *pleonexia*, in *Gorgias* as a vice of individuals, in *Republic* (423) as a vice of states.

Thus the doctrinal faults in the speaker's definition, from Plato's point of view, add to the errors of technique. But they also lead into doctrinal defects at a deeper level. The definition is supported with an argument, which is built on the premise that the human soul has two parts and two only: *epithymia* and *doxa*. Thus what the speaker represents as the ruling element in the soul is on a level with what, on Plato's account (*Rep.* 439E ff.), can at best follow reason's rule. The rational element, Plato's *logistikon*, is conspicuously absent here. From a Platonic point of view, then, this must count as a truncated psychology. But it is precisely the one to be found in Isocrates everywhere. It is expressed and applied to the question here at issue, namely the 'rule' of one or another element within the soul, at *To Nicocles,* 29, when Isocrates advises his prince that the "most kingly" value is that sort of control over appetites which will make him "seem to others to be better." As against the value of storing up a material estate, such a "fair reputation" (*doxa kale*) is immortal (32). Nor was Isocrates unaware of the anti-Platonic tendency of this exaltation of *doxa*: in *Against the Sophists* 2-8 he rejects *episteme* in favor of *doxa* in a passage quite clearly aimed, if not aimed solely, at Plato.[9] Isocrates never tired of pressing the anti-Platonic consequences for moral — or as he preferred to call it, "philosophical" — education. If accurate knowledge of a Platonic sort were at all possible, it would still be irrelevant to the matter of training the young for public life.

A strictly correlated and equally radical philosophical disagreement between Isocrates and Plato comes now to the surface: correlated to "acurate knowledge" in Plato is the grade of "real Being" (*to on ontos*). On this too Isocrates takes a position; in *Antidosis* 268 he reviews a series of speculations on the number and nature of real Beings. He runs the gamut from Anaxagoras' infinite multiplicity down through pluralist dictrines of different types, terminating in the Parmenidean One and Gorgianic None. Isocrates' view is that

---

9. Howland has made this point, θρ- βι]·' as has Jaeger, in *Padeia*, Highet trans. (Oxford, 1961), III, pp. 56-59.

there may be as many as infinitely many, or as few as none, without the "philosophical" educator's having to make any allowances whatever. He shrugs off such "dialectical" questions as nonchalantly as Protagoras did before him. H. I. Marrou captures the anti-Platonic spirit in this philosophy accurately in his paraphrase of *To Nicocles* 41:

> There is no point in attempting to mount into the heaven of Ideas or in playing about with paradoxes: for the purpose of living properly what we need is not new and surprising ideas but established good sense, traditional wisdom. (*A History of Education in Antiquity,* p. 133).

Let us return to the middle speech, bearing in mind this deeper level of philosophical doctrine, the ontology underlying the psychology. Are there any signs of the speaker's position? Indeed there are: the speaker uses the word *ousia* and another word precious to Plato, *philosophia,* in such a way as to reflect a similar "philo-doxy" in matters ontological. The words have unmistakable Platonic overtones, but Plato has his speaker use them to quite unPlatonic purposes. Most notably this is the case with the term *ousia,* which is used in two quite disjoint senses. At first the being in question is quite Platonic: one must define the *ousia* of his topic first, the speaker says. But the congruence with Plato is only momentary. The speaker's critique of love includes the point that it jeopardizes the beloved's *ousia* i.e. his material possessions! (240A) He drums on this point, always using the favorite Platonic word to refer perversely to the unPlatonic substance (240A2, 240A5, 241C3). Now this speaker is not the first to mention *ousia.* Lysias' speech uses it (232C7), but in such a way as to refer to worldly substance only: lovers will bc jealous of and vicious toward 'men of substance'. since these can trade on it to buy the affections of the beloved. But both of the earlier speeches of the dialogue are dealing in relatively insubstantial substances, as the platonizing Socrates is soon to reveal. The term *ousia* echoes again[10] in the Great Speech, but this time stripped of every trace of worldliness. It stands now for those singularly Platonic entities from the hyperheavenly region, the colorless, intangible, figureless *ousia ontos,* as he puts it in his ecstatic formula (247C).

10. R. G. Bury makes a similar point about the "responsions" of earlier speeches in Socrates' speech of *Symposium* (*The Symposium of Plato,* pp. lvii-lxiv). Terms of earlier speakers are picked up by Socrates, but used to different ends. Thus he concedes some nominal rightness to the earlier speakers, even while arguing their real error.

The *ousia* which is nothing more than material possessions is simply scorned in this speech; such substance is set at naught by the true and inspired lover, along with such not ordinarily naughty things as mothers, brothers and sisters, and friends (252A). So we see that the Middle Speaker comes out precisely in a middle position also on matters ontological: neither does he remain on the gross sensual level of Lysias, recognizing only the kind of substance one can fill one's purse or lure a boy with, nor does he rise to the bait of the otherworldly substance with the winged soul of the Platonic lover is to feed on. The Middle Speaker recognizes both the grossly material *ousia* and an immaterial one, but can achieve no enthusiasm for the immaterial.[11]

The other favorite term used, and from Plato's point of view abused, by the speaker is *philosophia* (239B4). No doubt the speaker's use of this term fits well enough with one generally accepted use: the one exemplified in Pericles' Funeral Oration in Thucydides (II, 40). But this is only a sign of how poorly it must fit with Plato's quite special meaning, his light that never was, on sea or land. In Plato *philosophia* is unthinkable without accurate knowledge of the really real. The *Republic* defines the philosopher in terms of the reality of his objects of knowledge (479f) and longing (490AB). In the hedonistic, utilitarian, "philodoxical" world of the Middle Speech, such philosophical visions and longings and such "real realities" obviously have no place.

Now even when Plato is not putting such ambiguous terms into the mouth of some "crafty fellow," he is quite capable of calling attention to their ambiguity. In the *Cratylus* he analyses the word 'episteme' two ways, once getting etymological components which imply a moving knower (412A), once a knower at rest (437A). The doubleness of meaning in this most important term is acknowledged in the second passage: it is 'amphibolous' (*ibid.*) Thus R. Robinson, although he is generally disposed to *deny* that Plato ever became conscious of fallacies of ambiguity, concedes that there Plato

---

11. Jaeger finds an altogether similar echoing of the language of Platonism in Isocrates' *Against the Sophists* 4, especially in phrases like *sympasa he arete* or 'total virtue': "Obviously Isocrates is aiming some of his sharpest shafts at the terminological peculiarities of the new philosophical method: he tracks them down with the subtle instinct of the stylist for everything which seems odd or ludicrous to the average educated man ..." (*Op. cit.*, III, p 57).

"almost gives a name" to them.[12] And here in *Phaedrus,* when Socrates finishes his two speeches on Eros, he calls attention to the fact that they only *appear* to contradict one another since the Eros in the one is only a "homonym' of the Eros in the other (266A). In other words, Plato is producing a specimen of the sort of sophistic homonymy at which Aristotle aims the proviso about contradiction in *On Interpretation* 6: "I speak of statements as contradictory when they affirm and deny the same thing of the same thing — not homonymously, together with all other such conditions that we add to counter the troublesome objections of sophists."[13]

What is Plato getting at, then, by representing this lover of opinion using Plato's own favorite ontological language in such an ambiguous way? It is worth noticing that Isocrates sponsors, in theory and in his own practice, what he calls *amphiboloi logoi.* The theory is stated in a late work, the *Panathenaicus,* where he presents the principle through the person of one of his disciples. He has a student catching him in a doctrinal inconsistency, but then extracting from this a principle of deliberate double meanings. Amphibolous talk is "disgraceful and a sign of an unusual perversity" when used in speeches designed for court cases. But when one is writing on "human nature and the nature of things," it becomes "beautiful and philosophical" (240). Amphiboly of this recommended sort works through describing things of a controversial sort — about which there is as much to blame as to praise — and seeming at the same time to praise them to their partisans, and blame them to their detractors (240f). The express aim is to create the effect of simplicity and easy access for those who read the speech without care, while concealing from such readers what will be revealed to those in on the secret: "freighted with allusions to history and philosophy," the message will now be seen to be difficult and original, and of course quite opposed to the surface message (246). The immediate purpose in view in the *Panathenaicus* is to make sense of a speech by Isocrates in which Sparta is glorified and yet his fellow Athenians can find a fundamental note of praise for themselves. The uncommonly loud applause

12. R. Robinson, "Plato's Consiousness of Fallacy," now reprinted in *Essays in Greek Philosophy* (Oxford, 1969), pp. 27, 38. Robinson laments Plato's lack of "some such word as *amphibolia* to provide a spark" (38), but has earlier conceded the importance of his calling epistome 'amphibolous' (27).

13. *Categories and De Interpretatione,* J. L. Ackrill trans. (Oxford, 1963), p. 47. Cf. fn. 38.

which greets the disciple's discovery of amphiboly, and the fact that the students are represented as then urging it on Isocrates, tend to confirm the point that Isocrates is himself (with due indirection) sponsoring the principle.

Isocrates' practice of amphiboly is well illustrated by the passage of *Nicocles* referred to above, where he has his young king boast about his own justice and temperance. The amphiboly is the more relevant to our argument in that it trades on Platonized language. The king has measured his justice by the rapid improvement he produced in the royal treasury without violence (31). The measure of his temperance is his refusal to cohabit with anyone but his own wife (36). To indulge, he comments, only makes for enemies within the palace (41). But when he first presents these quite unPlatonic ideas of justice and temperance, Isocrates has his ruler indulge in phrasing that is perfectly Platonic: justice and temperance are useful "in themselves" (*kath'hautas*), and further we can see "from examining their natures, powers and uses" that "those things which do not participate in these ideas" (*tas men me metechousas touton ton ideon*) are causes of great harm (30). The method of "examining the natures, powers and uses" recalls Plato's Hippocratic prescription for an intellectualist rhetoric in *Phaedrus*: it will proceed from a knowledge of the natures and powers of various souls and the uses of various sorts of speech in moving this or that sort of soul (271AB). But the striking amphiboly occurs of course in the talk about "participation" and "ideas." Obviously the king's temperance is nothing more than prudent calculation; yet he invites us to construe it as implying a Platonic other world, an intellectualistic "idea" in which his actions "participate."[14] Thus the very worldly point about not fouling one's own nest can be made to the gratification of the worldly wise, while at the same time the Platonist is disarmed by the amphibolous concession to the eternal.

Now *doubles entendres* can cut more ways than one, and he who amphibolizes must be agile as well as ambidextrous. Plato, if he is parodying such an amphibolous "juggling act," could very appropriately picture his rhetorician outsmarting himself, getting his doubleness only at the cost of misunderstanding on his own part. No doubt

---

14. In the Great Speech, and perhaps as "responsion" to the mistreatment of Justice and Temperance in the Middle Speech, Plato describes them as the first of the otherworldly entities espied after absolute beauty (250B).

the best parody of a juggler is the maladroit fellow who drops a piece on his own foot — preferably a heavy one, like *ousia.*

The speaker's attack on love is premised on a conception of the soul's good, that is the virtues, which is debased in a characteristic way. The speaker catalogues four virtues in the beloved which he claims will be damaged by the lover: the beloved will no longer be wise, courageous, rhetorical or shrewd (*sophos, andreios, rhetorikos, anchinous*: 239A). We propose to show that this list is a variation of a distinctive sort on the standard four virtues, which also underpin Plato's *Republic.* The variation consists in the two notable substitutions. In the position of Justice, we find its *eidolon* and counterfeit, Rhetoric: exactly the counterfeit which Plato charges practioners of rhetorical culture with passing off for the real thing in *Gorgias* (465C). Moreover Plato finds the rhetorical account of the virtues corrupted at exactly the two points where the Middle Speaker's account is corrupted. In the *Gorgias* he has Callicles recognize the worth of wisdom and courage as he is about to reject scornfully justice and temperance (491Df). Callicles permits himself some amphibolous talk too: if we can take 'justice' to mean 'getting the better of' others, or, within one's own soul, using sagacity and courage to secure the gratification of every appetite — if we call that justice, then Callicles is all for it. Being smart and courageous, in other words, fits in with a "pleonektic" morality of self-assertion, whereas justice and temperance, because they imply self-denial, must be rejected (or amphibolously endorsed).

Is the speaker's *anchinous* a variant form (corrupt from Plato's point of view) of the fourth of the standard set, temperance? Plato's account in *Phaedo* of the popular form of *sophrosyne,* although it does not use the exact term, does bring it close to *anchinoia* in the sense of that mental quickness appropriate to shrewd calculations of pleasures and pains. The *sophron* in this sense does not achieve Platonic indifference to bodily pleasures, but rather develops skill at trading one for another, like a man good at trading a less for a more valuable coin (69A). In the *Charmides* Socrates refutes the effort at defining temperance as calmness by showing that quickness (*anchinoia*) is as much temperance as calmness is (159E). Thus while Plato does not simply assert that *anchinoia* is an ersat form of *sophrosyne,* he identifies the two dialectically, and refuses to credit the identity. The Middle Speaker's doctrine of the virtues, then, fits in with his other doctrines and stands squarely opposed to Plato's own. A soul whose highest function is *doxa* in a world which excludes real being can aspire to nothing nobler than power to persuade and shrewdness.

We are not here insisting on finding Isocrates himself behind the middle speech of the *Phaedrus*. For the present case it suffices to show that rhetorical culture generally, with its tendency to reject Platonic intellectualism, tended also to reject its intellectualist definition of the virtues and education. The rejection need not, however, be open or direct. It could as well be expressed indirectly, by praise for virtues defined in non-intellectualist terms, such as pleasure, utility or public opinion. Especially in the cases of justice and temperance, which in their susual meanings are inconsistent with an aggressive worldliness bent on self-seeking and "getting more," there seems to have been a standing, and irritating, disagreement between Plato and the exponents of rhetorical culture. If the rhetoricians borrow from intellectualist language in order to debase its intended meaning, this 'amphiboly' only makes their position more irritating because deceptively expressed. However he may mask it, the position of the middle speaker is wholeheartedly 'demotic'.[15]

The Middle speech, then, after paying tribute to the importance of definition, defines love as a disorder of the soul, which soul is capable only of appetite and opinion. The soul's good is thus reduced to 'demotic' proportions too, to the kind of honesty and the calculating sort of sobriety which such a conception represents. If terms like *ousia* and *philosophia* are put into the speaker's mouth by Plato, it is not to reflect any serious respect for, or even genuine comprehension of, their Platonic referents. At most they stand for the willingness of such rhetorical educators to indulge in amphibolous talk.

The speaker is thus a self-proclaimed educator, voicing concern with the state of the boy's soul and with the cultivation of its virtues (239B, 241C). He is an educator who can, as we have suggested, be assigned to a recognizable and well-defined intellectual milieu. This

---

15. I. M. Crombie (*An Examination of Plato's Doctrines* [London, 1962], I, pp. 150 f.) expresses the Platonic distinction aptly as follows:
> There is 'demotic virtue which is enough to make a man live soberly and honestly [temperately and justly] because he sees that injustice does not pay; but beyond that there is 'the love of wisdom' which provides an altogether different motivation towards virtue ... being the assertion of the soul's true nature as a spiritual being.

milieu we may characterize for convenience as that of the sophistical-rhetorical culture of fifth and fourth century Athens.[16] The speaker's views on epistemology and ontology, his psychology and his theory of virtues, and, more particularly suggestive of Isocrates, his claims to expertise regarding *philosophia* (239B) all point to this conclusion. The structural relationship, moreover, which obtains between the three speeches of the *Phaedrus,* by which the middle speech is made to share the premises of Lysias' oration and is rejected along with it, also suggest the same intellectual affiliations.

With these general points in mind it is possible to clarify several further problems in the interpretation of the middle speech. First, why does Plato, in the brief prooimion, tell us that the speaker, despite what he will say, is a lover of the boy? Now, from Plato's point of view (and we must keep in mind that, whoever the "subject" of the portrait, he is being seen through Plato's eyes) all intel-

---

16. In this paper the terms sophist and rhetor have been used more or less interchangeably. Some scholars argue that Plato kept these two activities distinct, e.g. H. Raeder, "Plato und die Sophistik," *Danske Vidensk. Selskab. Hist.-filol. Meddekekser* 26.9 (1939), pp. 5-12 and Dodds, *Gorgias* (Oxford, 1959), pp. 6-7. According to Raeder and Dodds we should not give the name sophist to figures such as Gorgias (Raeder and Dodds) and Thrasymachus (Raeder), because Plato nowhere does. Plato did, to be sure, make a sharp *theoretical* distinction in the *Gorgias* between the two acitivities, but it should not be overlooked that there are two passages in this same dialogue which show that *in practice* the distinction could not be rigidly maintained (465C, 520A). The sophists and rhetors, as Socrates points out, were virtually indistinguishable, and only a theoretical scheme which glossed over actual contradictions could separate them. Much the same lack of concern about the two terms is in evidence at *Phaedrus* 257C-D, where logographer and sophist are clearly the same.

Plato's difficulty, of course, reflects the historical situation. Even if we accede to Dodd's skepticism about Gorgias, as a serious thinker, it will still be impossible to deny that Thrasymachus was both a rhetorician and sophist. Perhaps, in theory, this should not be so, but Thrasymachus, the historical figure, was both. Raeder's attempt to deny Thrasymachus the title of sophist on the grounds that his opinions would not have met with the approval of the sophists is preposterous, as a comparison with Antiphon's fragments shows. Moreover, Navarre's *Essai sur la rhetorique grecque* (Paris, 1900), pp. 24-78, and Kroll's article "Rhetorik," *RE* Supplementbd. 7 (1940), pp. 1043-1048, show that almost all the sophists were, to some degree, concerned with rhetorical studies. We may also recall that in the *Sophist* (268B-C) it is only in the *last* of a long series of divisions that the sophist and rhetor are clearly differentiated (cf. Cornford on *Sophist* 221C-223B [*Plato's Theory of Knowledge,* p. 174]).

lectual education can be understood as a species of erotic relationship in which the educator is the lover and the disciple the beloved. Socrates' relationship with young men such as Alcibiades, Agathon, Charmides and Meno are all cases in point.[17] From all of these it is also clear that although Plato is most explicit and emphatic on the need for chastity on the part of the philosopher (*Phaedrus* 253C-256E, *Symposium* 218B-219D), there is no reason at all to believe that the metaphor of the philosopher as lover rests on a merely non-essential point of comparison. For Plato, the activity of thought and the arousal of reflection in others both draw on the same deep sources of passion which animate our sexual natures. Socrates' relationship with the series of brilliant young men in the dialogues is to be sure not physical, but it is, at the same time, unequivocally erotic.

In this view, as in so much else, Plato is merely rendering more explicit an already existing cultural pattern. The notion of the educator as lover, the fusion in the attitude of the teacher of an erotic interest in a young student with a concern for his intellectual training, are by no means peculiar to Plato. H. I. Marrou, among others, has written illuminatingly on this aspect of Greek education.[18] One may compare, from among many other examples, Isocrates' account of the leave-taking of his students (*Antidosis* 87-88), strangely close to the mood of Sappho's poem in description of a similar occasion (Fr. 94 L-P).

But these are general considerations. More particularly suggestive of the situation portrayed in the middle speech is the work considered above, which is addressed to one of Isocrates' most celebrated pupils, Nicocles, son of the great Evagoras. In this protreptic discourse Isocrates, casting himself in the role of moral educator, warns Nicocles that though there are many others who come to him bearing gifts in search of royal favor and with mercenary intentions, he differently from the rest has come to advise the young king in a spirit of high-minded disinterestedness and with a gift that will not only never lose its value, but will grow more valuable with time (*To Nicocles*, 1-2, 54). In the same way the middle speaker, having to

---

17. The fusion of the erotic and philosophical, not necessarily in a narrowly educational context, is a frequent element in Plato's dialogues; cf. *Phaedrus* 248D, 249A and D, *Symp.* 209E-212A, *Rep.* 475B-C.

18. H. I. Marrou, *History of Education in Antiquity*, tr. G. Lamb (New York, 1964), pp. 150-162.

compete with many others for the favor of the young boy, declares his fundamental non-involvement; he alone among the suitors is a nonlover, free from the fault of selfishness which figures so prominently in his portrayal of the lover. The *To Nicocles* is not only important, however, because it allows us a glimpse of Isocrates in the role of a rival suitor for the attentions of a wealthy young monarch. It is also important because it lifts us from the realm of purely private education to that of society in its larger, political aspect.

In this enlarged context, the metaphor of educator as lover is subjected by Plato to a complex development. A connection between the world of the rhetorical lover, who lays claim to expertise in philosophical education and endeavors to win young men over to his point of view, and that of the worldly politician, is in fact hinted at in the *Phaedrus* 257E-258B (f. *Pol.* 303D). Socrates is making the paradoxical observation that the politicians, despite their scorn for the speechwriters, are really such themselves. The politicians are described as enamored (ερωσι) of writing. The difference is that their compositions are laws not speeches. Moreover, the politician, in his lawmaking, has such a fondness for those who praise his compositions that he prefixes their names, *demos* and *boule*, to each and every work. Similarly, when Socrates turns to a wider critique of the two earlier speeches, the natural contexts to which he directs his considerations are the political and dicanic (259E-260C). In Greek terms this double aspect of persuasion, i.e. the public and the private, is a familiar way of conceiving the matter.

Familiar, and closely connected, is Plato's conviction that both philosophers and practical men of the world, whether these latter be politicians, sophists, or rhetoricians, must be thought of not only as the lovers of their disiciples, but of some larger ideal as well. Such lovers, turned in two directions at once, act as intermediaries whose endeavor is to win over their beloved disciples to a cherished ideal of life. A passage in the *Gorgias* (481C-482A) is explicit on this point. Socrates is addressing Callicles about the objects of their respective loves. For Socrates the beloved are Philosophy and Alcibiades, for Callicles the Athenian People and Demos, the well-born son of Pyrilampes.[19] Now, it is not stated that it is an inseparable aspect of

19. In a more precise sense the object of the philosopher's love is not philosophy, but the ultimate goal of philosophical endeavor, i.e. being; cf. *Rep.* 475B-D, 489D and Shorey's note (b), 490B and Shorey's note (a); *Phaedrus* 249D-E; *Symposium* 209C, 210E-212A.

Socrates' love for Alcibiades that he should desire to turn the young man to a life of philosophy. But in the light of dialogues such as the *Symposium*, which is particularly concerned with Alcibiades, and the *Phaedrus* itself, such an inference is irresistible. Less immediately certain, but highly plausible in the light of social and psychological considerations, is the inference that when Callicles, and men like him, cultivate their proteges it is at least in part for the purpose of introducing them to the way of life to which they have given their own passionate allegiance.[20] Again one finds a parallel in Isocrates. In the *Antidosis* (132) and the *To Nicocles* (15-16), Isocrates urges upon Timotheus and Bicocles the view (inconsistently, as we shall see later) that in the practical conduct of the state it is necessary to be a lover of the *polis* and solicitous of the multitude.

III

Before proceeding to support our stronger thesis, which identifies the middle speaker with Isocrates, it would not be out of place to discuss briefly the question of the unity of the *Phaedrus*. The question in its most basic form is this, "Is there any intrinsic connection between the two parts of the dialogue, i.e. the first consisting of three discourses on love and the second of a theoretical examination of rhetoric?" Put in another way, "Is there an intrinsic connection between the themes of eros and rhetoric?" Jaeger is surely correct when he observes that in fact both halves of the dialogue are concerned with rhetoric: in the first half the subject is approached through examples. while the second is devoted to a theoretical critique. This is true, but this solution ignores the important question why love, *and not some other topic*, was chosen as subject. A number of answers have been given, but they are all, it seems to us, lacking in an attainable precision.[21] If our preceding arguments are

---

20. Cf. *Rep.* 495C-496A, where sophists are pseudo-suitors of Philosophy. Socrates' remarks concerning the object of Callicles' love are reminiscent of Pericles' exhortation to the Athenians that they become the lovers of their city (II, 43). Close, too, is the central situation of Aristophanes' *Knights,* in which the Athenian demos is portrayed as the object of the fervent attentions of two rival citizens. Similarly, though an explicitly erotic vocabulary is lacking, the advocates of sophistical-rhetorical culture, committed to a pragmatic point of view and to the pursuit of immediate political goals, are characterized in the *Republic* as suitors of the *demos* (494A).

21. *Paideia*, III, pp. 183-184. Jaeger suggests that the choice of subject is

sound, the solution to the problem of the unity of the same young men will pay to learn the verbal skill; will later imitate this sophistic jugglery of words in assembly and court of law, bringing to the most serious business of the city the sophist's zeal for victory in disregard of truth.

If, then, we may justly take the phrase "to make the weaker argument defeat the stronger" as a summary of Plato's complaint against the Sophists, it might be useful to state fully the crime which provokes the charge.

When put to the Socratic test, the Sophist, like the poet and the politician, reveals his ignorance. But this cannot be the root of Plato's animus, for in his ignorance the Sophist differs not from any other man. Nor can it be that, though ignorant, he persists in argument — for this too is true of every man, including Socrates. But ignorant men, in the Socrates sense, may seek the truth and *speak* the truth. Though Plato early insists upon and later elaborates the difference between genuine knowledge and opinion or belief, he never limits *truth* to the expression of knowledge. Socrates, who disavows all knowledge, does not hesitate to claim to speak the truth, nor to be able to distinguish truth from falsity. His claim is put most strongly in the *Apology*: "From me you shall hear the whole truth"; "Think only of the truth of my words and give heed to that."[1] The *truths* which Socrates then speaks are predominantly truths abouts events in Athens, the encounters and relations of men. They are, that is, truths about "appearances," about sensible objects in the empirical world, that world of "becoming" which Plato will later identify as the object of "opinion." But this does not, for Plato exclude the possibility that they are true.

Throughout the dialogues, as early as the *Meno* and as late as Book IX of the *Laws*, Plato clearly expresses the view that, however

---

largely fortuitous; but there are surely reasons beyond a presumed popularity of the subject with 5th century rhetoricians (259). Kennedy, *The Art of Persuasion in Greece* (Princeton, 1963), p. 75, sees the connection in the fact that "love beautifully exemplifies what . . . [Plato] . . . has in mind about rhetoric: rather than being a purely objective rational or artistic matter it involves the soul of the disputants." Robin, *Phedre* (Paris, 1933), 1, and R. Hackforth, Plato's *Phaedrus*, pp. 9-10, among others, see the reason for the choice of love in the basic affinity of love and philosophy, a position for which the *Symposium* is, of course, the major item of proof.

opinion may differ from knowledge, some opinions are true.[2] "True" in this context is neither metaphorical nor imprecise. There may be degrees of truth for Plato[3] but there are not kinds. Plato's theory of knowledge develops, of course, from problems which arise only if some opinions are acknowledged to be true. It is the truth of some opinions, such as that Simmias is taller than Socrates but shorter that Phaedo,[4] which leads Plato to distinguish form from sensible object, being from becoming reality from appearance, knowledge from opinion, and to talk of sensible objects "participating" in forms. And when a sensible object does participate in a form, say Simmias in tallness, then the statement expressing the opinion that it (he) does is true — it is a true opinion. Plato is usually clear about this, though his commentators have not always been. We may then say that, at least in the early dialogues, there is for Plato a truth of appearances or opinion as well as that more vital fundamental truth of things "in themselves" — the truth of improvement over Lysias', but also a clarification of human realities only hinted at in the earlier speech and a revelation of a level of self-awareness of which Lysias' speaker is simply not capable. On this interpretation, Socrates will be portraying a man with the same aims as Lysias' suitor, but possessed, at the same time, of greater acuity of mind; rather sinister, and less naive, he knows that he lusts after the boy (237B), and is willing, in order to win him over, to employ deceit and slander the god of love.[2 5]

> In the speech of Lysias, the basic disposition of the speaker was left indefinite, and Lysias might well have counted this indefiniteness an advantage. Socrates, however, clearly defines the situation in an opening summary such as was retained for these ficitious speeches in later rhetoric. The admirer (a

---

22. In the first speech of the *Apology* there are some thirty passages in which Socrates proclaims either that what he says is true or that what his accusers have said is false. Similar references to truth occur in many dialogues, e.g., *Charmides* 160, 161, 162; *Lysis* 213; *Laches* 194; *Protagoras* 348, 352. *Meno* 75; etc.

23. One can have a true opinion, we recall, about the road to Larissa (*Meno* 97 ff.). Cf. also *Symposium* 202, *Timaeus* 37, *Theaetetus* 187 ff. (where the claim that true opinion is knowledge is perhaps refuted, but the claim that there are true opinions is never questioned), *Philebus* 66, and *Laws* 864.

24. Cf. *Republic* 511.

25. Or the opinions that the Greek who remains at his post and fights is courageous but so also is the Scythian who fights flying (*Laches* 190).

25. P. Friedländer, *op. cit.*, pp. 222-226.

"wily flatterer") of a handsome young man who is much loved has falsely persuaded the youth that he does not love him. Thus, the theme taken over from Lysias is not posed paradoxically, for the more clearly delineated description serves a psychologically determined strategy. (222-223)

and

Here in the *Phaedrus*, the wily friend (239B) asserts that the lover keeps the beloved away from "divine philosophy." He must know, for he himself is caught up in this kind of love, after all, as much as he conceals it. Thus, it should not be said that a specific mode of life determined by false love is refuted here. What happens, rather, is that this specific mode of life is led to reveal itself in its true nature. This is the substance and meaning of the first speech of Socrates. (225-226)

We suggest that this portrait fits Isocrates closely. Before we bring forward our evidence, however, it is necessary to clarify one point. In the prologue of the middle speech Plato explicitly apprises the reader of the fact, however it is to be interpreted, that the speaker *consciously* keeps his true feelings concealed. Can the same be demonstrated of Isocrates' behavior toward his own pupils or toward the wider audience to which his works are directed? Most likely not, at least not with any certainty. The case we made out for Isocrates' 'amphiboly' at most opens up the possibility. We are, after all, dealing with psychological and moral nuances of a most fugitive nature. Nonetheless, there still unmistakably remains, as we hope to show, an aura of slyness and hypocrisy in the character of this, at first glance, flat and tedious man.[26]

The situation of the middle speech can be thought of otherwise than as representing a consciously assumed pose covering over real intentions clearly perceived by the actor. If we allow Friedländer's interpretation, we may also think of it as Plato's device for bringing into clearer view the true motives which animate such men, motives about which, we can be sure, they are most often themselves far from clear. After all, few men are so honest or shameless as to admit, as does the middle speaker, to such total selfishness. Most, like the speaker in Lysias' discourse, tend, rather, to conceive of themselves as realistic, enlightened, and sophisticated.[27] The contrast, from the perspective of Friedländer's interpretation, would be that between a

26. It is therefore not, on the face of it, absurd to reject the suggested identification of Callicles with Isocrates, as Dodds does, *op. cit.*, p. 12.
27. Cf. the remarks of Josef Pieper, *Euthusiasm and Divine Madness*, tr. Richard and Clara Winston (New York, 1964), pp. 6-12.

self-deluded certainty about the reasons for one's actions, as is the case with Lysias' speaker, and objectively perceived, far less flattering motives for these same actions. We will have moved from the mind of the actor to the mind of the observer. And this should not be a surprising ambiquity of perspective. In common usage, after all, the reproach of hypocrisy just as often refers to contradictions of which the "hypocrite" is unaware, but which others perceive, as to conscious disparity between word and deed.

Isocrates's self-proclaimed view is that he is the "teacher and counsellor" of the people (*Antidosis*, 102), a cut, we may presume, above the normal run of politician. In the same spirit, he advises Nicocles to set himself up as a moral paradigm for the edification of his subjects and to see to it that their lives are conducted with justice and moderation (*To Nicocles*, 31, cf. 11, 16-19). And yet it is also clear that from Plato's point of view Isocrates' position is flawed with an irredeemable contradiction. For in the very same works in which Isocrates smugly presents himself as educator and uplifter of the multitude he also propounds the view (*Antidosis*, 132-133), commending it to Nicocles as well (*To Nicocles*, 15-16), that to be a successful ruler one must govern in such a way as to gratify the masses! Now one may consider this a defensible political position involving no real contradiction. But surely Plato did not. He may have attributed the contradictions in Isocrates' view to muddle-headedness rather than to deliberate hypocrisy, but the line taken by Isocrates, i.e. that a genuine ruler should seek to gratify the desires of the governed, is, of course, rejected outright by Plato. It would have seemed to Plato a case of someone eager to achieve popular success masking his ambition with high-sounding pretensions about virtue and philosophy.

The *To Nicocles* also evidences the same moral ambiguity. This discourse, conceived in a high moral tone, is particularly aimed at devaluing, to the gain of Isocrates' priceless advice, the material gifts with which his rivals seek to gain Nicocles' favor and to be rewarded (1-2, 54). A commendable view, to be sure. Who would dispute the superiority of wisdom over material wealth? Yet, in this same work, Isocrates takes pains at several points to impress upon his young disciple the need for generosity. He does not, to be sure, explicitly ask repayment for his wise counsels, but it is extremely difficult to suppose that this is not hinted at in the several passages in which he urges Nicocles to reward friends (19) and view talented advisors with special favor (53, cf. 20, 22, 28). There is evidence for believing, moreover, that Isocrates was not above this kind of mercenary relationship with his most intimate students, especially men of wealth and power, since he seems to have charged Timotheus and Nicocles sizable sums of money for compositions which he wrote for them.[28]

Deviousness of this sort is not restricted to Isocrates' political activities, as Buchheit has convincingly shown in his study of Isocrates' *Helen*.[29] It is Buchheit's view that Isocrates is guilty of having attempted, in an underhanded and unconsciously way, to misrepresent the intentions of Gorgias, his older rival and, perhaps, teacher, whom vanity impelled him to attack, but whom he lacked the courage to confront in an open way.

This view of the matter presents us with two Isocrates: the one tediously familiar to all readers — preachy, high-minded, rather pompous; the other peering out from between the lines — a figure of slyness, greed, vanity, and ambition. Ancient tradition, in fact, knew of his less attractive Isocrates, and there is reason to think that his contemporaries found his vanity and pomposity overwhelmingly attractive targets.[30] More directly relevant to the matter at hand, Klaus Ries has shown in a recent study of Plato and Isocrates that a figure very like the duplicitous Isocrates we have been describing is present in Plato's account, in Books 5 and 6 of the *Republic,* of the corrupting influence of society on the gifted young and, more particularly, in his exposition of the view that the sophists, though professed teachers of the multitude, are in reality its willing slaves.[31] It is most likely that in Plato's view, Isocrates was preeminent among such men; and, as Ries argues, he is clearly alluded to at several crucial points in this section of the *Republic*. This contradiction (some might call it hypocrisy) between professed aims and actual conduct is, it should be noted, precisely the one to which we pointed in our earlier discussion of The *Antidosis* and *To Nicocles*. There is thus, to revert to the chief subject of our discussion, some plausibility in the view that the middle speaker, who is in other respects so

    28. Vid. pseudo-Plutarch, *Lives of the Ten Orators,* 837A, 838A.
    29. V. Buchheit, *op. cit.,* pp. 54-64.
    30. Vid. pseudo-Plutarch, *op. cit.,* 839A; for contemporaries, vid. J. Coulter, *op. cit.,* pp. 225-236.
    31. K. Ries, *op. cit.*

exactly reminiscent of Isocrates, is also, in the matter of his slyness and dishonesty, not very far from the mark.

IV

In conclusion, we return to our less ambitious thesis, which attempts only to locate the character of the middle speaker in a generic way. That thesis is considerably confirmed by a passage in the *Sophist* (221C-223B), a work probably written not very far in time from the *Phaedrus*. The subject immediately under discussion is the definition of the sophist as *hunter*: the sophist is a hunter of young men of rank and distinction; he works not by violence, but by persuasion; he practices his craft among private individuals; unlike the lover, who *gives* gifts, he *takes* a fee;[32] lastly, he affects a concern for the education of his charge to virtue. In Plato's eyes he is, of course, a proponent of a spurious form of education (*doxopaideutike*); Now this sketch corresponds with remarkable closeness to the figure which has emerged from our interpretation of the middle speech. The speaker of the *Phaedrus* is, to be sure, a lover, whereas the subject of Plato's sketch in the *Sophist* is, by his own account, an educator. But in the light of our earlier discussion of the close affinity between these two figures, of the self-proclaimed educational role of the middle speaker, and of the clear conceptual connection that Plato forms here in the *Sophist* passage, exhibiting the logical kinship between the two, this is a difference without any importance.[33]

The conception of love argued by this "left-handed" lover is, as is

---

32. Vid. Cornford, *op. cit.* (above, note 17), pp. 174, 182.

33. There is an extraordinarily precise clue which links the two passages. We saw earlier that the epithet which Plato applies to the middle speaker is αμυλος. The ancient etymologists understood the word to be a diminutive of the Homeric word αἵμων, which occurs uniquely at Iliad V,49 with a sense that is quite uncertain. (For a collection of ancient etymologies see *Lexikon fes frühgriechischen Epos,* ed. B. Snell *et al.* [Göttingen, 1955], s.v.). It occurs in the phrase αἵμονα θήρας generally understood in antiquity to mean "skilled at the hunt." Now it is arguable that Plato did not himself think of αἱμύλος as the diminutive of αἵμων, or that, if he had, he would not inevitably have recalled this passage in the *Iliad.* But it is a most suggestive fact that the only other passage in Plato where the word occurs is in a discussion of hunting (Laws 7. 832D). In the light of this consideration, one is tempted to say that in order to bring out all the nuances of the word *in this passage* one must paraphrase αἱμύλος as a "stealthy hunter of young men."

the entire complex of rhetorical-sophistical culture of which it is the heart, totally and passionately repudiated by Socrates in the final speech. Such a lover only knows liaisons of brief duration. He is destructively possessive, lacking in trust, jealous of any independence or maturity on the part of his beloved. He is a "realist," whose decisions concerning human attachments are calculated on the basis only of pleasure and utility. He is, lastly, a man obsessed with *necessity*.[34]

As often, Aristotle provides us with a discursive treatment of a matter which serves as a kind of guide to Plato's dramatic treatment of it. In his discussion of the three types of friendship at the beginning of Book VIII of the *Nichomachean Ethics* (1155b10-1157b6), Aristotle defines the two inferior grades of friendship — in fact, they are not really friendship at all except thanks to an ambiguity[35] — as based either on pleasure or utility. These, as we saw earlier, are central notions in the middle speech. These false forms of friendship he rejects in favor of an enduring friendship which rest on a reciprocal love of virtue. One of the just causes for breaking off a friendship which Aristotle cites in Book IX is precisely the sort of deception which characterizes the person of the middle speech: the deliberate pretense of a concern for the boy's character in order to conceal the baser causes of the attachment, pleasure or utility. Such a pretender is worse than a counterfeiter, Aristotle comments, in proportion as the thing he debases (friendship) is more valuable (1165b4ff). Aristotle is also aware (1157a27-28) of the political analogues to the forms of personal friendship under discussion: "we speak of 'friendly' states, though we all know that political alliances are formed on

---

34. 238E, 239A (twice), 239B, 239C, 240A, 240C, 240D, 240E, 241B (twice), 240C. Is this the same necessity some mistake for the Good at *Rep.* 493C?

35. In the *Eudemian Ethics,* probably written when Plato was still alive (cf. Düring, "Aristoteles," RE Supplementband XI[1968], p. 333), Aristotle discusses the same topic of friends, putting emphasis on the logical point about plurality of meanings. Also close to the *Phaedrus* in time is the *Categories,* in which Aristotle seems to be codifying results of explorations of homonymy in *Topics.* In any case, when one adds Aristotle's pleasure-based to his utility-based friendship, he gets the "left-handed" eros of the *Phaedrus,* and especially of the Middle Speech. But this is the eros which Plato calls a "homonym" (266A) of the Platonic eros of the Great Speech. These matters bear on the studies G. E. L. Owen had done on the developments of Plato and Aristotle.

calculations of expediency." This point is extremely useful in reinforcing our earlier observations about the wider political dimensions implicit in what seemed an exclusively private and personal situation. Indeed Plato must have heard many men in Greek political life who operated on the same premises and talked the same language as the left-handed lover of the middle speech. They too were "realists," looking at the world in a clear-eyed and disabused way, weighing dispassionately what was profitable and expedient, free from "foolish" and "useless" illusions. Although most were surely without the self-awareness with which Plato credits the speaker in the prologue. Thucydides is, of course, full of speeches by such men.[36] The only difference is that they are wooing not a young boy but the Athenian people or a potentially valuable ally.

We earlier examined the philosophical position of the middle speaker. It is important to note that for Plato it is no accident that a man who *thinks* the way the left-handed lover does should also conceive of love the way he does. There is a kind of logical necessity which operates to bring this about. For Plato the saying in the gospel holds true. "Where your treasure is, there will your heart be also." There is also a factual necessity which holds such a man in its grip. It is, in fact, a point that Plato makes several times that the politician must, if he is to survive, be assimilated to the object of his love (*Gorgias* 512E-513C, *Rep.* 493D,494E).[37]

In this paper we do not mean to imply any "reduction" of the *Phaedrus* to a mere rhetorical polemic. Among the reasons against any such reduction is the violence it would do to important, and in *Phaedrus* importantly new, matters of logic such as the nature of

---

36. See especially the speeches of the Corcyrean ambassador (I. 32-36), Diodotus (III, 43-48), and Euphemus (VI, 76-80). Although a detailed comparative study is out of place here, it can be shown through an examination of specific argumentative terms and concepts that there exists a very close affinity between the minds of these speakers and that of the middle speaker of the *Phaedrus.* Especially important are notions such as *ophelia, blabe* and *sophrosyne.* Compare also Creon's argument in the *Antigone* for preferring 'friends' in the political sense to personal friends: only thus does one expand one's country (ll. 182-190). The friendship which Ismene pledges to Antigone (ll. 98 f.) is not in the same family, except logically.

37. This should be contrasted with the philosopher's voluntary striving to assimilate himself to the God within (*Phaedrus* 252C-E); cf. *Theat.* 176A, *Rep.* 500C.

paradox, ambiguity and definition. Although we make no effort to go into these complicated questions here, it appears that the ambiguity discovered in *Phaedrus* in the case of the two or more meanings of "eros" has important continuities with some of the theorizing about meaning in the Academy during Plato's later years. This would give still other basis for unifying the *Phaedrus* internally, and then for unifying it with what is gradually getting clarified about Plato and the Academy in the mid-fourth century.[38]

---

38. The article by Jonathan Barnes ("Homonymy in Aristotle and Speusippus," *CQ*, n.s. XXI [1971] 65-80) carries out a thorough new research on some of the issues touched on here. It appeared too late to be given more than a brief mention. It may be noted, however, that, although it is a general thesis of Barnes' article that "homonymy" is *not* said, by either Speusippus or Aristotle, to lodge in linguistic items, but rather in their *denotata*, the article does concede exceptions, such as this one from *De Int.* 6 and a similar one from *Rhet.* III, 2 (p. 79). These passages in Aristotle are pointed at sophistical rhetoricians.

THE ATTACK ON ISOCRATES IN THE PHAEDRUS*

By R. L. Howland

The most famous and successful teacher of rhetoric at Athens in the fourth century was Isocrates, and he claimed for rhetoric an educational importance which Plato considered to be unmerited and misleading. He made rhetoric the basis of his whole educational system and claimed to teach his pupils to become not only good rhetoricians but good citizens. Plato attacked both aspects of this theory of education. In the *Gorgias* he exposed the claim of rhetoric to be considered valuable as an instrument of education by showing that rhetoricial excellence had no necessary connection with moral excellence. In the *Protagoras* he exposes the inconsistency of those who claimed to teach men to be good citizens − to teach πολιτικὴ τέχνη − without an absolute standard of moral values. Even if we believe that in the *Gorgias* and the *Protagoras*, as in other dialogues, Plato is representing faithfully the constructive views of the historic Socrates, we can hardly believe that he was unaware of the contemporary relevance of those views, and it is significant that he thought fit to publish them in the form of an attack on a teacher of rhetoric and an attack on a teacher of πολιτικὴ τέχνη. At any rate it is reasonable to suppose that the Athenian reading public would expect to find such a contemporary relevance and that they would interpret these attacks as being, in some measure at least, directed against Isocrates.

As far as the *Gorgias* is concerned it would probably be generally admitted that the attack on rhetoric is intended to refer to Isocrates as the most influential contemporary teacher of it. It is perhaps not so easy to allow that the *Protagoras* is also largely directed against Isocrates, as a teacher of πολιτικὴ τέχνη; but at least the *Protagoras* had this effect, that it drew a counter-attack from Isocrates. For it

---

* By R.L. Howland, From the *CLASSICAL QUARTERLY,* vol. 31 (1937), 551-559, Reprinted by permission of the Oxford University Press.

seems to me that the irrelevant introduction to the *Helen* can best be explained as primarily (though not exclusively) an attack on Plato, and in particular on the *Protagoras*. It opens with the statement that there are certain persons who pride themselves on maintaining obscure and paradoxical hypotheses, and that there are some who have spent their lives (καταγεγηράκασιν) showing that Courage and Wisdom and Justice are one and the same (208B1) and that men do not possess these virtues φύσει, μία δ' ἐπιστήμη καθ' ἁπάντων ἐστίν (208B2). Now this is a very fair summary of the suggestions of many of Plato's earlier dialogues and epitomizes accurately the positive doctrine of the *Protagoras*, where the unity of the virtues is first formulated and proved. Isocrates then goes on to ask whether there is anyone whose education has been so neglected (τίς ἐστι οὕτως ὀψιμαθής) that he does not know that Protagoras and the sophists of his day left us τοιαῦτα καὶ πολὺ τούτων πρεγματωδέστερα συγγράμματα (208C2). He adds Gorgias, and then Zeno and Melissus, as masters of paradoxical obscurities, and it is significant that Protagoras heads the list and has a sentence to himself, although he is certainly not such a good example as Zeno or Melissus. The point that Isocrates is making is this. An historically accurate portrait of the great sophist should have allowed him this kind of skill. By showing Socrates as superior in this type of argument Plato has been guilty of gross misrepresentation, and he certainly cannot claim for himself any distinction for spending so much time in doing what others had done better — and 'better' here means ·πραγ ̄ ματωδέστερα', for obscurity and difficulty are the only merits which such exercises can claim. Persons who are inclined to this type of argument, however, ought to abandon such nonsense and educate their associates (παιδαυειν τοὺς συνόντας 209A4) in matters of practical importance. Isocrates indicates that it is those who profess to be educators whom he has mind, and he makes this quite clear a little later (209C4) when he says that men can be forgiven if they are delight in these useless arguments, but τοῖς παιδεύειν προσποιουμένοις ἄξιον ἐπιτιμᾶν because τοὺς συνόντας μάλιστα βλάπτουσιν (209D1). They ought, he says, τὴν ἀλήθειαν διώκειν ... ἐνθυμουμένους ουι πολὺ κρεῖττόν ἐστιν περὶ τῶν χρχσίμων ἐπιεικῶς δοξάξειν ἢ περὶ τῶν εχρηστων ἀκριβῶς ἐπίστασθαι, καὶ μικρὸν προέχειν ἐν τοῖς μεμαλοις μᾶλλον ἢ πολὺ διαφέρειν ἐν τοῖς μικροῖς καὶ τοῖς μηδὲν πρὸς τὸν βίον ὠφελοῦσιν. This is surely a direct criticism of the Platonic thesis of the superiority of ἐπιστήμη to δόξα, and even if it is no specifically directed against the *Protagoras* it has at least a distinct relevance to that dialogue. It is somewhat vitiated, of course, by its opening words, which urge the necessity of τὴν ἀλήθειαν διώκειν, and this inconsistency is thoroughly exposed in the *Phaedrus,* where the whole passage is subjected to a relentless criticism.

But whatever we may believe to have been Isocrates' object in the introduction to the *Helen,* it certainly seems that Plato considered it to refer to himself, and he makes an exhaustive reply in the *Phaedrus.* The attack on Isocrates in this dialogue takes the form of an attack on the principles and teaching of rhetoric. Several commentators[1] have noticed in the *Phaedrus* polemic against Isocrates an verbal reminiscences of his writings; but there is more to it than that. The whole dialogue must be considered primarily as a direct and comprehensive attack on the educational system of Isocrates, in which Isocrates' own words and methods, particularly those which he uses in the *Helen,* are turned against himself. The following analysis will, I hope, make this clear.

The dialogue opens with a meeting between Socrates and Phaedrus. Phaedrus has just heard and been much impressed by a discourse of Lysias, a rhetorical exercise on the theme that it is better to grant favours to a suitor who is not really in love than to the true lover, on the ground that the true lover is a madman and must therefore be harmful to the object of his affection. Phaedrus is persuaded to give Socrates an account of it, though he protests that he cannot do more than give a summary. Socrates then discovers that Phaedrus has a written copy of the discourse with him, and the important point is thus established that the discourse, although it may be read or delivered as a speech, is in reality a written work.

Before the discourse is read a discussion of the charm of the scenery and the legend connected with the place leads to the remark of Phaedrus that Socrates is a strange creature in that he never leaves the city. Socrates replies (230D3) Συγγίγνωσκέ μοι, ὦ εριστε. φιλομαθής γάρ εἰμι. Only men in the city and not trees and the countryside can teach him anything. Now there is a tradition that Isocrates (in the words of Roger Ascham) 'did cause to be written at

---

1. Especially L. Robin in his introduction to this Dialogue in the *Bude* collection (Paris, 1933) (vide particularly pp. clx-clxxv). Cf. Raeder, *Platons philosophische Entwickelung* (Leipzig, 1905), pp. 265-279.

the entrie of his schole in golden letters this golden sentence 'Σὰν ᾖς φιλομαθής, ἔσει πολυμαθής', and whether this tradition is founded upon fact or not this sentence does actually occur in the *Ad Femonicum* of Isocrates. The Athenian public would be reminded by the phrase φιλομαθὴς γάρ εἰμι of Isocrates' 'golden sentence', particularly if it attained the prominence which tradition asserts, and it is a most appropriate excuse for Socrates to give to Phaedrus, who throughout the dialogue represents the intelligent follower of Isocrates.

The discourse of Lysias is then read.

Socrates says that he was impressed, but as much by the enthusiasm of the reader as by anything else. The suggestion is that the written discourse needs a vivid presentation in order to make its effect. Phaedrus asks (234E3) whether Socrates thinks that anyone else could have said ἕτερα του]ων μείζω καὶ πλείω περὶ τοῦ αὐτο πράγματος. Socrates expresses surprise that they are expected to praise the discourse (234E5) ὡς τὰ δέοντα εἰρηκότος τοῦ ποιητοῦ, ελλ' οὐκ ἐκείνῃ μόνον ὅτι σαφῆ καὶ στρογγύλα καὶ ἀκριβῶς ἕκαστα τῶν ὀνομάτων ἀποτετόρνευται. He means that he thought he was only expected to pay attention to those aspects of the discourse which he imagined that Phaedrus, as a pure rhetorician, would consider important.

We shall probably be right in recognizing here, as Raeder suggests, a reference to a passage in the κατὰ τῶν Σοφιστῶν (294C), where Isocrates, speaking of the aspects of oratory which the pupil has to learn, says that he must be able τοῖς ἐνθυμήμασιν πρεπόντως ὅλον τὸν λόγον καταποικῖλαι καὶ τοῖς ὀνόμασιν εὐρύθμως καὶ μουσικῶς εἰπεῖν. The continuation of this passage has also an important, though indirect, bearing on the Ρκεξλη ⁻· Isocrates proceeds immediately (294D2) to summarize the essential characteristics of the good pupil and the good teacher. The attributes of the pupil are distinctly referred to later in the *Phaedrus* (269D), and we may pass them over for the moment. As for the teacher, he must be able to expound everything that can be taught, and for the rest set such an example to his pupils that they may improve their own style by imitating his (294E). The teacher of rhetoric, therefore, must be able to practice what he preaches and to show his pupils how it should be done. Now Isocrates has extended the scope of this precept and employed it in the *Busiris* and the *Helen* as a method of literary criticism. In those works he first of all offers a few general comments on the encomia by other authors and then produces his 'fair copy', ἵνα μὴ δοκῶ τὸ ῥᾷστον ποιεῖν, as he says in the *Helen* (211A2). (The formula is the same in the *Busiris* except that προχειρότατον is substituted for ῥᾷστον.) This is a form of criticism which perhaps shows more courage than critical ability, but the point of immediate importance is that Plato has imitated it exactly in the *Phaedrus*. The discourse of Lysias is briefly criticized and Socrates produces a 'fair copy' on the same theme.[3] The whole procedure is then in its turn examined, and the critical method itself is found to be defective because it assumes the possibility of producing a good discourse on a given theme. Socrates has meanwhile produced the real 'fair copy' on the subject of Ἔρως, in which the theme is exactly the opposite of that of the two preceding discourses, whose thesis is shown to be tenable only if the canons of correct discourse are not observed.

To return to the discourse of Lysias. Socrates offers his apologies if he is guilty of having paid attention to the wrong aspects of the speech. He was only paying attention to τὸ ῥητορικόν and he thought that in this respect the discourse was not quite up to the standard which Lysias himself would approve (235A2). The author appeared to repeat himself and to take a beginner's delight (ναενιεύεσθαι, 235A6) in saying the same things in two different ways, both equally excellent. Phaedrus says that this is really the merit of the speech; nothing has been omitted. Socrates does not accept this favourable view. He thinks he has heard better discourses on the subject and feels that he could do better himself. Of course he would derive all he could say from other sources, for he could not invent anything himself συνειδὼς ἐμαυτῷ ἀμαθίαν (235C8). Apart from the general irony of the suggestion that Socrates has nothing general to say about Ἔρως it is perhaps admissible to see here an ironical reference in the word ἀμαθία to the πολυμαθία which is promised to the pupils of Isocrates.

Phaedrus insists that Socrates should make a speech on the same theme, τῶν ἐν τῷ βιβλίῳ βελτίω τε καὶ μὴ ἐλάττω ἕτερα ὑπόσχες εἰκεῖν, τούτων ἀπεχόμενος (235D6). Again there is emphasis on the

---

2. It is perhaps worth pointing out that Plato had already done something of the kind before (though the imitation is not there so obvious or specific) in the *Symposium*, where the interrogation of Agathon is in fact a criticism of his encomium of Ἔρως and leads up to the discourse of Diotima, which is the 'fair copy'.

fact that Lysias' discourse is written, but it is the phrase τούτων ἀπεχόμενος – avoiding τὰ ἐν τῷ βιβλίῳ – which is important. Socrates says that this is an impossible condition and that anyone speaking on this theme must be allowed to say the obvious and essential things (ἀναγκαῖα). He then proceeds (236A4) καὶ τῶν μὲν τοιούτων οὐ τὴν εὔτεσιν ἀλλα τὴν διαθεσιν ἐκαινετεον, τῶν δὲ ημ ἀναγκαίων καὶ χαλεπῶν εὑρεῖν πρὸς τη διαθέσει καὶ τὴν εὕρεσιν. Here we have a double criticism of Isocrates and the reference is to the *Helen*. (211 A4), where he says that he well make his encomium παραλιπὼν τὰ τοις ἄλλοις εἰρημένα.[4] In the second place the proof of the absurdity of the condition is itself a criticism of another statement of Isocrates in the *Helen* (210B2) οἱ δὲ κοινοὶ καὶ πιστοὶ καὶ τούτοις ὅμοιοι τῶν λόγων διὰ πολλῶν ἰδεῶν καὶ καιρῶν δυσκαταμαθήτων εὑρίσκβνται καὶ λέγονται καὶ τοσούτῳ χαλεπωτέραν ἔχουσι τὴν σύνθεσιν, ὅσωπερ τὸ σεμνύνεσθαι του σπώπτειν καὶ τὸ σπουλαζειν τοῦ παίζειν ἐπιπονώτερόν ἐστιν. The passage in the *Phaedrus* shows that Isocrates has here failed to distinguish between two types of argument, those which owe their merit solely to their method of presentation (διάθεσις) Plato, σύνθεσις Isocrates) and those which owe it to their originality as well (εὔρεστις). It is this confusion of thought on the part of Isocrates which has led him to impose on himself such an absurd condition.

Socrates then summons the Muses to his aid and makes his discourse. He proves that it is bad to grant favours to the lover who is really in love but cannot quite bring himself to draw explicitly, as Lysias has done, what Phaedrus believes to be the necessary conclusion. The arrangement of the matter in this discourse is better, and the haphazard arguments of Lysias are reduced to something like order.

Socrates has done as much as Phaedrus expects and is about to make his way home when he is stopped by τὸ δαιμόνιόν τε καὶ εἰωθὸς σημεῖον (235B7), a sure indication that we are now coming to the essentially Socratic or Platonic part of the dialogue. The discourse of Lysias and what Socrates afterwards calls the discourse of Phaedrus (the attribution is significant) have blasphemed against the god Ἔρως and restitution must be made. Fortunately there is a

---

3. Isocrates did not apparently always insist on this condition, and he does not do so in the *Busiris,* so that perhaps the refence here to the *Helen* may be considered to be the more explicit.

καθαρμὸς ἀρχαῖος (253,Α4), ὃν Ὅμηρος μὲν οὐκ ᾔσθετο, Στησίχορος δέ. τῶν γὰρ ὀμμάτων στερηθεὶς διὰ τχν Ἑλέοης κακηγορίαν ... καὶ ποιήσας δὴ ᾳσαν τὴν καλουμένην παλινῳδίαν, παραχρῆμα ἀνέβλεψεν. Athenian readers would appreciate the ingenuity with which Plato has designed the dialogue so that his real views on Ἔρως are expressed in the form of a palinode, and the subtlety with which the direct reference to Helen is introduced. Moreover the subject-matter, Ἔρως, of the palinode, as, of course, of the preceding discourse, has a relevance to the *Helen*. At 212B6 Isocrates says that he will praise Helen by showing the superiority of τοὺς ἀγαπήσαντας καὶ θαυμάσαντας ἐκείνην. Ἔρως is therefore to a large extent the subject of the encomium; but the subject is treated in a muddled way. The δύναμις of Helen over Stesichorus, for instance, which is mentioned at the end of the encomium, is certainly not love, though that is what her δυναμις has meant up to that point (218D5). Isocrates says that Stesichorus ἐβλασφήμησέν τι περὶ αὐτῆς (218E1) and then made a recantation. Plato is unkind enough to quote the opening lines of the palinode, to show that Stesichorus' recantation was a denial of the usual story about Helen. Apparently his blasphemy had been to accept the common tradition; but Isocrates has also done this, and we are meant to notice that he has therefore by implication referred to a great part of his own encomium as blasphemy. It is perhaps not much more than a 'debating point', but Plato does not let Isocrates off, and I think his readers would have appreciated it. Socrates then proceeds to his recantation (244A1), ὁ μὲν πρότερος ἦν λόγος Φαίδρου τοῦ Πυθοκλέους ὃν δὲ μέλλω λέγειν Στησιχόρου τοῦ Εὐφήμου.[5]

Phaedrus admires the discourse and says that he is afraid that Lysias will not be able to compete, and that in any case he may not want to do so. In fact it is quite likely that he will refrain altogether from writing discourses in the future because he has recently been insulted by someone who persistently called him a λογογράφος

---

4. About this discourse of Socrates there is one small point which is of interest if not of great significance. The comparison of the soul with a chariot had already been made by Isocrates. It may be a case of unconscious plagiarism and Plato has certainly made the simile his own, but the following passage does occur in the *Ad Demonicum* (9A3), where Isocrates is talking on the evil effects of wine: ὅταν γὰρ ὁ ᾽οῦς ὑπ᾽ οἴνον διαφθαρῇ, ταὐτὰ πάσχει τοῖς ἅρμασι τοῖς ἡνιόχους ἀποβαλοῦσιν. ἐκεῖνά τε γὰρ ἀτάκτως φέρεται διαμαρτάνοντα τῶν εὐθυνόντων, ἥ τε ψυχὴ πολλὰ σφάλλεται διαφθαρείσης τῆς διανοίας.

(257C6). It is difficult to see the point of this remark if we take it to refer exclusively to Lysias. Lysias can hardly have taken umbrage at being called a λογογράφος because that is precisely what he had been and professed to be. On the other hand Isocrates had also at one time been a λογογράφος and the absence of all mention in his writings at this stage of his career and his derogatory remarks about law-court oratory in general are usually taken to mean that he was ashamed of the fact.[6] But Socrates goes on to show that Lysias (or Isocrates) is in what he would consider good company, for all those who introduce laws are in a sense λογογράφοι. They prefix their names to the decrees they bring forward and the name of those who approve of it (the βουλη or the δημος or both) and are proud rather than ashamed of being λογογραφοί. It is not true, as Phaedrus has suggested (257D7), that the greatest men in the state refrain from publishing λόγοι for fear of being called σοφισταί by posterity. Of course Plato has shamelessly made use of the etymology of the word λογογράφος and does not allow it the more specific meaning of 'writer of speeches for the law-courts', which is what it would normally mean to the Athenian public. The implication is that even if Isocrates confines his attention to broad political issues, and becomes as eminent as Solon or Lycurgus or Darius, he is still a λογογράφος and his art is generally the same as that which he practised when he was a λογογράφος in the narrower and idiomatic sense. He is, in fact, in the same class as Lysias and cannot despise his type of oratory.

After thus mildly ridiculing Isocrates Plato goes on to make his point, which is this (258D1): τοῦτο μὲν ἄρα παντὶ δῆλον, ὅτι οὐκ αἰσχρὸν αὐτό γε τὸ γράφειν λόγους. ἀλλ᾽ ἐκεῖνο οἶμαι αἰσχρὸν ἤδη, τὸ μὴ καλῶς λέγειν τε καὶ γράφειν ἀλλ᾽ αἰσχρῶς τε καὶ κακῶς. It is not said that the writing of discourses is in any way praiseworthy, but only that there is nothing αἰσχρόν in writing them unless they are written αἰσχρῶς. A more positive estimate of the value of such an exercise comes later.[7]

So much then for the preliminaries. We now come to the first of the two chief topics of this part of the dialogue' (258D7) τίς οὖν ὁ τρόπος τοῦ καλῶς τε καὶ μὴ γράφειν; Phaedrus asks what object men

---

5. Alternatively, the ἔσαγχος τῶν πολιτικῶν who insulted Lysias by calling him a λογογράφος may represent Isocrates. The effect is the same, namely that Isocrates is not entitled to distinguish himself from λογογράφοι.

6. 276E.

can have for living if not for the pleasures of discourse. 'There is time for that', says Socrates (258E6), and that is, in fact, the second topic of this part of the dialogue. Plato prepares us for it here but puts off discussion of it until the first question has been dealt with.

The answer to this question is, first of all, that a man must know τἀληθὲς ὧν ἂν ἐρεῖν πέρι μέλλῃ (259E5). He must know the truth about his subject. Phaedrus says that he has heard that it is not necessary to know τα τῳ οντι δικαια (260A1) but only τὰ δγξαντα ἂν πλήθει οἵπερ δικάσουσιν. Socrates easily disposes of this argument. If he persuaded Phaedrus to equip himself for war by obtaining a horse and was aware that Phaedrus did not know what a horse was, except that he thought it had longer ears than any other animal, Phaedrus would be in a pretty plight if, being under this misapprehension, he acquired a donkey and called it horse. That is γελοιον, but it is a serious matter if an orator who is persuading an audience panders to their misapprehension to such an extent that he persuades them to do evil instead of good. It seems a fairly obvious point and it is reasonable to ask why Plato thought it necessary to argue it in such detail. Once again the explanation is that Isocrates did actually put forward the suggestion that Phaedrus says he has heard. In the *Ad Nicoclem* (23D2-24D3) he says that men do not like the most salutary counsels any more than they like the foods which are best for them, and the orator who wishes to carry his audience with him must imitate Homer and the tragedians who recognized the importance of making their work as attractive as possible. His conclusion is this: τούτων οὖν παραδειγμάτων ὑπαρχόντων δέδεικται τοῖς ἐπιθυμοῦσιν τοὺς ἀκρωμένους ψυχαγωγεῖν, ὅτι ρου μὲν νουθετεῖν καὶ συμβουλεύειν ἀφεκτέον, τὰ δὲ τοιαῦτα λεκτέον οἷς ὁρῶσι τοὺς ὄχλους μάλιστα χαίροντας.[8] Plato interprets this, not without some justification, as meaning that the function of rhetoric is to please the audience and that the successful orator has to know how to do this rather than to know τἀληθές.

Socrates then suggests that rhetoric is perhaps not a τέχνη at all but only an ἄτεχνος τριβή (260E5). Ἆρ' οὖν οὐ τὸ μὲν ὅλον ἡ ῥητορικὴ ἂν εἴη τέχνη ψυχαγωγία τις διὰ λόγων; (261A8) he says, recalling, I think, the ψυχαγωγεῖν of Isocrates. Rhetoric, however, Socrates continues, is generically the same whether it is employed in public or in private, about important or unimportant matters

---

7. Cf. *Evagoras* 191A-B.

(μεγάλα or σμικρά). It is not possible to differentiate, as Phaedrus wants to do, between speeches in the law courts or περὶ δημηγορίας and other kinds of discourse. Palamedes employs rhetoric as much as Nestor or Odysseus, and the Eleatic Palamedes (Zeno) as much as Gorgias and Thrasymachus, the modern counterparts of Nestor and Odysseus, It is a good point and Isocrates has laid himself open to it. At the beginning of the *Helen* he has bracketed Gorgias and Zeno as masters of sophistic obscurities, and now Plato replies by bracketing them as employers of rhetoric. Plato, however, is still not prepared to admit the existence of an art of rhetoric, but he insists (261E1) περὶ πάντα τὰ λεγόμενα μία τις τέχνη, εἴπερ ἔστιν. The point is then elaborated that knowledge is the essential requisite of the orator. It is only the man who has accurate knowledge who can make or notice those slight deviations from the truth which are the hardest to detect and the most likely to win over an audience by their verisimilitude. The conclusion is (262B10) λόγων ἄρα τέχνην, ὢ εταιρξ, ὁ τὴν ἀλήθειαν μὴ εἰδώς, δόξας δὲ τεθηρευκώς, γελοίαν τινά, ὡς ἔοικε, καὶ ἄτεχνον παρέξεται. Isocrates' contention in the *Helen* (269A5) that it is better δοξάζειν about important matters than ἐπίστασθαι about unimportant matters is thus thoroughly refuted on two counts. Firstly, it is not legitimate to distinguish, as far as the employment of rhetoric is concerned, between μεγάλα and σμικρά, for the art, if there is one, is independent of the nature of the theme; and secondly, knowledge is always better than opinion.

Phaedrus feels that they are arguing ψιλῶς πως in the abstract. They need παραδείγματα. πατα τύχην γέ τινα (262C10) the discourses of Lysias and Socrates (that is to say the discourse of Lysias and the discourse proper of Socrates, not that which has been called the discourse of Phaedrus) offer us an example of the way in which muddled thinking can lead us into error, and clear thinking can lead us to the truth. Ἔρως is one of those words which require a definition when we use it. All men, for instance, know exactly what is meant by silver or iron, but they do not know exactly what is meant by words like δίκαιον and ἀγαθόν. Such words need a definition before we can know what is meant by them, and Ἔρως is a word like that. Lysias made a mistake in not defining what he meant by Ἔρως. Socrates, under the influence of the Nymphs of Achelous and Pan the son of Hermes, did better and defined Ἔρως fully. Φεῦ, ὅσῳ λέγεις τ ε χ ν ι κ ω τ έ ρ ε ς Νύμφας τὰς Ἀχελῴου καὶ Πᾶνα τὸν Ἑρμοῦ Λυσίου τοῦ Κεφάλου πρὸς λόγους εἶναι (263D5). The nymps were *technically* more correct than Lysias.

It is important to emphasize that the discourse of Lysias is in this part of the dialogue criticized not for the immorality of its theme but for its technical defects. Some of these defects were remedied by the so-called discourse of Phaedrus, but not all of them, notably the failure to define Ἔρως. The fact is that neither of these discourses could have been made if Ἔρως had been defined. It is not possible to make a good discourse on a theme which can only be maintained, as in this case, on the basis of a confusion of thought in the mind of the author or his audience. Isocrates' method of criticism, whereby he undertakes to produce a 'fair copy' on a given theme, cannot be effective, or rather can only be effective so long as it is incomplete. It is only when we clarify our ideas and define our terms that we can know whether the theme can be maintained. In this case it cannot, and Plato of course implies that no immoral theme can be successfully maintained, if the author has the requisite knowledge and makes his knowledge clear in the discourse. The way to dispose of an immoral argument, therefore, is not to rant against its immorality but to point out the technical fault, for there must inevitably be one, upon which the thesis rests. The only man who can make a good discourse is the man who knows the truth, and if a discourse is founded on truth it will be good. Even in the realm of literature knowledge is goodness and is the first essential for the making of good literature.[9]

Socrates then goes on to show his strictly correct technique enabled him to make his discourse. The arguments were put together in a logical order so that the discourse had a proper organic structure. Ἔρως was defined and he emphasizes the manner in which the definition was made. It was done by a process of division, by dividing μανία into several kinds and identifying Ἔρως with one of them, and this method foreshadows that which was later to be so fully illustrated in the *Sophistes*. The examination of the way in which Ἔρως was defined leads to the conclusion that there are two things which the maker of discourses must be able to do. He must firstly be

---

8. The relevance of the discourse of Socrates, and of its myth, to the rest of the dialogue now becomes more evident. It is an outstanding example of Plato's thesis that knowledge of the subject and a strict regard for essential truth result in a finde discourse.

able εἰς μίαν ἰδέαν συνορῶντα ἄγειν τὰ πολλαχῇ διεσπαρμένα (265D3) and secondly καλιν κατ' εἴδη δύνασθαι τέμνειν (265E2). But this is dialectic. What is τὸ λειπόμενον τῆς ῥητορικῆς? (266D4). Phaedrus says that there is a great deal in the textbooks about the προοίμιον, the διήγησις μαρτυρίας and so on. Socrates calls these τὰ κομψὰ τῆς τέχνης. There is considerable discussion of them because they were generally thought to be important, but they are ultimately dismissed as of little value. There is one passage (267A6ff.) which concerns us because most commentators, quite rightly, see in it a reminiscence of a passage in Isocrates. Socrates says Τισίαν δὲ Γοργίαν τε ἐασομεν εὕδεην (a sufficiently contemptuous dismissal) who makes small things appears great and great things small διὰ ῥώμην λογγυ and who say κᾳινά τε ἀρχαως τά τ' ἐναντία καινῶς and can speak very briefly or at length on all subjects. Isocrates makes exactly this claim for oratory in the *Panegyricus* (42C), and whether it is an original claim of Isocrates, which is probable, or is taken from Gorgias, as some commentators think, the point is that Isocrates claims it as a merit whereas Plato ridicules it. Finally (267D8) Socrates says that that is all he has to say even if Phaedrus has anything to add. Phaedrus says that he could only add Σμικρά γε καὶ οὐκ ἄξια λέγειν. Ἐῶμεν δὴ τὰ σμικρὰ says Socrates, in ironical deference to Isocrates.

A knowledge of those technicalities, however, is of no real use. You do not become a tragedian like Sophocles or Eurioides (268C6) because you can περὶ συικροῦ πρεγματος ῥήσεις παμμήκεις ποιεῖν καὶ περὶ μεγελου πάνυ σμικράς and so on. (It is worth noticing how the contrast between τὰ μεγάλα and τὰ ομικρά occurs again and again. It is never allowed to stand and is generally ridiculed.) Perhaps they are necessary for the complete orator, but the essential points are these: (269D6) εἰ μέν σοι ὑπάρχει φύσει ῥητορικῷ εἶναι, ἔσει ῥήτωρ ἐλλόγιμος (perhaps the form of the sentence is intended to recall Isocrates' ἔσει πολυμεθής) προσλαβὼν ἐπιστήμν τε καὶ υελετην· ὅτου δ' ἂν ἐλλίπης ταύτων, ταύτη ατελης εσει. Now this is exactly what Isocrates says in the passage from the κατὰ τῶν Σοφιστῶν (294D3), to which I referred above, when he speaks of what is necessary for the pupil who is leaning rhetoric. δεῖν τὸν μὲν μαθητήν, πρὸς τῷ τχν φύσιν ἔχειν οἵαν χρή, τὰ μὲν εἴδη τὰ τῶν λόγων μαθεῖν (Plato's ἐπιστήμη), περὶ δὲ τὰς χρήσεις αὐτῶν γυμνασηναι (Plato's μελέτη). The correspondence is quite remarkable, particularly if, passing over the essentials of the good teacher which have already been dealt with, we proceed to the last sentence of Isocrates' paragraph (295A1) καθ' ὃ δ' ἂν ἐλλειφθῇ τι τῶν εἰρημένων, ἀνάγκη ταύτῃ χεῖρον διακεῖσθαι τοὺς πλησιάζοντας. (Plato's ὅτου δ' ἂν ἐλλίπῃς τού]ων etc.)

Socrates continues (269D6) ὅσον δὲ αὐτοῦ τέχνη does not lie in the direction of Tisias or Thrasymachus (or, by implication, of Isocrates). We must take as our example Pericles, the greatest of orators (269E1). He devoted himself to scientific study under Anaxagoras, and Socrates with his usual irony claims that this was the cause of his rhetorical excellence. Ironical as this may appear to be, however, it remains true that the orator must study φύσις. As the doctor studies the φύσις of the body, so the orator must study the φύσις of the soul, to find out how he may best work upon the souls of those who listen to him. Once again Isocrates is made to pay for his use of the word ψυχαγωοεῖν (271C10). Ἐπειδὴ λόγου δύναμις τυγχάνει ψυχαγωγία οὖσα, τὸν μέλλοντα ῥητορικὸν ἔσεσθαι ἀνάγκη εἰδέναι ψυχὴ ὅσα εἴδη ἔχει. Whatever the experts may say about persuasiveness rather than truth being the virtue of the orator, we cannot agree with them. There is no other way by which a man can become a successful orator than by a long and exhaustive study of souls. That is enough about the τσχνη τε καὶ ἀτεχνία λόγων (274B2).

What it comes to is this. Taking his own account of the qualities required by a learner of rhetoric, Isocrates is working on wrong lines. He is not teaching them ἐπιστήμη or emphasizing its importance; or at best he is teaching them ἐπιστήμη of entirely unimportant matters (σμικρά), a procedure which he has himself condemned. The refutation of Isocrates' arguments in the *Helen* is complete.

We come now to the second of the two chief topics of this part of the dialogue. Is the writing of discourses a valuable exercise, and is it a subject worth teaching? The story of Theuth, who invented writing for the Egyptians, shows that writing is harmful rather than helpful because it implants λήθη in the soul and makes men δοξόσοφοι ἀντὶ σοφῶν (275B2). Written discourses, too, are like paintings; they look real enough but they cannot answer questions about themselves. The only discourse which is of value is that ὃς μετ' ἐπιστήμης γράφεται ἐν τοῦ μανθάνοντος ψυχῇ (276A5). As far as the writing of discourses is concerned we may assess its positive value thus. It is a splendid recreation, far superior to symposia and the like, a παγκαλή παιδία (276E1) but infinitely inferior to the καλλίων σπουδή (276E5) which makes a man write his discourses in the soul of a kindred spirit, using the art of dialectic.

There are thus two general criticisms of Isocrates. First, that he does not teach rhetoric properly because he does not make ἐπιστήμη the essential basis of it (in fact he does not teach dialectic), and second, that rhetoric, the art of *writing* discourses, is of no serious value, because at best it is a καιδία and not a σπουδή.

Phaedrus then asks for a summary of the argument – πάλιν δὲ ὑπόμνησόν με πῶς (277B4) – and Socrates sums up the matter. Firstly the man who does not understand the nature of the souls of men and how to make his discourses fit those souls, ποικίλη μὲν ποικίλους ... ἁπλοῦς δὲ ἁπλῇ (277C1) – a further criticism, I think, of the statement of Isocrates in the κατὰ τῶν Σοφίστων quoted above, that the orator must be able always ὅλον τὸν λόγον καταποικῖλαι (214D1) – will not be δύνατος τέχνῃ οὔτε πρὸς τὸ διδάξαι οὔτξ τι πρὸς τὸ πεῖσαι (277C4). Secondly (277D6) if Lysias ἢ τις ἄλλος πώποτε ἔγραψεν ἢ γράψει, ἰδίᾳ ἢ δημοσίᾳ, συγγραμμα πολιτικον γραφων και μαγαλυν τινα εν αυτω βεβαιοτητα ηγουμενος καὶ σαφήνειαν, οὕτω μὲν ὄνειδος τῷ γράφοντι εἴτε τίς φησιν εἴτε μή, for ignorance about the nature of justice and injustice, good and evil, is disgraceful to a man even if ὁ πᾶς ὄχλος αὐτὸ ἐπαινέσῃ (another reference to the passage in the *Ad Nicoclem* (24D3) where Isocrates says τὰ τοιαῦτα λεκτέον οἷς ὁρῶσι τοὺς ὄχλους μάλιστα χαίροντας).

There is nothing disgraceful, therefore, in writing discourses if we realize that this is only a παιδία. The σπουδαῖος knows that discourses about justice and beauty and goodness implanted first in his own soul and then in the souls of others are the only valuable and lasting discourses. The man who realizes this we will call, not σοφός, for that title belongs to God alone, but φιλόσοφος (278D). In other words Plato's teaching, and not Isocrates', is φιλοσοφία. Anyone who has nothing better to offer us than his writings we shall be justified in calling (278E1) ποιητὴν ἢ λόγων συγγραφέα ἢ νομογράφον. The objectionable word λογογράφος is avoided, because Plato does not want the association of the word with the law-courts to obscure the issue, but the use of νομογράφος is a stroke of genius.

Finally, so that there may be no doubt about the object of all this criticism, Isocrates is mentioned by name (278D8). Quite likely, says Socrates, he may make a name for himself as a writer of discourses, if he persists in that occupation, for he has better talent than Lysias.

But in fact he might progress to even greater things φύσει γάρ, ὦ φίλε, ἔνεστι τις φιλοσοφία τῇ τοῦ ἀνδρὸς διανοίᾳ (279A9). Some scholars appear to take this as a friendly reference; but when it was published,[10] which is the relevant point, Isocrates was the world-famous head of a world-famous school and had for years claimed that his teaching was φιλοσοφία. Plato allows that φύσει he has φιλοσοφία τις. Even if we take this as the expressed view of the historic Socrates, it only adds to the sting that Plato thinks fit to recall and publish it now. It is surely the most comprehensive damnation with the faintest possible praise.

9. The *Phaedrus* is certainly not an early work, It must have been published after the *Ad Nicoclem* of Isocrates, to which it refers (v. supra), and the *Ad Nicoclem* cannot have been published before 374, the year in which Nicocles succeeded his father Evagoras, and probably appeared about 372. The *Nicocles*, published a few years later, opens with a long attack on those who decry oratory, and this may be Isocrates' attempt to reply to the *Phaedrus*. The date of the *Phaedrus* would then fall between the dates of these two works of Isocrates, that is approximately between 372 and 368.

IRONY AND ALLEGORY IN THE *PHAEDRUS**

V. Tejera

Aristotle's discussion of stylistic propriety in Book III, chapter vii of the *Rhetoric* notices that, in seeking to be proportionate and adequate to his subject matter, an excited or enthusiastic speaker may use exaggeration. But he may have to admit his excess, or his inspiration, in order to preserve his effect. The inspired style, says Aristotle, is especially effective in poetry or when the audience is sympathetic. But it can also be used, he concludes, "with irony, as ... in the speeches in the *Phaedrus*." In the person of the young Phaedrus, Socrates certainly has a sympathetic audience in that dialogue. But it has not been accepted as equally certain that Socrates is as ironic as he is inspired in the two speeches which he invents for Phaedrus in the dialogue.

The Initial Interaction

The first thing that happens in the *Phaedrus* is that Socrates sees through the affectation and harmless pretenses of a young man suffering the symptoms of that expectant state known as being in love with love. It appears that Lysias the speechwriter (λογογράφος, 275C)[1] is in love with him. As an apprentice intellectual who has

*Reprinted by permission of the author and publishers of *Philosophy and Rhetoric*, 8 (1975), 71-87. This article is also scheduled as a chapter in the author's forthcoming book, *Why Plato wrote Dialogues*.
 1. The only speech that Lysias ever *spoke* was the one in his own defense *Against Eratosthenes*. A victim of the Tyranny of the Thirty and a metic, Lysias had to resort to the art of composing speeches for others in order to make a living in the democracy. He is thus more properly called a speechwriter than an orator, Of course, *at the time* of the "dramatic date" of the conversation he was only a man of affairs. Plato, the author, has the perspective of a turn-of-the-century observer, not that of a contemporary of the historical Socrates. In his critique of writing, therefore, Plato's Socrates has at least as much reference to Lysias the writer as to Lysias the orator. We will also have to consider the element of self-irony included by Plato, the writer, in this critique.

been discussing the art of speech with Lysias, Phaedrus is very pleased to meet Socrates, and takes him on a walk outside the walls of Athens. Socrates, fitting his mood to that of the youngster, accommodatingly professes to be love-sick from his own passion for language and argument (227B-C).[2] Phaedrus now has a friend with whom to share the love-speech he got from Lysias; but he is coy about trying to repeat it verbatim to Socrates.

Socrates insists on hearing it. As they walk towards the shady spot where Phaedrus wants to sit and read it, he asks Socrates whether he believes that the myth is true that Boreas abducted Oreithyia from the river bank nearby? When I am not yet able *to know myself* as the oracle enjoins, Phaedrus, how can you expect me to worry about other inquiries? Oh Socrates, says Phaedrus, you are such a stranger to the countryside. Only dangle a discourse in a book before me, Socrates answers, and I would follow anywhere.

Phaedrus reads the speech. Don't you think it's superb, Socrates? Listening to you was quite divine, Socrates answers, I caught your beautiful enthusiasm. Please be serious Socrates, don't you think it's the best speech by any Greek on this subject? No, I found it repetitious and self-conscious about its own skill. I am somehow sure that better things to say exist somewhere, different and quotable — if only I could remember who said them (235C). You mean you could make a better and quite different speech on the same subject, Socrates? I'll dedicate a statue at Delphi if you do. Yes, Phaedrus, but no speech on this subject can be entirely original. Good enough, but if you don't make it I swear I will never read or speak to you again. As a lover of language and argument then, says Socrates with tongue in cheek, I will have to do as you say.

But Socrates finds that to be able to make his speech he has to hide his head from embarrassment or shame (μὺ αἰσχύνης, 237A). Why is this? What is going on here that has made Socrates ashamed of himself? The behavioral clue that Plato has given shows that Socrates is physically resisting a tendency to sexism in his response to the beautiful young Phaedrus. So would an ancient Greek contemporary, it seems to me, have understood the gesture and so would

---

2. Socrates is not simply a "lover of discourse," as the translators would have it here (228C). A λόγος was both a reasoning and a discourse. If μισόλογος means "one who hates speech and argument" (*Phaedo* 89C,C; "*Republic*" 411D), then a lover of λόγων was a lover of speeches and reasonings.

he have appreciated the reality of Socrates's restraint (σωφροσύνη). But Socrates cannot, or does not, hold back from giving some intellectual expression to the erotic stimulation he has felt. Hence the failure of his first discourse, as *philosophy*. It is a pleading not different in kind from Lysias' attempt to win the favors of the admired beloved. It is only better done up to a point. It is more honest only in the sense that, while Socrates's suitor also pretends he is not in love, the speech as a whole is less directly an erotic plea in that it is encased in a narrative *about* a suitor and his suit which recognizes that the suitor is really a lover and not a non-lover. Still, the fact that Socrates lapses into dithyrambics from the stimulus he is under makes it all the more manifest that Dionysian desire rather than intelligence is governing his speech. While the lover and the Socrates behind him seem slightly less self-interested than Lysias and his clever suitor, Socrates's speech nonetheless outdoes Lysias in Lysias's own terms. And these not only are *not* philosophical terms in the best sense, they turn out to be in Socrates's considered judgment an offense to the god of love,

That the speech is not philosophical but sophistical can be seen from the deceitfulness of the suitor's claim that the lover keeps his beloved away from the enlightenment of philosophy and, for it, substitutes his own authority (239B). It is deceitful because the suitor is himself really just another lover and, in so far, will do the very same passion-guided things that he is pretending to warn his beloved against. But why is the speech an offense against the god? Socrates recognizes the speech to have been impious because, just like Lysias, he has said that the lover is a bad thing. But if love is something sacred (Θεῖος), as Socrates and Phaedrus believe it is, then it is false that love is bad. And Socrates must atone for, and cleanse himself of, his blasphemy.

Normal Madness and Formless Essence

Socrates will purify himself with a palinode, or avertive recantation, under the inspiration of the poet Stesichorus. Stesichorus too had once offended against love in verses about Helen of Troy, but succeeded in rectifying both the ill he had spoken and the harm he had suffered, Socrates will make himself the outlet for a repetition of the well-spoken precedent of Stesichorus, and thus neutralize his blasphemy against love before any harm comes to *him*.

Socrates starts the palinode off in a spirit of great humourousness and with an outbreak of punning. The reader becomes conscious of the connotations of the name Stesichorus, or "choral leader," and of the beautiful meaning of the name of the beautiful youngster, the "shining one." He is the son of the "fame-seeker" (Pythocles) from "Wreatheville" (Myrrhinous), while the repentant poet is the son of "Mr. Finespeak" (Euphemos) from "Longinhton" (Himera). The lie is given, at once, to the proposition that the non-lover should be favored over the lover because the latter is mad. In fact, says Socrates, there are four kinds of madness all of which are regularly accounted superior to ordinary sanity, and true love is one of them. The lover is, therefore, superior to the non-lover (243E-244B).

Socrates expatiates with wit but not without reverence. In calling the art which foretells the future the mantic art, we do not recognize, he says, that the mania or madness on which it is based is honorable? The prophet is certainly more honored than the birdwatching augurer whose great pretensions are legitimated. Socrates slyly implies, by a more far-fetched and forced etymology. The tortuous etymology in question is obligingly supplied by Socrates himself as he merrily pursues his point. And the madness that sometimes overtook the subjects of great plagues or tragedies, has it not eventuated in exemplary rituals of release for themselves and their tribal successors? To this day whoever is truly touched, in his troubles, by the expiatory madness finds deliverance from affliction. Then there is the inspired madness of the Muse-possessed poet who surpasses by far his sane and uninspired counterpart, the mere master of poetic technique. I will prove, Socrates continues, that it is a madness much like these that the gods have given to man for the benefit of all true lovers (244B-245C).

Socrates now undertakes a lovingly elaborate and ironic allegory (245C-257B) which will, when completed, constitute an apt account of a general human phenomenon, the mad love of sense beauty — the passion against which he, in particular, has been wrestling for the good of the youngster who has inspired it and for the sake of his own, almost-betrayed integrity. As a piece of detailed intellectualization it will also, on completion, have relieved him of, and tamed, the appetitive stirrings unwittingly awakened. The dramatic, motivating tension of the dialogue is to be found in just this fact that the disciplined and older knowledge-seeker has been truly surprised —

indeed, erotically assaulted — by the poetry of the circumstances and the beauty of the youngster. So what does Socrates do about it, once he has pulled himself together in the wake of his misguided first discourse? Characteristically, what he does is methodically inspired and overwhelmingly intellectual. He takes, in the second discourse, a mixed bag of conceptual materials ranging from nature-philosophy and Pythagorean doctrine, through the heuristic use of visualized Olympian myth and Orphic allusion, to the folklore of passion and the aesthetic-ascetic basic of ideality, and transforms them into a story about the genesis of reflectiveness, or intellectuality, in the discipline of true love. Because his myth does honor to the gods and the man who can imitate them as well as to mind and those who honor it, he can offer his invention to the god of love in the spirit of a suppliant seeking purification and protection.

But the enthusiastic invention must nonetheless be called ironic because it keeps Phaedrus, to whom it is addressed, from noticing what has really been troubling Socrates and that it is he, Phaedrus, who "caused" the trouble, not the weaknesses in Lysias's speech. Socrates is being quite accurate when he tells Phaedrus that he is the cause of the first discourse, but he is also being ironical because it remains hidden to Phaedrus that he was the erotic, as distinguished from the studious, generator of the discursive response. The case is similar with Socrates's second, vastly superior effect. Here he has competed with, or been inspired by, the example of Stesichorus where before he had unfortunately stooped to beating Lysias at his own rhetorical game of disguised lustfulness. But he still "blames" Phaedrus, in the second discourse, for the poetical expressions he has been "compelled" to employ (257A). Socrates, that is, has poetically adapted his words to the situation and preserved the student-teacher relationship between himself and Phaedrus; but he is characteristically unwilling to be identified with his old enemies the poets.

In a richly ambiguous conclusion, which needs examining, Socrates prays the god of love not to take from him (πηρωσης) that art of love (τὴν ἐρωτικὴν τέχνην) and that capacity for love which the god has given him. He also prays not to be less honored than before by those who are beautiful! He prays to the god to turn Lysias towards philosophy rather than rhetoric, and to free Phaedrus from his present clinging to two diverse things (ἐπαμφοτερίζη) so that he may undividedly (απλως) devote himself to love ('Ερωτα) in a rational, philosophical way (μετὰ φιλοσόφων λόγων)³. Here we should not translate (as Jowett, Fowler, and Cooper do) "devote himself to love *and* (as, 'along with') philosophical discourses"; this is to miss the point and the irony. Use of the conjunction "and" does not remove Phaedrus from doing two still distinct things. Socrates is hoping that the young Phaedrus will become a philosophical lover (as Socrates has just shown himself to be); it would not be right for him to want Phaedrus, at this stage, to be anything else or more. Phaedrus is destined to be loved and to be a lover; Socrates can only require him to become philosophical. To let him be concerned with love *and* with speechmaking is to pray for him to become like the Lysias they have criticized and left behind because he was neither a philosophical speaker nor a philosophical lover, but only a rhetorical speaker and an insincere lover.

Thus, the "proof" which Socrates had promised of the fact that love is a god-given madness turns out to be a beautiful myth about the development and basis of intelligence (σωφροσύνη) in the most intimate relationship of which humans are capable. What I will call the discipline of true love turns out to be, in Santanayana's phrase, a kind of "normal madness." To take Socrates's discourse in this dialogue as dressed-up logical argumentation, and to ask how what he says in them can be made to fit the doctrinal system of Platonism is to have missed the overall structure of the dialogue and the nature of the interaction between Phaedrus and Socrates. It is, precisely, to have been made a victim of Socrates's irony by failing to see it. Our loveless appetite for disputation and our nonphilosophical ways of loving have kept the commentators from overcoming the same schizoid plight for which Lysias was condemned. For, the positive point of Socrates's many ironies so far is the mythopoetic or dramatic validation by Plato of the *indivisibility* of appetite or want (ποθος, 253E) and intellect and responsiveness or spirit (Θυμός) as the precondition of human happiness. In the case of the Socrates of the *Phaedrus,* Plato has him come close in practice to identifying good philosophizing with true love.

And while it is true that Socrates mentions (249C) the ability to unify impressions into rational classes, as if invoking the theory of ideas, what he has been talking about is the soul-nourishing vision which the procession of the gods, in his story, loves to enjoy and

3. Or, "devote himself to love without philosophical reason."

which upward-toiling humans strive to glimpse. But this vision is in fact described as an ἀσχημάτιστος ... οὐσία (247C), a completely *formless* essence! Thus, it cannot be a question here of the theory of forms.

Socrates's Critique of Speaking and Writing

Phaedrus feels that Socrates's second discourse is much more beautiful than his first and that Lysias will not be able to equal it. An abusive politician, he says, recently called Lysias a speechwriter; so perhaps Lysias will want to refrain from writing, out of injured pride or for the sake of his reputation. This is somewhat disloyal of Phaedrus, but it signals that he has now become a disciple of Socrates. There is also a kind of vague return to historicity in the remark since it implies that Lysias was still a gentleman and not yet a *logographos*, as was the actual fact at the time of this fictional conversational encounter. You under-estimate your friend's tough-mindedness, Socrates answers, the disgrace consists in writing and speaking *badly*, not in writing or speaking themselves (258D).

Socrates then asks, what is the method (ὁ τρόπος) of good writing? Socrates has, in the preceding, given us an example of good speechmaking. It is fair to assume that Socrates's second discourse has met his own standards of human and philosophical validity, else he would not feel purified by it nor would he have offered it to the god. The fact that it also succeeds in converting Phaedrus from Lysias to Socrates may perhaps be taken to indicate that it is also a good example of *techne,* or informed art and knowledgeable practice. Whether to how far it is so can in any case be verified by reference to the explicit discussion which now follows about the nature of good and bad speaking and writing.[4] We are not told, within the limits of the dialogue, whether the speech can be credited with more than setting Phaedrus on the road to philosophical rhetoric and loving.

Phaedrus reaffirms that, for himself, the study of discourse is the greatest and purest of pleasures. In undertaking this study, says Socrates, the noonday locusts will surely notice our devotion to the Muse of Philosophy and that we have not succumbed like tired peasants to the charm of their Siren voices; they will perhaps hand

---

4. Socrates himself suggests it be examined in this way at 262C.

on to us the gift they got from the Muses they serve, that of never needing food or drink to support their lives of song. So let us examine (σκέψασθαι) the rationale (τὸν λόγον) of good and bad speaking and writing.

In working through the conception of rhetoric which Socrates now puts forward, we will get most from our dialogue if, in juxtaposition with this conception, we keep in mind the metaphorical, narrative, and "dialectical" techniques actually used by Socrates in his second and successful discourse. If we feel impelled to make explicit to ourselves the conception of truth and philosophy implicit in what is a great philosophical discourse, it is because the dialogue is having its effect on us and already structuring our response.

The claims which Socrates makes on behalf of the art of speaking τὴν τῶν λόγων τέχνην) are that knowledge of the truth does not guarantee persuasiveness (260D) and that for a speech to be good the speaker must know the truth about the matters of which he is to speak (259E). In other words, Socrates has so far said that knowledge of truth is a necessary but not a sufficient condition of good speechmaking. Conversely, it follows that if a speech is to be good it will at least have to be based on knowledge of the truth. But much as we can agree to this, a difficulty arises when we remember that in so many of the dialogues Socrates claims not to know, or to be sure of, what the truth is. Nor is the difficulty alleviated by the fact that the philosophical discourse Socrates has just regaled us with is itself so allegorical and so poetical. As Phaedrus says farther on,[5] Socrates very easily makes up stories (λόγοι) about anything he likes. The answer which emerges, for this particular dialogue, seems to be that as long as one's basic distinctions are well drawn or dialectically and ontologically apt, one is proceeding convincingly and philosophically and not away from the direction of truth.

To understand what is going on in the rest of our dialogue, we must notice that the discussion which now ensues (259E-278B) is definitely not a consideration of style in literature in general, as some commentators have thought. The discussion is in the end addressed to the more specific question of the difficulties associated with an art of oratory which had come, as a matter of history, to be based on

---

5. (275B). And as we should remark about Plato's Socrates throughout, if we are to get an accurate sense of the philosophical and critical uses to which his creator puts him in the dialogues. These uses are quite varied and diverse.

writing or logography. This emerges from pages 274B and following in which the harmful effect of writing upon memory is elaborated by Socrates in a myth, and in which the superior effectiveness of the spoken word in dialectical intercourse is emphasized for purposes of good teaching. We must hew to the central line of dramatic development, to the internal dynamic, of the conversation as a whole if we are to avoid being distracted by the many other interesting points which arise in the instructive conversation with Phaedrus.

Socrates had started out, in this last part of the dialogue, wanting Phaedrus to respond to some arguments that will persuade him that "only by philosophizing properly will he ever be able to speak about anything adequately" (εαν μη ιχανως φιλοσοφηαη κτα). Socrates is broadening the conception of rhetoric in a way unheard of by Phaedrus (261B8), but which Isocrates was to make familiar to the Athenians with the programmatic statement in his speech *Against the Sophists* published in connection with the opening of his school, seven years after the death of Socrates. Socrates asks Phaedrus hasn't he heard of the clever Eleatic's[6] practice of the art of refutation and antilogism, outside of the law courts in public and intellectual life?

But to be able to mislead others and escape deception himself a speaker will have to be able to distinguish (διειδέναι) similarities and differences with sureness. Therefore, a speaker who has no knowledge of the way things are and who appeals to mere opinions cannot be said to be in possession of an art, or science, of rhetoric (262B-C). Thus are refuted the people quoted by Phaedrus (260B) who say that an art of persuasion has to be based on what *seems* to be true and not on the truth: it would be laughable to call that a science which is not based on knowledge, and whose manipulations and deceptions are not based on knowledge. So let us look, says Socrates, at Lysias's love-speech and at mine for examples of unscientific (ἄτεχνον) and Scientific (ἐντέχνον) practice.

When Socrates now goes on to say (using the dual number) that the discourse just spoken (262D) are an example of how one who knows the truth may lead his audience on by flatteringly playing with words (προσπαίζων) – it has not been clear to readers and

---

6. Zeno presumably, or not impossible, Parmenides — since it is Plato's Parmenides who is dramatized as constructing a full-scale antilogy; while all we know of Zeno are his paradoxes and his refutative practice of the method of *reductio ad absurdum*.

translators which two of the three speeches Socrates has in mind. Of the three speeches, the one by Lysias and the first by Socrates, are not *both* examples composed by "one who knows the truth" — unless we turn Lysias into a man of knowledge. But the development of the dialogue does not allow this, as we see from 257B where he is censured as unfriendly to true love and as unphilosophical. Socrates's second discourse cannot be paired with Lysias's either, for the additional reason that though it "leads on" to philosophy it does not "mislead" like Lysias's. This leaves the two by Socrates, which meet the conditions required except for an apparent difficulty. They are both by "one who knows" and they are both "playful," unlike Lysias's which intended to seduce where Socrates's first speech only played at being seductive. We have to become more precise and observe that the latter speech was repudiated only because it praised the non-lover and falsely separated, in idea, the lover and the philosopher who should be united in the same person. Socrates's first speech is not really "misleading": it was launched as a story *about* a non-lover's speech; and it did start off correctly with a definition. It was only wrong in identifying "the lover" as one in whom passion forcefully overrides right opinion (238A-C). But it was right in showing the bad consequences of consorting with such a lover; while the man who was called the non-lover does not keep the beloved from philosophy and wisdom. Finally, that the two discourses in question are the two by Socrates is confirmed by the fact that both were spoken (ἐρρηθητην, 262D1) and only spoken (dramatically speaking), in contrast to Lysias's which was first written out and then read (ἀναγιγνώσκειν, 228E, 230E).

Not only should a good speech begin with a clear idea, or definition, of the subject of discourse; rhetoric must also teach, as a matter of method, how to distinguish clearly all equivocal or essentially controversial concepts (263B). "Love" is such a concept; Lysias was not clear about it, and did not get to it until the end of his discourse. Pan and the Nymphs who inspired Socrates were more methodical than that. Again, there was no ordering principle at work in Lysias's speech organically determining the sequence of its parts. It was like the four-verse epitaph of Midas the Phrygian, in which the lines can be put in any order without changing the meaning. Phaedrus objects that Socrates is jeering (σκώπτεις) at the speech, showing incidentally that he has not succeeded in making a clean break with it (264E).

Dialectic and Rhetoric, Philosophy and Writing

So Socrates turns to his own speeches which defined love as a kind of good madness. The second of them, he says, began with some clear distinctions "and somehow succeeded in projecting a likeness of the occurrence of love which might lead us up to truth or away from it; and having mixed a not unpotable account we had fun, in a measured and well-spoken way, with a rather mythical hymn to Love, my lord and yours, Phaedrus, and the guardian of beautiful children."[7] In other words, in the account which Socrates has given of love, love could be a starting point for the search after truth. And the account, for all the effort and seriousness that went into it, is characterized as an enjoyable virtuoso entertainment honoring love under the aspect in which it can lead the young towards truth,

Socrates's words, here, make explicit both the serious philosophical intent of his speech and the playful and aesthetic means by which he pursues his purpose. It is in the tension between the aesthetic design of the speech and its ethical purpose that its irony resides. Yet, given the character of Socrates's interlocutor and his interest in the study of discourse, the means is beautifully suited to the end. This is Plato's Socrates at his ironic best, achieving in the second speech an intelligent fusion of what he does with what he ought to do and enjoying the moral and artistic effort that this kind of integrity demands. It is no wonder that Aristotle could take this dialogue so seriously for purposes of his treatise on rhetoric, yet recognize that the speeches in it were ironic. Out of his own abundant talents, Plato has skillfully endowed his Socrates with what the renaissance Italians called "sprezzatura," the ability to achieve the difficult with the easy grace that makes it beautiful. Thus, when he describes his performance as wit or playfulness (παιδιά, 265D) we see that it is simply an instance of the self-depreciation which Socrates sometimes practices. That he is not running down his speech but only himself is shown by the fact that he now proceeds to draw technical principles from it.

Socrates abstracts, as a first precondition of good speech-making,

---

7. καὶ οὐκ οἶδ' ὅπη τὸ ἐρωτικὸν πάθος ἀπεικάζοντες, ἴσως μὲν ἀληθοῦς τινος ἐφαπτόμενοι, τάχα δ' ἂν χαὶ ἄλλοσε παραιραρόμανοι, κεράσαντες οὐ παντάπασιν ἀπίηανον λόγον, μυθικόν τινα ὕμνον προσεπαίσαμεν μετρίως τε καὶ εὐφήμος τὸν ἐμὸν τε καὶ σὸν δεσπότην ῎Ερωτα, ὦ φαῖδρε, καλῶν παίδων ἔιφορον.

the power of accurate conceptualization. This is the ability to gather under one relevant heading, or general notion, a number of scattered particulars; is is the power to provide clear definitions early in the composition. The other prerequisite is skill in making distinctions; the good distinction-maker, like the good carver, will divide things up along the lines of the natural jointings in his subject matter (265E). Socrates admiringly calls the masters of this twofold skill "dialecticians," and suggests that it comprises almost the whole of the art of rhetoric (266D). But Phaedrus wants to talk about the other things, as well, that the rhetoric books cover. These other things are all listed in quick succession, and in conjunction with the particular rhetorician who most or first insisted on them, under the heading of "niceties of the art" between 266E and 268. In point of their effectiveness, Socrates finds that all these niceties or devices constitute no more than the preliminaries of the art and not the art itself (269A); they do not suffice to define rhetoric.

In fact, rhetoric will never be rightly defined by those ignorant of the dialectical process just described. It is just the things least taught to learners, namely, the apt *application* of the artifices and the *organizing* of the speech into an integral *whole,* that are the core and dynamism of the art for Socrates. – It must be, we note, because they are respectively based on analysis (of the situation) with synthesis (of the materials) that Socrates identifies them with dialectical activity. – So how and from whom, says Phaedrus, can I get the rhetorical art of persuasion? Not from Lysias and Thrasymachus, Socrates answers, for their methods fail to constitute an art. You must be gifted to begin with, you must care and practice, and you must acquire the science ($\dot{\epsilon}\pi\iota\sigma\tau\acute{\eta}\mu\eta$) of it. The most accomplished of orators is perhaps Pericles (269E), if you must have an example.

We are now obliged to notice that what Socrates says about Pericles here appears to contradict what is said about him on pages 503 and 504 of the *Gorgias;* just as what Socrates has said about Tragedy at 268C-E also contradicts what was said about it on page 502 of that Dialogue. But it was Pericles as a *politician,* not as a speechmaker. that was being criticized in the *Gorgias.* And it was in the context of the point that the politician is (inevitably) in the same unhappy relation to his public as the Sophist is to his ungrateful pupils. The political leader who gives the public much of what it wants must neglect the true business of the statesman which, according to Socrates, is to promote justice in and among the people.

Insofar as giving the public what it thinks it wants is flattery and ignores justice, the rhetoric of the political leader cannot be serving the true science of politics; it serves only Sophistic politics. It cannot look beyond the order or techniques of speechmaking to the order which would bring men to justness. Thus what Plato's Socrates makes Pericles illustrate in the *Gorgias* is that the successful politican cannot, in the nature of the case, practice the true science of rhetoric because his rhetoric does not serve the true art-and-science of statesmanship. Like the Sophists he is limited to practicing rhetoric as an *empeiria* or mere set of skills. Of course this need not prevent him from being a virtuoso speechmaker; it is just that, from the standpoint of the true science of statesmanship, to give primacy to virtuoso speechmaking is a mistake. So, in the *Phaedrus,* it is strictly in the context of greatness in the techniques of composition that Pericles's name was invoked. Just as in the *Gorgias* Socrates did not say that Pericles's rhetoric led the people towards justice, so in the *Phaedrus* he does not say that his rhetoric leads the hearer towards ideality or truth. Taking the *Gorgias* and the *Phaedrus* together, while scrupulously respecting their contexts, Plato's Socrates can be seen to be saying that in the true art-and-science of rhetoric the techniques of organizing a speech into a beautiful and effective whole must be informed by the purpose of promoting either justness or truthfulness in the hearer, and this whether the initial motive was political or erotic. Without this, rhetoric remains a mere skill; and the only questions that can arise about it are questions of technique.

The important technical question that was being discussed when the subject of Tragedy came up at 268C-E was that of how to produce speeches that are well-ordered wholes. This is especially interesting because one of the important questions which the *Phaedrus* as a whole leaves outstanding in the reader's mind is whether a speech can have a good dialectical basis (as Socrates has just described the "dialectic") and remain unphilosophical, i.e., not be directed towards justness and truth? Can what Socrates calls the dialectical distinctions upon which a discourse is based, and which are constitutive of its wholeness, be good ones if they do not tally with those that would follow from a knowledge of the nature of human excellence? We get no explicit general answer in the dialogue, and it would not be wise to want one. Rather, only those will be on their way to wisdom in this respect who can accept from Plato the gift of the question as a question, as one, that is, which will now become an operating part of their minds, causing them to hold all discourse henceforth accountable to the search for the conditions which will make men good.

As for what Socrates actually says in the *Phaedrus* about Tragedy, the contrast with the *Gorgias* is marked. He implies, with his question at 268C, that a Tragedy cannot be reduced to the aggregate of mimetic speeches in it. And he accepts from Phaedrus that the art of Sophocles and Euripides requires in addition a power of synthesis and apt harmonization. Socrates adds, however, that no master of any art would want to discourage a beginner because he only knew the preliminaries of his art; the master would surely put him on the road to acquiring the other more difficult and constitutive things required by the art. So it is with rhetoric: the learner must add to his knowledge of what is in the textbooks a dialectical power of putting it all together on the basis of apt distinctions and good generalizations. Pericles's rhetorical ability, Socrates adds half humorously, was probably connected to the philosophical largeness of mind he developed in converse with his friend Anaxagoras.

But the best way to develop your rhetorical skill (*empeiria*) into a real art-and-science (*techne*) is to make the soul the object of your concern (270B). But we cannot understand the nature of the soul without first learning about the whole nature of man. We must be inductive and methodical about the whole thing, like Hippocrates the physician. If the function of rhetoric is to produce conviction in the soul (271A), then the scientific teacher of rhetoric will have to discuss the nature and constitution of the soul. He will also have to understand what it responds to and toward what it is directed. Thirdly, he will have to use his knowledge of these causes (αἰτίαι) to show how to correlate (διαταξάμενος) a given kind of speaking with a given kind of soul so as to produce the desired effect. This knowledge of soul, however, is not to be found in the current treatises on rhetoric even though rhetoric cannot be a science (*techne*) without it. Furthermore, a man must also learn that there is a time when it is best to be silent and that there is a best time to speak; he must know when to be brief, when compassionate, when clever or impressive, and so on if he is to be completely artful or scientific. It's a long and arduous task, Phaedrus, says Socrates, unless you know of a shortcut; perhaps Lysias showed you one? No, he didn't.

Well, says Socrates, some people claim that it is not necessary to be so solemn about it nor to get so far in pursuit of first principles (272D). They say that all that is needed is to attend to "probabilities" and to stick to what is accepted as most likely in each case. But this advice reduces to absurdity, Phaedrus, when a speaker is forced to avoid the defensible truth of a case and is required to defend the false alternatives only because they *seem* more likely. The fact of the matter is that the man who can understand probabilities and invent plausibilities best is just the man who knows the truth best. And the man who knows the truth is the man who is a good observer of souls and has incisive dialectical ability (273A). It is a long course to take, Phaedrus, for the sake of great ends; it is not the way you thought it was.[8] Enough said, then, of speaking as an art and as less than an art; we have still to discuss what writing is good for.

Do you know Phaedrus what is the best way to please God in the conduct of arguments (274B)? Since I'm not sure myself, let me tell you something the Ancients said about it. When the divine Thamus was king of Egypt under the god Ammon, Theuth the inventor came to him with many mathematical inventions. Thamus praised some of them and blamed others. But he especially condemned the invention of a script, or writing, on the grounds that it would weaken men's memories and make them forgetful. There you go again, Socrates, making up stories about anything you like. Perhaps I am prophesying, Phaedrus, please learn to consider *only* whether what is said is true or false (275C-D). You are right to rebuke me. Socrates, and what Thamus said is true.

Whoever believes he can perpetuate some real art (*techne*) in a piece of writing, or that he can be clear and certain about anything in writing, is wrong. Written words are like portraits, if you put a question to them they cannot answer or defend themselves; and you never know into what insensitive hands they may fall. But the spoken word of the man of knowledge, planted in a receptive mind under suitable conditions in a dialectical exchange, will not only be

---

8. H. N. Fowler contradicts himself, and mistranslates, here when he writes (274A) "this path ... must be trodden for great ends, not for those you have in mind. Yet your ends also, as our argument says, will best be gained in this way, if one so desires." Phaedrus's end is to become a good rhetorician: it does not differ from the end of the course (περίοδος) described by Socrates, as Fowler's translation implies.

able to defend itself, it will bear further fruit. Writing cannot be so serious, it can stand only as a reminder of our best thoughts and for the beguilement of our later years. But to be able to speak or write well a man must know the truth about his subject and be able to distinguish things clearly as they are in themselves. And he must understand about souls and the kinds of discourse to which they will respond (277B-E).

We see that for Plato's Socrates the *material* upon which art is to take effect is the attentive human being, and nothing less than the whole human being. Socrates does not allow the status of science or art to anything that will not have an enduring effect for the good upon the auditor. Now Plato, the creator of this Socrates, can also be felt by the reader to be having his effect upon him with his dialogues. But the difference between Plato and his Socrates in this respect is that the *proximate* material which Plato's art must give shape to, is in the main purely conceptual and discursive. It is true that his art of characterization is indispensable to the achievement of the design of many of the dialogues. But the love of knowledge, i.e., *the critical activity* called philosophy which both Plato and Socrates practiced, takes its effect more indirectly on Plato's reader than upon Socrates's live auditor. It is because Socrates sees himself relating so immediately to his hearer with questions, words, and arguments that he condemns writing; for, writing cannot be effective in this dialectical way. The written word gets very quickly out of the control of its formulator; it is too easily misunderstood and made into something uncritical. The ironical horror of it was just this, that no sooner was Plato dead than his own Academy began to take his works in the most uncritical possible way as a kind of masked presentation of the dogmatic system of neopythagorean belief which came to be called Platonism. To the degree that Plato saw himself already misunderstood in his lifetime. Socrates's critique of writing in the *Phaedrus* is a restrained and prophetic piece of self-irony on Plato's part.

It is also a playful rehearsal of what the historical Socrates *might* have said to his young new disciple Plato, on perceiving his incurable addiction to writing. Again, it is possible that Plato was also alluding to the historical case of his contemporary, Isocrates, the speechwriter and statesmanly educator who, precisely because he wrote out his speeches, was never able to be a *dialectical* orator of the kind Socrates is here portrayed to be. He was never able, that is, to confront an audience on his feet, to insist on the right questions and invent the distinctions and explanations most appropriate to the situation, while not forgetting the basic human values to which we must hew if we are to become or remain good men. The written word has a harder time becoming a part of the hearer than the spoken (278A).

Plato's Socrates, however, is not being as negative about Isocrates as he was about Lysias. Tell the poets, the lawmakers, and the speechwriters, Phaedrus, that the Muses have this day taught us that they are not wise unless they can support what they have written dialectically, orally, and ethically. Tell this to Lysias. But what will you, Socrates, tell *your* friend the fair Isocrates? I prophesy that, because of his nobler character and better nature, he will want to go beyond the technical study of rhetoric into the pursuit of knowledge; there is already something philosophical about his mind.

We conclude that in telling Phaedrus to take this message to Isocrates, Socrates is in fact suggesting that the latter will be a better model for the student of discourse than the older and unphilosophical Lysias. Of course, while this is confirmed up to a point by the extant speeches of the two writers, Isocrates, as a matter of historical fact, never did develop into the fully dialectical and philosophical *speaker* that the dramatic Socrates has been depicting. There is no evidence that Plato himself achieved this norm either. But the fact of the dialogues themselves leaves no doubt that Plato achieved, in the medium of writing, a dialectical mastery and philosophical criticality that *refutes* his master's pessimism about the effectiveness of writing. Unfortunately, the regressive dogmatic activities of Plato's earliest Academic successors also completely *justify* the prophetic pessimism of Plato's Socrates.

Bibliography

Plato. *Phaedrus.* Text, English Notes & Dissertations. W. H. Thompson (London: Whittaker & Co. and G. Bell (1868).
— *Phedre.* Notice. Texte etabli et traduit par Leon Robin (Paris: Soc. d'Edition "Les Belles Lettres" 1966).
— *Euthyphor. Apology. Crito. Phaedo. Phaedrus.* Text & Translation. H. N. Fowler (London: Heinemann 1914).
— *Phaedrus.* Translation & Commentary. R. Hackforth (Cambridge: The University Press 1952).
— *Phaedrus, Ion, Gorgias and Symposium.* Translation. Lane Cooper (Ithaca: Cornell University Press 1955).

Aristotle, *Rhetoric. Text & Commentary. 3 volumes.* E. M. Cope. Rev. & Ed. by J. E. Sandys (Cambridge: The University Press 1877).
Isocrates, *Rhetoric.* Text & Translation. 3 volumes. G. Norlin and La Rue Van Hook (London: Heinemann 1928-1945).
Lysias. *Orations.* Text & Translation. W. R. M. Lamb (London: Heinemann 1930).
Frenkian, A. M. *La Methode Hippocratique dans le Phedre de Platon* (Bucharest: Imprimöerie Nationale 1941).
Linforth, I. M. *Telestic Madness in Plato, Phaedrus 244DE* (Berkeley: U. of Calif. Publ. in Class. Philology vol. 13, no. 6).
Pieper, J. *Love and Inspiration. A Study of Plato's "Phaedrus."* Transl. by R. & C. Winston (London: Faber & Faber 1965).
Ruiloba, Palazuelos, F. *Epilogo al Fedro* (Santa Cruz de Tenerife: Universidad de la Laguna 1952).
Schmelzer, C. *Studien zur Redekunst.* Bd. I. Commentar zu Platon's Phaedrus. (Guben: Ehrlich 1869).
Themistius. *Plaidoyer d'un Socratique conte le Phedre de Platon. Intro. Text* öetabli et traduit par H. Kesters. (Louvain: Nauwelaerts 1959).
De Vries, G. J. *A Commentary on the Phaedrus of Plato* (Amsterdam: Hakkert 1969).

PLATO'S CONCEPTION OF *DISPOSITIO**

Floyd Douglas Anderson & Ray Lynn Anderson

The "living creature" image of Plato's Phaedrus *has typically been interpreted either as a formalized schema of* Dispositio *or as a declaration in behalf of "organic unity" of rhetorical and literary composition. In this article, it is argued that both of these interpretations are inconsistent with major aspects of Platonic philosophy and rhetorical theory. An alternative interpretation of the image is presentend.*

"Any discourse ought to be constructed like a living creature, with its own body, as it were; it must not lack either head or feet; it must have a middle and extremities so composed as to suit each other and the whole work."[1] Few statements from the corpus of classical rhetorical theory are quoted as often as this one from Plato's *Phaedrus*. Writers of textbooks on composition and public speaking frequently quote the statement to show that no less an authority than Plato recognized the efficacy of dividing a discourse into three parts, an introduction, a body, and a conclusion. Students of rhetorical and literary theory and criticism often note Plato's comment as both a significant dictum on the importance of form generally and as an ingenious description of good (i.e., "organic") rhetorical and literary form.[2]

---

*Reprinted by permission of the Southern Speech Communication Association from *The Southern Speech Journal*, 36 (Spring, 1971), 195-208.

1. *Phaedrus*, trans. R. Hackforth, 246C.
2. For the prevailing interpretations of Plato's views on *dispositio*, see Everett Lee Hunt, "Plato and Aristotle on Rhetoric and Rhetoricians, *Studies in Rhetoric and Public Speaking in Honor of James A. Winans* (New York: Century, 1925), p. 37; Werner Jaeger, *Paidea: The Ideals of Greek Culture*, trans. Gilbert Highet (New York: Oxford UNiversity Press, 1944), III, 192; George Kennedy, *The Art of Persuasion in Greece* (Princeton: Princeton University Press, 1963), p. 78; Lester Thonssen and A. Craig Baird, *Speech Criticism* (New York: Ronald Press, 1948), p. 397.

Our thesis in this article is that the prevailing interpretations of Plato's statement — i.e., as an attempt to methodize form into three parts and as a declaration on behalf of organic unity in artistic composition — are basically incorrect. Rather, Plato's "living creature" analogy alludes to a deeper, philosophical-psychological notion of rhetorical form. The assumptions underlying Platonic rhetorical theory, in fact, permit neither a formalized schema of *dispositio* nor any serious discussion of composition rules which relate solely to the arrangement of one part of a discourse to another. For Plato, *dispositio* must aid in guiding men to right opinion, persuading them by arguments ordered not according simply to the nature of the arguments themselves but also according to the make-up of the individual auditor's souls. That this is indeed Plato's view is apparent, however, only when his "living creature" figure is considered in the context of other aspects of his rhetorical theory.

Plato's Noble Orator As Philosopher-Psychologist

Plato's views on rhetoric appear in several of his works, with his conception of a "noble" art of rhetoric presented primarily in the Phaedrus. The "nobility" of the rhetoric depicted in this work arises from two essential requirements: (1) that the orator be a philosopher, and (2) that he also be a psychologist, with this second requirement entailed in the first.

In Platonic metaphysics the only truth or reality is an Idea or Form in the mind of God. All else is appearance. Since only the philosopher is able to distinguish between appearance and reality, Plato's insistence than an orator know the "truth" about the matters he intends to discuss is tantamount to stating that the "noble" orator must be a philosopher. Orators who are not also philosophers live as though chained inside a darkened cave beholding mere "shadows"[3] and are capable of persuading their auditors only about "the shadow of an ass" which they confound with a horse, or, what is much worse, about the shadow of injustice which they confound with justice.[4]

The philosopher-orator, perceiving "truth" himself, must never-

---

3. *Republic,* trans. B. Jowett, 514-521; also see *Charmides,* trans. B. Jowett, 170. *Phaedo,* trans. Hugh Tredennick, 75.
4. *Gorgias,* trans. W. C. Hembold, 456, 459-460.

theless take care not to present it directly to his underling auditors.[5] Since non-philosophers have grown accustomed to mere "shadows" — just as one's eyes would eventually adjust to the darkness inside a cave — they would be "blinded" by direct exposure to "truth" or "reality." Plato's philosopher-orator therefore often practices an "art of deception" in which, by presenting resemblances to truth, proceeding by degrees from one resemblance to another,[6] he "deceives" inferiors into believing something which approximates it.[7]

To discover the "truth" about the subjects on which he speaks, Plato's "noble" rhetor must employ dialectic: "Dialectic, and dialectic alone, goes directly to the first principle and is the only science which does away with hypothesis in order to make her ground secure."[8] Hence, Socrates criticizes Lysias' speech in the *Phaedrus* for his failure to define his terms or distinguish between particulars and universals or debatable and non-debatable propositions.[9] Being unskilled in dialectic, Lysias is unable to do so. For Plato, as Hunt observes, "dialectic was the whole process of rational analysis by which the soul was led into the knowledge of ideas."[10]

Yet if the philosopher-orator is to succesfully "touch" the minds of his auditors in this fashion, he must also know the nature of the human "soul."[11] For certain dispositions of character demand persuasive techniques especially chosen to suit them. The philosopher-orator must therefore adapt his speech to each of the individual members of his audience in a manner not unlike that in which the discussant in dialectic adapts his arguments to his counterpart.[12] Without a thorough knowledge of human psychology there can be no meaningful practice of rhetoric:

> Then it is plain that Thrasymachus, or anyone else who seriously proffers a scientific rhetoric, will, in the first place, describe the soul very precisely, and let us see whether it is single and uniform in nature or, analogously to the

---

5. *Republic*, 517-518.
6. *Phaedrus*, 244-257C, 275C.
7. Cf. Kennedy, p. 70.
8. *Republic*, 533-534; also see *Phaedrus*, 265-266.
9. *Phaedrus*, 263.
10. Hunt, p. 53.
11. *Phaedrus*, 270-272.
12. For an excellent treatment of Socratic dialectic, see William Sattler. "Socratic Dialectic and Modern Group Discussion," *QJS*, XXIX (April 1943), 152-157.

body, complex. For to do that is, we maintain, to show a thing's nature... And secondly he will describe the natural capacity it has to act upon what, and through what means, or by what it can be acted upon... Thirdly, he will classify the types of discourse and the types of souls, and the various ways in which souls are affected, explaining the reasons in each case, suggesting the type of speech appropriate to each type of soul, and showing what kind of speech can be relied on to create belief in one soul and disbelief in another, and why.[13]

Traditional Interpretations of Plato's Conception of *Dispositio*

As we have noted, the often quoted Platonic figure concerning arrangement, that every discourse ought to be like a living creature, possessing a body, head and feet, has traditionally been interpreted as either a simple attempt to methodize the arrangement of speech materials into three main divisions or as an injunction for organic unity in artistic composition. Both interpretations, however, fail to relate Plato's remarks on *dispositio* to his insistence that an orator be both a philosopher and a psychologist; that the user of any legitimate *techne* or art of his subject matter and knowledge of the souls of his auditors. These dual requirements are crucial for an understanding of any aspect of Plato's theory of rhetoric; with them Plato insists that a rule of speech composition is legitimate only if it posits a relationship (known to be true by the philosopher-orator) between the orator's subject matter and the mind or soul of his auditor. But these prevailing interpretations of Plato's "living creature" figure point up relationships only between parts of the rhetor's subject matter; the simplest interpretation calling for three distinct and natural parts, the more complex interpretation suggesting that whatever the parts of a discourse, they should be arranged such that, if inspected from part-to-whole or from whole-to-part, the discourse has a vital unity, a oneness in its plurality.

The significant question before us, then, is one of consistency; Did Plato construct an "ideal" rhetoric which demanded that legitimate rules of speech composition reveal accurate relationships between subject matter and auditor, and then, in dealing with *dispositio*, himself suggest an illegitimate rule of composition? It would seem that acceptance of either of the traditional interpretations of the "living creature" figure amounts implicitly to accusing Plato of a

---

13. *Phaedrus,* 271A-B.

major theoretical inconsistency. A substantial amount of evidence exists within the *Phaedrus,* however, which suggests that neither of the traditional interpretations of Plato's conception of *dispositio* represents what he had in mind when setting forth his "living creature" image.

Plato's Objection to the Methodized Systems of *Dispositio* of His Contemporaries

That Plato intended the "living creature" image as a dictum for a tri-partite methodization of rhetorical form seems highly improbable for two reasons. The first is his disapproval of the formalized systems of *dispositio* advanced by the professional rhetoricians of his day. This disapproval is dramatically expressed in the *Phaedrus,* where Socrates launches into a rather lengthy tirade against the handbooks of the various professional rhetoricians, ridiculing several of the standard doctrines and precepts outlined in such handbooks.[14] One of the doctrines that he ridicules is the standard division of a speech into prescribed or formalized parts:

> *Phaedr.* Well, Socrates, of course there is plenty of matter in the rhetorical manuals.
> *Socr.* Thank you for the reminder. The first point, I suppose, is that a speech must begin with a preamble. You are referring, are you not, to such niceties of the art?
> *Phaedr.* Yes.
> *Socr.* And next comes exposition accompanied by direct evidence: thridly, indirect evidence; fourthly, probabilities; besides which there are the proof and supplementary proof mentioned by the Byzantine master of rhetorical artifice.
> *Phaedr.* You mean the worthy Theodorus?
> *Socr.* Of course. And we are to have a refutation and supplementary refutation both for prosecution and defense.[15]

Having thus scorned the professional rhetoricians' methodization of rhetorical form, it seems unlikely that Plato would turn right around and offer his own methodized system. Moreover, although Socrates himself employed the methodological divisions of the rhetoricians (i.e., exordium statement of the case, confirmation, and epilogue) in

---

14. *Phaedrus,* 266-269.
15. *Phaedrus,* 266-267A; cf. Aristotle's criticism of the professional rhetorians' treatment of arrangement in the *Rhetoric,* 1414B.

his first speech in the *Phaedrus*, a speech which he himself condemned as "false" rhetoric, he did not employ such divisions in his second speech, which was intended to serve as an illustration of "noble" rhetoric.

Plato's Objection to Rhetorical Methodization of any Kind

A second and even more important problem with the interpretation of the "living creature" figure as a formalized schema of *dispositio* is that Plato viewed methodization of any kind as the ultimate barrier to communication. This view is made abundantly clear by Plato's discussion in *Phaedrus* — and in several other works — of the inherent inferiority of the written word. Plato saw the written word as the paradigmatic case of faulty communication — faulty because it represented the ultimate in methodization. By its very nature, written discourse could not meet the criteria of truly serious (living) discourse; discourse which goes together with knowledge. Plato therefore labeled written discourse as "dead" discourse;[16] the antithesis of "living" communication. Plato criticized written discourse because it both subverted man's capacity of memory[17] and lacked the essential plasticity of truly discourse.[18] The written word was permanent and rigid. It could neither adjust itself to the souls of individual auditors nor adapt itself to the questioning process necessary to the discovery of non-debatable propositions.

> It is the same with written works; they seem to talk to you as though they were intelligent, but if you ask them anything about what they say, from a desire to be instructed, they go on telling you just the same thing forever. And once a thing is put in writing, the composition, whatever it may be drifts all over the place, getting into the hands not only of those who understand it, but equally of those who have no business with it; it doesn't know how the address the right people, and not address the wrong.[19]

If the "deadness" of the written word results from its rigidified and methodized communicative approach, Plato's likening of *dispositio* to a "living" thing suggests that it could not also involve methodization. That Plato saw the written word as the paradigm of faulty

16. *Phaedrus*, 276A-B.
17. *Phaedrus*, 275A.
18. See Plato's discussion of the "flexible" nature of "serious" discourse in *Phaedrus*, 277C-278A. Also see the *Letters*, trans. L. A. Post, 344C.
19. *Phaedrus*, 275D-E.

communication because of its suffocating methodization is also revealed in the *Protagoras* where the actions of ignorant orarors are compared to the undesirable characteristics of books.

> It is true that if a man talked on these matters with any of our popular orators, he might possibly hear similar discourses from Pericles or some other proficient speaker, but if one asks any of them an additional question, like books they cannot either answer or ask a question on their own account. Ask them the smallest thing supplementary to what they have said, and like a gong which booms out when you strike it and goes on until you lay a hand on it, so our orators have a tiny question spin out a regular marathon of speech.[20]

Socrates' severe criticism in *Phaedrus* of the arrangement of Lysias' speech can then be regarded as the natural consequent of Plato's general bias against the methodized approach to rhetoric.[21] After all, Lysias' speech is in the form of a *manuscript* and because it has fallen into the hands of people "who have no business with it," "it doesn't know how to address the right people, and not address the wrong."

The Inadequacy of the "Organic Unity" Interpretation of Plato's Conception of *Dispositio*

If Plato's "living creature" image cannot be interpreted as a formal schema of *dispositio*, should we then take it as a recommendation that each speaker and writer "shape the several parts of his discourse into an organic and vital unity of an artistic composition?"[22] The problem with this widely-accepted interpretation is that it treats mere discourse, in the Platonic sense as an entity in its own right; an entity which, when properly constructed, has parts so divided that any alternation would dismember or destroy its inherent vitality, its life. But Plato never proclaims that discourse *qua* discourse possesses organistic qualities. These properties are reserved only for discourse which is both true and attuned to the disposition of particular auditors. It is unlikely that Plato would ever have criticized a discourse simply because it did not meet certain paper and pencil tests

---

20. *Protagoras,* trans. W. K. C. Guthrie, 329A-B.
21. See *Menexenus,* trans. B. Jowett, 235A-E. Here Plato criticizes the "methodized" invention of contemporary orators who deliver "ready-made" speeches; orations "long ago prepared."
22. W. Rhys Roberts, *Greek Rhetoric and Literary Criticism* (New York: Longmans, Green, 1963), p. 7.

relating to the aesthetic unity of paragraphs or the balance of arguments. To engage in such a practice would be attending to dimensions of subject matter while dismissing auditor considerations, which, incidently, may prevent aesthetically unified paragraphs or balanced arguments. Even when Socrates instructs Phaedrus to first define his terms and then find divisions according to natural formation (i.e., "not to hack off parts like a clumsy butcher"),[23] he is speaking of more than the relations between various parts of a discourse which might be displayed on a piece of paper or a modern tape recording. He is referring to the relations between parts of discourse as they in turn relate to the minds of men. Socrates assures us here that this proces of division is what he has "hitherto been in the habit" of calling dialectic;[24] that process which aims at touching God's mind (and so comprehending *Eidios*) through the patient and continual touching ("loving" in the context of *Phaedrus*) of mortal minds. For Plato, then, an orator must employ his understanding of human psychology as well as of his subject matter to produce discourse which may be called "organic." Plato thus instructs us that the orator "must have a corresponding discernment of the nature of the soul, discover the type of speech appropriate to each nature, and order and arrange his discourse accordingly, addressing a variegated soul in a variegated style ... and a simple soul in a simple style."[25] The faults of arrangement which Plato has Socrates criticize in Lysias' speech are faults stemming from Lysias being neither philosopher nor psychologist:

> No, he doesn't seem to get anywhere near what we are looking for; he goes about it like a man swimming on his back, in reverse, and starts from the end instead of the beginning; his opening words are what the lover would naturally say to his boy only when he had finished ... And to pass to other points, doesn't his matter strike you as thrown at haphazard? Do you find any cogent reason for his next remark, or indeed any of his remarks, occupying the place it does? I myself, in my ignorance, thought that the writer, with a fine abandon, put down just what came into his head. Can you find any cogent principle of composition which he observed in setting down his observations in this particular order?[26]

What is significant in this critical commentary is not the observation

23. *Phaedrus*, 265E.
24. *Phaedrus*, 266B.
25. *Phaedrus*, 277B-C.
26. *Phaedrus*, 264A-B.

that Lysias' speech lacks logical structure, but the reasons why it has none: (1) the order of the elements of the discourse do not naturally correspond to how one would address such a youthful lover; and (2) the subject matter seems "thrown out at haphazard."

Plato furthermore makes it clear that the structural superiority of Socrates' second speech in the dialogue stems from his knowledge of philosophy and psychology.[27] As a philosopher, he has proceeded dialectically to discover the truth about his subject and to make necessary logical distinctions, and has then arranged his arguments in accordance with this knowledge. As a psychologist, he has carefully analyzed his audience, in this case the youthful Phaedrus, and has then arranged his materials in the manner most suited to correspond with and thus induce persuasion in Phaedrus' soul. Socrates' speech has a beginning, a middle and an end — "head, body and feet" — but its pattern of arrangement is the result of Socrates' philosophical-psychological understanding of the rhetrotical situation, not the result of a strict adherence to a formal schema of *dispositio* or of such measured adjustments within the text of his speech so as to give it an internal wholeness and unity.

The Broader Context of the "Living Creature" Image

The inadequacies of the standard interpretations of Plato's conception of *dispositio* arise largely from their failure to encompass the borader context of the "living creature" image. More specifically, the formal schema and organic unity interpretations suffer from the fact that they both spring from viewing the image *spatially*; that is, by literally forming in one's mind an image of a human body which invariantly places the head above the body and the body above the feet, and then inferring from this literal image that the proper arrangement of discourse follows the *natural* and *stable* relations pertaining between the component parts of the physical body. The assumption of a physical model explains why proponents of a formal schema insist that the proper arrangement of discourse is to move from head (introduction) to body, to feet (conclusion) as well as why adherents of the literary unity position are concerned with maintaining a balanced and vital geometry of parts within any discourse.

But there are no inherently compelling reasons within the confines

---

27. See especially *Phaedrus*, 263-264, 265-266, 269, 277.

of Platonic philosophy for regarding the "living creature" image as an analogy between the disposition of a physical body and the proper arrangement of discourse. Indeed, there is much evidence that the "living creature" figure is used primarily, as is Plato's custom, to refer to something beyond the physical representation it denotes. Plato's images do not court analysis in terms of photographic representation or exact correspondence. They are more often than not vehicles to something beyond, revealing semblances and likenesses of an artistic nature.

Lifting the "living creature" figure above the level of spatial illustration produces a rather exciting result: the image represents an analogy between the disposition of discourse and the disposition of that thing which for Plato makes any creature a "living" thing, the soul. Plato's suggestion that discourse should be likened to a "living creature" would mean, therefore, that the *dispositio* of rhetorical discourse ought to correspond to that of the auditor's soul.

The support for this alternative hypothesis is manifold. This interpretation, first of all, is wholly in keeping with Plato's prime requirements that the noble orator be both a philosopher and a psychologist. It is a legitimate rule of speech composition in that it posits a relationship (known to be true by the noble orator) between the rhetor's subject matter and the soul of his auditor.

Aside from these requirements this interpretation also seems more consonant with the special meaning that Plato reserves for the notion of "living creature." A "living creature" for Plato always entails something more than a fully endowed physical body. In the *Phaedo*, for example, Plato insists that the only thing that makes any creature a "living" entity is that it possesses a soul.[28] Plato explicitly states in the *Epinomis* that "the name 'living creature' is most properly used in the case when a single complex of soul and body gives birth to a single form."[29] And in the *Phaedrus* also he argues that "this composite structure of soul and body is called a living being . . ."[30]

It is important in this connection that we recall the medical analogy sustained throughout *Gorgias*, the *Laws*, and the *Phaedrus*.[31] Here Plato makes it eminently clear that medicine gives

28. *Phaedo*, trans. Hugh Tredennick, 105C.
29. *Epinomis*, trans. A. E. Taylor, 981A.
30. *Phaedrus*, 271A.
31. See *Gorgias*, 465B, *Laws*, trans. A. E. Taylor, 857D, and *Phaedrus*, 270B.

strength and health to the body while rhetoric aims at importing *pietho* and *arete* to the soul. Drugs are to the body what discourses is to the soul. But "nursing" in the rhetorical sense implies a knowledge of the soul's affliction so that the proper mixture of mental drugs (resemblances) may be ministered to the ailing creature. Given the distinction set out by the medical analogy, then, it is quite understandable that Socrates, advising Phaedrus on the necessity of knowing the souls of those to whom he would minister, would again use a variation of the medical analogy: "in the first place, describe the soul very precisely and let us see whether it is single and uniform in nature or, *analogously to the body, complex*" [italics added].[32] Now if man's soul is indeed complex, "analogously to the body," it would only be natural that it would have identifiable parts (i.e., it would perhaps have a head, a body, and feet or counterparts for head, body, and feet). Although Plato discusses the nature of the soul in several different places, perhaps the most revealing analysis appears in the *Timaeus*.

> Now of the divine, he himself was the creator, but the creation of the mortal he committed to his offspring. And they, imitating him, received from him the immortal principle of the soul, and around this they proceeded to fashion a mortal body, and made it to be the vehicle of the soul, and constructed within the body a soul of another nature which was mortal, subject to terrible and irresistable afflections ... these they mingled with irrational sense and with all-daring love according to necessary laws, and so framed man. Wherefore, fearing to pollute the divine any more than was absolutely unavoidable, they gave to the mortal nature a separate habitation in another part of the body, placing the neck between them to be the isthmus and boundary, which they constructed between the head and breast, to keep them apart. And mortal soul, divided the cavity of the thorax into two parts ... That part of the inferior soul which is endowed with courage and passion and loves contention, they settled nearer the head, midway between the midriff and the neck, in order that being obedient to the rule of reason it might join with it in controlling and restraining the desires when they are no longer willing of their own accord to obey the word of command issuing from the citadel.

The significance of this analysis is, of course, that it relates the components of Plato's idea of the soul — involving reason, passion, and appetites or will — to the architecture of the body complex. Relating the "living creature" image to Plato's description of the bodily parts and the incasement function they have with respect to the soul in the *Timaeus*, the head corresponds to reason, the body to

32. *Phaedrus*, 271A.
33. *Timaeus*, trans. B. Jowett, 69C-70A.

the passions (located above the midriff), and the feet — since Plato continually associates the lowest part of the mortal soul with the principle of locomotion[34] — logically correspond to the will.[35]

If we now relate the "living creature" figure to the meaning and centrality of the "winged charioteer" myth in the *Phaedrus*, we discover what Plato probably conceived as valid rhetorical *dispositio*. Both the "winged charioteer" myth, relating to the nature of rhetoric, and the "living creature" figure, referring to the concept of *dispositio*, point to the necessary correlation between soul and *Eidos*, the focal point of all Plato's philosophy. The three parts of the "winged charioteer" image are the same as those mentioned in the *Republic*[36] and the three parts of the "living creature" figure are the same as those mentioned in the *Timaeus*: the three elements of both images are synonymous with Plato's three-part division of the soul. The winged charioteer corresponds to reason, the white horse to will or appetite, the black horse to the passions.[37] Just as love is the perpetual struggle for harmony between the component parts of the soul, so rhetoric (the discourse of love) is for Plato the act of assisting the auditor in establishing the proper controlled or harmonious relation between the charioteer and his horses. Just as our overall "manner of discourse" should be "likened to the union of powers in a team of winged steeds and their winged charioteer,"[38] so should the arrangement of our discourse be likened to a "living creature" with a head, body and feet, each suited to the other.

Conclusion

Without an understanding of the broader context of Plato's "living creature" image, the critic fails to appreciate the full significance of his view of *dispositio*. For Plato, the "winged charioteer" figure provided an artistic statement of the function of rhetoric: discourse aimed at rising to true knowledge by the charioteer (reason) bridling

34. *Timaeus*, 44D, 69C.
35. *Timaeus*, 34C, 69E, 89C, 90A, 91E.
36. *Republic*, 580, 588; also see *Laws*, 863B.
37. *Republic*, 580, 588.
38. *Phaedrus*, 246A.
39. *Timaeus*, 91E. For an excellent analysis of the "winged charioteer" image see Paul Friedländer, *Plato* (New York: Pantheon Books, 1958), pp. 192-198.

the two horses into balance. With the "living creature" figure Plato illustrated how discourse could be arranged to facilitate the attainment of the rhetor's end: discourse must be tailor-made to the existing disposition of the auditor's soul, for only then can the head (reason) give guidance to "those parts of the soul which are in the breast"; and below. With this image Plato dramatically informs us that the clumsy butchering of a "living creature" is an infinitely greater crime than unknowingly scrambling a logically correct speech outline. The bungling butcher distinguishes himself by his ministering to another's affliction of soul in such a way as to alienate that soul from *Eidos*.

RHETORIC AS SEDUCTION*

William G. Kelly Jr.

In his *Symposium* and *Phaedrus* Plato makes a sophisticated inquiry into the erotic nature of communication and reveals his vision of communication as love-sharing or love-making, which one achieves as he approaches Truth. In doing so, Plato grasps at a fundamental definition of communicative acts, relating them to the basic and primary physical ones which give us all life and sustain us. In this essay I examine the sex-talk relationship in one of its dimensions — the manner in which Plato viewed communication as an erotic encounter.

In the *Phaedrus,* concealed in the pinions of Socrates' expansively beautiful second speech on love, lies the key to an understanding of the *Phaedrus* and the *Symposium*.[1] Socrates says of the soul, "To tell what it really is would be a theme of a divine and a very long discourse; what it resembles, however, may be expressed more briefly and in human language."[2] It is as though Plato realizes the impossible task of describing communication, and he chooses, therefore, to tell us metaphorically what it resembles in two dialogues which revolve tightly around the theme of erotic love. Plato's realization is suggestive of Norman O. Brown's in *Love's Body* when he suggests that "to make in ourselves a new consciousness, an erotic sense of reality, is to become conscious of symbolism. Symbolism is mind making connections (correspondences) rather than distinctions (separations). Symbolism makes conscious interconnections and unions that were unconscious and repressed."[3] Richard Weaver,

---

*Reprinted with permission by *Philosophy and Rhetoric,* 6 (1973), 69-80.
  1. Wayne N. Thompson calls for rhetorical study of the *Symposium* in his article, "The Symposium: A Neglected Source of Plato's Ideas on Rhetoric," *The Southern Speech Communication Journal,* 37 (Spring, 1972), 219-32.
  2. Plato, *Phaedrus,* trans. W. C. Helmbold and W. G. Rabinowitz (New York: Bobbs-Merrill, 1956), 246, p. 28.
  3. Norman O. Brown, *Love's Body* (New York; Vintage Books, 1966). pp. 81-82.

writing about the *Phaedrus* in *The Ethics of Rhetoric*, reveals that he has caught the metaphorical vision of the work. He says of the dialogue: "The central idea is that all speech, which is the means the gods have given man to express his soul, is a form of eros, in the proper interpretation of the word."[4] In Brown's sense and in Weaver's, I undertake in this essay to re-synthesize, remake, the correspondences between communication and love which imbue Plato's writing on rhetoric with erotic vigor.

In his *Symposium* and his *Phaedrus,* Plato discusses this sex-talk relationship in the most subtle fashion, in a manner like seduction itself, which leaves the reader delighted with the consequences only after he has succumbed to the author's ploys. There are immediate clues to what Plato is about. Ostensibly, both dialogues contain vociferous discussions of rhetoric and of love — this in spite of the often rather superfluous advice about speech making. For instance, at the outset of the *Phaedrus* the substance of Socrates' complaints against Lysias' speech focus on relatively minor matters such as its redundancy.[5] The *Symposium* offers even less direct advice to the rhetor, and it makes less pretense to offering such counsel. After all, Plato holds the discipline of rhetoric in obvious contempt. He is doing more than merely offering rhetorical nostrums; these extensive discussions of speeches and speech making serve as a veneer for the more important substructure, a facade for the more subtle and significant undertaking — the construction of extended metaphors about the erotic nature of communication.

THE *SYMPOSIUM*

Early, at the banquet, Eryximachos suggests "that each one may drink as much as he likes, but no one *must* drink," and "that the piping-girl who has just come in may go out again, and play to herself, or if she pleases to the women inside, and that today we entertain each other with talk."[6] More specifically, he suggests that they, in their turns, eulogize an ignored god — who else but Love?

---

4. Richard Weaver, *The Ethics of Rhetoric* (Chicago: Henry Regnery Co., 1965), p. 5.

5. *Phaedrus,* 235, p. 13.

6. Plato, *Symposium,* trans. W. H. D. Rouse, in *Great Dialogues of Plato* (New York: Mentor, 1956), 177E, p. 75.

Socrates answers that he could not refuse, because "love is the only thing I profess to know about."[7] Thus at the outset, Plato establishes the theme he is to develop throughout the dialogue, that whenever Socrates speaks, he speaks of love, whether love of men or of wisdom.

When he finally enters Agathon's house, Socrates feels he must flatter his host, but he does so in a way most important to an understanding of this dialogue. He launches into a discussion of tactility in communication, talking about the exchange of wisdom as if it were a physical commodity passing between two bodies. He says,

> What a blessing it would be, Agathon, if wisdom could run from the fuller amongst us to the emptier, while we touch one another, as when two cups are placed side by side a bit of wool conveys water from the fuller to the emptier! If wisdom is like that, I think it precious to be beside you, for I think I shall be filled up with fine wisdom. Mine would be poor stuff and questionable, like a dream, but yours brilliant and fast growing; see how it has blazed out of you while you are still young, and showed itself to us the other day before over thirty thousand of our nation![8]

A notable feature of this speech is, of course, Socrates' unabashed attempt at flattery, but equally remarkable is the view of communication it reflects. He alludes to a spiritual kind of communication in which an effortless change of wisdom passes from person to person like a substance passing by a wick from vessel to vessel — a transfer brought about by proximity and a physical link. If there is an ideal to be wished for, this is the one for which Socrates opts, because it forever eliminates the necessity for the intermediary of words and subsequently for rhetoric. Surely these opening lines of the *Symposium* cannot be diminished in significance, for they set the stage for what is to come.

A bit later in the dialogue, in Pausanias' speech, Plato's view of the sexual nature of rhetoric becomes yet clearer when Pausanias discusses the license afforded lovers seeking their ends. He says,

> For if, wishing to get money from someone, or to win public office, or to get any other power, a man should behave as lovers do towards their beloved, begging and beseeching them in their petitions, and swearing solemn oaths, and sleeping at their doors, and being willing to do slavish services such as no slave would do, he would be hindered both by friends and by enemies from doing his business thus ....[9]

7. *Ibid.*
8. *Ibid.*, 175D, p. 74.
9. *Ibid.*, 182D, p. 80.

Here Pausanias openly mentions various functions of rhetoric (selling, winning public office, etc.) in the same context, in fact in comparison with, the activities of lovers. He leaves little question as to his perception of rhetorical communication as analogous to courtship.

Alcibiades' appearance at the banquet provides the strongest argument yet for perceiving the *Symposium* as a metaphor on the sexual nature of rhetoric. It is not Socrates, but Alcibiades, who is the key to the intricacies of the *Symposium*. Alcibiades enters on cue directly following Socrates' speech. According to the account, he was "very drunk and shouting loud, . . . crowned with a thick wreath of ivy and violets and wearing a great lot of ribands on his head" and wanting to put a garland on Agathon.[10] He seems quite aware of his drunken condition as he asks his friends, "Will you laugh at me because I'm drunk?"[11] Then he notices Socrates, and after declaring his delight and surprise, Alcibiades jealously complains that Socrates is lying beside Agathon. He carps, "but you managed to get beside the handsomest of the company."[12] A significant point lies in Socrates' reply to Alcibiades' jealousy. Perhaps half in jest, Socrates pleads for help from Agathon saying,

> Agathon won't you defend me? I find that this person's love has become quite a serious thing. From the time when I fell in love with him, I am no longer allowed to look at or talk with a handsome person, not even one, or this jealous and envious creature treats me outrageously, and abuses me, and hardly keeps his hands off me. They don't let him try it on now, but do reconcile us, or if he uses force, defend me, for I'm fairly terrified at his madness and passion.[13]

Socrates spurns Alcibiades for his apparent shallowness, his pettiness, and his capacity for the sham. As Alcibiades continues, he lets everyone know that he has the greatest admiration for Socrates and wishes nothing more than to be his lover again, He calls Socrates "the man who beats all the world at talking," and compares him to the renowned player of pipes, Marsyas, the Satyr, who "used to bewitch men through instruments by the power of his mouth."[14] In commenting on Socrates' propensity for talk what greater insult could he

---

10. *Ibid.*, 213D, pp. 106-107.
11. *Ibid.*, p. 107.
12. *Ibid.*
13. *Ibid.*
14. *Ibid.*, 215D, pp. 108-09.

hurl, even in jest, than to compare him to the master of sensual love and seduction, the satyr? He says further that the tunes of Marsyas "enravish us," and to Socrates he says, "You do the very same without instruments by bare words!"[15] There is no clearer statement of the link between rhetoric and seduction in the *Symposium* than this analogy between Socrates' eloquence and the satyr's cunning. Alcibiades pursues Socrates' affections with vigor, but Socrates spurns him — not because he has any aversion to Alcibiades *per se*, but because Socrates does not wish to be *seduced* by the buffoon. Socrates spurns the love of the body alone, and Phaedrus articulates the principle on which Socrates operates when he says, "A base man is that common lover who loves the body rather than the soul for he is not lasting since he loves a thing not lasting."[16] Thus rhetoric understood as seduction is fakery of the worst sort and is analogous to love of the basest kind. The seduction metaphor is perhaps the most odious Plato could muster in that by pretense, seduction proffers the hollow, the most banal, as if the greatest good — love itself. The seducer foists appearances on the unwary; as Phaedrus says about the shams of the would-be orator: "It is from what seems to be true that persuasion comes, not from the real truth."[17]

A further example of what Socrates finds despicable in the seductive rhetor appears in the speech of Pausanias, himself a disciple of Prodicos, the Sophist. In an attempt to order the proceedings at the banquet, Pausanias demonstrates some concern for the necessity to delineate various kinds of love rather than to "just simply belaud Love," as he says. He distinguishes two loves, the one, common love, he associates with Common Aphrodite; the other, heavenly love, he associates with Heavenly Aphrodite. Then he says of common love,

> The Love, then, which belongs to Common Aphrodite is really and truly common and works at random; and this is the love which inferior men feel. Such persons love firstly women as well as boys; next, when they love they love bodies rather than souls; and next, they choose the most foolish persons they can, for they look only to getting something done, and care nothing whether well or not. So what happens to them is that they act at random, whether they do good or whether they do its opposite; for this Love springs from the goddess which is much younger than the order (Common Aphrodite

---

15. *Ibid.*, 109.
16. *Ibid.*, 182D, p. 80.
17. *Phaedrus.* 260, p. 46.

is younger than Heavenly Aphrodite), and in her birth had a share of both female and male.[18]

Randomness, then, is the abhorrent habit of the man who does not know good from evil. He is the seductive orator, taking up any cause or any side of an issue and arguing with equal ferocity and sincerity.

Let us now compare this discussion of the evil nature of randomness with Socrates' statements on the same theme in the *Phaedrus*.

THE *PHAEDRUS*

In the *Phaedrus,* Socrates' friend is in doubt as to the orator's responsibility to truth. Socrates patiently pleads for Phaedrus' allegiance to truth in the following passage:

> Socr. Suppose I tried to persuade you to buy a horse and go to war and neither of us knew what a horse was while I knew just this much about you: Phaedrus thinks a horse is a domestic animal that has the longest ears—
> Phaedr. It would be quite ridiculous, Socrates.
> Socr. Not yet; but if in all seriousness, I should try to persuade you by composing a speech in praise of the ass yet calling it a horse and declaring that it was a beast entirely adapted to service both domestic and military where it was useful as a mount against the enemy, and was capable besides of carrying equipment and of doing many other things—
> Phaedr. It would now be utterly asinine!
> Socr. Is it not, then, better to be ridiculous and friendly than clever and hostile?
> Phaedr. So it seems.
> Socr. Then when an orator who knows nothing about good or evil undertakes to persuade a city in the same state of ignorance, not by singing the praises of an ass's shadow masquerading as a horse, but by recommending evil as though it were good (for he has studied the opinions of the mob and can persuade it to do evil in place of good), under such circumstances what sort of a harvest do you think rhetoric would reap from the seed she has sown?
> Phaedr. Not a very acceptable one.[19]

This passage illustrates Socrates' aversion to deceptive rhetorics prime ingredient of seduction as represented in the *Symposium*. Socrates proposes in the *Phaedrus* to sell his friend an ass in lieu of a horse, as Pausanias in the *Symposium* describes a man who loves randomly with the aim of merely "getting something done." In both cases, the men chose the poorer course because they did not know or

18. φδωρθ'ιηω' 180E, p. 78.
19. *Phaedrus,* 260, pp. 46-47.

chose not to distinguish the best from the worst they acted randomly. Such rhetoric — like such love — can only be undesirable, because of its fickleness and its unpredictability. We hesitate to commit love to those who would as soon love anyone as us, for that love does not last, because, by definition, it is fluctuating and ephemeral.

Several other things in the *Phaderus* suggest that the dialogue is more than the discussion of speech making or of love that it pretends to be. The *Phaedrus,* perhaps more strongly than the *Symposium,* argues the erotic nature of communication. Socrates encounters Phaedrus on an Athen's street one warm summer afternoon and seems at once enamoured with him. Phaedrus tells Socrates he has come from Lysias' house and that, "the topic than engaged us was, in a way, love."[20] The following exchange ensues:

> Phaedr. Lysias, you must know, has put in writing the attempted seduction of a handsome boy, but not by a lover of his! That was, in fact what made it so ingenious, the point being that one should rather surrender to a non-lover than to a lover.
> Socr. Well now, how splendid. Still, I wish he'd stated that it should rather be a poor man than a rich one, to an oldster rather than a youngster — to say nothing of all my own characteristics and those of the run of us. Such a topic would really suit the city and help democracy![21]

Thus early in the dialogue, Phaedrus introduces two important concepts: seduction itself and the preference of the lover over the non-lover. A theme of contrast between truth and sham like that in the *Symposium* is established at the outset. Socrates is hardly subtle as he flirtingly suggests his own outstanding qualities (poverty and age) which he believes should qualify him as Phaedrus' lover. While he surely intends to direct mirthful sarcasm at the want of gravity in the talk at Lysias' house, Socrates also sets the mood of the entire dialogue — one in which talk of communication will occur *within* a metaphorical discussion of eroticism.

Plato also methodically develops the physical setting in which Socrates and his young friend talk. The dialogue takes place near the spot where, as legend has it, Boreas carried off and ravished the young girl, Oreithyia. Certainly, the reference to that legend presages the extraordinary nature of this discussion of rhetoric. And one of the most beautiful passages in the dialogue is Socrates' description of

20. *Ibid.,* 227, p. 3.
21. *Ibid.,* pp. 3-4.

the place where the two finally come to rest on that summer afternoon. He says,

> And a fine retreat it is. Here is a lofty, spreading plane tree and the agnus cactus, high clustering with delightful shade. Now that it is in full bloom, the whole place will be wonderfully fragrant; and the stream that flows beneath the plane is delightfully cool to the feet. To judge from the figurines and images, this must be a spot sacred to Achalous and the Nymphs. And please note how welcome and sweet the fresh air is, resounding with the summer chirping of the cicada chorus. But the finest thing of all is the grass, thick enough on the gentle slope to rest one's head most comfortably. It turns out, dear Phaedrus, that you're the best of guides for a stranger.[22]

It is a rendezvous for lovers, to lie and talk and dangle their bare feet in the cool stream! Notice too, what Socrates says about the setting when Phaedrus interrupts Socrates' first attempt at a speech: "Then listen to me in silence; for this place gives the impression of being truly divine, so much so that if, as the speech proceeds, I often seem to be in a frenzy, don't be surprised. Already my words are almost dithyrambic."[23] If nothing before had established the erotic nature of this dialogue on rhetoric, Socrates' assertion surely does so as he identifies his speech making with the wild Bacchanalian hymn.

Socrates' frenzy in this speech is akin to the kinds of "divine madness" he alludes to at the end of the dialogue where he identifies kinds of madness with four gods: "to Apollo we ascribed prophetic inspiration, to Dionysus mystic madness, to the Muses poetic afflatus; while to Aphrodite and Eros we gave the fourth love-madness, declaring it to be the best."[24] Perhaps in this case Socrates' divine frenzy is most like the madness he speaks of as "my master and yours, Phaedrus: Love, the guardian of beautiful boys."[25] At the least, Socrates is referring to excitement in his speech as a kind of rhetorical frenzy and comparing it to that encountered in the worship of Bacchus.

The speech by Phaedrus and the first speech by Socrates contain further evidence of Plato's covert intent in the dialogue. The speeches, of course, are diatribes on the benefits of the non-lover as opposed to the lover or of making love to one who does not love you in preference to one who does. Seen as parts of Plato's entire meta-

22. *Ibid.*, 230, p. 7.
23. *Ibid.*, 238, p. 18.
24. *Ibid.*, 265, p. 54.
25. *Ibid.*

phor, the absurdity of the speeches becomes overwhelming. They function as a sarcastic, almost comical, *reductus ad absurdum* argument against rhetoric as seduction. To argue that one should love a person who has no love for him is demented in Plato's view, and he has Socrates say as much when in mock surprise, he "discovers" his error. Socrates declares his sin saying,

> Socr. Phaedrus, it was a dreadful, dreadful speech both the one you brought and the one you forced me to deliver.
> Phaedr. How, please?
> Socr. It was fatuous, and also concealed something impious. What could be more dreadful than that? [26]

He pronounces a more scathing indictment upon his speech by calling it "fatuous," associating it with the silliness of infatuation. Later, Socrates amplifies his denunciation of his acts against Aphrodite and attempts to expunge his sins by explaining,

> Their [the 'speeches'] fatuousness was really charming: they put on airs as if they amounted to something, while not uttering a syllable of sense or truth — as though, if you please, they could win applause from a couple of little manikins by deceiving them.[27]

And he further characterizes the kind of love they have praised in their speeches as like that "taken from some haunt of sailors who had never known a generous, decent love."[28] Thus, not only does Plato create an unavoidable *reductio ad absurdum* argument against loving a non-lover, but he reiterates the absurdity time and again. As he was doing this, the sly Socrates was vigorously at work on another level, even as he spoke in favor of the non-lover. With great skill he shows poor Phaedrus the foibles of the sophist, who, like the one who randomly loves, speaks without conscience on any side of an issue — even against that beloved of gods, Aphrodite.

Elsewhere in the dialogue the contrast between the kinds of love appears vividly, especially in Socrates' description of the nature of the soul. If we understand Socrates' metaphor of the wings to be about communication of Truth, then we have an illuminating analogy in his last speech. For Socrates, when the soul communicates well, when it approaches Truth, it flies mystically, somewhat like the soul's expression in speech which Weaver mentions. Plato declares that "the natural function of a wing is to raise what is heavy and soar

26. *Ibid.*, 242, p. 23.
27. *Ibid.*
28. *Ibid.*, 243, p. 24.

with it to where the race of god dwells."²⁹ In this heavenly place where the soul may soar "Reality lives, without shape or color, intangible, visible only to reason, the soul's pilot; and all true knowledge is knowledge of her."³⁰ While I construe the wings as suggesting some kind of successful communication, Socrates himself makes clear his comparison of reason to the soul's pilot, further justifying my own symbolic flight. He relates a vision of one who sees his lover, is reminded of the true heavenly beauty he once experienced before this life, and is eager to experience the bygone relationship with reality. Socrates compares this anxiety with that of sprouting wings. He says fancifully:

> While they are sprouting, he is eager to fly, but he cannot. He gazes upward as though he were a bird and cares nothing for what is here below, so that he is accused of being mad. . . . The man who partakes of this madness and loves beauty is called a lover.³¹

Interestingly, we do not begin to sprout wings until we have a vision of at least an earthly appearance of beauty or truth; some association with such perfection is apparently necessary. Supposedly that attraction to Truth comes in one way when the lover sees the one he loves. Plato says that when the charioteer of the soul "beholds the love-inspiring sight . . . his whole soul is warmed by the vision and becomes filled with the tickling and pricking of desire." This takes place because "at this sight the charioteer's memory is borne back to the form of real beauty" abiding in the heavens.³² Unfortunately, those who ate not philosophers do not catch sight of wisdom, a vision of loveliness, and consequently do not soar up to that heavenly love of which Socrates speaks. As this poor soul must be contented with sham love, so must the sophist grovel with something less than truth.

For Socrates, the lover of truth, the philosopher, is preferable over the rhetorician, and like the true erotic lover who must love the soul as well as the body, the lover of truth must be engaged in "stargazing, if you will, about the nature of things."³³ The mundane practical matters are not the primary concerns of the philosopher; they are those of the rhetorician, the seducer bogged down with the

29. *Ibid.*, 246, p. 29.
30. *Ibid.*, 247, p. 30.
31. *Ibid.*, 249, p. 33.
32. *Ibid.*, 254, p. 38.
33. *Ibid.*, 270, p. 60.

body not the soul. The sophists have no love of the Truth, no affinity for the ethereal loveliness, no propensity for True communication; they are "sailors who had never known a generous, decent love."

CONCLUSION

In the *Symposium* and in the *Phaedrus,* Socrates admonishes against rhetoric as a form of seduction. The pejorative criticism reveals Plato's obvious disdain for sophistry. He abhors its lack of commitment to Truth in part, at least, because its evil is ultimate; while the seducer pretends to the greatest good (love), he perpetrates the greatest evil (deceit) on his victim. Seductive rhetoric is comparably insidious for it arises from a philosophical stance endorsing deceit or sham; it loves the body and not the soul, it seeks and creates the ephemeral and not that which endures. Through the two dialogues recurs the ultimate image of untruth — false love, fakery, seduction. The ratio developing out of both dialogues is this: Love is to seduction as Truth is to rhetoric. Rhetoric is the semblance of wisdom as seduction is the semblance of love.

For Plato, the baseness of rhetoric grows out of its inherent randomness; in it there is no abiding affection for Truth. In the end, Plato links the indictment, like the first, to the ephemeral nature of deceptive communication. In these dialogues Plato weaves strand after strand of metaphorical thread into a strong, if delicate, tapestry portraying a most subtle poetic relationship between seduction and the practice of the sophists.

THE *SYMPOSIUM*: A NEGLECTED SOURCE FOR PLATO'S IDEAS ON RHETORIC*

Wayne N. Thompson

An analysis of the Symposium *is one way to supplement the knowledge of Plato's rhetoric obtained from the more familiar* Phaedrus *and* Gorgias. *The present investigation provides support for the following conclusions: (1) Plato confirms the insistence on truth to be found in the* Phaedrus. *(2) The clearcut ideas on the proper arrangement and content of the speech of praise cover rhetorical matters that are not taken up in the* Phaedrus *or the* Gorgias *and that are consistent with the ideas that Aristotle recorded later. (3) In certain other aspects of convention Plato also is consistent with the theories and the practices of Aristotle and other Greeks of the fourth century. (4) Finally and most importantly, the Socrates-Diotima presentation is the best available example of Plato's ideal speech.*

The *Symposium* has been studied extensively as a literary masterpiece and as a significant philosophic statement, but so far as the writer can determine there has been no thorough analysis of it from the standpoint of rhetoric. This neglect is surprising; for as the dialogue that provides the most varied and extensive sample of Plato's writings as a logographer, the *Symposium* is a promising source for ideas of rhetorical significance.

Some sections that follow include comparisons of Plato and Aristotle, but the primary concern of this paper is not Greek rhetoric generally but Plato as rhetorical theorist and practitioner. Whether other Greek logographers did or did not follow the same practices would be another study. The restriction is justified as well as necessary, for Plato is such an important figure in the history of rhetoric that any clarification, modification, or expansion of our knowledge of his views should be significant. The principal comparisons that

* Reprinted by permission of the Southern Speech Communication Journal, *37* (Spring, 1972), 219-232.

follow, therefore, are not with other classical Greeks but with Plato's other rhetorical works, notably the *Phaedrus*. Both that work and the *Gorgias* are philosophic statements about sophism and rhetoric that leave many aspects of a full theory of speechmaking unclear or unspecified.

The Insistence on Truth

That the *Symposium* takes the position that the speaker should know and respect truth is scarcely a contribution to knowledge, for the emphasis on this position in the *Phaedrus* has long been well known.[1] However, the centrality of this attitude to Plato's treatment of rhetoric makes a brief examination of this confirmation a good starting point for this analysis of the *Symposium* from the rhetorical viewpoint.

Particularly of interest is the exact parallel between the two works in method. To review the *Phaedrus*, the first speech by Socrates is an admirable example of sophistic rhetoric, the succeeding section is a dialogue in which Socrates specifies the crucial flaw that marks both his address and that of Lysias, and after that is the presentation by Socrates of a true masterpiece — one combining truth with the skills of the sophist-rhetorician.

In the *Symposium* the structure of the climactic section is identical. The speech by Agathon by sophistic standards is a rhetorical masterpiece. Clear, tightly structured, and filled with plausible enthymemes, it reveals invention that is imaginative and resourceful, and in imagery much of it soars to heights of poetic beauty. Agathon's virtuosity overwhelms those present except for Socrates. "When Agathon had finished speaking," reports Aristodemus, "all who were there applauded loudly; the young man obviously had spoken in a manner worthy of himself and of the god" (198)".[2] And Socrates, though he immediately thereafter speaks in ironic criticism

---

1. For example, see Lester Thonssen and A. Craig Baird, *Speech Criticism* (New York: Ronald Press, 1948), pp. 54-55. Thonssen and Baird, in turn cite Everett Lee Hunt, "Plato and Aristotle on Rhetoric and Rhetoricians" in *Studies in Rhetoric and Public Speaking in Honor of James A. Winans* (New York: Appleton-Century-Crofts, 1925), pp. 37-38.

2. Numbers in parentheses are references to the *Symposium* or the *Phaedrus*. Unless otherwise indicated, quotations are from the translation by Lane Cooper.

of Agathon's effort, acknowledges some admirable qualities: "And how ... shall I be otherwise than at a loss, I or anybody else you please, who has to speak after a discourse as beautiful and varied as this has been delivered? And if the rest was not in equal measure wonderful, yet who could listen to the close without amazement at the beauty of the epithets and phrases? " (198)

Then, as in the *Phaedrus,* dialogue intervenes between the two speeches — the sophistic masterpiece and the true masterpiece. In both works the criticism— the neglect of truth — is the same; only the mechanism of expression is different. In the *Symposium* the method is a mixture of irony and direct statement:

> In fact, I was stupid enough to think that in every case one ought to tell the truth about the subject of the praise, and that this must serve as basis. ... And I felt very proud indeed to think how well I was going to speak because I knew the real way of praising anything. But, seemingly, this was not the way of praising anything whatever finely. No! The way was to attribute to the object the greatest and the finest things one could conceive of, whether they were so or not. If false, that was no matter (198).

For further emphasis Socrates adds that he will not speak if it means "good-bye to the truth" (199).

Finally, to complete the parallel, the *Symposium* continues after the critical dialogue with an example of excellence in speechmaking. In the two dialogues, therefore, argument and sequence, as the following summary shows, are alike:

Phaedrus		*Symposium*
237-241	A masterpiece of sophistic oratory	195-197
242-243	A critique of the sophistic masterpiece	198-201
244-257	A true masterpiece	201-212

Without doubt, the emphasis on the importance of knowing truth is as strong in the *Symposium* as in the *Phaedrus.*

Arrangement for the Speech of Praise

Plato apparently had definite ideas on what the speech of praise should include and on the proper pattern of development. Four statements on this are consistent, even though they are made through two speakers and are in the different contexts of (1) generalizing about speechmaking, (2) summarizing a particular speech, and (3) serving as the basis for criticism.

Says Agathon: "Yet the one right method, in every form of praise on every topic, is, namely, to explain the nature of the agent who is the subject of the speech, through which such and such effects are brought about. This therefore is the proper way for us to praise the God of Love, to tell first of his nature, then of his gifts" (195). In the summary of his speech Agathon indicates that he has followed his own advice: ". . . Eros seems to me *to be,* first, in himself the fairest and the best, and, after that, *to be the cause* of benefits like these to others."[3]

Plato repeats this precept of arrangement when Socrates speaks. "Dear Agathon," he says, "you certainly did well, in my opinion, to usher in your speech by saying that one must in the first place, show what sort of being Eros is, and afterwards tell of his works. That way of opening I very much approve" (199). Later he repeats: "The right procedure, Agathon, as you explained, is first to tell what Eros is, and what he is like, and then tell of his works" (201).

This clear statement on the principal topics and their arrangement in the speech of praise is an addition to the rhetorical theory presented in the *Gorgias* and the *Phaedrus.* Although the latter work includes a substantial section on arrangement (264-267), it does not include any instruction as specific as that in the *Symposium.* In the *Phaedrus* Plato writes of the importance of orderliness (264), of the functions of synthesis and division (265-266), and of the presence in rhetorical theory of the parts of a speech (266-267); but nowhere in that work does he write about the content of the body of the speech of praise or, for that matter, of any other type of address.

The statement in the *Symposium,* also, is much plainer than anything to be found in Aristotle's *Rhetoric* on the sequence of ideas in the speech of praise. Although Aristotle identifies qualities and deeds as *topoi* in i.9 (1367B9-13) and in iii.16 (1416B23-26), he does not specify as does Plato the particular order to follow, and he does not indicate that these *topoi* are necessary to the speech of praise or that the two taken together are the total of such a speech. From the materials one cannot determine whether Aristotle was indeed more flexible in his conception than was Plato or whether he was only less exact in his statements.

3. *Symposium* 197. Italics added.

Invention in the *Symposium*

Space in a journal article does not permit a full analysis of the inventional practices of the *Symposium*, but a general observation and three subsections on major features should provide an overall characterization. To look at invention broadly, the materials for these seven speeches praising a god are about what one would expect. Mythology is the major source for the stories and the examples, and most of the illustrative and supporting passages come from the works of the earlier Greek authors, notably Hesiod and Homer.

Qualities of the Speech of Praise

Mythology and Greek literature, of course, are potential sources for a great variety of specific materials. What picture of the speech of praise governed Plato as he developed the addresses and chose their specifics? For information on Plato's view of this form of speech-making, the critic can turn both to direct statements of rhetorical theory in the *Symposium* and to analyses of the content of the speeches. Conclusions based on either source will be additions to knowledge of Plato's rhetoric, for prior studies, usually of the *Gorgias* and the *Phaedrus*, do not include statements on speeches of praise. Moreover this information adds one additional element to the overall assessment of the ways in which Aristotle was in accord with Plato and of the ways in which he differed.

As a broad characterization, Plato's rhetoric of the speech of praise was a preview of the fuller, more analytical treatment in the *Rhetoric* i.9. No way exists to prove a causal relation between the *Symposium* and certain important elements of Aristotle's i.9, but a comparison of the two works shows similarities in the basic conception of the speech of praise, in the qualities to include, and in *topoi* for adding impressiveness.

The basic conception already has been noticed. In specifying the sequence of the parts of the speech, Agathon and Socrates also were indicating the proper content: qualities of the person being praised and his deeds. Aristotle, though less clear-cut essentially is in agreement: "Praise is the expression in words of the eminence of a man's good qualities, and therefore we must display his actions as the product of such qualities" (1367B27-28).

Similarities also are evident in the details of the two works. In both the virtues as critical inventional elements, and the two lists are much alike. Aristotle, who was *setting forth* rhetorical theory, enumerates nine virtues: justice, courage, temperance, magnificence, magnanimity, liberality, gentleness, prudence, and wisdom (1366B1-3). Plato, who was *exemplifying* theory, utilizes about the same ones. In Agathon's speech, for example, justice, temperance, courage, and wisdom are topics for distinct sections (196-197). Moreover, a section on tenderness (195) presents a quality much like Aristotle's gentleness, and a later section extols Love as being non-violent. Of Aristotle's nine forms of virtue, a sixth appears in this speech in the *Symposium* when Agathon mentions in the exordium the quality of liberality.

Although the correspondence is less striking in the other addresses in the *Symposium,* the qualities that the other speakers use in praise are compatible with the analysis presented in the *Rhetoric.* The basic considerations in praise and blame wrote Aristotle, are virtue and vice, the noble and the base (1266A23-24). One of the nine forms of virtue, he stated, is prudence, which "is that virtue of the understanding which enables men to come to wise decisions about the relation to happiness of the goods and evils" (1366B20-22).

In relation to the foregoing statements of rhetorical theory, the rhetorical practices of Plato's speakers in the *Symposium* make an interesting comparison. Phaedrus develops as his central argument the idea that Eros causes men to act so as to attain virtue and happiness. In the development of this idea the courage of lovers and their willingness to self-sacrifice are major subpoints. Pausanias likewise makes virtue the major constituent in the summary of his presentation: "So it is unconditionally beautiful to grant one's favors just for the sake of virtue. This is the Eros . . . who forces both the lover for his own sake and the loved one to give great heed to virtue" (185). So it is also in the speech next in order in the *Symposium,* the one by Eryximachus, whose allusions to temperance, justice, and happiness include several items that Aristotle was to list as forms of virtue: "But the Eros who employs himself with temperance and justice in working good, alike among us and the gods, this Eros has the greatest power, and is the source of all our happiness" (188). Aristophanes, likewise, closes with emphasis on happiness: The God of Love "serves us most by leading us into our proper state, and for the future, who endows us with the greatest hopes, if we are dutiful to the gods, that he will re-establish us in our original nature, and, healing us, he will give us happiness and bliss" (189). Finally, Alcibiades, who is praising Socrates rather than Eros, begins with a story showing temperance despite great temptations (217-219). Later anecdotes in this address, besides showing endurance and manliness, point out courage (220-221), magnanimity (220-221), and wisdom (221-222) — all qualities to be enumerated later in the *Rhetoric*.

The *Symposium* also included examples that are predecessors of at least two of Aristotle's *topoi* for heightening the effects of praise. "Again, if you cannot find enough to say of a man himself," advises the Stagyrite, "you may pit him against others. . . . The comparison should be with famous men" (1368A19-21). This method is exemplified by Alcibiades, who testifies that Socrates' utterances affect him far more than do the speeches of Pericles and other able orators (215). Near the end of the same speech the same device appears, though somewhat subtly, when the orator states that Socrates is dissimilar to all other men whereas even such great figures as Achilles and Pericles could be likened to others (221).

A second line of argument common to the *Rhetoric* and the *Symposium* is proof of greatness through the existence of statues or encomia (*Rhetoric* 1368A15-18), Aristophanes uses the argument in negative form when he uses the nonerection of temples as support for the contention that the power of Eros is unappreciated (189).

Enthymemes

A second way to examine Plato's invention is to look at his enthymemes, which Aristotle later was to describe as the substance of rhetorical persuasion (i.1.1354A14-15). As with the significance of virtues to the speech of praise, Aristotle's theory of the enthymeme was consistent with that of Plato, as implied from the latter's practices. Again, evidence does not exist for claiming a causal connection, but the practices in the *Symposium* and the theories of the *Rhetoric* are alike.

The nature of Aristotle's enthymeme, of course, has been analyzed many times and much disputed. A review of this extensive literature is beyond the scope of the present article, but it is necessary to indicate the view that the writer holds. His own reading of the *Rhetoric* leads to the conception to be found in the writings of

Lloyd Bitzer,[4] James H. McBurney,[5] E. M. Cope,[6] and still others.[7] The essence of this view of Aristotle's enthymeme is this: Successful arguments are founded on "notions possessed by everybody,"[8] and they lead the listener to the desired conclusion by connecting the speaker's premise with a belief or value that the auditor presumably already holds. Space does not permit a lengthy list of the enthythemes Plato devised for his speakers, but the four examples that follow indicate that his invention included deductive arguments whose nature is consistent with the theory that Aristotle was later to record:

Belief: The eldest is the best.

Argument: Eros, who is the eldest, is the best among the gods (speech by Phaedrus, 178).

Belief: Whatever is a force for honor and bravery is praiseworthy.

Argument: Love, which is a force for honor and bravery, is praiseworthy (speech by Phaedrus, 178-179).

Belief: Healing brings the greatest happiness to mankind.

Argument: Eros, who is a healer of ills, is man's greatest friend (speech by Aristophanes, 189).

Belief: The god who is fairest and best is the most blessed.

Argument: Eros, because he is fairest and best, is the most blessed (speech by Agathon, 195).

Devices for Clarification and Emphasis

Third, Plato's invention can be described through an examination of his special devices. Here the most striking conclusion is the absence of novelty; despite the distinctness of Plato's philosophy of rhetoric, at the operational level his methods of amplifying and

---

4. Bitzer, "Aristotle's Enthymeme Revisited," *Quarterly Journal of Seech* XLV (Dec., 1959) 399-408.

5. McBurney, "The Place of the Enthymeme in Rhetorical Theory," *Speech Monographs*, III (1936), 49-74.

6. Cope, *An Introduction to Aristotle's Rhetoric* (London: Macmillan and Co., 1867), p. 93 *et passim*.

7. Among the others are both ancient writers and modern ones, such as Minucian and Charles S. Mudd. See Prentice A. Meador, Jr., tr., "Minucian *On Epicheiremes*: An Introduction and a Translation," *Speech Monographs* XXXI (March, 1964), 59; Mudd, "The Enthymeme and Logical Validity," *Quarterly Journal of Speech*, XLV (Dec., 1959), 409-414.

8. *Rhetoric* i.1.1355A27-28. Similar statements appear at ii.22.1395-53, 1369A-1 and ii.25.1402A32-33.

intensifying are much like those of his colleagues. This was a period, states George Kennedy, when "There was ... a general desire to create a literary prose";[9] and in epideictic rhetoric in particular, the primary objective was "the display of beautiful prose."[10] Or, as Kennedy observes, "Epideictic is the form of oratory closest in style and function to poetry"[11] and in some cases "it has a degree of stylistic ornamentation" that makes the address an exercise by "an oratorical virtuoso."[12]

Plato's practices in the *Symposium* are in accord with this tradition, whose most noteworthy contemporary exponent was Isocrates. Both the profusion and the variety of devices are striking. To cite examples of each of these would be tedious, but the writer has found in the *Symposium* one or more instances of each of the following: the use of witnesses and authorities; the same allusion in the conclusion as in the introduction: argument by residue; historical allusion; proverbs; extended narrative; hypothetical example; hypothetical conversation, digression for the sake of audience adaptation; the aciom snatches of verse for embellishment; invented dialogue; a promising to take an oath; personal testimony; and narrative examples. The last two of these are major practices in the speech by Alcibiades.

The device that appears much the most often in the *Symposum*, also, is consistent with Greek preferences. According to Kennedy, the Greeks of the fifth century B.C. had a "marked love of antithesis";[13] this stylistic feature, he proceeds to point out, was prominent in the earliest work of Antiphon, in the oratrions appearing in the history of Thucydides, and in the plays of Euripides and Sophocles. "The habit of antithesis" Kennedy concludes, "was deeply ingrained in the Greek character."[14] Aristotle writes of the usefulness of the device and tries to explain the basis for its effectiveness.[15] As understood by the Greeks, antithesis pertained to op-

9. Kennedy, *The Art of Persuasion in Greece* (Princeton, N.J.: Princeton University Press, 1963), p. 66.
10. Frank Byron Jevons, *A History of Greek Literature*, 2nd ed. (London: Charles Griffin and Company, 1889), p. 395.
11. Kennedy, p. 153.
12. Kennedy, p. 152.
13. Kennedy, p. 33.
14. Kennedy, p. 34.
15. *Rhetoric* iii.9.1409B33-1410B5 and iii.11.1412B22-24.

position in wording, in thought, or preferably in both.[16] Since the following examples are in translation, only contrast in thought will be considered; but even with this restriction the range in the *Symposium* is broad. At least two distinct uses are identifiable. First, some antitheses serve to sharpen the thought and to clarify. Thus Alcibiades says, "but the purpose of the image will be truth and not amusement" (215). Aristophanes uses the same device when he contrasts the fate of the man who alienates the gods with the gloss that come when ". . . once we have become friends with Eros, and made our peace with him" (193).

Somewhat more complex is the antithesis that puts two distinct concepts into opposition for the purpose of emphasizing the thought expressed in the second of the two. Plato has Phaedrus use this device to stress the significance of the impact of love: ". . . neither kindred, dignities, nor wealth, nor any other thing can implant in us as love does" (178). Similarly, Alcibiades adds force to his praise of Socrates by creating an opposition. Achilles and Pericles can be compared to other men, he argues, but in contrast Socrates can be compared to no mortal (221).

Closely related to contrast is comparison, which Plato in some places employs as logical argument. An especially interesting example in the speech by Eryximachus includes an antithesis within each half of the comparison: ". . . and as Pausanias was just now saying that to indulge good men is honourable, and bad men dishonourable: — so too in the body the good and healthy elements are to be indulged, and the bad elements and the elements of disease are not to be indulged" (186).[17] Diotima also arrives at a position through comparison. As a very good rhetorician, she follows the sound procedure of moving from the concrete and observable to the abstract and arguable. After pointing out that from youth to old age there are bodily changes even though the individual continues to bear the same name, she says, "And that is true not merely of the body, but also of the soul; true of our ways, our character, our notions, longings, pleasures, pains, and fears; not one of these remains the same in any individual, but some of them are being born while others are passing away" (207).

16. *Rhetoric to Alexander* 1435B27-37; see also Aristotle *Rhetoric* iii.1409B35-1410A22.
17. Benjamin Jowett translation.

Finally, Plato in the *Symposium* shows inventiveness by creating figurative analogies that clarify, vivify, and emphasize. The following are examples:

Aristophanes: "He soake, and cut mankind in two, like people cutting quinces for preserves, or as you cut an egg through with a hair" (190).

Alcibiades: The pain suffered at being bitten by Socrates' philosophic discourse is like the pain that anybody suffers when bitten by an adder (217).

Alcibiades: "I maintain that he [Socrates] is altogether like the seated statues of Silenus in the shops of sculptors, the figures the artists represent with pipe or flute, which, when they are opened down the middle, are seen to have within them little images of gods" (215).

Alcibiades: ". . . my heart beats far more wildly than the hearts of the Corybantic revelers" (215).

Such practices as the foregoing enrich the speeches that comprise the *Symposium* and reinforce the conclusion that Plato was resourceful and skilled in the use of the rhetorical devices that were prevalent in his own time.

Plato's Ideal Speech

The final way in which an analysis of the *Symposium* adds to our knowledge of Plato's rhetoric is that it provides an example of Plato's ideal speech. For this position there have been several contenders. Kennedy offers the speech in the *Menexenus* as the ideal and notes its clarity of definition, logical divisions and knowledge of the psychology of the audience.[18] Elvena Green nominates the address by Socrates that closes the *Gorgias* as "Plato's . . . demonstration of a true rhetoric."[19] An even more obvious candidate for designation as the ideal speech is the second address by Socrates in the *Phaedrus,* which avowedly is a corrective to the moral badness of the first address just as the first was a corrective to the rhetorical faultiness of the speech by Lysias.

18. Kennedy, p. 161. Kennedy gives credit for some of these ideas to Alfred Croiset, "Sur le *Menexene* de Platon," *Melanges Perrot,* Paris, 1931, 59ff.

19. Green, "Plato's Use of Three Dramatic Elements in *Gorgias* as means to Demonstrate His Thought," *Southern Speech Journal,* XXXIII (Summer, 1968), 214.

But to all of these claimants there are major objections. Kennedy notes that the oration in the *Menexenus* fails to meet the requirement that the contents of a speech be true.[20] The final addresses in the *Phaedrus* and the *Gorgias*, of course, do not have this shortcoming, but they fall short by a second criterion, which also is central to Plato's thought.

Specifically, both of these final addresses are continuous discourses. As such, they cannot illustrate how the dialectic process can serve as the instrument for clarifying and correcting misapprehensions. That dialectic should perform this function in rhetorical discourse has already been noted. One of the seven qualities of rhetoric that Everett Lee Hunt abstracts from the *Phaedrus* is the preference for dialogue to a continuous presentation,[21] and even more relevant to the present paper is the analysis of Oscar L. Brownstein, whose title states his central point: "Plato's *Phaedrus*: Dialectic as the Genuine Art of Speaking." ". . . the third speech has the limitations of any continuous discourse," Brownstein states; "it cannot be perfected by cross-examination."[22] This is the precise deficiency that the present writer is noting.

Surmounting the foregoing difficulty is the Socrates-Diotima presentation in the *Symposium*. The nature of this "speech" and Plato's strategies for overcoming the critical weakness of the speeches in the *Gorgias* and the *Phaedrus* are worthy of examination. Socrates, beginning his turn by examining Agathon dialectically, uses the dialogue method to expose the falsity of the preceding address and to show the true nature of Eros. After that he explains that he will use for his speech the remarks that he once heard from Diotima. This device, though at times Diotima is quoted at some length, permits Plato to present a "speech" that is largely in question-and-answer form. As the learner, Socrates poses questions that make it possible to explore the topic of love systematically. Following the orderly sequence that Agathon and Socrates recommend, Diotima defines Eros, states his functions, explains his parents and origin, and, after an internal summary, answers operationally the question "What value has Eros for mankind?" Diotima then finishes with an uninterrupted passage of about 2,000 words in translation. At this point Plato

20. Kennedy, p. 161.
21. Hunt, pp. 37-38.
22. Brownstein, *Quarterly Journal of Speech*, LI (Dec., 1965), 393.

suggests an association in his mind between continuous discourse and sophistic rhetoric. "And she, replying like a finished Sophist," comments Socrates as he introduces this longest monologue of their joint contribution (208). The speech now reaches a climax that unifies the preceding ideas. The passage is one of poetic beauty, and its content is the culmination of the philosophic inquiry.

The Socrates-Diotima addess is admirable in many ways. It is clear, pointed, inventive, well arranged, and beautifully poetic. But, more important, Plato illustrates not only the *presentation* of truth but also the *development* of truth through dialectic inquiry. The ideal speech, thus, is a combination of rhetoric, dialectic, and poetic-rhetoric in purpose, dialectic in content, and poetic in expression, imaginativeness, and universality. Moreover, this presentation is highly conversational — in many ways a nonspeech. Rhetorical devices, although the sophisticated analyst can identify them, by most standards are unobtrusive. Subordinate to the ideas, they clarify and heighten the thought and are not used for their own sake. Unlike in sophistic rhetoric, their functions are not those of conforming to rules or displaying the speaker's virtuosity.

What was Plato's ideal rhetoric, then? It was a presentation of a dialectic inquiry exploring a topic and unfolding truths it was a conversational "nonspeech" whose rhetorical devices were unobstrusive. It brought dialectic, poetic, and rhetoric together. It did not abstain from rhetorical techniques, but it used them to further truth and not for ostentatious display.

Conclusion

The *Symposium*, in summary, is a rich and neglected source for further information on several aspects of Plato's rhetoric. Not only does it confirm the insistence on knowing the truth to be found in the *Phaedrus,* but also it adds similarity of method to similarity of thought.

In the *Symposium* Plato provides an unusually clear statement of the arrangement of major ideas in the speech of praise, and the dialogue adds to the existing information of the relation of Aristotle's ideas to Plato's in important aspects of both arrangement and invention. As a rhetorician using devices for amplification, clarification, and emphasis, Plato was versatile, skillful, and thoroughly

Greek. Like many of his contemporaries and predecessors, notably Isocrates and Gorgias, he used antithesis extensively and for more than one purpose.

Finally, and perhaps most importantly, the Socrates-Diotima address is superior as an example of Plato's ideal speech to the addresses in the *Menexenus,* the *Gorgias,* and the *Phaedrus.* In combining dialectic investigation with rhetorical purpose in this climactic speech of the *Symposium,* Plato goes beyond his other works in recording an accurate example of a rhetoric that he approves. Thus, a rhetorical presentation of a dialectic search for truth not only is possible in theory but also can be exemplified.

PLATO'S CONCEPTION OF PERSUASION*

Glenn R. Morrow

There are two ways, recognized in all ages, by which social order may be brought about: persuasion and compulsion. These two terms appear frequently conjoined in Plato's text, so often as to give the appearance of a proverb, or a cliche.[2] There is obviously a place for compulsion in Plato's philosophy. It is almost an axiom in political theory than any organized government has the right to employ force on occasion, and it must do so if it intends to remain a government. Force becomes violence when it is illegitimately exercised, either by public officials acting *ultra vires,* or by private citizens in rebellion against constituted authority. But Plato had a particular horror of the factional violence between democrats and oligarchs with which the Greek cities of the late fifth and early fourth centuries were sadly familiar. Nor did he countenance the other kind of violence, the use of illegitimate force by public officers. It is one of the main purposes of the *Laws* to insist upon the supremacy of law, even over officials of government. What his followers may have done in positions of power, or what Plato himself might have done in positions of power, or what Plato himself might have done in such a position, is not a part of his teaching. If we can believe his words, his main reliance was upon persuasion. This is evident from the emphasis upon education in both the *Republic* and the *Laws,* in each case for the purpose of producing citizens who have learned to like what the law enjoins and dislike what it forbids. In the later work we even find a provision, almost unique in political philosophy, that the laws themselves should be prefaced by preambles of a "persuasive" sort, so that those

---

*Reprinted by permission of the *Philosophical Review,* 62 (1953), 234-50.

1. This is a revised version of a paper read before a joint meeting of the Philosophy Club and the Erasmus Club at Duke University on April 7, 1952.

2. Some instances of this conjunction of terms: *Republic* 411D, 519E, 548B; *Sophist* 222C; *Statesman* 304D; *Philebus* 58A; *Laws* 660A; 661C; 718B; 722C; 753A. Cf. also Aristotle, *Politics* 1324b 30; *Eudemian Ethics* 1224a 15, b 39.

who are expected to obey will understand the purpose of the law and become more disposed to recognize its authority. Plato's intention clearly is to bring about what he calls "the natural rule of law, without force over willing subjects" (*Laws,* 690C).

But Mr. Karl Popper, in his recent book,³ looks upon Plato's "persuasion," as upon almost all other aspects of Plato's thought, with profound distrust. Plato, he thinks, was a propagandist, a fundamentally dishonest leader of the "revolt against civilization." The Greek word translated by "persuasion" can mean, he says, either (a) persuasion by fair means or (b) talking over by foul means; and it is the latter which he believes Plato is recommending as a political instrument.⁴ "Plato compromised his integrity with every step he took. He was forced to combat free thought, and the pursuit of truth. He was led to defend lying, political miralces, tabooistic superstition, the suppression of truth, and ultimately brutal violence."⁵

These are obviously foul means. Whether Plato used them, or advocated their use, is a matter which the emotional overtones in these phrases would prevent us from deciding readily. But this technique that Plato calls persuasion might perhaps be investigated more carefully than is done by Mr. Popper. It will be evident, I think, that even without the foul means that Mr. Popper mentions, persuasion, as understood by Plato, involves ominous consequences and that this technique may be particularly dangerous when it is employed by persons whose motives, by any commonly recognized standard, are not above reproach.

The Greeks, from Homer onwards, seem to have had an ambivalent attitude toward the devices of persuasion.⁶ The word we trans-

---

3. *The Open Society and Its Enemies* (London, 1945), two volumes; second (revised) edition, in one volume (Princeton, 1950).

4. *Ibid.,* chap. xiii, n. 10.

5. *Ibid.,* (2nd ed.), p. 194. In his preface to the second edition Mr. Popper remarks about the earlier edition: "some of its criticism strikes me today as more emotional and harsher in tone than I could wish." But I do not find that he has altered any of his original contentions.

6. *Kaiom* was traditionally regarded as something like a divinity (Hesiod, *Works and Days,* 73; *Theogony,* 349), sometimes in contrast with another divinity, Ἀναγκαίη, Necessity (Herodotus VIII, 111). But the πότνια Πειθώ of Hesiod is treated with scant respect by Aeschylus. He calls her "willy" (πειθώ δολία, Choephoroe, 726), "the insufferable child of scheming Ate," (*Agamemnon,* 385-386), and makes Prometheus protest that he will not be

late as "persuade" is the active voice (πείθω) of the verb whose passive voice (πείθομαι) means "obey," or "trust". It means getting a person to do something you want him to do, by the use of almost any means short of physical compulsion. Its usual means of operation is of course words, though words may be accompanied by gifts,[7] or may even contain threats. One who knew how to "talk people over" was obviously a very useful and powerful man; and with the rise of democracies, when large numbers of people had to be talked over in assemblies, skill in persuasion became one of the principal requirements for political leadership.[8] Hence the rise of rhetoric, which by its Sicilian master, Gorgias, was explicitly called the "art of persuasion," and came to be cultivated by all the smart young men who aspired to a career in public life.

Plato, as we know, had no high opinion of the rhetoricians, and at least in his early dialogues the art which they professed was to him equally contemptible. In the *Gorgias* it is called a "sham" — a pseudo-art that professes to guide men without claiming to know the principles upon which wise counsel can be based. But between the *Gorgias* and the *Phaedrus* Plato's attitude toward rhetoric apparently underwent a remarkable change. From the *Phaedrus* we learn that when practiced properly it is a very great art indeed; it is the art of leading souls (psychology).[9] This is not to say that Plato's opinion of the rhetoricians had altered. In his opinion they were still far from being masters of this great art, and one of his purposes in this dialogue is to lay down the principles that must be mastered if one would be a genuine rhetorician. Since the function of rhetoric is to lead souls, the master of this art must first of all know the nature of this thing, the soul, on which his art is exercices. Is the soul one and uniform everywhere, or are there various kinds of souls, i.e.,

charmed by the "honey-tongued incantations of Persuasion" that Zeus is employing (*Prometheus* 172-173). The μελιγλώσσοι ἐπαοιδαί of Aeschylus have a clear echo in the ἐπῳδαί of Plato's *Laws*. See below.

7. Cf. the proverb: "Gifts persuade even the gods." Euripides, *Medea* 964; Plato, *Republic* 390E; and note πεπεισμένους μισθοῖς, *Laws* 804D.

8. The comic poet, Eupolis, says of Pericles (fr. 94, 5): "Persuasion sat upon his lips."

9. *Phaedrus* 261A. This word ψυχεγωγία, with its cognate verb, came later to be used to denote the leading of departed souls to the nether world, or the evoking of the dead by special rites. There is a hint of the magical implications in *Laws* 909B.

persons? And if there are different kinds of souls, what power of acting or of being acted upon belongs to each, and by what agencies can each be affected? Only when he has got the answers to these questions will the rhetorician be able to proceed as a genuine artist, with a clear knowledge of the materials he is working with, the effects he wishes to produce, and the means, or causes, which will necessarily (ἐξ ἀνάγκης) bring about the result he wishes (*Phaedrus* 270C-272B).

The implications of this technique are appalling. A leader who knew human nature as thoroughly as Plato's genuine rhetorician, would have a truly divine or diabolical power to do with human beings as he wished. I say divine *or* diabolical; for here we come to a new distinction that Plato makes in this dialogue — the distinction between the philosophical and the nonphilosophical uses of this art. The genuine rhetorician, Plato says, must also know the truth of the matters which he is persuading people to believe. A man has to know the difference between a horse and an ass if he is going to persuade men that the horse is a more useful animal than the ass, and equally so if he wants to persuade them that the ass is more useful than the horse. This is a homely Socratic illustration of the difference between the philosophical rhetorician, in whom the resources of rhetoric supplement and make effective the insights he has reached through dialectic, and the ignorant or unscrupulous practioner of the art.

These pages of the *Phaedrus* contain in germ Aristotle's treatise on rhetoric, which sometimes shocks the unsophisticated reader with its seemingly unscrupulous advice to the rhetorician on how to employ his knowledge of human nature to win his case. Plato's conception is the germ of all later techniques of persuasion, from the handbooks of argumentation used in college courses to the arts of the advertiser, the promotor, the politician, and even the educator. All of these operate on a "scientific knowledge" of human nature, and today they have at their disposal the resources of modern psychology, with its more exact understanding of our vulnerable points. These are some of the implications of the art which Plato outlines here so clearly. Most people who read these pages of the *Phaedrus* probably overlook these implications and never dream of attributing to Plato the intention of practicing such an art. But in fact this seems to have been precisely his intention. In the *Statesman* he mentions a certain kind of rhetoric that has a status akin to the royal science, for it "persuades men to do justice and assists in guiding the helm of the state" (*Statesman* 303E; cf. 304D-E).

But the fullest evidence that Plato intended to use this art is afforded by the detailed provisions in the *Republic* and the *Laws*. The scheme of elementary education described in the *Republic* is but an application of the art of psychagogy. Plato is proposing that his philosophical rulers design and control the means of instruction so as to lead the souls of their citizens along the paths of conduct that philosophical wisdom shows to be right. With sound psychology he sees that the foundations of character are laid in infancy and early childhood. Recognizing the importance of the feelings, he sees that the child must be trained to love good and hate evil. And since the feelings develop before the reason, it is to the training of the sentiments that the educator's efforts are first directed. Believing that the child tends to imitate examples of character and conduct, and knowing from his own experience the power of poetic fancy on the child's imagination, he proposes to censor the poets. The musician likewise must be restricted to composition in certain "modes" only, those that represent and are conducive to manly and philosophical virtue. In short, the educator chooses the kind of character he wishes to produce and directs his efforts artfully, and scientifically, to that end.

The same conception of education appears in the *Laws*: it is essentially a training of the sentiments, from earliest years inward, into accord with the standards set by the law (653BC). But in the later work we are given a clearer view of what Plato thought this training involves. He calls it explicitly and repeatedly a process of "enchantment." On the first appearance of this term one is disposed to think that Plato is simply indulging in one of his plays on words. "In order to produce this effect [i.e., conformity of the sentiments with the law] chants (ᾠδαί) appear to have been invented, which are really enchantments (ἐπῳδαί), and are designed to implant that harmony of which we speak" (659DE). But the word επωδαι and its cognates appear with notable frequency in all later discussions of education, and we can only conclude that Plato is deliberately emphasizing a definite technique.[10] And this is strange, for επωδαι are most com-

---

10. Ἐπῳδαί, ἐπῳδός, ἐπᾴδειν. The most important passages in which these terms occur in connection with education or persuasion are the following: 659E, 664B, 665C, 666C, 670C, 671A, 773D, 812C, 837E, 887D, 903B, 944B.

monly connected, elsewhere in Plato and in Greek writers generally, with magic or sorcery. They are the spells with which the sorcerer charms snakes, or drives away diseases, or averts divine wrath (*Euthydemus* 289E; *Republic* 364B, 426B; cf. *Symposium* 202E).[11] For our purposes the *Euthydemus* passage is peculiarly significant, for Socrates there disdainfully describes the art of the rhetoricians (the λογοποιοί) as a part of the sorcerer's art. The rhetorician charms juries, as the sorcerer charms snakes. The adoption of this art of enchantment as his fundamental procedure in the *Laws* shows that the conception of rhetoric advanced in the *Phaedrus* is seriously meant; he intends to use to the full this art of persuasion, only he will use it as a philosopher should, i.e., as a means of molding human nature aright.

The enchantments used on children are the melodies and rhythms of the songs they sing and the dances they perform. Looking at it psychologically, Plato describes this as an ordering of the young creature's desire for perpetual movement and of his spontaneous delight in sounds and rhythms. Since melodies and rhythms, and the words connected with them, vary greatly in the kinds of life they portray, poets and musicians must be compelled to write only in approved strains, those that portray courage, temperance, and the other virtues (660A-663D). The constant participation in such songs and dances, in play and at the state festivals, will presumably establish the corresponding sentiments in the children and make them steadfast against temptation (665C). The device of enchantment is applied to adults as well. The daily religious sacrifices are occasions on which certain precepts are reiterated with solemnity, and the prayers said at these sacrifices must be rigorously censored, so that no ill-omened word will be uttered (800C-801E). Besides the daily sacrifices, there are numerous religious festivals – monthly, semi-monthly, annual, and biennal – at which the citizens come together, sometimes by tribes and sometimes in a single concourse, for a day of friendship and ceremony. For each of these festivals certain dances and songs are consecrated, and no one, under penalty of indictment for impiety, may offer any other dance or hymn to the

---

11. The analogy to moral exhortation does occasionally occur elsewhere in Plato, as when Socrates' discourse with Charmides on temperance professes to be a kind of charm (*Charmides* 156ff), or when Glaucon and Adeimantus are advised to rehearse the argument about poetry as a charm against the praises of Homer (*Republic* 608A). Cf. also *Phaedo* 114D.

gods (799A-800A). The songs deemed appropriate for these occasions are hymns selected or adapted from the composition of the older poets, with the addition of such newer compositions as win the approval of the judges; all others are resolutely excluded (802B-D). Again at the monthly athletic contests, poets shall celebrate the victors — but no one may sing who is not at least fifty years of age, and of proved character (829CD). Plato makes provision also for musical contests, also carefully regulated (834E-835B). In general, no one is allowed to enter into competition a piece that has not been approved in advance. The judges of these contests are not the audience and the spectators, but specially elected experts (764D-765D).[12] They are to consider not only what the author intended to represent, and whether or not his execution was succesful, but also whether it was worth doing (667B-669B). All these are ways of enchanting, or casting a spell over, the minds of the citizens. By such means, the Athenian Stranger says, "We shall persuade those who need persuading more effectively than we could by any other words" (664C).

It turns out that the persuasive preambles also are considered by Plato a species of enchantment. The clue to understanding the kind of art they embody and the way in which they influence the citizen, is given in the passage in which Plato explains how the poet is to be induced to sing and write according to the canons. Just as the child must be charmed by music and rhythm to a love of virtue and orderliness, so the poet must be "persuaded" by "noble and laudatory phrases" (ῥήματα καλὰ καὶ ἐπαινετά, 660A), i.e., by phrases praising the word of the virtues he is to represent. Now the preambles in Plato's text are just such laudatory compositions extolling the goods that the law seeks to realize in the life of the citizen and appealing to all that is noble in him to co-operate with the law. These preambles and the laws that follow them are not to be stored away in some scribe's library and known only to the officials. They are to be frequently read and listened to by all, since they are one of the few examples of prose literature that may be safely put into the hands of the schoolboy and the citizen (811C-E).

There are many such preambles in the *Laws,* and among them are

---

12. Plato remarks elsewhere (*Laws* 701A) that the decline in Athenian customs began when the standards of excellence in music and the drama came to be determined by the applause of the audience. Cf. 659B.

some of the finest passages that Plato ever wrote. The great preamble in Books IV and V covers the whole duty of man, to the gods, to his fellowmen and to himself, setting forth in proper order the objects he should admire and value, with the reasons which Plato draws from his long experience of life for this ordering of them. For example:

> Listen, all ye who have just now heard the laws about gods and about our death forefathers. Of all the things which a man has, next to the gods, his soul is the most divine and the most truly his own. Now in every man there are two parts, the better and superior, which rules, and the worse and inferior, which serves; and the ruling part of him is always to be preferred to the subject. Wherefore I am right in bidding every one next to the gods, who are our masters, and those who in order follow them [i.e. the demons], to honor his own soul, which everyone seems to honor, but no one honors as he ought; for honor is a divine good, and no evil thing is dishonorable; and he who thinks that he can honor the soul by word or gift, or any sort of compliance, without making her in any way better, seems to honor her but honors her not at all [726E ff].

Then follows a list of the ways in which a man falsely honors his soul: by praising himself, by making excuses, by self-indulgence, by want of endurance, by excessive love of life, by preferring beauty to virtue. This is clearly what Plato means by a laudatory composition. It is one prolonged enchantment, one may say, and whoever reads it cannot help feeling the spell of Plato's eloquence and moral fervor. The same enchanting effect is produced by the other shorter preambles, as well as by the ostensibly formal demonstration of the existence and nature of the gods (Book X), which serves as a preamble to the law of heresy. Besides the enchanting character of this argument as a whole, there are special enchantments at various stages (887C ff; 903B ff; and 904E ff). Note, for example, this discourse (explicitly called an $\epsilon\pi\omega\delta\acute{\eta}$) addressed to the man who doubts the providence of the gods.

> The ruler of the universe has ordered all things with a view to the excellence and preservation of the whole, and each part, as far as may be, has an action and passion appropriate to it.... One of these portions of the universe is thine own, unhappy man, which, however little, contributes to the whole; and you do not seem to be aware that this and every other creation is for the sake of the whole, and in order that the life of the whole may be blessed; and that you are created for the sake of the whole, and not the whole for the sake of you.... And you are annoyed because you are ignorant how what is best for you happens to you and to the universe, as far as the laws of the common creation permit [903B-D].

In saying that these are enchantments I do not wish to imply, nor I think would Plato, that they make no appeal to reason. They are intelligently persuasive; they are persuasion at the high level of rational insight suffused with emotion.

The purpose of these enchantments is to bring about conformity to the law, not merely in the public relations of citizen to citizen, but in all the details, even the most intimate, of private life. Much that in Athenian life was left to the control of "unwritten law" or "ancestral customs" — such as the relations between husband and wife, the care of young children, family worship, funerals — is made in Plato's state a matter of explicit enactment. This is partly because the citizens of his new state will have no common ancestral customs to appeal to, but mainly because these customs are the mortice, or the props, of the social fabric. Without due regulation of private life, the foundations of public law cannot be made secure (790B). "Reflecting on this, Cleinias," says the Athenian Stranger, "you ought to bind together the new state in every possible way, omitting nothing, whether great or small, of what are called laws, or customs, or usages, for by these means a city is bound together" (793CD). Plato's legislation is, in short, one vast system of total persuasion, the climactic fulfillment of the art of psychagogy that he had outlined in the *Phaedrus*.

Knowing all this, who could fail to share Mr. Popper's apprehension at this device that Plato calls persuasion? We recognize in it the first realistic application of an art which can be put, as we now see all too well, to diabolical ends. But can we say, as Mr. Popper does, that Plato is sacrificing his integrity in making these proposals, or that he is consciously and deliberately advocating foul means of persuasion? It is one thing, as Richard Robinson has pointed out, to assert the dangerous nature of Plato's doctrine, and another thing to condemn him as a criminal and speculatively attribute to him the worst motives for teaching it.[13] Formally, Plato's integrity can be amply defended. The persuasion employed in his state is unquestionably concerned with instructing, i.e., inculcating true beliefs, as Plato thought them to be. There are two sorts of physicians, Plato says. One kind prescribes what mere experience suggests, as if he had exact knowledge, and when he has given his order, like a tyrant, he rushes off with equal assurance to the next patient. The other kind of doctors enters into discussion with his patient and his family; he is at

13. "Dr. Popper's Defense of Democracy," *Philos. Rev.*, LX (1951), 498.

once getting information from the sick man and also instructing him, as far is possible, and he will not prescribe until he has first convinced him (720CD). "The man who treats of laws in the way we are doing is schooling the citizens, rather than legislating" (857E; cf. 880E). If we object that no statesman can possibly know as certainly what is conducive to moral health as the physician knows how to improve the body's condition, we cannot deny that Plato thought he knew, and that is the point at issue here. "I am as certain of these things," says the Athenian Stranger, "as I am that Crete is an island" (662B). And not many of us would really doubt the validity of the moral principles that Plato wishes his citizens to accept and live by; most of this doctrine is completely obvious,

One might still object that the methods used are unfair, because they involve so much attention to the sentiments and make so little use of rational proofs. Yet (here again defending Plato) it is obvious that a mature man also has his sentiments and these are usually the most potent forces in him. Furthermore, it may be contended that the truth of principles of conduct or of legal procedure is as much a matter of sentiment as of reason. Our acceptance of them, their truth as we apprehend it, rests ultimately on judgments of value, in which sentiments of appreciation are an essential ingredient. Socrates had persistently asked the question, "Can virtue be taught?" And no answer is given us in the earlier, more Socratic, dialogues. Plato's answer is: "Yes. Virtue can be taught, but not by instruction in the narrow meaning of the term. To learn, or acquire, virtue means the training of the feelings, the discipline of the passions, the formation of habits. Such habituation and training under the guidance of intellectual insight is moral instruction." This is also Aristotle's teaching, and that of countless educators since their time who have been concerned with the training of character. We cannot in truth condemn Plato's methods as unfair means of persuasion without at the same time condemning most of what has ever taken place under the guise of moral instruction. It is exactly what we try to do in our homes, in the church, in every organization or group that wishes to produce and perpetuate a type of character and behavior. We try to enchant the soul so that it will instinctively love that which intelligent judgment pronounces best.

The tragedy of Plato, we can see, is not the conflict between noble words and ignoble and treacherous intentions. It is the conflict between his desire for the moral health of his fellowmen and the love of reason, critical reason, in human affairs. Plato never renounced either of these objects of his devotion; but they are not easy to reconcile, and the form of the synthesis he gives them in his later days really means the victory of morality and the suppression of reason. Let us see how this is so.

Nowhere in his writings does Plato express more frequently than in the *Laws* his desire for the supremacy of reason in human affairs. The chief of all the virues is *Nous*, or intelligence, and it is this that all the other virtues serve (963A). Our state is to be called, not a monarchy, nor a democracy, but by some term indicative of that power which is supreme in it, viz., Nous (713A). This Nous is what is truly divine in the cosmos; it is Plato's God. This divine Nous furnishes the standards for all legislation, and the laws are sovereign only because they have this reason in them. Plato no longer suggests — in fact he explicitly rejects — the conception of personal absolutism. All officials are themselves subject to the law, and there are numerous special devices to assure that this sovereignty of the law be maintained. Plato is in fact the earliest protagonist of a principle that modern legislators, particularly of the Anglo-Saxon tradition, regard as of primary importance, the "rule of law."[14] He also anticipates another principle that became of great importance later in western culture, the conception of a higher law, a "law of nature," from which all positive law derives whatever authority it has.[15] Plato draws heavily upon history and contemporary institutions for the contents of his own system. But it is the gifted legislator, and he alone, who can see in human history the elements of eternal reason that can be used in legislation. Even the gifted legislator may not see truly or fully. Plato recognizes this too, hence leaves a place for amending and supplementing his law. But these amendments are presumably not to be very great; for after a period of ten years (772B) the legislation is to be fixed and immutable, a living image of that eternal law that sets the standard for all human life.

The reason that Plato venerates is therefore the reason embodied in the law. "We give to reason's ordering the name of law" (714A).

---

14. For the evidence, see my article, "Plato and the Rule of Law," *Philos. Rev.,* L (1941), 105-126.

15. Cf. my article, "Plato and the Law of Nature," in *Essays in Political Theory Presented to George H. Sabine,* edited by Konvitz and Murphy, (Ithaca N.Y., 1948), pp. 17-44.

So that as he looks at human beings, the problem of making their reason supreme over their passions becomes the problem of assuring the supremacy of the law in their conduct and beliefs. This is the clear import of the famous passage in which he describes human beings as puppets of the gods, and compares the affections in us to the cords and strings that move the puppet.

> There is one among these cords which every man ought to grasp and never let go, but to pull with it against all the rest: and this is *the sacred and golden cord of reason, called by us the common law of the state.* There are others which are hard and of iron, but this one is soft, because golden; and there are several other kinds. Now we ought always to cooperate with the lead of the best, which is law. For inasmuch as reason is beautiful and gentle, and not violent, her rule must needs have ministers in order to help the golden principle in vanquishing the others [644E-645A].

This image reminds us of the myth Plato had used much earlier in the *Republic* to set forth the different natures of men — some have gold in their nature, some silver, some brass and iron. Here, as in the *Republic*, the golden element is the λογισμός or λογισικόν. But whereas in the *Republic* we are taught to think of the λογισικόν as a faculty of exploring all time and all existence, here it seems to have a lesser function, that of apprehending the public law of the city. The rational man is he who obeys this golden cord of the law. Not blindly, nor reluctantly, for this cord is incapable of compelling. It must have ministers (ὑπηρεταί), i.e., it must be supported by opinions and customs and all the artifices of persuasion we have mentioned.

Whoever understands this conception of reason will not be surprised that there are so few provisions in Plato's state for the development of what *we* would call the powers of reason and rational choice. The course of study outlined for the youth in Plato's new institution, the compulsory public school, is limited in its scope, and instruction is strictly regulated and supervised. Plato's remarks show his concern lest character be corrupted by too much knowledge, and if he sees the need of quickening the mental powers at this stage of development, there is almost no provision for it in his text. Beginning at the age of ten the youth are to devote three years to the study of "letters," three years more to the lyre, and finally comes the study of arithmetic, mensuration, and the motions of the heavenly bodies (809E, 817E). Dancing, gymnastics, and military exercises are apparently a part of the program at all stages (813B ff). Plato opposes the prevailing Athenian opinion that the youth should drink deeply of their rich poetic literature, from Homer to Aristophanes. "The poets have said much that is good and much that is bad, and this being so, a wide range of learning is a danger to young people" (810E ff). Of prose literature Plato says only that "some dangerous books have been bequeathed us by our predecessors" (810C) – probably thinking here of the writings of the Ionian physicists, the "new wise men" who are criticized in the tenth book (888E ff) as having given currency to atheistic ideas. The Athenian Stranger ends this discussion of letters by referring to the laws which he and his companions have been composing. These with their preludes form an admirable example of what young people should learn. They will therefore constitute the materials of instruction, together with any compositions like them which are officially approved (811E; cf. 858C-E). No criticism of these compositions is to be tolerated. The teacher, under pain of dismissal, is required to approve and "praise" them (enchantment again).

In mathematics the aims are little, if any, higher than in letters and music. Since this is education for the multitude, these studies should not be pursued with minute accuracy (818A). Arithmetic, or theory of numbers, has a peculiar power to rouse the sluggish intellect (747B), yet the study of it is to be pursued only so far as is necessary for war, household management, and civic administration (809C, 819BC). The study of astronomy provides an understanding of the calendar (809CD), and also serves to dispel the erroneous impression that the so-called planets are "wanderers," and otherwise to give correct ideas regarding the relative positions and speeds of the heavenly bodies (821B-822A). This is clearly connected with Plato's hope to substitute a rational worship of the stars for the traditional and often immoral cults of the Olympian deities. Plato's most promising suggestion is the proposal to include in the study of mensuration the theory of incommensurables, in order to correct what he regards as shameful and widespread ignorance among the Greeks (819D-820C). But this proposal is made tentatively, and the general tone of this discussion of mathematics is best represented by Plato's opening comment: "Complete ignorance [of this kind of knowledge] is not so terrible or extreme an evil; far more harmful is wide learning and experience combined with a bad bringing up" (819A).

At one point in this discussion Plato mentions a "certain few" for whom a higher education is planned, and promises an account of it later (818A). This is found presumably in the passage at the end of Book XII where he discusses the constitution of that new body called the Nocturnal Council, which meets at the break of day to study the laws and the principles behind them. Here Plato asserts definitely the need of higher learning, particularly in mathematics and theology, if the state is to have a continuing life, yet no clear provisions are made for it, and the impression forces itself upon us that the scantiness of his account is due, not to the weariness of old age, but to a realization that the task was an impossible one. This Council consists of the Director of Education and the best of the other high officials, together with an equal number of carefully selected younger citizens between thirty and forty years of age (951E). Here, if anywhere, we should expect to find that dialectical and philosophical inquiry into first principles on which Plato in the *Republic* had laid such stress. But it is hard to imagine how any citizen who had been subjected for thirty years or more to the strictly supervised regimen we have described could retain the critical power and the freedom of mind required for such study. It should be recalled that even in the *Republic* Plato would have his selected guardians introduced to dialectic only at the age of thirty. Socrates (of all persons!) remarks upon the harm done by philosophical discussion — how it infects people with a spirit of lawlessness (537E). "You must have seen how youngsters, when they got their first taste of it, treat argument as a form of sport solely for purposes of contradiction ... delighting, like puppies, in tugging and tearing at anyone who comes near them." This is why, Socrates says, he speaks so vigorously "against the present practice of admitting anybody, however unfit, to philosophic discussions, and about the need for disciplined and steadfast character" (539B-D).

"Disciplined and steadfast character" seems then to be the main purpose of Plato's education.[16] Character can be made steadfast only by being anchored to the reason in the law, and if the law is to serve this purpose it must be as unchanging as the divine reason itself, or as nearly so as is possible in this world of becoming (798AB; cf. 960D ff). This means that criticism of the laws is tolerated only

---

16. This throws light on *Republic* 358A, where the moral virtues, which are both intrinsically and instrumentally good, seem to be ranked highest in the scale of goods, whereas Aristotle ranks them second, precisely because they are instrumental to the attainment of the intellectual virtues.

within very narrow limits, if at all. The Athenian Stranger remarks that one excellent feature of the Cretan law is the provision that no youth shall inquire which laws are right and which are wrong, and that if any old man has any strictures to pass on any of them, he must not utter in the presence of the young, but only before a magistrate or a person of his own age (634E). Plato's law goes even further than this. It is hard to find any persons, even officials, in Plato's state who may criticize the laws with impunity, after the ten-year period of testing is over. The highest officials are to be known as Guardian of the Laws (νομοφύλακες) – an apt title, for their function is mainly to oversee the administration of the laws by the other officials, and, in general, to assure the observance of the laws by all the citizens.

The crowning expression of this spirit of conformity is to be found in Plato's restrictions on foreign travel. No man under forty years of age shall be permitted to go abroad to any place whatsoever; and no man, whatever his age, shall go abroad in a private capacity; but only as a herald, or as a member of an official embassy, or as what Plato calls an officially approved "observer" (θεωρός). Heralds and ambassadors shall be selected from among the nobles and best citizens, in order to gain repute for the state abroad, and when they return home they shall teach the youth that the institutions of other countries are "second-rate" as compared with their own (950D ff). To remedy what must have seemed even to Plato a serious defect, he authorizes the visit of "observers" to foreign countries; for, he says, a state that is isolated can never become fully civilized, nor would it be able to safeguard its laws unless it grasped them, not by habit only, but also by conviction (951B). But such an observer must be "incorruptible"; he must be more than fifty years of age and have proved himself a man of high repute both in military and other affairs. When he has completed his tour abroad he shall sit with the Nocturnal Council and communicate to them what he has learned. If he Council finds him to be a better man that when he left home (nothing is said about the value of his new ideas) he shall receive high commendation. If, on the other hand, he appears to have been corrupted by his travels, in spite of his pretentions to wisdom, he shall be forbidden to associate with anyone, young or old; and if he does not submit, he shall be put to death for meddling with education and the laws (951C-952D).

Persuasion, even as Plato understands the term, could hardly go farther. This passage shows in all its grimness the monolithic power of the official doctrine and the impotence of the individual to challenge it. It reveals also the tragedy of Plato's intellectual predicament. He sees that the laws, however excellent, cannot be maintained in their perfection unless they are held by conviction, not by habit alone; and he sees that no human institution, not even his own legislation, is beyond the need of correction. But he has deprived himself of the sole means of correction, viz., the free play of individual criticism. Socrates in prison, discussing with Crito the propriety of escaping, invokes (according to Plato's account) the image of the laws themselves are arguing with him. "We have given you, Socrates," the Laws say, "a choice between alternatives; either to persuade us that we are wrong, or to obey us." This is the spirit of genuine persuasion, the willingness to be persuaded as well as to persuade. Plato, with his concern for the "care of the soul" which he had learned from Socrates, could not allow any soul to doubt the authority of the regime in which alone, as he thought, that soul could safely reach maturity. Thereby he blinded himself to the deeper meaning of that Socratic concern for the soul. The most penetrating judgment we can make on Plato's state is in those memorable words that he himself put in the mouth of Socrates at his trial: "The life lived without criticism is not fit for a man to live."

TRUE AND FALSE SPEECH IN PLATO'S *CRATYLUS* 385 B-C*

W. M. Pfeiffer

In 385B-C of the *Cratylus,* Plato appears to be formulating a version of the correspondence theory of truth, in such a way that it applies not only to discourse, but to individual names as well. However commentators who have remarked on this passage, either take exception to the reasoning, or find it necessary to interpret the conclusion with qualifications that Plato never could have intended. Richard Robinson, for example, on p. 328 of "A Criticism of Plato's *Cratylus*",[1] sums up the argument thus:

> ... since statements have a truthvalue, their parts, including names, must have a truthvalue too. Therefore names are true or false.

and criticises it for involving a fallacy of division. Lorenz and Mittelstrasse,[2] by contrast, construe the argument as validly proceeding from the true-false distinction of sentences to a corresponding true-false distinction of their parts. But, like Robinson, they regard truth and falsehood as characteristics of statements or sentences, and are obliged to save the reasoning by claiming that Plato conceived of names (ονοματα) as predicates, so that the truth and falsehood of names is to be understood as the respective truth value of elementary sentences which affirm these predicates of individuals given by context. And most recently, R. Weingartner,[3] interpreting the passage in the same way as Robinson, insists that the argument is bad, and that Socrates (who is represented as making it) thought its conclusion to be false.

---

*Reprinted with permission from Volume II, no. 1 of the *Canadian Journal of Philosophy,* pp. 87-104, by the Canadian Association for Publishing in Philosophy.

1. *Phil. Rev.,* 1956, pp. 324-341.
2. In ther paper "On Rational Philosophy of Language: The Programme in Plato's *Cratylus* Reconsidered", *Mind,* 1967, pp. 1-20. They discuss this argument on pp. 5-6.
3. In his "Making Sense of the Cratylus",*Phronesis,* 1970, pp. 5-25. His remarks on this argument are on pp. 14-15.

In fact, this argument is not concerned, in any particular way, with statements or sentences; nor does it establish the independent existence of true and false names. But it does comprise a formulation — probably the first articulate one in the history of Western thought — of a correspondence theory of truth for discourse generally,[4] and it establishes that names can be spoken as true or false within the context of discourse. Moreover it can be validly construed if understood in terms of the background against which it was written, and as Plato expressed it. The main issues in interpreting it, are the proper expansion of the statament of the conditions for false discourse (step four), and the sense in which Plato is using the term 'λογος'. Though the latter issue affects the whole argument, it will be discussed in detail in connection with some of the later steps.

The argument occurs in the *Cratylus* in the course of a discussion of the view that names are purely conventional, the arbitrary products of human activity, rather than natural and necessarily corresponding to the true nature of things. Hermogenes, the champion of the conventionalist position, has put forward the extreme thesis that the caprice of an individual, even when it inverts generally accepted (i.e. conventional) usage, will yield names that are genuine — at least relative to the individual (ιδια) who posits them. For example, an individual can call 'horse' what everybody else calls 'man'. Such appellations, though always right in one's "private language", are by the same token not names in the ordinary sense, so Socrates, the interlocutor in the dialogue, constructs the argument in 385B-C to show that there is an objective criterion of truth and falsity for names, independent of individual *fiat*.

The argument is carried out in two stages: the first (385B) establishes the possibility of true and false discourse in general, and explains how it is true and false; and the second (385C) applies these results to names. The best way to examine the argument is to consider each stage separately, first displaying the steps, and then commenting on them and on the reasoning and results. All the steps are proposed by Socrates: Hermogenes merely affirms them, but adds nothing except degrees of emphasis.

---

4. Some passages in earlier literature which may contain attempts to deal with a theory of this sort, are discussed inf. on pp. 97-98.

1. True and False Discourse (385B)

Socrates begins by asking Hermogenes:
1. Would you say there is such a thing as
    καλεῖς τι
  (a) saying true things
    ἀληθῆ λέγειν
  (b) and false ones?
    καὶ ψευδῆ;

When Hermogenes agrees, Socrates goes on to infer:
2, Then there would be
    οὐκοῦν εἴη ἂν
  (a) true speech,
    λόγος ἀληθής,
  (b) and false?
    ὁ δὲ ψευδής;

Hermogenes assents readily, so Socrates proceeds to explain what true and false speech are, defining what he means by these expressions:
3. Well, then,
    ἆρ' οὖν
  (a) that which says the things that are
    as they are,
      is true;
    οὗτος ὃς ἂν τὰ ὄντα λέγῃ
    ὡς ἔστιν αληθης.
  (b) and that (which says them) as they are not, false?
    ος δ' αν
    ὡς οὐκ ἔστιν, ψευδής;

Hermogenes affirms this point too. Now, having worked in a reference to "the things that are" or reality (τα οντα), Socrates confirms the relation between them and language:
4. This, then, is possible:
    ἔστιν ἄρα τοῦτο·
    in discourse (a) to say the things that are
    λόγῳ λέγειν τὰ ὄντα
      and (b) not to?
        τε και υη;

Once more Hermogenes assents readily, concluding the first stage of the argument.

Plato began the argument by recognizing the existence (καλεῖς τι) of the activity of speaking in the most general sense, in terms of the infinitive 'λέγειν', but he immediately introduced the notions of truth and falsity as characteristics of things, not of the activity, using the neuter plural of the adjectives 'ἀληθῆ' and 'ψευδῆ'. Had he wished to express truth and falsity as modifications of the act, i.e., as different ways of speaking, he could have used the adverbs 'ἀληθῶς' and 'ψευδῶς' – the terms, at any rate, were available. Moreover, even if 'ἀληθῆ' and 'ψευδῆ' are being used adverbially, as the neuter forms of adjectives frequently are, they would be "accusatives of the internal object" or "object effected", and so would be regarded as standing in apposition to an unexpressed object of the verb.[5] They are, however, very likely accusatives of the external object or object affected. But in either case, truth and falsity are treated as a matter of *what* is said, not how it is said.

In the second step, Plato moves from the existence of saying true and false things, to assert the existence (ειη) of the internal object, λόγος, which is now directly described as being either true or false. The term 'λόγος' has to be understood here in the broad sense of *speech* or *discourse in general,* rather than taken as referring to any particular instances such as stories, sentences, etc.[6] The adjectives 'ἀληθής' and 'ψευδής' indicate that it, λόγος, can be of two kinds: true, or false.

---

5. Cf. H. W. Smyth, *Greek Grammar* (Cambridge: Harvard University Press, 1959), §1607.

6. Cf. *LSJ.* s.v. IX,1 = *expression, utterance, speech*; by contrast to IX.3.b = *sentence, complete statement.*

There is no precise English equivalent for 'λόγος' as Plato is using the term throughout this passage. The closest sense is probably that expressed by the French *'le langage',* as that term is used in recent linguistic studies. Cf. S. Ullmann, *Semantics: An Introduction to the Science of Meaning* (Oxford: Blackwell, 1964), pp. 19sqq. *'le langage',* Ullmann notes (p. 19, n. 1), "embraces the faculty of language in all its various forms and manifestations". This notion includes *la langue* – the vehicle of communication or "code" –, and *la parole* – the encoding of a particular message on a given occasion.

In this part of the *Cratylus* Plato is trying to shift attention away from *la parole,* from the user and the circumstances surrounding the occasion of an utterance (i.e. away from the pragmatics of language), but he does not have the technical notion of language as a code. On this see further the discussion of 'λόγος' immediately following the presentation of the second stage of the argument.

Step three explains how these two kinds of λόγος differ: both refer to existing things or the things that are (τὰ γντα), but true discourse says[7] them as they in fact are (ὡς ἔστιν), and false discourse as they are not (ὡς οὐκ ἔστιν). Thus the ἀληθῆ of step one become φα ὄντα stated ὡς ἔστιν, and the ψευδη come out also as τα οντα, but stated ὡς οὐκ ἔστιν. Two apparently different kind of things (αληθῆ, ψευδῆ) are explained as one kind (τα βντα) differently stated (ὡς ἔστιν, ὡς οὐκ ἔστιν), in two corresponding different kinds of discourse (λόγος ἀληθής, λόγος ψευδής).

The fourth step, like the first and second, asserts the existence, or at least the possibility, of something (ἔστιν ἄρα τοῦτο) — in this case of the states of affairs described in step three. That step was explanatory, enlarging on what was asserted in the second step, and step four is thus necessary to formally incorporate the items of the explanation into the argument. This is no idle point: the possibility of expressing reality (τὰ ὄντα) in discourse (λόγος) is explicitly denied in the third thesis of Gorgias' notorious "Concerning Notbeing or Nature", on the grounds of the irreducible difference between discourse (which is just something we utter), and reality (which is composed of the things that truly exist).[8] Plato has to take into account this sort of argument, since the investigation in the *Cratylus* is concerned with discovering just what is the relationship between discourse and whatever it is about — whether reality or the conventional world of appearance.

But in the case of this step in the argument, the matter is further complicated in that Plato is dealing with two kinds of discourse, true and false, and with reality accordingly stated in two different ways. Thus he has to give a dual set of conditions in step four, corresponding to the dual explanations, in step three. For (a) truth, there is no special problem: that discourse which states the things that are, as they are, depends simply on the possibility of stating, in discourse, the things that are. But (b) false discourse, which differs in stating the things that are, as they are not (ὡς οὐκ ἔστιν), requires the

---

7. 'λέγω', like English 'say', has *inter alia* the two senses: (i) *to say* or *speak,* i.e. *to utter an articulate sound,* and (ii) *to mean* or *intend,* i.e. *to have a definite signification.* Cf. LSJ. s.v. *III, esp. 1 and 9. The sense* mean is probably predominant in this occurrence of 'λέγη', but the ambiguous 'says' is used in this translation as it has a better sound in English at this point.

8. As reported in Sextus Empiricus, *Adv. math.* VIII,83-87.

addition of the negative idea to the statement of the conditions for true discourse. Exactly how this is done, is the first issue critical to the interpretation of this part of the *Cratylus*.

Plato expresses the negative idea in step four by the elliptical phrase 'τε καὶ νή'. Translators, almost uniformly, and uncritically, render this "that which is not",[9] as though it were to be expanded as the otherwise familiar 'τὰ|μὴ ὄντα'. But this would raise the problem of not-being, which Plato seems to be trying to avoid in the *Cratylus*. He eventually does take up that problem in the *Sophistes*: pp. 236-245 and 255-264 of that dialogue are the *locus classicus* for his discussion of how it is possible to make false statements without positing the existence of not-being (ὑποθέσθαι τὸ μὴ ὂν εἶναι) (237A). There he works out the solution that false statements assert "other things than those which are" (ἕτερα τῶν ὄντων), and in the sense they assert "the things that are not [those that are]" — being other — "as though they were" (τὰ μὴ ὄντ' ἄρα ὡς ὄντα) (263B). But in the *Cratylus* Plato is not dealing specifically with statements, and moreover he *starts* with the admission that it is possible to say false things (ψευδῆ λέγειν), and argues only to the point of distinguishing, on the one hand, the relationship that holds between this kind of discourse and reality, from that between true discourse and reality, on the other. He does not examine what is involved in the negation of reality (not-being), although later in the dialogue (385E-387A) he does undertake an extensive analysis of being.

The clue to the correct expansion of the statement of the conditions for false discourse is found later in the *Cratylus*, where the same issue comes up again. Cratylus, the champion of the nature-theory, has been maintaining that no genuine name can be incorrect or false, and at 429C-D Socrates asks him whether it is not possible to say false things (ψευδῆ λέγειν). This is the (b) part of the premise that was accepted by Hermogenes as step one of the argument in 385B, but Cratylus in his turn rejects it, on the basis of this sophism:

How would anyone who says that which he says
not say that which is?

---

9. Sc. Fowler in the Loeb edition; and similarly Meridier in the Bude, Buccellato in his edition, and Ast in his Latin translation, to give but a few examples. Otto Apelt, however, retains the literal sense of the original: „*Also ist es möglich durch die Rede das Seiende zu bestimmen und auch wieder n i c h t ?* " [Emphatic spacing added.]

Or isn't 'saying false things' this,
    viz. 'not saying the things that are'? [10]
πῶς γὰρ ἄν ... λέγων γέ τις τουτο ὃ λέγει,
    μὴ τὸ ὂν λέγοι;
ἢ οὐ τοῦτό ἐστιν τὸ ψευδῆ λέγειν,
    τὸ μὴ τὰ ὄντα λέγειν;

The explicit equivalence in the last two lines of this little argument (i) provide the conditions for false discourse, while (ii) avoiding the problem of not-being. For (i) 'μὴ τὰ ὄντα λέγειν' is the simple negation of 'λέγειν τὰ ὄντα': the 'μὴ' negates neither the 'ὄντα' nor the 'λεγειν' separately,[11] but the whole expression[12] — which, unnegated, is the corresponding condition for true discourse. And (ii) 'μὴ τὰ ὄνταλεγειν' is a very different expression from 'ὑποθέσθαι τὸ μὴ ὂν εἶναι' of the *Sophistes* — which does raise the problem of not-being. In its fully expanded form, step four thus provides the conditions for (a) true, and (b) false, discourse, as:

10. Most translators, however, render this passage incorrectly: even Apelt, who alone of those referred to in the preceding note, translated the similar occurrence in 385B accurately, gives the last two lines here as: „Oder heisst lügen nicht so viel als d a s N i c h t s e i e n d e sagen? [Emphatic spacing added.] *Meridier translates the present passage correctly:*
    ... en disant ce qu'on dit
        comment ne pas dire ce qui est?
    Parler faux ne consiste-t-il pas a
    ne pas dire ce qui est?
but perhaps only because of the French idiom; for in his note *ad* the second line he remarks "...Μη (et non, ου) s'explique comme se rapportant non a l'ensemble de la phrase, mais a τὸ ὄν (cf. plus loin τὰ μὴ ὄντα)." But surely he cannot be referring to 'μ ὴ τ ὰ βντα' in the fourth line, yet there are no other occurrences of 'ὄντα' with any negative in the rest of the dialogue!

11. In the *Sophistes,* both these cases generate problems: the negation of 'ὄν' seems to imply the existence of not-being, although the expression cannot be applied to any existing thing (237A-D); and the very attempt to formulate it is taken to result, not in speaking but saying nothing (λέγειν μέν, λέγειν ἰστοι μηδέν), but in not speaking at all (οὐδὲ λέγειν (237E)! 'οὐ λιγω' was apparently not understood on the anthology of 'οὐ φημί'.

12. Cf. the similar ellipsis in 387C of the *Cratylus,* where the adversative-negative expression 'ἂν δὲ μή' is used to distinguish the conditions for unsuccessful speaking, from those for successful. The latter are given in the complex statement 'ἐὰν μὲν ᾖ πέφυκα τε πράγματα λέγειν τε καὶ λέγεσθαι επι ᾧ, ταύτῃ καὶ τούτῳ λέγῃ' and the former by the negation of this whole set of conditions in the expression quoted. Yet no one would expand the statement of them as αν δε η πεθεκε ηα μη πραγματα λεγειν ηε και λεγεσθαι —'.,

(4) This, then, is possible:

ἔστιν ἄρα]ουτο·

in discourse (a) to say the things that are

λόγῳ λέγειν τὰ ὄντα

and (b) not [to say the things that are].

καὶ μὴ [τὰ ὄντα λέγειν].

The argument up to this point clearly establishes the conditions necessary for a correspondence theory of truth. According to this type of theory, there are two parallel realms: discourse, and reality; and truth and falsity are a function of the relation between them. Truth is a characteristic possessed by discourse when this relation is one of correspondence; when there is a lack of correspondence, discourse is false. This is exactly the situation described in step three: there are λόγος, and τα οντα; and the relation between them is that λόγος states (λέγη τὰ ὄντα in one of two ways, and is true or false accordingly. The expressions 'ὡς ἔστιν' and 'ὡς οὐκ εσ]ιν', which specify the ways as involving correspondence or not, are adverbial and modify the relation.[13]

Professor A. Mourelatos of the University of Texas, who looked at an earlier draft of this paper, pointed out that ας' cannot automatically be taken as adverbial, and called attention to the alternative interpretation according to which the 'ἔστι' is taken as "veridical" in C. H. Kahn's sense. (This sense of 'εἶναι' is discussed inf., in note 20.)

On p. 253 of his article "The Greek Verb 'to be' and the Concept of Being" (*Foundations of Language,* 1966), Kahn renders a summary statement of the Greek concept of truth, conflated from this passage in the *Cratylus,* and from *Sophistes* 263B, and Aristotle *Met.* 1011 b27 as:

to say of the things that are (the case) *that* they are and of the things that are not *that* they are not. [Italics added.]

But his n. 5 *ad loc.* seems to reverse this position, and thereby support the interpretation given in this paper. In that note he remarks that "The translation given in [his] texts reflects the natural syntax of ὡς ιστιν, e.g., in Protagoras or Aristotle. Plato, however, often seems to play on the alternative construction (taking ὡς as adverb rather than as conjunction) and thus to take the formula as meaning: "to speak of the things which are just as they are...". "[Italics added.]".

Cornford remarks on the ambiguity of the expression, but observes that "the difference is grammatical rather than substantial" (*PTK.,* p. 310). To put it another way, the original Greek 'ὡς ἔστι' is identical in form, whichever function it may have, and our contemporary distinction between the conjunction 'that' and the adverb 'as', cannot be urged with equivalent force in Classical Greek. But in any case, evidence that the expressions function adverbially in the

This newly formulated correspondence theory differs significantly from the old, traditional, view which formed the background for Plato. Traditionally, truth and falsity were regarded not so much as dependent on the occurrence, or lack, of correspondence between discourse and reality, but rather as a measure of the degree of reality revealed, or concealed, in an action or utterance.[14] In the early Greek world-view,[15] all the things that are (τὰ ἐόντα) were con-

present occurrences, is provided by parallel contexts: in the *Euthydemus*, where Plato first raises the issue (as discussed at the end of Part I of this paper), the expressions occupying the corresponding position in the statement suggesting how false speaking should be described, are 'τρόπον τινά', and 'ὥς γε ἔχει', and can only be adverbial: also, later in the *Cratylus* where Plato examines the relationship between speaking (and naming), and reality, by means of the craft analogy (387A sqq.), he uses adverbial expressions in similar positions in his statements assessing the various ways that speaking and naming can be carried out (cf. e.g. 'ὡς ἂν ἡμεῖς βουλώμεθα', 'ᾧ ἂν βουληθῶμεν', κτα.).

14. Something of this sense is reflected in the derivation of 'ἀληθής', and 'ἀλήθεια', from a privative and the stem of 'ληθχ' ('λανθάνω') = escaping notice; according to which derivation, truth is literally *not-escaping notice, not-concealed, un-hidden*, etc. Cf. *LSJ* s.v. 'ἀληθής'.

The etymological approach to interpreting this notion has lost favour since Heidegger pushed it to a non-Greek extreme, claiming that the "original" meaning of the term was the "unhiddenness (*Unverborgenheit*) of Being", which he construed as a purely ontological characteristic, opposed to the epistemological one of "correctness of apprehension". Cf. his *Sein und Zeit*, pp. 219sqq., and *Platons Lehre von der Wahrheit*, pp. 46 sqq.

But there is no justification for taking the etymology in an exclusively ontological sense: as P. Friedländer points out in his discussion of this issue (Ch. XI of his *Plato: An Introduction*), the single case, surviving from the early Greek period, in which 'ἀληθής' is understood as 'α-ληθής' (viz. Hesiod, ‡κξθνθχδ 233), has to do with the (epistemological) characteristic of not-forgetting or not-neglecting. He notes, moreover that the essential contrary to truth was, for the Greeks, always, lying deception, conscious distortion, etc. — in short, everything that disturbs, distorts, slants, or conceals the true and real.

The extent to which the etymology does, in fact, provide a useful insight into the conception of truth in the Ancient Greek world, will become clear from the outline of the Ancient Greek worldview, of which it was an integral part, as given in the text of this paper.

15. This *Weltbild* can be reconstructed from descriptions and usages in Homer, Hesiod, the Lyric poets and early dramatists. It is based initially on some suggestions and ideas from Professor L. E. Woodbury of the Department of Classics, University College, Toronto. On another occasion I hope to present it in greater detail; it is not possible here to do more than sketch the relevant aspects of a much oversimplified picture.

sidered to have an αρχή or φύσις or ενεσις, a *source or growth or origin*; and also a τέλος or τελευτή or πέρας, an *end or goal*. The former were in the "past", among "the things that are before" (τὰ προεόντα), the latter among "the things that are to be" (τὰ ἐσόμενα). The full truth about anything involved a full disclosure or revelation of it, based on knowledge of the origin from which it grows, and of the goal toward which it is growing, since both help determine what it is.[16] But such knowledge was possible only for divine, superhuman beings who spanned the three "time" periods of reality, and held "the ends of all things" (πέρατα πάντων): mere mortals were limited to present experience, to the things that are here and now. At best a few selected individuals, by means of the divine gift of "memory" (μνήμη, the opposite of λήθη), could have access to the things that are before and so trace the genealogy of heroes (as did Pindar, for example) or even of the world-creature (Hesiod), revealing present circumstances and achievements as the necessary outcome of past growth or development. But the things that are to be, remained always inscrutable: there was no divine gift corresponding to "memory" which could be used effectively by mortals to penetrate that fated but unknowable realm.[17] Nor was the superior ability, possessed by the divine beings, to gain access to the full truth, any guarantee that they would reveal it to lesser humans: though Parmenides justifies the Way of Truth, in part, by putting it in the mouth of a goddess, Hesiod's Muses quite candidly warn him, at the beginning of the *Theogony*, that they can speak lies as though they were true, or utter truths when they so pleased.[18]

Gradually, however, this theocentric world-view was shifted to the

---

16. Thus Solon, in the story told by Herodotus in Bk. 1, 30-33, was unable to say that Croesus was the happiest of mortals, without first discovering whether, in addition to his present fortunate circumstances, he would end his life well too (πρι τελευτήσαντα καλῶς τὸν αἰῶνα πύθωμαι).

17. This is illustrated by the story of Cassandra, whose gift of prophecy was vitiated by the fact that no one ever believed her. The story required that kind of twist in order to be consistent with what the Greeks felt could be brought within human power.

18. Cf. ll. 27-28:
ἴδμεν ψεύδεα πολλὰ λέγειν ἐτύμοισν ὁμοῖα,
ἴδμεν δ', εὖτ' ἐθέλωμεν, ἀληθέα γηρύσασθαι.
We know how to speak many false things as though they were true,
But we also know how, when we wish, to utter true things.

anthropocentric one of Sophistic times epitomized in Protagoras' *homo mensura* doctrine, and truth could now be treated as a characteristic of human knowledge and discourse about things, together with the extension of human powers to many areas formerly reserved for the gods.[19] Parmenides struck the greatest blow leading in this direction, when he compressed the old tripartite view of being into one, continuous (ἔν, συνεχές – B8.6), uniform (ὁμοῦ πᾶν –B8.5) bulk (ὄγκωι – B8.43); refusing to acknowledge any distinctions or divisions in being (οὐδὲ διαιρετόν ἐστιν – N8.22) between things that are present here and now (παρεόντα – B4.1) and things putatively absent (ἀπεόντα – B4.1; which would include both the old προεντα and ἐσόμενα). As a result, generation or coming into being, and unknowable coming to an end, are put right out of the picture (τωγενεσις μὲν ἀπέσβεσται καὶ ἄπυστος ὄλεθρος – B8.21); being neither comes into being nor passes from being (οὔτε γενέσθαι/οὔτ' ὄλλυσθαι – B8.13-14), but is ungenerated or without beginning (ἀγένητον – B8.3; αναρχον – B8.27) and without end or goal (ἀνώλεθρον – B8.3; ἀτέλεστον – B8.4). For Parmenides, truth and being coincide, because there is nothing other than being to be revealed.

But an articulate, methodical account of truth was not possible until Plato relocated the old explanatory aspects of things in an intelligible region – the νοητὸς τόπος of *Republic* 508C. He thereby shifted the concern from the origin or generation (γένεσις) of being to its *genera* (γένη), from the source or growth (αρχή in the old sense, or φύσις) to the form or idea, or distinctive character (εἶδος, ἰδέα, οὐσία); and from the elusive end or goal (τέλος, τελευτή,

---

19. Cf., for example, the sentiment in the first part of fgt. B234 of Democritus, where he observes that "men (ἄνθρωποι) ask in prayers for health from the gods (παρὰθεῶν) and do not know that they have in themselves the power for this (τχν δὲ ταύτης δύναμιν ἐν ἑαυτοῖς ἔχοντες οὐκ ἴσασιν.).

The trend toward human independence in matters of truth may have begun with Xenophanes, if, in his frgt. B18, there is a genuine opposition between revealing (ὑπέδειξαν), which the gods are responsible for, and discovering (ἐψευρίσκουσιν), which mortals may undertake. But these may be just two aspects of the traditional disclosure which is wholly within the purview of the gods alone: for in B34 Xenophanes seems to be suggesting that even if a mortal (ευηρ) were, quite by accident (τύχοι), to utter the most complete [truth] (τὰ μάλιστα ... τετελεσμένον εἰπών) he would not even realize it himself (αὐτὸς ὅμως οὐκ οἶδε).

πέρας) to the hypotheses and stepping stones (ὑποθέσεις οαμαι) which lead ultimately to the unconditioned principle of everything (τὸ ἀνυπόθετον, ἡ τοῦ παντὸς ἀρχή – *Republic* 511C). Truth is no longer something the attainment of which is physically outside the sphere of human competence, and dependent on the disclosure of things in regions thought of as being elsewhere in space and time; but rather it is present in the things that are, to be discovered by the powers of the intellect operating here and now, and to be expressed in utterances which can be evaluated in terms of their correspondence with the things that are available to all thinking men.

From step one of this argument in the *Cratylus,* Plato seems to be trying to dissociate truth and falsity from the act of speaking in the sense of the old act of revelation, and, more importantly, from the speaker, the agent whose usage it is, whether god or man. He proposes instead a view of truth and falsity as characteristics of what is uttered, to be assessed in terms of objective criteria, independently of the utterer. When, in step three, he brings into the argument the adverbial expressions 'ὡς ἔστιν' and 'ὡς οὐκ ἔστιν' to explain the difference between truth and falsity, they modify not the act of uttering by an agent, but rather the 'λέγῃ', the *meaning* relation that holds between the utterance and the reality referred to in the utterance, and that determines, by its correspondence or lack of correspondence, whether the utterance is true or false.

In this passage, Plato can be seen to be making the first self-conscious and deliberate attempt to methodically work out this conception of truth as a rational theory,[20] even to the point of iden-

---

20. As Professor Mourelatos pointed out, the *conception* of truth as involving a correspondence between knowledge and reality, or language and reality, is present earlier than Plato's treatment of it in the *Cratylus,* especially by implication, in, for example, Herodotus. F. M. Cornford, in his *Plato's Theory of Knowledge,* describes the view as current and popular (p. 310); cf. also J. V. Luce, "The Date of the *Cratylus*", *Am. J. Philol.,* 1964, p. 151.

For that matter, a correspondence theory seems to be built into the very conception of being which Kahn, in the article referred to in n. 13 *sup.,* identifies as underlying the most fundamental value of 'εἶναι' (and of the Indo-European *es). This "veridical" usage, as he designates it on p. 252, is not simply to be or to exist, but to be so (p. 250); and is essentially ambiguous, meaning *to be true* with respect to statements made in words, and *to be the case* with respect to facts or situations, in the world (p. 252). Kahn further explains that the ambiguity is likely based on the one-to-one correspondence between what is the case and the truth of the statement that it is the case (p. 252).

tifying the metaphysical presuppositions which underlie it (cf. step four of the argument). Plato himself indicates this by developing the theory in an argument that stands independently in the discussion in the *Cratylus*, formally introduced by the direction to consider a new point (φέρε δή μοι τόδε εἰπέ).

Prior to Plato, surviving evidence indicates that Heracleitus may have attempted to formulate the conception of correspondence, and to use it in explaining true (i.e. *overt,* or *fully-revealing*) words and actions, though he certainly cannot be said to have worked it out as a theory. Cf., for example, B112, where he defines "wisdom" (σοφίη) as:

saying and doing true things,
understanding according to natural growth.
εληθεα λέγειν καὶ ποιεῖν
κατὰ φύσιν ἐπαίοντας.

Here, 'κατά' expresses the notion of correspondence, and 'φύσιν' refers to the traditional explanatory principle of "original being", as it has "grown to be", Cf. also B1, ll.5-6, where Heracleitus, who has a divine understanding of things through his grasp of the common λόγος, describes his own activity as:

distinguishing each thing according to
    natural growth
and declaring of what kind it is.
κατὰ φυσιν διαιρεων ακαστον
καὶ φρεζων ὅκως ἔχει-

'φράζων', stronger than 'λέγων', here means *declare* or even *reveal;* and 'ὅκως ἔχει', which is equivalent to 'ὁκοῖον εστι', means *of what sort* or *kind* something is, i.e., what *species* or division of being it belongs to. W. J. Verdenius, on p. 74 of his *Parmenides* (Amsterdam: Hakkert, 1964), notes that in this fragment Heracleitus explains κατὰ φύσιν by ὅκως ἔχει.

Oarmenides presupposes a correspondence view of truth at the basis of his whole approach, in setting up the way of truth (ἀληθείης – B1.29) which leads to genuine being (ἐὸν ἔμμεναι – B6.1; ἐτήτυμον εἶναι – B8.18), and which is opposed to the way of mortal opinions (βροτῶν δόξας – B1.30) that leads to appearances (τὰ δοκοῦντα – B1.31). But although he several times pairs off the key expressions involved, in contexts where he is discussing knowing, and speaking about, genuine being (e.g., B2.3-4; B8.17-18, 38sqq.), he nowhere formulates the conception or tries to work it out as a theory.

Plato first raised the issue in 283E-284C of the *Euthydemus,* but there he concentrated mainly on problems associated with attempting to explain false speaking by means of correspondence, and directed sophistical objections against the suggestions that this could be done in terms of actually saying what one is talking about (283E-284B), or in terms which involved dealing in any way whatsoever with "the things that are not" (τὰ μὴ ὄντα) (284B-C). He ended the argument with the hint that saying false things (ψευδῆ λέγει) might be explained as "saying the things that are in a sort of way, but not, however, as they are" (τὰ ὄντα μὲν τρόπον τινὰ λέγει· οὐ μέντοι ὥς γε ἔχοι – 284V). This hint is developed in the *Cratylus*; the very different problem of dealing with τε μὴ ὄντα is not taken up until later, in the *Sophistes,* as has been noted.

II. Saying True and False Names (385C)

In the second stage of this argument in the *Cratylus,* Socrates proceeds from what has been proved for discourse generally, to establish that it holds also for all occurrences of discourse, whatever their size, including single words.

He begins:
5. Consider that discourse which is true:
ὁ λόγος δ' ἔστιν ὁ ἀληθής
 whether it is true all together
 ποτερον μεν ολος αληθης,
  but the bits of it not true?
 τὰ μόρια δ' αὐτοῦ οὐκ ἀληθῆ;
Hermogenes denies that discourse is only true all together, and agrees with the implicit alternative to the "whether", asserting that the bits will also be true (ἀλλὰ καὶ τὰ μόρια), so Socrates continues, putting the next step in the form of an explicit alternative:
6. Again, are the large bits true
πότερον δὲ τὰ μὲν μέγαλα μόρια ἀληθῆ
 but the small ones not
 τὰ δα σμικρὰ οὔ·
or all?
ἢ πάντα;
Hermogenes chooses the obvious alternative (παντα), whereupon

Socrates introduces the name into the argument in the same way as he started it off, i.e., by asking Hermogenes:

7. Is there anything that you would say is
   ἔστιν οὖν ὅ τι λέγεις
   > a smaller bit of discourse, other than a name?
   > λόγου σμικρότερον μόριον ἄλλο ἢ ὄνομα;

Hermogenes affirms that there is not, the name is the smallest (τοῦτο σμικρότατον), so Socrates determines whether the characteristics of speech or discourse in general, apply to this smallest bit:

8. And the name, then
   καὶ τὸ ὄνομα ἄρα
   > (a) that occurs in true speech (i) is spoken (99) as true,
   > τὸ τοῦ ἐληθοῦς λόγου λέγεται ἀληθές,
   > (b) and isn't the bit of false discourse
   > τὸ δὲ τοῦ ψεύδους μόριον οὐ ψεῦδος;

Hermogenes agrees, so Socrates concludes the argument:

9. It is possible, then
   ἔστιν ἄρα
   > to say a name as false and as true
   > ὄνομα ψεῦδος καὶ ἀληθὲς λέγειν
   — if it is also possible for speech?
   — ἔιπερ καὶ λογον;

Hermogenes cannot but agree.

It is in this second stage of the argument that the fallacy of division, remarked on at the start of this paper, might appear to occur. But the approaches to the *Cratylus* which give that interpretation err in two ways: first in taking 'λόγος' to mean *sentence* (or *statement* or *proposition* or *judgement*), the combination of words which can be used to make an assertion and in this way be true or false, i.e., the grammatical entity which in much present-day theory of logic is treated as the unit of truth and falsity; and second, in rendering 'ὅλον' as *whole*, 'μόρια' as *parts,* and then applying our present-day concept according to which a whole is not just the aggregate of its parts, but takes on an identity of its own, with characteristics not contributed by the parts individually. Once this interpretation has been given, the attribution, of any properties which belong to sentences in virtue of their being complete sentences, to their parts, is inescapably fallacious.

The present translation gives a reading of the Greek which avoids these errors.[21] For clearly 'λόγος', which at no point in this passage occurs in the plural,[22] can only mean *speech* or *discourse in general*, and not any specific instances of discourse, such as sentences. Furthermore, 'λόγος' cannot mean *language* in the sense of a structured entity or whole which has its own peculiar properties in virtue of its structure.[23] On the contrary, steps five and six of the argument make it clear that Plato here conceived of λόγος as something all of whose bits or "shares" (μόρια — cf. μείρομαι could have, along with it, the property of being spoken as true or false.[24] The concep-

---

21. Most translators, in fact, render 'λόγος' correctly: e.g. Fowler by 'speech', Meridier by 'le discours', Apelt by 'die Rede'. It is commentators, such as those mentioned at the beginning of this paper, who treat the errors in their analyses of the argument. This is evidence that the errors are the result of interpretation, i.e. of bringing presuppositions to the reading of Plato, rather than looking at what he actually said.

22. Most commentators who construe the argument as having a plural subject, ignore this fact. But D. D. Heath, who takes the argument as being about propositions, even inserts the term 'λόγοι' into his discussion, as though it occurred in the original text. This is surprising in that his article ("On Plato's Cratylus", *J. Philol.*, 1888, pp. 192-218) is one of the more insightful studies of the *Cratylus* that has appeared.

23. This is what is usually investigated in contemporary philosophical studies of language. N. L. Wilson, for example, in *The Concept of Language* (Toronto: University of Toronto Press, 1959) argues that 'language' is an "individuative" rather than a "bulk" term (cf. 'water'), and language a thing or entitiy of a certain kind, not a kind of stuff (pp. 3-4). His book is an investigation of the structure and functioning of language; Plato, by contrast, in the *Cratylus*, is investigating the functioning of discourse or speech, and is concerned with "stuff", not structure. (But cf. n. 25 *inf.*).

24. 'ὅλος' cannot here mean *whole* in the sense of structured entity or organic whole, for then the rest of step five would not make sense, Meridier, perhaps aware of this, renders, *'dans l'ensemble'*; Apelt, 'als Ganzes'.

Plato does not seem to be perfectly clear about the different ways in which bits of stuff, and parts of structured entities, are totalled into an "all", and a whole, respectively. Even in the *Theaetetus* (203E-205A) he identifies the notion of *all* the bits of something, and that of the *totality* (τὰ δι γε πάνταμέρη τὸ πᾶν εἶναι — 204E), and, though suggesting that the *whole* differs in being a unitary conception distinct from the sum of the parts (τὸ ὅλον ἐκ τῶν μερῶν λέγεις γεγονὸς ἕν τι εισος ἕτερον τῶν πάντων μερῶν — 204A), he argues that since both totality and whole are that from which nothing is lacking, they are identical (205A)! This is, of course, not to deny that he may have been aware of the distinction without working it out explicitly. It is presupposed, for example, in the doctrine of the ερ[ξται or virtues in the *Republic,* and figures in the difference between moderation and justice; the former is appropriate or peculiar

tion of λόγος which makes sense of these steps, is, to borrow a set of illustrations from the *Protagoras* 329D: not like that of the face, whose parts (μόρια) are nose, mouth, eyes and ears; but like gold, whose bits differ neither from each other, nor from the whole, except in greatness and smallness (τὰ ... μόρια οὐδὲν διαφέρει τὰ ἕτερα τῶν ἑτέρων, ἀλλήλων καὶ τοῦ ὅλου, ἀλλ' ἢ μεμεθει καὶ σμικρότητι). In this part of the *Cratylus,* the term 'λόγος', to put it another way, refers not to a unitary entity, but to a collection or set of collections of bits, all similar to each other and to any collection of them, in being statable as true or false.

Taking these considerations into account, the reasoning in the second stage of the argument becomes fairly straightforward. Plato moves from the existence of discourse generally which can be asserted as true or false, according to whether it states the things that are as they are or as they are not, to the notion of the smallest bits of discourse – ὀνόματα – which share in the characteristic of being statable as true or false. Step five, the first step in this stage of the argument, established that λόγος is the kind of thing which has bits that share in what has been demonstrated in the preceding four steps to hold in general of it. Step six, affirming that all bits or shares qualify, small as well as large, emphasizes the pervasiveness of truth and falsity through discourse as conceived by Plato, and may also reflect his awareness of the importance of two ranges of size of discourse: sentences, and simple words or ὀνόματα[25] The designa-

---

virtue of each citizen and each division of the soul individually, and permits each to keep to its own function; the latter is the appropriate virtue of the lot collectively – the state and the soul, – and consists in facilitating circumstances in which each individual or division can perform its own function.

25. These ranges must differ in degree only, not in kind, if the characteristic of truth or falsity is to be equally applicable to both. In the *Sophistes* 261D-262E, Plato argues that λόγος is composed of combinations of two kinds of words: ὀνόματα and ῥήματα and the smallest such combination is a λόγος, the shortest form of discourse (.. πρὶν ἄν τις τοῖς ὀνόμασι τὰ ῥήματα κετάση· τότι ἑ ηροσεν τε και λ ο γ ο ς ἐγένετο εοθυς ἡ πρώτη συμπλοκή, σχεδὸν τῶν λόγων ὁ πρωδ τε καὶ σμικρότατος. – 262C). But at this point in the *Cratylus* he seems to treat both sentences and woes as the same in being bits of discourse, and differing only with respect to the size of the bits. He does not appear to attach any special significance to the fact that the bigger bits are composed of a minimum of two different types of smaller bits, not even to distinguish such types, though later in the dialogue at 431B, he does say that λόγοι are αξυνθεαις of ὀνόματα and ῥήματα, λόγοι in that passage may be sentences.

tion of the ὄνομα as not only the smaller sort of bit, but the smallest (σμικρότατον), may be intended to avoid the necessity of attributing truth and falsity to mere sounds smaller than words; however it suggests that Plato conceived of ονοματα as being in some way the *units* of discourse.

Step seven works names into the argument as Hermogenes agrees that he would say (λεγεις) that they were the smallest bits of discourse; then in step eight, Socrates (i) first establishes that the mode of existence of names consists in being said (λέγεται), and then (ii) he explains the relationship of names to the two kinds of discourse identified in the first stage: those said in true discourse are said or spoken as true, and similarly for false. This step is roughly analogous to step three above, though Plato does not, at this point, go on to express the relationship between ονοματα and reality, as he did for discourse.[26]

The conclusion of the argument with respect to names is put in the form not that there exist false, and true, names, but rather that there exists the possibility of saying (λέγειν) a name as false, and as true; even this possibility is subject to the possibility of the same thing for discourse (ειπξρ καὶ λόγον [ψευδῆ καὶ αληθῆ λέγειν]). It is significant that, although in step two Plato has established the existence of true and false discourse without reference to its being spoken, he nonetheless compares the case of names to that of discourse as spoken. The conclusion of the argument, in other words, is not only not categorical, being drawn subject to the opening premise of the whole argument, but also, it does not assert the unqualified existence of true and false names, but only that they can be so spoken. Steps five and six, which do describe the bits or shares of discourse as ἀληθῆ unqualifiedly, do not assert the independent existence of such; rather it is the nature of these μόρια to be μόρια *of* (τὰ μόρια δ' αὐτοῦ [sc. λόγου).[27] Names, then, come out as true or

---

26. From what argument is given, however, it is clear that names should state individual things as they are true, and not if false. Since λόγος εληθς is that which τα ὄντα λέγῃ ὡς ἔστιν, and ψευδής εεις οὐκ ἔστιν, and an ὄνομα can be spoken in both kinds of λόγος, it would seem that daan ὄνομα in τοῦ ελnθους λόγου would λέγῃ εκ στον των ὄντων ὡς ἔστιν, and be one in τουψευδος would also λέγῃ ἕκαστον τῶν ὄντων, but ὡς οὐκ ἔστιν. In fact, later in the dialogue, a correct ὄνομα is discovered to be of the sort which reveals the nature or the being of things, and in 430D Plato equates the correct assignment of names to things, with their true assignment, and incorrect with false.

27. G. J. de Vries *ad loc.,* in his "Notes on some Passages of the *Cratylus*"

false only within the context of discourse, as its smallest units, and in no wise independently, which is possible only for discourse.

What Plato seems to be after, in this stage of the argument, is a criterion for objectively evaluating usages, especially names. In the ancient Greek world, the same traditional forces which tended to the view that truth is to be found in an act of revelation on the part of specially qualified agents, also tended towards the complementary view that there existed sets of usages unknown to ordinary mortals, which were, by virtue of their divine provenance, necessarily true.[28] Thus, in the remainder of the *Cratylus,* after sketching, by analogy to various crafts, the construction of an ideal language in which names would be "κατὰ φύσιν", i.e. would correspond to the fundamental being of things (387A-390E), Plato proceeds to carry out an extended examination of different sets of actual usages, in an attempt to determine what, if any, conception of reality is embodied in them (391C-427D). However, he concludes, after trying to explain the correspondence relation by treating the name as an imitation (μίμημα) or image (εἰκών) of things (422E-439B), that the truth can be neither revealed nor evaluated on the basis of its image, but rather must be learned in its own right, and the image evaluated by comparison with the truth (μανθάνειν ... ἐκ τῆς ἀληθείας αὐτήν τε αὐτὴν καὶ τὴν εἰνόνα αὐτῆς, εἰ πτ[εποντως εἰργασται) (439B).

(Mnemosyne, 1955, pp. 290-297), notes that here the partitive genitive seems to stress the ονομα as being a part of the εληθης λόγος, But he, too, describes the argument as involving fallacious reasoning, because Socrates seems to be attributing logical correctness [sic] not to judgment, but to ονοματα.

28. Cf. 400D of the *Cratylus,* where Socrates notes that mortals know nothing of the gods, nor of the panes the gods use, but that it is clear that they use the true ones (δῆλον γὰρ ὅτι ἐκεῖνοί γε ταληθθη

GENUINE SPEECH vs. CHATTER: A SOCRATIC PROBLEMATIC*

Stephen Skousgaard

In today's political scene in which double-talk and "advertising" or "public relations" rhetoric confront a democratic citizenry whose ability to make wise decisions depends upon truthful discourse, it is urgent that philosophers turn from esoteric "linguistic analysis" toward a larger problematic of language. In this light it may be fruitful to assume as an interpretive stance toward Plato's "Socratic Dialogues" a problematic of language in which forms of genuine speech are contrasted with the chaos of the Sophist's rhetoric. Such an interpretation may shed light on the role of language and philosophy *within* a political community.

Perhaps it will prove beneficial to attend to dialogue as a literary genre, that genre in which Plato presents the Socratic drama. This drama in the dialogue genre has an antecedent in the genre of the tragic poets. Let us understand Greek tragedy as a ritual in the cult of the goddess Dike. The dramatic performance of a tragedy is a ritual for those who experience the dramatic movement. This ritual becomes political when the members of a society experience the paradigm of just order for their own souls in the ritual-experience; however, such a political cult loses its meaning when the people for whom these tragedies are performed no longer experience the ritual as informing their souls with Justice. It should be noted that in the Athens of Socrates and Plato the dramatic tension of order and

---

*Reprinted by permission, *Kinesis,* 6 (1974), 87-94.

*I am indebted to many sources for the following paper: in particular, Edward G. Ballard, *Socratic Ignorance* (The Hague: Martinus Nijhoff, 1967) and Eric Voegelin, *The World of the Polis* (Baton Rouge: Louisiana State University Press, 1957). I have not made specific references in the text for I have appropriated their ideas for my own use; of course, I assume full responsibility for such distortion. Readers of these and other authors may recognize my indebtedness and distortions.

passion had been broken; the performance of tragedy had ceased functioning as an effective political ritual. A new ritual is required.

Socrates' answer to this need is the ritual of dialogue through which he attempts to create order in his own soul and in his society. He attempts to persuade others to join his search for wisdom through the performance of the dialogical-ritual. The Platonic Dialogues instantiate in literary form the dialogical-ritual of Socrates much the same as the genre of tragic poetry instantiates the ritual of value-reconstruction. Dialogue may be taken as the successor to tragedy as a political ritual; only the new ritual is for the new political conditions in which Socrates and Plato find themselves.

If this interpretation of the dialogue ritual is correct, then the question arises — to whom is this new genre addressed? The decisive public does not want to listen: the people of Socrates' and Plato's Athens no longer experience their own souls as the stage for the ritual of the struggle between order and chaos. In the answer to this question lies, I believe, the genius of Plato's creation of the new, appropriate genre. The dialogue is a literary work available to anyone willing to read it. In other words, when the actual political condition has disintegrated to the extent that the public cannot experience the tension between order and passion in the public performances of tragic poetry, then a new form of language which can perform for the willing individual must be found. When the *paideia* apparatus of Athens no longer provides order in the historical existence of men and society, then Socrates must try infusing order through individual dialogical-ritual. This dialogical-ritual is continued through the instrument of the literary genre, dialogue, created by Plato. The literary work preserves through history the ritual of dialogue. Is it, then, too much to suggest that Plato's genre itself is an attempt to concretize the Form of the Socratic dialogical-ritual?

Upon examination we see that this genre is animated by the ritual of Socrates' dialogical encounter with fellow citizens. It is easy to identify the technique of question and answer as the source of movement within the genre of Dialogue. But is this all there is to the speech form of dialogue? Is it merely a technique? And why is dialogue a ritual? Let us begin to answer these questions by turning to the *Apology*.

Apology opens the Socratic drama, and in it we find him reaffirming his role, hence himself. The Delphic oracle has announced that Socrates is the wisest of men; but the oracle of Delphi has also summarized human wisdom in the command "know thyself." In following both pronouncements, it would seem that Socrates should discover wisdom in discovering himself. Yet he is only too conscious of his own ignorance, so he goes about questioning those whom his society regards as wise in order to discover the meaning of the Delphic pronouncements. Socrates engages, then, in dialogue with his fellow citizens in order to discover himself and the meaning of human wisdom. The self he discovers is the one who is wisest precisely because he is aware of his own ignorance.

The Socratic activity of dialogue has a two-fold effect. On the one hand, his self-examination through dialogue constitutes his wisdom, that is, constitutes himself as *who* the Delphic oracle pronounced him to be. His engaging the citizenry in his self-constitution not only reveals himself, but also it reveals the character of his interlocutors. And the character of the Athenian citizens expresses the character of the community whose corruptness is revealed by the condamnation of Socrates. Since dialogue is by nature a social activity, his self-constitution through dialogue was a great political opportunity for Athens. The oracle had sent Socrates as a gadfly into their midst; quite literally, then, he was a gift of the god.

Though Athenian society is no longer ordered through the ritual of tragedy, it rejects the ritual of dialogue. The spirit of the community has been lost, and the public speech of performed tragedy fails to provide the private experience of order in the souls of the citizens. Dialogue is the new form of regenerative political speech brought by Socrates into the community. As such it is genuine speech; dialogue is the new speech form for order because it is through this linguistic *activity* that Socrates constitutes himself as wise and it is through this same dialogue that he provides the means for others to do the same. Dialogue by its very essence is a political act.

The opening lines of the *Apology* reveal that the crucial issue is joined between dialogue and oratory; the issue is precisely whether moral and political decisions are to be made through the medium of genuine or corrupt talk. On the surface the jurors are to decide the "guilt" of Socrates — implicitly they decide whether to silence genuine speech by cutting out the one who engages in dialogue. In *Apology*, then, dialogue is pitted against oratory; dialogue is on trial and rhetoric is its accuser. His accusers have indicted Socrates in the language of oratory of which he says, "I was almost carried away by them — their arguments were so convincing. On the other hand, scarcely a word of what they said was true" (17A). Socrates opens his defense speech by placing on trial the character of speech itself as it is spoken in Athens, for its emphasis is on persuasion and winning debates in law courts, while truth is not even considered. In opposition to his accusers' speech form, Socrates speaks of himself: he says that from him will be heard "the whole truth ... in the same language it has been [his] custom to use" (17C), that is, dialogical speech. The judges must choose; they must either listen to oratory and rhetoric, the language of disorder, or they will listen to dialogue, the language of order and wisdom. A more thorough account of these opposing speech forms will be given in the following; for now it need only be seen that they are at stake in the trial of Socrates.

As Socrates points out, he has incurred the wrath of the community by his gadfly activity. His speech reveals the truth, one discovers oneself in dialogical activity, whereas rhetoric allows one to give oneself outward appearance of dignity and wisdom. Through his speech Socrates has forced men to see the truth of their ignorance, and the hiatus between their true selves and their appearance is unbearably ugly. They condemn Socrates.

The argument between accuser and defendant is not merely in words. At stake is *who* they are. The decision of the judges is not a mere verbal announcement, and Socrates does not allow the opportunity of his condemnation to pass without bringing to light the fact that speech is *logos* of the soul, hence *logos* of society.

Perhaps this point is best illustrated as follows. Socrates' accusers did not intend for him to come to trial; rather they wanted him either to flee the city or to evade the death penalty by choosing exile. Should Socrates flee or choose exile, he would silence himself, thus vindicating the status quo in Athens. Not only would the disruptive element be cut out with the removal of Socrates, but his entire way of life, his speech form, would be discredited. Socrates recognizes what is at stake; he remains to take hemlock when he could have escaped before trial, before sentencing, or before execution. By remaining in Athens and taking hemlock, he forces the judges' decision to its conclusion. Thereby the external events reveal the inner character of the Athenian spirit. Furthermore, if the political ritual successor to tragedy is to work, the hero of its drama must at least be existentially consistent with his speech; his death must complete the argument of his life. Socrates' life and death in their manner of being are chosen through dialogue; that is, he constitutes his death by choosing it freely. By forcing his judges into the open, Socrates turns his condemnation into a political victory; for his actions make possible the new literary genre, dialogue. The corrupt society could not silence dialogical speech merely by condemning and executing an individual philosopher, for the new literary genre comes as the "others" of Socrates' prediction. The literary genre dialogue, then, preserves the ordering force of the dialogical ritual: it is there for all in any crises of any order.

Let us turn now to *Euthydemus* in which the distinction between philosophical and sophistical speech is sharpened. Despite the comic overtone, the crucial import of this dialogue cannot be underestimated: who should educate the young — the rhetorician or the philosopher? The education of the young will determine the political future. We see the contest between dialogue and oratory in its full consequences, namely, the two forms of speech are two forms of life.

Socrates invites the two Sophists to prove the value of their discovery of "eristics" by convincing the future political leader, the promising lad Clinias, that he must strive to be a thoroughly good man. Socrates introduces the use of "protreptics," that is, discourse whose aim is to lead the hearer to commit himself to the search for wisdom. By contra-posing Socrates with the teachers of "eristics" — that is, the trick of catching one's interlocutor in contradictions resulting from the natural ambiguities of language — Plato clearly shows the chasm between the two kinds of speech. The two brothers accept Socrates' invitation and gleefully set about producing antinomies. To be sure, the deduction of contradictory conclusions from premises is legitimate activity in testing presuppositions; but in "eristics" the method of question and answer merely *appears* to be engaged in this activity. The two Sophists intend merely to confute others, thereby making themselves look clever and advertising the teaching they sell. On the other hand, Socrates' arguments are an attempt to lead the youth to knowledge, on which right conduct and statesmanship depend.

We can see the importance of *Euthydemus* for our interpretation. Both Socrates and Sophists engage in the method of question and answer; but the resemblance is only superficial, for in the hands of Socrates it is an instrument of criticism while in the hands of Euthydemus it is a sophistic weapon used to silence others. Eristics silences speech by catching others — who perhaps legitimately seek wisdom through dialogue — in seeming contradictions and making them appear foolish. Why is this silencing so dangerous? Applied to the impressionable young, who cannot yet distinguish between the form of dialogue and eristics, such a technique will influence future political leaders to turn away from dialogue for fear of appearing foolish. Rather than risk the confrontation of questions and answers, the young will turn to rhetoric and oratory, for these speech forms are persuasive in law courts and keep them safe from appearing foolish as a result of eristic tricks (or safe from discovering one's own real foolishness). The trial of Socrates is a grim reminder of the corrupting resulting from the community's acceptance of rhetoric over dialogue. Yet, to an undiscerning witness, the dialogue of Socrates must have seemed on a par with the "eristics" of Euthydemus.

It is in Socrates' debate with Gorgias that such undiscerning witnesses can be seen with their full consequences for social order. In the *Gorgias* the explicitly political import of the corruption of speech is recognized. Already in the drama of Socrates we have learned that dialogue is the ritual for self-constitution and that this feat is not achieved in splendid isolation but through dialogical encounter with others. That is, self-constitution is a political act. In the *Gorgias* we find an emphasis on the political consequences of speech forms; the claim that self-constitution occurs through dialogue is broadened into the explicit claim that dialogue is the speech form for good political-constitution. Furthermore, the consequence of this claim is expressed: Socrates *is* the true ruler of the community despite its rejection of him. The contradistinction between dialogue and rhetoric is the vehicle through which Plato introduces this discovery.

The debate in this dialogue begins when Socrates learns that Gorgias is answering any and all questions. He asks Gorgias "who he *is*." We are alerted immediately that the issue is an existential one. Gorgias' simple reply is that he is a teacher of rhetoric, the art of persuasion, the art a young man needs for a "successful" career. Through questioning however, Socrates quickly leads the Sophist to admit that rhetoric is merely a persuasive instrument and not the pursuit of truth. Gorgias is clever enough to see the danger of his position — namely, his students can easily turn his art to vulgar uses — hence, he tries to absolve himself of responsibility for the consequences of the speech form he teaches. Again Socrates quickly leads him into contradiction through dialogue.

When Gorgias admits defeat in the debate, his followers leap to his rescue. Polus accuses Socrates of verbal trickery; obviously he cannot distinguish between dialogue and eristics. Socrates recognizes that he must demonstrate this distinction to reveal personal and political consequences of non-protreptic speech forms. However, before dialogue can begin, Socrates must secure agreement from Polus that he will follow wherever the argument leads. With agreement secured, Socrates leads the discussion to explicit political tones. Polus claims that rhetoric makes a man politically powerful for, with this art, he can persuade, hence control, the masses. In short, with rhetoric one can be a tyrant: his will is master. But Socrates dialogically questions this position. If a tyrant commits evil to others by his use of rhetoric, if he is a selfish ruler, then he harms others and acts against his own interest, for evil citizens turn on a ruler. Hence, the tyrant is powerless with his rhetoric unless he uses it for the good of other men and society. To be sure, rhetoric *appears* to be a powerful art, for it can be used to take one's enemies to court and it can flatter the mob. But rhetoric does not do the speaker any good unless it makes his soul good. Socrates claims that doing injustice is worse than suffering injustice and if one does injustice he should persuade the courts to punish him so that he will be better. Rhetoric is, therefore, powerless unless it is used for good purposes, that is, unless it is protreptic, not merely eristic. In his debate with Polus Socrates defeats the position of the rhetor by defeating the common assumption that men should "take care of themselves at all costs."

Here Callicles interrupts. He insists that Socrates is joking, for if he is correct then men everywhere live inverted to their true natures. He still believes men should use speech for private gain regardless of justice. Socrates openly declares that the issue is between their two forms of existence. He declares that he is in love with the search for *sophia,* while Callicles loves the masses (*demos*). Callicles constantly shifts to and fro, always changing opinion to avoid displeasing the *demos,* his favorite, which itself constantly shifts and sways. Socrates' favorite, *sophia,* remains steady and true. Thus, a dimension is added to the struggle between the forms of speech. The contradistinction of the two speech forms is seen as that between the flux of the mob's opinions and the stable truth of the philosopher: *philodocia* as opposed to *philosophia.*

The level of communication, that which distinguishes dialogue from eristics, lies deeper than correct argument. A Sophist can engage in correct argument and yet dialogue does not necessarily occur. This deeper level is *pathos*. *Pathos* is what all men share regardless of their speech form, whether their intellectual position is faithful to it or not. In their exposure to *pathos* all men are equal, though they may differ widely in the manner in which they come to grips with it and build the experience onto their lives. One such shared experience is eros. Socrates builds his experience into love of wisdom or philosophical inquiry; Callicles sells his for "success" with the mob, he loves opinion. Yet behind the encrusted attitudes which separate men lies the shared *pathos*. However false an intellectual position, the *pathos* at the core of human existence has the truth of immediate experience. Socrates must believe this; otherwise the following debate with Callicles would be senseless. The possibility, however remote, of breaking through to their shared *pathos* must be open; otherwise dialogue could not occur and the chaos of Sophistry would be the truth of existence.

Callicles rejects the appeal of *pathos*, calling it a demagogic trick trading on the conflict between nature, which is "rule by the powerful," and convention, which is the alliance of the weak. Philosophers may argue that doing evil is worse than suffering evil, but men of strength know otherwise. Callicles warns Socrates that his philosophizing is a *nice* accomplishment and it may impress young men in parlors, but men of affairs know better. To these men, who rule and make events happen, philosophical argument is foolish; "they know better." Callicles then warns Socrates that he should learn the art of rhetoric and forget protreptic dialogue; otherwise he will find himself powerless if his enemies take him to court. Socrates can only answer this slur on philosophy with an appeal to courage: the philosopher is immune to Callicles' threat. To a man like Socrates, who is willing to suffer the injustice of death rather than commit injustice himself, Callicles' argument has no force because it rests on an inverted view of existence.

With philosophy thus established by the appeal of a philosopher's courage, Socrates raises the question: who on philosophical principle is the good statesman? Philosophy defines good and evil in terms of advancing or decomposing the order in the soul. Thus, a statesman is good if under his rule the citizens grow better; he is a bad ruler if citizens become disordered in their souls. This is the conclusion which follows from the long debate between the two men. Callicles, however, cannot break through the crust of his own rhetoric to the shared *pathos*: he cannot defeat the dialogical encounter, but he will not submit to its truth. Rather, he repeats his ominous warnings to Socrates that the consequences of dialogue will be unpleasant for the philosopher. It is still lost on Callicles that Socrates would rather suffer the ultimate injustice of his own death than contribute to disorder by conforming to the established speech form of rhetoric. Socrates even agrees that it would not be at all surprising if he were put to death and states the reason for his expectation:

> I think that I am one of the very few Athenians, not to say the only one, engaged in the true political art, and that of the men of today I alone practice statesmanship. Since therefore when I speak on any occasion it is not with a view to winning favor, but I aim at what is best, not what is most pleasant, and since I am unwilling to engage in those "dainty devices" that you recommend, I shall have nothing to say for myself when in court. (521D)

In these lines Socrates has made the fantastic claim that *he* is the true ruler by virtue of being the only one who practices statesmanship. Callicles and the other orators, the controlling politicians, have no true authority. Socrates has transferred to himself, through dialogue, the authority of society. His authority is based in the true order of his own soul constituted by dialogue.

There follows Socrates' myth of the "Judgement of the Dead," according to which, after death souls stand naked before the gods for judgment. Here rhetoric and oratory are of no use for they cannot hide behind a veneer of pleasant speech. In death a judgment is shared by all mankind, regardless of the appearances of respectability. Death, like eros, is *pathos*; it is in all men's experience. Dialogue is the attempt to force others to face this judgment in their lives. The attempt is precisely to break through the crust of rhetoric, to penetrate to the shared *pathos* at the core of everyone's soul. Socrates is the true ruler for he strives to restore order in men's souls, to make them better, by having men submit freely to the judgment of death during their historical lives. Death is a catharsis liberating men in their historical life if they will live in the presence of its judgment. To live permanently in the state of this judgment is the goal of dialogue, of philosophy. The life of virtue, which is the philosopher's goal, is trans-historical, and it is reached through dialogue and preserved in this speech form as articulated in the literary genre, dialogue. Thus, the philosopher is the true ruler despite his historical situation.

PLATO ON THE RHETORIC OF POETRY*

Morris Henry Partee

Plato's mistrust of unalterable discourse underlies both his banishment of poetry from the Republic and his ambivalent attitude towards his own works. The ambiguity of the dialogue form helps resolve the tension between immutable knowledge and tentative language. A close attention to language of any sort involves the mind in a trivial, if not dangerous exercise, for knowledge exists as independently of language as of society. The *Cratylus* argues that since language at best is an intelligent imitation of nature, the study of language cannot substitute for the direct and immediate examination of truth itself.[1] Both original confusion and present conventions render language unworthy of serious philosophical consideration. Only the dialectician, the one using the words, currently, can judge the worth of the original word-artisan's production. Any fixed language, whether written treatises or memorized poetry, can hinder as much as stimulate thought.

Since truth or falsity for Plato extend even to the level of letters and sounds, any linguistic ornaments are mere obfuscation. By thus eviscerating poetry of its verbal organs, Plato can refuse to admit artistic language to be a legitimate expression of human values. Poets, in common with sophists and rhapsodes, use their stylistic powers to call attention to their discourse. But although Plato explicitly contrasts good and bad rhetorical principles, he consistently denies any value whatsoever to the particular embodiment of thought. Utterances so brief as to be formless are best; the continuity of speech must not obscure the continuity of reasoning. Plato saw that human art — like physical nature — tends to be amoral. Man responds to any beauty with his entire soul even though his reaction to earthly

---

*Reprinted with permission from *Journal of Aesthetics and Art Criticism*, 33 (Winter, 1974), 205-212, by The Cleveland Museum of Art.

1. See my "Plato's Theory of Language," *Foundations of Language*, 8 (1972), 113-32.

beauty consists either of nonproductive pleasure or pain. Man perceives the higher beauty with the total rapture of philosophy; Plato's distinctions between the two sorts of total inspiration are subtle indeed.[2]

Language has an inherently seductive power which interferes with both philosophical activity and true poetic response. The pursuit of wisdom is for Plato an essentially private enterprise; public utterances are best when impersonal. A man's personal authority can render his discourse liable to misinterpretation and confusion. As the probably authentic "Seventh Letter" states, fixed discourse is always treacherous: "The best safeguard is to avoid writing and to commit things to memory. For when a thing has once been committed to writing, it is impossible to prevent it from gaining publicity. It is for this reason that I myself have never written anything on these subjects. There is not, and there never will be, a written treatise of Plato's. Those that are called his are really the teaching of Socrates restored to youth and beauty"(314).[3] It is no wonder, therefore, that the *Republic X* allows only straightforward didactic discourse to exist in the noble commonwealth.[4] Yet the artistry of the dialogues testifies that Plato felt no need to restrict himself to this modest end.[5]

But writing need not be excluded completely. A man may provide himself with an amusement for when his real powers fail. Plato re-

---

2. I have discussed this point more fully in "Inspiration in the Aesthetics of Plato," *JAAC*, 30 (1971), 87-95.

3. *The Platonic Epistles*, trans. J. Harward (Cambridge, 1932), p. 103. See Herman L. Sinaido, *Love Knowledge, and Discourse in Plato* (Chicago, 1965), pp. 3-10.

4. See Paul Friedländer, *Plato: An Introduction*, trans. Hans Meyerhoff (New York, 1958), pp. 121-4.

5. R. G. Collingwood in "Plato's Philosophy of Art," *Mind*, 34 (1925) focuses on *Republic X* 595-608, which he feels typical of Plato's thought elsewhere. He states, "If it is asked why Socrates permits certain forms of art to be retained in the ideal state instead of consistently banishing them all alike, the answer is surely obvious: these are, in the opinion of Socrates, the forms which art will take in the hands of men who understand its true nature" (pp. 156-7). Collingwood's reasoning would argue, however, that one can cheerfully accept an injection of the Black Death if he has sufficient streptomycin in his system. Leonard Moss in "Plato and the *Poetics*", *Philological Quarterly*, 50 (1971), 533-42 provides a useful summary of scholarly positions on Plato's theory of imitation and the admissibility of art into the state.

cognizes human failings, but he never admits them as excuses. He uses an image of a farmer sowing seeds to extend his concept of words as living, responding entities. Like a farmer, a thinker may legitimately seek amusement. But he will not seriously write them in water or that black fluid called ink, for his pen would sow words which can neither speak in their own defense, nor present the truth adequately. The written word can refresh but not replace the human memory: "He will sow his seed in literary gardens, I take it, and write when he does write by way of pastime, collecting a store of refreshment both for his own memory, against the day 'when age oblivious come,' and for all such as tread in his footsteps; and he will take pleasure in watching the tender plants grow up. And when other men resort to other pastimes, regaling themselves with drinking parties and such like, he will doubtless prefer to indulge in the recreation I refer to" (*Phaedrus* 276). Even old men may want to exchange ideas. These writings will provide a worthwhile recreation when the man has lost the power of active thought. Elsewhere, Plato says "A man may sometimes set aside meditations about eternal things, and for recreation turn to consider the truths of generation which are

---

6. See Eric Havelock, *Preface to Plato*, (Cambridge, Mass., 1963), pp. 3-19.

7. Usually, fame should be despised: "You are aware that the greatest and most influential statesmen are ashamed of writing speeches and leaving them in a written form, lest they should be called sophists by posterity" (*Phaedrus* 257). On the other hand, some creations may bring fame without stigma: "Who, when he thinks of Homer and Hesiod and other great poets, would not rather have their children than ordinary human ones? Who would not emulate them in the creation of children such as theirs, which have preserved their memory and given them everlasting glory?" (*Symposium* 209).

8. The myths of Plato are subject enough for several books. Plato obviously feels myths are useful. In the *Gorgias*, Socrates tells Callicles that he will regard his account as a fable; he, Socrates, regards it as reasonable (523). Similarly, the *Phaedo* states that myths deal with the most likely or probably (114). J. Tate in "Plato and Allegorical Interpretation," *Classical Quarterly*, 23 (1929), 146 reemphasizes this point Plato himself comments in what he regards as the proper interpretation of a myth. Socrates neither accepts nor rejects the myth in which Boreas is said to have carried off Orithnyia from the bank of the Ilissus (*Phaedrus* 229-30). Sinaido refers to the importance of this myth for understanding the entire *Phaedrus* (p. 13). [See Page 22A] Ludwig Edelstein in "The Function of Myth in Plato's Philosophy," *Journal of the History of Ideas*, 10 (1949), 463-81 distinguishes between the ethical myths which are an addition to rational knowledge and the historical and scientific myths which serve where such knowledge does not exist (p. 473).

probable only; he will thus gain a pleasure not to be repented of, and secure for himself while he lives a wise and moderate pastime" (*Timaeus* 59). Certainly the written monuments to one's own past thought are more noble than idle banqueting. But one should not confuse innocent pastimes with a search for the eternal verities.

The writing of discourses about justice and other noble topics can be an acceptable pastime. But these individual amusements are useless as far as real philosophy is concerned. Nor can these recreations be shared; even in play a man keeps to himself. The serious treatment of great issues requires the art of dialectic. "The dialectician selects a soul of the right type, and in it he plants and sows his words founded on knowledge, words which can defend both themselves and him who planted them, words which instead of remaining barren contain a seed whence new words grow up in new characters; whereby the seed is vouchsafed immortality, and its possessor the fullest measure of blessedness that man can attain unto" (*Phaedrus* 276-7). Plato attributes great power to the properly applied word. As in the *Cratylus*, the dialectician is the true and effective user of language. He responds to a waiting spirit and fills him with these forceful words. The very act of giving the words aids the giver as well as the responder. These words have a social value; they do not exist in a vacuum. Moreover, these words have the animate property of reproduction; the seed lies within the word and given proper treatment, will respond immortally. Human words are static and need their creator to defend them. But words implanted by the dialectic pass from one soul to another.[1 2]

9. Sophists, like the rhapsodes of the *Ion* claim all sorts of knowledge. See, for instance, *Euthydemus* 273.

10. Plato knows the rules for good rhetoric. Lysias, on the other hand, begins at what properly should be the end. Socrates observes, "Then as to the other topics — are they not thrown down anyhow? Is there any principle in them? Why should the next topic follow next in order, or any other topic? I cannot help fancying in my ignorance that he wrote off boldly just what came into his head, but I dare say that you would recognize a rhetorical necessity in the succession of the several parts of the composition" (*Phaedrus* 264). Still, brief passages are best (*Protagoras* 342-3). Plato develops only the second of these two positions.

11. Roy L. Hart in "The Imagination in Plato," *IPQ*, 5 (1965), astutely observes, "That Plato did not elaborate an explicit doctrine of the imagination is owing less to his only slightly developed psychology than to his appreciation of the ontological compexity of such a doctrine" (p. 436).

12. The *Symposium* 209 also suggests a wordless conception: "Souls which

Plato now brings his discussion back to the immediate cause of the argument. A rhetorician must know the audience, his subject matter, and all the applicable rules of logic, particularly when he commits his idea to writing. Lysias' speech is condemned, not because of his evil praise of lust, but because of muddy thinking and inept artistry. The deliberate composition and delivery of speeches are not necessarily a matter of reproach, but his conclusions "have shown that any work, in the past or in the future, whether by Lysias or anyone else, whether composed in a private capacity or in the role of a public man who by proposing a law becomes the author of a political composition, is a matter of reproach to its author (whether or not the reproach is actually voiced) if he regards it as containing important truth of permanent validity. For ignorance of what is a waving vision and what is a mere dream image of justice and injustice, good and evil, cannot truly be acquitted of involving reproach, even if the mass of men extol it" (*Phaedrus* 277). Popularity can no more justify bad poetry. Indeed presenting one's ideas to the masses increases the danger of being swayed by vulgar adulation. Certainty and clearness of discourse depend on knowledge, not on techniques of style.

Thus, Plato identifies writing with eloquent speaking; both tend to be superficial persuasion. All language must inspire criticism and instruction; fixed language is frivolous — language is either believed or criticized, not simply enjoyed. A written discourse on any subject must necessarily contain much useless material. Indeed, written verse or prose merits little serious attention. The same strictures apply to the set speech. Declamation usually is mere persuasion without any questioning or exposition. Such compositions are at best a means of reminding those who know the truth already.

On the other hand, Plato realizes that some communication is not only necessary, but desirable. But he ignores the medium altogether.

are pregnant — for there certainly are men who are more creative in their souls than in their bodies — conceive that which is proper for the soul to conceive or contain. And what are these conceptions? Wisdom and virtue in general. And such creators are poets and all artists who are deserving of the name inventors. But the greatest and fairest sort of wisdom by far is that which is concerned with the ordering of states and families, and which is called temperance and justice." The state of mind is all important to the outward expression: "Since there has been shown to be false speech and false opinion, there may be imitations of real existence, and out of this condition of the mind an art of deception may arise" (*Sophist* 264).

The true speaker first establishes the truth within himself. His discourses are then legitimate children, creatures with a life of their own (*Phaedrus* 264, 277-8). This creation must be reinforced by correct instincts. With the proper purpose, a statement on justice, honor, goodness, or such topics can have a noble lucidity and seriousness. These spiritual children do not enter into another. Rather the sons and brothers go into the souls of other men (*Phaedrus* 278). There, the good discourse is engraved correctly, thus encouraging the listener to paint true images in his mind. Clearly, oral communication is far superior to its imitation in the written word. Only in personal contact can discourse be truly graven on another's soul. Personal, living knowledge must immediately precede all forms of discourse; writing can be only a faint echo of living speech.[13]

II

The spoken word of poetry shares the subordinate status of writing. A man may write well or badly, but no matter what his skill, he cannot directly convey knowledge to his hearer. Plato's readiness to link truth with visual images[14] may explain why poetry cannot contain more than its surface texture will hold. Perception comes from envisioning reality, not from understanding language. The *Phaedrus* recognizes that man can aspire to the highest heaven, a realm no earthly poet can justly describe. Yet motivated by the high subject matter, Plato boldly makes the attempt through his metaphors of flight and vision. "In the place beyond the heavens, true Being dwells, without color or shape, not susceptible to touch. Reason alone, the soul's pilot can behold it, and all true knowledge is knowledge thereof. Now even as the mind of a god is nourished by reason and knowledge, so also is it with every soul that has a care to receive her proper food; wherefore when at

---

13. G. R. Levy in his introduction to J. A. Stewart's *Myths of Plato* (Carbondale, Ill., 1960) states that "Plato's whole plan for the dissemination of philosophy in writing was a continuation of personal relationships, not the perpetuation of doctrine" (p. 5).

14. John Warry in *Greek Aesthetic Theory* (New York, 1962), correctly states, "It is worthy remembering that the word for 'seeing' in Greek is etymologically germane to that which denotes 'learning,' and the same is true in other Indo-European languages. If pressed to name the second 'clearest' sense, Plato would hardly have done other than name that of hearing, for after the eye the ear is indisputably the finest minister to the intellect" (p. 29).

last she has beheld Being she is well content, and contemplating truth she is nourished and prospers, until the heaven's revolution brings her back full circle" (*Phaedrus* 247). During the travels of the soul, she perceives the very essence of justice, temperance, and knowledge. In this rapture the soul rises above the knowledge, which, as neighbor to Becoming, varies with man's unintelligent perception of various objects. "And when she has contemplated likewise and feasted upon all else that has true being, she descends again within the hevanes and comes back home. And having so come, her charioteer sets his steeds at their manger, and puts ambrosia before them and draught of nectar to drink withal" (*Phaedrus* 247). The soul which has seen the most of being becomes a philosopher; less vision makes a poet or other imitative artist. As in the *Symposium* 211 and the *Republic* VII 517-8, Plato has the inspired soul return to the lower world. But this return does not result necessarily in effective work in this world of shadows.

Most people have lost the memory of the holy things they once saw. Some had the vision only for a moment; others forsook the "holy objects of their vision." The image of fading sight can describe the process of forgetting. "Few indeed are left that can still remember much: but when these discern some likeness of the things yonder, they are amazed, and no longer masters of themselves, and know not what is come upon them by reason of their perception being dim. Now in the earthly likeness of justice and temperance and all other prized possessions of the soul there dwells no luster; nay, so dull are the organs where with men approach their images that hardly can a few behold that which is imaged" (*Phaedrus* 250). True rapture makes a man gaze around like a bird. On the other hand, a partial vision may result in merely the dull response of ignorant amazement. Any man whose senses are not dead can respond, but he cannot understand his own reaction. The perception involves some effort on the part of the individual. Images of reality can enrapture, but few people have the power to rise above this unintellectual rapture to see the truth itself.[15]

15. Douglas Morgan in *Love: Plato, the Bible and Freud* (Englewood Cliffs, 1964) states, "Seeing is sometimes believing, but believing is never knowing. What we see, we do not know. What we know, we do not see. This is the first and fundamental law of Plato's philosophy. It seems odd only to men whose understanding is beclouded by their senses, and who by habit close the eye of the mind to see only with the eye in the head" (p. 15).

The metaphor of eye as soul evokes a corresponding image of beauty as wisdom. The eye of the mind of course has a far greater power than that of the body, but both are windows of perception. The soul before imprisonment in the body had an unblemished vision of all sorts of revelations: "Now beauty, as we said, shone bright amidst these visions, and in this world below we apprehend it through the clearest of our senses, clear and resplendent. For sight is the keenest mode of perception vouchsafed us through the body; wisdom, indeed, we cannot see thereby — how passionate had been our desire for her, if she had granted us so clear an image of herself to gaze upon — not yet any other of those beloved objects, save only beauty; for beauty alone this has been ordained, to be most manifest to sense and most lovely of them all" (*Phaedrus* 250). Plato could easily have allowed beauty of all sorts to lift man to a vision of true beauty. And indeed, artifacts and beautiful humans can serve this function. But art first calls attention to itself as a physical object and does not necessarily stimulate further vision. Earthly beauty causes not true rapture, but selfish pleasure. Wisdom cannot be seen in this mundane existence, for the mere sight would be overwhelming.

Language can create only the basic condition for man's achieving this vision of absolute wisdom and beauty. The quest for truth does not begin from nothing; the mind must interact with tradition.[16] The sayings of the ancients have grace and beauty. These bits of lore contain an important inactive wisdom. Respect for the traditional runs throughout the dialogues — usually expressed by deference to the ancients or by allusions to poetry. Plato's inquiry often begins from a word from the past.[17] For example, Plato says "Not to be lightly rejected, Phaedrus, is any word of the wise; perhaps they are right: one has to see. And in particular this present assertion must

---

16. But even good information — laws, sayings, customs — is more antidote than treasure: "Of all kinds of knowledge the knowledge of good laws has the greatest power of improving the learner; otherwise there would be no meaning in the divine and admirable law possessing a name akin to mind ($νους$, $νομος$). And of all other words, such as the praises and censures of individuals which occur in poetry and also in prose, whether written down or uttered in daily conversation, whether men dispute about them in the spirit of contention or weakly assent to them, as is often the case — of all these the one sure test is the writings of the legislator, which the righteous judge ought to have in his mind as the antidote of all other words" (*Laws XII* 957).

17. *Lysias* 214, *Phaedrus* 235, *Republic I* 332, *II* 364-5, *Protagoras* 339-347.

not be dismissed" (*Phaedrus* 260). But often great modifications and restrictions must be applied, for here Phaedrus has just advanced a widespread belief that "the intending orator is under no necessity of understanding what is truly just, but only what is likely to be thought just by the body of men who are to give judgment; nor need he know what is truly good or noble, but what will be thought so; since it is on the latter, not the former, that persuasion depends" (*Phaedrus* 259-60). So the sayings are only stable points for departure; one moves away from them, not to them.[18] The word must challenge rather than grip the soul.

Socrates' disclaiming of merit almost always accompanies his eloquence. Deferential references to the ancients abound when he waxes poetic. By removing his own personality from his speech, he reaffirms — in accordance with his identification of soul and true discourse — the tentative nature of his words. Socrates declares that if Phaedrus goes "as far as that I shall find it impossible to agree with you; if I were to assent out of politeness, I should be confuted by the wise men and women who in past ages have spoken and written on this theme" (*Phaedrus* 235). Socrates characteristically cannot remember who, but he knows that "there is something welling up within my breast, which makes me feel that I could find something different, and something better, to say. I am of course well aware it cannot be anything originating in my own mind, for I know my ignorance; so I supposed it can only be that it has been poured into me, through my ears, as into a vessel, from some external source; though in my stupid fashion I have actually forgotten how, and from whom, I heard it" (*Phaedrus* 235). Elsewhere Plato has stated that true discourse originated only in the soul of the speaker, yet Socrates declares his emptiness. His eloquence, the flowing outward of a speech earlier poured into his ears, merits no respect. But the images thus stimulated in the soul of another are the true offspring of the philosopher. Irony, the language which constantly refutes its direct statement, helps keep Plato's audience from passively absorbing doctrine.

III

Plato has explicitly denied worth to other's imaginative language and

18. Cf. *Meno* 81.

implicitly rejected the seriousness of his own dialogues. But the consummate artistry of his prose belies his casual dismissal of all but philosophical conversation. The example of the dialogues runs startlingly counter to the strictures both on creations of the imagination and on written words. Consistency to Plato's condemnation of art would certainly demand a repudiation of the dialogues in any good state.[19] But the tentative nature of the dialogues saves them from the damning dogmatism of other forms of discourse. Phaedrus should convey a message to composers of speeches, political tracts, and poets: "If any of them has done his work with a knowledge of the truth, can defend his statements when challenged, and can demonstrate the inferiority of his own writings out of his own mouth, he ought not to be designated by a name drawn from those writings, but by one that indicates his serious pursuit" (*Phaedrus* 278). Socrates will not call them possessors of wisdom, for only gods always have knowledge. Instead, he who can create and defend his creation will be called a lover of wisdom or a philosopher.[20] Through his use of irony. Plato has already recognized the inferiority of the dialogues to true personal discourse. By patterning his work as closely as possible to the interchange of ideas, Plato sets up attack and defence within the dialogues themselves.[21]

For Plato, speech is more plastic than wax or other such media.[22]

---

19. Carleton Lewis Brownson in *Plato's Studies and Criticisms of the Poets* (Boston, 1920) states that when Plato "pronounces his final judgment against the poets, he seems to forget or disregard the significance which he has given to μίμησις in X. For he banishes not all poetry which is mimetic in the wider sense of X, but preeminently that which is mimetic in the narrower sense of III. Hymns to the gods and encomia upon good men are admitted to the state. They might well have been excluded by the argument of X: they are not mimetic, however, if one adheres to the definition of III. The conclusion of X is consistent, therefore, with the premises of III, but not fully consistent with the premises of X" (pp. 93-4).

20. Cf. *Laws IX* 858-9.

21. Paul Shorey in *Platonism, Ancient and Modern* (Berkeley, 1938) states, "In Plato dialectics simply means discussion, argument; and the skill with Plato in his dialogues makes the written word perform the function of the spoken word, is, in this respect, one of the chief though least often recognized values of the study of Plato .... At its best, Plato's realistic reproduction of argumentative conversation is a real verification of, and check upon, the processes of thought" (pp. 37-8).

22. See *Republic IX* 588, *Laws IV* 712, *V* 746.

Thus he has only contempt for stylists, those who spend hours on phrases, twisting them around, pasting them together and pulling them apart. Directly seeking popular recognition, such men should be contemptuously called poets or speech-writers or law-givers. Literary craftsmanship, Plato thinks, consists of unintelligent word games. Obviously polished phrases show that their creator has been manipulating mere words rather than attending to truth itself.[23]

The *Timaeus* shows a similar distinction between the lovers of truth and the lovers of language. A man may certainly admire the nobility of his discourse, but this love must not lead to sterile complacency. Indeed, out of frustration comes further inquiry. The description of the perfect state, the dialogue *Republic,* gives Plato a certain measure of satisfaction. "I might compare myself to a person who, on beholding beautiful animals either created by the painter's art, or, better still, alive but at rest, is seized with a desire to see them in motion or engaged in some struggle or conflict to which their forms appear suited; this is my feeling about the State which we have been describing" (*Timaeus* 19). A painter can create beautiful works just as a philosopher can leave behind noble examples of his thought. But both creations are inferior to real animate creations or to the real philosophic process.[24] Plato would like to see his creation in existence, performing in its proper way. But just as a painting gives only a momentary glimpse of true being, a dialogue can only suggest the Form for the state.

Plato does not claim authority for his teaching, nor does he approve of anyone else, such as the poets or sophists, making such claims.[25] The poets are the self-appointed and generally recognized

---

23. Socrates always claims a plain, awkward style. He would ask a question, "and if I do this in a very inartistic and ridiculous manner, do not laugh at me, for I only venture to improvise before you because I am eager to hear your wisdom: and I must therefore ask you and your disciples to refrain from laughing" (*Euthydemus* 278).

24. There is some justification for D. R. Grey's paradoxical statement in "Art in the *Republic,*" *Philosophy,* 27 (1952) that "there is, properly, *no* place for art in the *Republic,* because the whole philosophical, political, and metaphysical conception is aesthetic from beginning to end" (p. 302). Plato allows the rulers of the Republic only the greatest of arts – statecraft (see *Republic III* 342 and *Euthydemus* 291). Statecraft is like coloring sculpture (*Republic IV* 420), like painting (*Laws VI* 769, *Republic VI* 484), and like composing a tragedy (*Laws VII* 817).

25. G. R. Levy states that "for every Myth he is accustomed to use a

teachers. But their art has no more permanence than Plato's, and their dogmatism discourages any intelligent response. The poets inescapably imitate human actions; they set both real and ideal deeds in the province of the old humanity. Bound by natural human limitations, no man can speak directly, yet significantly, to the human situation. Plato states, "I am conscious that I myself should never be able to celebrate the city and her citizens in a befitting manner, and I am not surprised at my own incapacity; to me the wonder is rather that the poets, present as well as past, are not better — not that I mean to depreciate them; but everyone can see that they are a tribe of imitators, and will imitate best and most easily the life in which they have been brought up; while that which is beyond the range of a man's education he finds hard to carry out in action, and still harder adequately to represent in language" (*Timaeus* 19). Poets tend to imitate without personal involvement or philosophical evaluation. These poets lie passively in their environment; their limited imagination does not allow them to improve upon what society has given them. And language proves more recalcitrant to meaningful expression than do actions. An action or thing may participate in some way with its corresponding Form. But there is no Form for language to resemble. Language can suggest all Forms, while being none of them truly.

The earlier tentative statements about the role of the dialogues becomes more definite in the *Laws*. The dialogues are indeed to be regarded as true poems, not the gripping poetry of conflict, but a serene embodiment of truth and beauty. Almost as an afterthought, the Stranger recognizes some merit in his long discourse (*Laws* VII 811-2):

> I think that I am not wholly in want of a pattern, for when I consider the words which we have spoken from early dawn until now, and which, as I believe, have been inspired by Heaven, they appear to me to be quite like a poem. When I reflected upon all these words of ours, I naturally felt pleasure, for of all the discourses which I have ever learnt or heard, either in poetry or prose, this seemed to me to be the justest, and most suitable for young men to hear; I cannot imagine any better pattern than this which the guardian of the

different means of introducing the break in the dramatic dialogue, and of disclaimit as his own creation, 'I am not good at inventing stories', says his spokesman Socrates. Stewart has gathered a bunch of these impersonal openings, whose diversity may hide a subjective, and therefore, perhaps a universal, origine" (p. 70).

law who is also the director of education can have. He cannot do better than advise the teachers to teach the young these words and any which are of a like nature, if he should happen to find them, either in poetry or prose, or if he come across unwritten discourses akin to ours, he should certainly preserve them, and commit them to writing.

Even here Plato does not claim authority for his creation. First, the words of the dialogue are to be used in conjunction with the personal direction of a teacher. And second, the principles and laws are not directly recommended for the world where the Athenian reasons with Cleinias and Megillus, but rather in the state set up by the dialogue. So in the second-best state, fallible men may need the aid of the written word. True poetry of the soul comes through a god-like communion with the eternal. But when the inspiration is not present, preserved discourses may give some direction to education.

Anyone who deals with the mere transmission of facts and customs must submit to the authority of one who truly knows, here the lawgiver. The teachers Plato envisions in the *Laws* primarily transmit sayings or discourses rather than ideas. For this reason, good discourses are of great importance. The teachers must learn and approve the dialogues. Those who will shall be employed; those objecting will be dismissed. But Plato carefully declares that the Athenian's ideas do not stem from a personal whim. The source of inspiration is the same for philosophy and for poetry. Good words are always inexplicable — they come from the muses. The seriousness of his intent and the intensity of his lifelong dedication to philosophy lead Plato to admit that his dialogues, being just, are suitable for the consideration of young men. But even here, his customary modesty leads him to suggest that the dialogue is only a fanciful tale.

Besides their role in education, written laws can help guide the state in its ordinary functions. Whatever its inadequacies, written discourse does have the advantage of allowing even the slowest man to absorb its meaning. The value of such discourse still comes from its being tested for contemporary relevance. Cleinias receives the approval of Megillus and the Athenian by saying that "the greatest help to rational legislation is that the laws when once written down are always at rest; they can be put to the test at any future time, and therefore, if on first hearing they seem difficult, there is no reason for apprehension about them, because any man however dull can go over them and consider them again and again; nor if they are tedious but useful, is there any reason or religion, as it seems to me, in any man refusing to maintain the principles of them to the utmost of his power" (*Laws* X 891). The state described by the *Laws* lacks the absolute order of the world set up by the *Republic*. The Athenian knows that heretical discourses have been scattered through the realm. The legislator himself must compose counterarguments. Thus, towards the end of his life, Plato begins to recognize that a wise man must fight error by some more direct method. The philosopher must not only bring down the dazzling vision of truth to this world, but he must clear away the murk of human ignorance. Nevertheless, Plato will not illumine and cleanse with the same instrument. To the last, the philosopher rejects this dangerous compromise.

BIBLIOGRAPHY

Anton, H. S., "Uber die Rhetorik bei Aristoteles in ihrem Verhältnis zu Platon's *Gorgias," Rheinisches Museum für Philologie,* 14 (1859), 570-98.
- "Die Dialoge *Gorgias* und *Phädrus," Zeitschrift für Philosophie und philologie Kritik,* 35 (1859), 81-113.

Apelt, Otto, *Observationes criticae in Platonis dialogos,* Progr. des Gymn. Weimar, 1880, 10 p.
- "Die Ideenlehre in Platos Sophistes," in *Beiträge zur Geschichte der griechischen Philosophie,* Leizpig, 1891, 67-99.
- "Platons Sophistes und die Ideenlehre," *Jahrbücher für classische Philologie,* 145 (1892) 529-540.
- "Platons Sophistes in geschichtlicher Beleuchtung," *Rheinisches Museum für Philologie,* 50 (1895), 394-452.
- "Die Definition des ὄν in Platons Sophistes," *Jahrbücher für classische Philologie,* 151 (1895), 257-72.

Arnim, H. von, *Platos Jugenddialoge und die Entststehungszeit des Phaidros.* Leipzig: Teubner, 1914. 224 p.

Arnold, Augustus, *Platon's Werke, einzeln erklärt und in ihrem Zusammenhange dargestellt.* Erfurt: Villaret, 1855.

Ast, F., *Phaedrus. Recens., Hermiae scholiis e Cod. Monac. XI. suisque commentariis illustravit Fr. Ast.* Lipsiae: Schwickert, 1810.
- *Phaedrus. Denuo recogn. brevique annotatione instruxit Fr. Ast.* Lipsiae: Weidmann, 1830.

Baar, A., *Darlegung der im Platonischen Dialog Gorgias vorkommenden Argumentationem und ihrer Resultate.* Znaim, 1873, 12p.

Bacher, Th. E., *Dramatische Composition und rhetorische Disposition der Platonischen Republik, I.* Augsburg, 1869. 34p.

Baiterus, Geo., "Gorgias, item incerti auctoris Io.," in *Platonis opera. Recognoverunt Ioa. Baiterus, Ioa. Casp. Orellius, Aug. Guil. Winckelmann.* Suttgart: Meyer und Zeller, (1839), 1851.

Baron, Carolus, "De l'unité de composition dans le *Phèdre* du Platon," *Revue des Études Grecques,* (1891), 58-62.

Baumann, Heinr., *Versuch einer Kritik über Platons Apologie nach dem jetzigen Stande der Wissenschaft.* Znaim, 1868, 15p.

Beare, J.I., "The *Phaedrus,* Its Structure," *Hermathena,* vol. 17, 312-334.

Beck, Chr., *"Gorgias, Ion, Philebus, Menon"* in *Ex rec. Henr. Stephani passim emendata adiectis scholiis et notat. crit. edid.* Lipsiae: C. Tauchnitz, 1816.

Beierle, G., *Disposition des Platonischen Dialogs Phaidros.* Troppau, 1872.

Bekker, Imm., Platonis *Dialogi* (Gr. et Lat.) *Ex recensione Imm. Bekker.* Berolini: G. Reimer, 1816, 1817; 1823.

Bellin, A. G., *Exposition des idées de Platon et d'Aristote, sur la nature et l'origine du langage.* Paris, 1842. 30 p.

Bénard, Charles, "Platon historien de la sophistique," *Séances et travaux de l'Académie des sciences morales et politiques,* 124 (1885), 339-363.

Bergemann, A. W., "Opbouw en bedoeling van Plato's dialog *Phaidros.*" *Tijdschrift voor Philosophie,* 24 (1962), 652-667.

Berger, J., *De rhetorica, quid sit secundum Platonem.* Parisiis, 1840, 28p.

Bianchi, L., "A proposito del giudizio di Platone sui *Gorgia,*" *Maia,* 6 (1953), 271-82.

Bielmeier, A., *Die neuplatonische Phaidrosinterpretation. Ihr Werdegang und ihre Eigenart.* Rhet. Studien 16, Paderborn, 1930, 96p.

Black, Friedrich, "Eine bedenkliche Stelle in Platons *Phaidros,*" *Commentationes in Lomorem G. Studemund.* Argentorati, 1889, 237-46.

Blackwood, R., J. Crossett, and H. Long, "*Gorgias* 482b," *Classical Journal,* 57 (1962), 318-19.

Bluck, R. S., "Plato, *Gorgias* 493c1-3," *Classical Review,* 13 (1963), 263-64.

— "The *Phaedrus* and Reincarnation," *American Journal of Philology,* 79 (1958), 156-64.

Böhringer, Adolf, *Der Platonische Gorgias.* Prog. d. Lyceums, Karlsruhe, 1870, 34 p.

Bondeson, W., "Plato's 'Sophist': Falsehoods and Images." *Apeiron,* 6 (1972), 1-6.

— "Plato's Sophist and the Significance and Truth-Value of Statements," *Apeiron,* 8 (1974), 41-47.

Bonghi, Ruggiero, "Lachete o della Fortezza. *Gorgia* o della retorica," in *Dialoghi di Platone tradotti da Ruggiero Bonghi.* Torino: Fat. Bocca e C., 1904, 126p.

Bonitz, Hermann, "*Gorgias.* Gedankengang und Gliederung des Gespräches. Zur Rechtfertigung der bezeichneten des Gespräches," in *Platonische Studien,* Berlin: Vahlen, 1858, 1-46.

Bourguet, E., "La composition dans le *Phèdre* de Platon," *Revue de métaph. et de Morale,* 26 (1919), 335-51.

Boutens, P. C., *Phaidros.* Rotterdam: Brusse, 1923.

Brambilla, A., and M. Robertazzi, *Fedro.* Milano: Signorelli, 1941.

Bratuscheck, Ernest, *Platonis Phaedri dispositio.* Dissertation, Berlin, 1865, 30p.

Bresler, F., *Uber den platonischen Phaedrus,* Danzig, 1867, 20p.

Brisca, Menapace, "La Rettorica di Francesco Patrizio o del Platonismo Anti-Aristotelico," *Siculorum Gymnasium,* 5 (1952), 434-61.

Brownstein, Oscar L., "Plato's *Phaedrus*: Dialectic as the Genuine Art of Speaking," *Quarterly Journal of Speech,* 51 (1965), 392-98.

Buccellato, M., "Un'aporia sofistica sulla communicabilità del sapere e la sua risonanza platonica," *Archivio di Filosofia,* (1950), 68-93.

— "La 'retorica' sofistica negli scritti di Platone," *Rivista critica di Storia della Filosofia,* 7 (1952), 81-103; 351-77; 431-446.

— *La retorica sofistica negli scritti di Platone.* Milano: Bocca, 1953, 201p.

— "La retorica sofistica negli scritti di Platone, IV: Il *Cratilo* e l'interesse dottrinàle della questione onomatologica," *Rivista critica di Storia della Filosofia,* 8 (1953), 14-35.

Buchheit, V., *Untersuchungen zur Theories des Genos epideiltikon von Gorgias bis Aristoteles.* München: Hueber, 1960. 260p.
Buchwald, W. von, *Phaidros.* München, 1964, 189p.
Budé, T., *Gorgias. Dialogue. Edition classique, précédée d'une notice littéraire.* Paris: Jules Delalain et fils, 1868.
Bury, John Bagnell, "Questions Connected with Plato's *Phaidros,*" *Journal of Philology,* 15 (1886), 80-85.
Busse, A., "Nochmals das Pindarzitat in Platons *Gorgias,*" *Hermes,* 66 (1931), 367-68.
— "Zum Pindarzitat in Platons *Gorgias,* 484b," *Hermes,* 66 (1931), 126.
Byker, Donald, "Plato's Philosophy of Natural Law as a Key to His View of Persuasion." Unpublished doctoral dissertation, University of Michigan, 1969. 132p.
Byl, S., "Platon et Aristote ont-ils professé des vues contradictories sur la vieillesse?" *Les Etudes Classiques,* 42 (1974), 113-26.
Calder, M. W., "Plato's Apology of Socrates: A Speech for the Defense," *Boston University Journal,* 20 (1972), 42-47.
Calonge, Ruiz, *Gorgias.* Clás. Polít. Madrid Inst. de Estud. polít., 1951. 123p.
Cambiano, G., "Dialettica, medicina, retorica nel *Fedro* platonico," *Rivista di Filosofia,* 57 (1966), 284-305.
Carmack, William R., "A History of Greek Rhetoric and Oratory," *Quarterly Journal of Speech,* 49 (1963), 325-28.
Cauer, P., "Platons *Menon* und sein Verhältnis zu Protagoras und Gorgias," *Rheinisches Museum für Philologie.* vol. 72, 284-306.
Chaillet, Janus Ludovicus, "Platonis *Menexenus,*" in *De orationibus, quae Athenis in funéribus publicis habebantur.* Dotecomiae: C. Misset, 1891.
Christ, Augustin Theodor, *Platons Gorgias.* Leipzig: G. Freytag, 1890. 163p.
Cobet, C. G., "Ad Platonis *Gorgias,*" *Mnemosyne,* 2 (1874), 113-61.
Cohn, G., *Platons Gorgias.* Copenhague: Tillge, 1911. 142p.
Cope, Edward Meredith, *Plato's Gorgias. Literally translated with an Introductory Essay, Containing a Summary of the Argument by Edward Meredith Cope.* London: Bell & Sons, 1864; 1884. 200 p.
Coulter, James A., "*Phaedrus* 279A: The Praise of Isocrates," *Greek, Roman, and Byzantine Studies,* 8 (1967), 225-36.
— "The Relation of the *Apology* of Socrates to Gorgias' *Defense of Palamedes* and Plato's Critique of Gorgianic Rhetoric," *Harvard Studies in Classical Philology,* 68 (1964), 269-303.
—, and Malcolm Brown, "The Middle Speech of Plato's *Phaedrus,*" *Journal of the History of Philosophy,* 9 (1971), 405-23.
Courcelle, Pierre, "Le corps-tombeau. Platon *Gorgias,* 493a, *Cratyle,* 400c, *Phèdre,* 250," *Revue des Etudes Anciennes,* 68 (1966), 101-22.
Cron, Christian, "Zur Frage nach der Gliederung des platonischen Dialogs *Gorgias,*" *Jahrbücher für classischen Philologie,* 133 (1886), 563-582; 141 (1890), 253-281.
— "Zu Platon's *Gorgias,* 453C," *Jahrbücher für classische Philologie,* 89 (1864), 520-23.

- *Beiträge zur Erklärung des Platonischen Gorgias im Ganzen und Einzelnen.* Leipzig: Teubner, 1870.
- "Zu Platon's *Gorgias* 456D," *Jahrbücher für classische Philologie,* 103 (1871), 581-82.
- "Zu Platon's *Gorgias,*" *Jahrbücher für classische Philologie,* 123 (1881), 815-816.

Croiset, A. and L. Bodin, *Protagoras, Gorgias, Ménon,* Paris, 1923.

Crusius, C. L., *De Platonis dicendi genere inter poesin atque prosam Orationem medio ad illustr. Diog. Laert. lib. III.* Vitembergae, 1763.

Cushman, Robert E., *Therapeia.* University of North Carolina, 1958.

Dalsjö, Magnus, "Platonis *Gorgias,*" in *Valda skrifter af Platon i svensk öfversättning af Magnus Dalsjö 6 delen.* Stockholm: L. J. Hiertas förlag, 1877.

Davies, G. A., "Plato, *Phaedro* 62A," *Classical Review,* (1915), 69-70.

De Fraine, J., "Rhetorische gemeenplaatsen in de voorrede van de l'*Apologia Socratis,*" *Philologische Studien,* (1942-43), 87-94.

Denis, Jacques, "Théorie idéaliste de l'art est-elle de Platon ou de Cicéron?" *Annales de la Faculté des Caen,* 1 (1887), 541-552.
- "Le Phèdre," *Annales de la Faculté des Lettres de Caen,* 7 (1890), 214-228.

Deuschle, Julius, *Gorgias. Platos ausgewählte Schriften.* Leipzig: B.G. Teubner, 1859; 1876. 194p.
- "Zum Platonischen *Gorgias,*" *Jahrbücher für classische Philologie,* 81 (1860), 486-500.
- "*Gorgias.*" *Zeitschrift für das Gymnasialwesen,* 15 (1861), 1-33.
- "Dispositionem von Dialogen und Reden des Platon und Demosthenes," *Zeitschrift für das Gymnasialwissenschaft,* 14 (1860), 353-76.
- *Dasselbe u. d. T.: Dispositionem der Apologie und des Gorgias von Platon und logische Analyse des Gorgias.* Leipzig: Teubner, 1867.
- *Platon, Auserlesene Werke.* Stuttgart: Metzler, 1869.

Deventer, Charles M., "Erotische dialogen van Plato. De *Phaedrus,*" *De Gids,* 4 (1894), 267-98.
- "De *Phaedrus,*" in *Platonische studien.* Amsterdam: S. L. van Looy, 1896, 152-91.

Dezeimeris, Reinhold, "Remarques critiques sur un passage des scholies grecques sur le *Gorgias* de Platon," *Annales de la Faculté des lettres de Bordeaux,* 1 (1879), 283-85.

Diès, A., *Autour de Platon.* 2 vols. Paris, 1927, pp. 402-32.

Dimock, George E., Jr., "Ἀλλὰ in Lysias and Plato's *Phaedrus,*" *American Journal of Philology,* 73 (1952), 381-396.

Dodds, E. R., *Gorgias.* Oxford: Clarendon Press, 1959. 406p.

Domino, Anna Maria, *Il Gorgia o della Retorica. Nuova versione di Anna Maria Domino.* Vercelli, S.A.V.I.T., 1942, 131p.

Dorter, Kenneth, "The Significance and Interconnection of the Speeches in Plato's *Symposium,*" *Philosophy and Rhetoric,* 2 (1969), 215-34.
- "Imagery and Philosophy in Plato's *Phaedrus,*" *Journal of the History of Philosophy,* 9 (1971), 279-88.

Dover, K.J., "Aristophanes' Speech in Plato's *Symposium*," *Journal of Hellenic Studies*, 86 (1966), 41-50.
Duchemin, J., "Remarques sur la composition du *Gorgias*," *Revue des Etudes Grecques*, 56 (1943), 265-86.
Dümmler, Ferdinand, *Antisthenika*. Berlin, 1882.
— Prolegomena zu Platons Staat und der platonischen und aristotelischen Staatslehre. *Basel 1891. 65p.*
Duerr, K., "Der Platonische Gorgias als Lektüre der Oberprima," *Neue Jahrbücher für Paedagogik*, (1923), 145-58.
Duncan, Roger, "The Dialectical Destruction of Rhetorical Figures: Platonic Response to John Kozy, Jr., *Philosophy and Rhetoric*, 4 (1971), 175-77.
Egermann, F., "Der Dialogus des Tacitus und Platons *Gorgias*," *Hermes*, 70 (1935), 424-30.
Engel, E. S., "Plato on Rhetoric and Writing," Unpublished doctoral dissertation, Yale University, 1973. 176p.
Erickson, Keith V., "Plato's Theory of Rhetoric: A Research Guide," *Rhetoric Society Quarterly*, 7 (1977) 78-90.
Eussner, Adam, "Zu Platon's *Gorgias*," *Blätter für des Bayer. Gymnasialschulwesen*, 10 (1874), 37-39.
Fehling, Detlev, *Die Wiederholungsfiguren und ihr Gebrauch bei den Griechen vor Gorgias*. Berlin: Walter de Gruyter, 1969. 358p.
Ferrai, Eugenio, *Il dialoghi di Platone nuovamente volgarizzati da Eugenio Ferrai*. Padova: Tip. del Seminario, 1873-1883.
Ferrante, D., "Curiosità etimologiche nel *Cratilo* di Platone e nel De lingua latina di Varrone," *Giornale Italiano di Filologia*, 15 (1962), 163-71;
Ferro, A., "Introduzione al *Fedro*," *Archivio di Storia delle Filosofia Italiana*, 4 (1935), 297-310.
Findeisenus, Ch. Gdfr., *Gorgias, Ad fidem Codd. Mss. August. et Meermann., versionisque Ficini rec., emendavit, explic. indicemque verborum Gr. adiecit Ch. Gdfr. Findeisenus*. Gothae: 1796.
Fischer, Albert, *De mythis Platonicis*. Dissertation, Königsberg, 1865. 68p.
Fisher, J., "Plato on Writing and Doing Philosophy," *Journal of the History of Ideas*, 27 (April, 1966), 163-72.
Fleshler, Helen, "Plato and Aristotle on Rhetoric and Dialectic," *Pennsylvania Speech Annual*, 20 (1963), 11-17.
Foerster, L. B., *Quaestiones de Platonis Phaedro pars prior*. Dissertation, Berlin: Ebeling und Plahn, 1869. 46p.
Foerster, R., "Platons *Phaidros* und Apuleius," *Philologus*, vol. 75, 134-35.
Fortenbaugh, William W., "Plato *Phaedrus* 235c3," *Classical Philology*, 6 (1966), 108-09.
Friedländer, Paul, *"Gorgias," Plato*. New York: Pantheon Books, 1964, 244-72.
— "Plato *Phaedrus* 245 A," *Classical Philology*, (1941), 51-52.
Fouillée, Alfred, *Il Menesseno di Platone e la orazione funébre di Pericle in Tucidide*. Lodi: C. Dell' Aro, 1880, 34p.
Frenkian, A. M., *La Méthode Hippocratique dans le Phèdre de Platon*. Bucharest: Imprimérie Nationale, 1941.
Friedrichs, Emil, *Platons Lehre von der Lust im Gorgias und Philebus*. Leipzig: Halle, 1890. 51p.

Gagarin, Michael, "The Purpose of Plato's *Protagoras,*" *American Philological Association Proceedings,* 100 (1969), 133-64.
Gallagher, Donald, K., "In Praise of Pausanias: Dialectic in the Second Speech of Plato's *Symposium,*" *Kinesis,* 6 (1974), 40-55.
Geffcken, J., "Studien zu Platons *Gorgias,*" *Hermes,* 65 (1930), 14-37.
Georgii, L., *Phaidros,* Stuttgart: Metzler, 1853.
Gercke, A., *Gorgias,* Berlin: Weidmann, 1897. 186p.
Gerhard, W. A., "Plato's Theory of Dialectic," *New Scholasticism,* 21 (April, 1947), 192-211.
Giuffrida, P., "Significati e limiti del neoatticismo," *Maia,* 7 (1955), 83-124.
Glogau, Gustav, "Gedankengang von Platons *Gorgias,*" *Archiv für Geschichte der Philosophie,* 8 (1895), 153-89.
Goldbacher, Alois, "Zur Erklärung und Kritik des platonischen Dialoges Lysis," *Analecta Graeciensia,* 1893, 123-40.
Golling, Ioan., *De Calliclis orationis, quae est in Gorgia Platonico sex locis commentatio.* Wien, 1875, 19p.
Gomperz, H., *Sophistik und Rhetorik.* Berlin: 1912.
González, Rólan T., "Breve introduccion a la problematica de los géneros literarios. Su clasificacíon en la antigüedad clasica," *Cuadernos de Filologia clásica,* 4 (1972), 213-37.
Gotschlich, E., *Ueber die Veranlassung des Platonischen Dialoges Gorgias und die Polemik in demselben.* Beuthen, 1871. 14p.
Green, Elvena M., "Plato's Use of Three Dramatic Elements in *Gorgias* as Means to Demonstrate His Thought," *Southern Speech Communication Journal,* 33 (1968), 307-315.
Greene, W. Charles, "The Spoken and the Written Word," *Harvard Studies in Classical Philology,* 60 (1951), 23-59.
Gross, N. P., *The Rhetoric of Love. Studies in Ancient Amatory Persuasion.* Unpublished dissertation, University of North Carolina, 1971.
Grote, G., *Plato and the Other Companions of Socrates.* London, 1888, 1-55.
Güthling, Otto, *Platon's Gorgias. Übersetzt von Friedrich Schleiermacher. Neu herausgegeben von Otto Güthling.* Leipzig, 1883. 44p.
Guzzo, C., *Fedro. Trad. di C. Guzzo, introd. e note di A. Guzzo.* Napoli: Loffredo, 1934, 205p.
Haenisch, E., *De oratione, quae sub nomine Lysiae in Platonis Phaedro legitur, utrum Lysiae an Platonis esse videatur.* Ratisbon, 1825, 39p.
Hamel, W., *Rhétorique ancienne. Analyse critique du Phèdre de Platon.* Toulouse, 1859.
– "Analyse critique du *Gorgias* de Platon," *Extr. des Mémoires de l'Acad. de Toulouse,* 1871.
Hamilton, W., *Gorgias.* Baltimore: The Penguin Books, 1960, 149p.
– *Plato, Phaedrus and Seventh and Eight Letters.* Hammondsworth, England, 1973.
Harrison, E. L., "Plato, *Gorgias* 449 D Foll.," *Eranos,* 61 (1963), 63-65.
– "Was Gorgias a Sophist? " *Phoenix,* 18 (1964), 183-92.
Hathaway, R. F., "Law and Moral Paradox in Plato's *Apology,*" *Journal of the History of Philosophy,* 8 (1970), 127-42.

Hauff, C., *Oratio de scientiarum amore Platonico*. Bonnae: Gandavi, 1830.
Havelock, Eric A., *Preface to Plato*. Oxford, 1963.
Heindrof, L. F., *Gorgias, Apologia Socratis, Charmides, Hippias maior*. Berolini: Nauck, 1805. 1825.
— *Phaedrus*. Lipsiae: Nauck, 1839.
Hellwig, A., *Untersuchungen zur Theorie der Rhetorik bei Platon und der Rhetorik Aristoteles*. Göttingen: Vandenhoeck & Ruprecht, 1973. 374p.
Hembold, W. C., and W. B. Holter, "The Unity of the *Phaedrus*," *University of California Publications in Classical Philology*, 14 (1952), 387-417.
Hermann, C. F., "Die Rede des Lysias in Plato's *Phaedros*," *Heidelburg Jahrbücher umgearb. in dessen Gesammelte Abhandlungen*, 17 (1828), 1-21.
— *Vindiciae disputationis de idea boni apud Platonem*. Marburg, 1839. 48p.
— *De interpretatione Timaei dialogi a Cicerone relicta disputatio*. Göttingae, 1841. 39p.
Hillbruner, Anthony, "Plato and Korzybski: Two Views of Truth and Rhetorical Theory," *Southern Speech Communication Journal*, 24 (Summer, 1959), 185-96.
Hinze, G., *Ueber Plan und Gedankengang in Plato's Phaedrus*, Dissertation, Regimonti, 1874.
Hirsch, E., *De Platonis Gorgia*. Breslau, 1865.
— *Probe einer Ubersetzung von Platons Gorgias*. Dissertation, 1870.
Hirschig, R. B., *Exploratio argumentationum Socraticarum, in quibus scribae labefactarunt medios Platonis dialogos Gorgiam et Philebum*. Traiecti ad Rh., 1859.
— *Opera*. Parisiis: Didot, 1856; 1873.
— *Gorgias, Syllogismo Socratico una cum grammaticae duce emendatus atque illustratus nec non prolegomenis et indice instructus in usum studiosae iuventutis*. Traiecti ad Rh., 1873.
Hirzel, Rud., *Ueber das Rhetorische und seine Bedeutung bei Plato*. Lipsiae, 1871. 75p.
Hoerber, R. G., "Love or Rhetoric in Plato's *Phaedrus*," *Classical Bulletin*, 34 (1958), 33.
Holzner, E., *Plato's Phaedrus und die Sophistenrede des Isokrates*. Prager Studien aus dem Gebiete der classischen Alterthumswissenschaft, (H. Dominicus Verl.), 1894, 50p.
Hope, Richard, *"Gorgias*: On the Purpose of Education," *The Personalist*, 20 (1939), no. 4.
Horn, Ferdinand, *Platonstudien*. Wien: F. Tempsky, 1902, 408p.
Hörstel, L., *Oder von der Redekunst, worin Plato zeigt, dass Socrates das Sittengesetz gegen die Volksverführer bis zum Tode behauptet und geübt hat*. Göttingen: Dieterich, 1797.
Höttermann, E., "Die Polemik Platons im *Phaidros*," *Zeitschrift für das Gymnasialwesen*, (1911), 385-410.
Howland, R. L., "The Attack on Isocrates in the *Phaedrus*," *Classical Quarterly*, 31 (1937), 151-59.
Hude, K., "Les oraisons funèbres de Lysias et Platon," *Danske Videnskabernes Selskabs historish-filologiske Meddelelser*, vol. I, 1-13.

Hudson-Williams, H., *Three Systems of Education: Some Reflections on the Implications of Plato's Phaedrus.* Inaugural Lecture, Kings College. University of Durham and Oxford University Press, 1954.
Huit, Charles, "Le *Gorgias*," *'L'Instruction publique,* 12 (1883), 622-24; 640-43; 656-58; 672-74; 688-90; 707-709; 725-26; 742-45; 759-61; 774-76; 784-86.
— *Le Gorgias, commentaire grammatical et littéraire des chapitres 37-83.* Paris: Lahure, 1884; 94p.
Hülsenbeck, J., *Ueber Plato's Gorgias und Phaedrus.* Iglau, 1869.
Humbert, J., "Polycratus, l'accusation de Socrate et le Gorgias," *Revue de Philologie,* (1931), 20-77.
Hunt, Everett Lee, "Plato on Rhetoric and Rhetoricians," *Quarterly Journal of Speech,* 6 (June, 1920), 35-56.
— "Plato and Aristotle on Rhetoric and Rhetoricians," *Studies in Rhetoric and Public Speaking in Honor of James Albert Winans.* New York, 1962. pp. 3-60.
Jaeger, Werner, "Plato's *Phaedrus:* Philosophy and Rhetoric," *Paideia: The Ideals of Greek Culture.* New York: Oxford University Press, 1944, 182-96.
Jahn, E., *Gorgias, mit Einleitung und Anmerkungen.* Wien, 1859.
Joja, Crizantema, "Le Sens Moderne De la Διανοια, Ou L'univers Du Discours' chez Platon," *Philosophie et Logique,* 17 (1973), 359-70.
Joly, Robert, "La question Hippocratique et le Témoignage du *Phèdre,*" *Revue des Etudes Grecques,* 74 (1961), 349-50; 69-92.
Jowett, Benjamin, *The Dialogus of Plato translated into English with Analysis and Introductions by Benjamin Jowett.* 5 vols. Oxford: Clarendon Press, 1871; 1892; New York, 1953.
Kaku, A., "What is Plato's Motive in *Gorgias,*" *Journal of Classical Studies,* 8 (1960), 28-42. (In Japanese).
Karris, Robert J., "The Background and Significance of the Pastoral Epistles," *Journal of Biblical Literature,* 92 (1974), 549-64.
Kassner, R., *Phaidros.* Jena: Diederichs, 1922, 96p.
Kermavner, V., *Die Allegorien in Platons Gorgias.* Czernowitz, 1863. 17p.
Kesters, H., *Plaidoyer d'un Socratique contre le Phèdre de Platon.* Louvain: Nauwelaerts, 1959.
— "De ware redekunst volgens Platoons *Phaidros.*" *Tijdschrift voor Filosofie,* 25 (1963), 651-87; 26 (1964), 33-68, 405-441.
Kindelmann, Thomas, "Der philosophische Gehalt des Mythus in Platons *Phaedrus,* dargelegt mit Rücksicht auf seine Seelenlehre," *Progr. des Gymn. Kremsier,* 8 (1881), 3-35.
Kirk, J. W., "Lucian and the Rhetoric of the Second Century," *Southern Speech Communication Journal,* 26 (Fall, 1960), 70-80.
Kirsche, A.B., *Ueber Platon's Phaedros.* Göttingen, 1848.
Klein, Willette, "A Restatement of Plato's Contribution to the Theory of Persuasion." Unpublished Masters thesis, Brooklyn College, 1937.
Kleist, James, "Aesop and *Phaedrus,*" *Classical Bulletin,* 27 (1950), 7-8.
Kleve, Knut, "The Unum Verabilissimum and Plato's Mystical Style," *Symbolae Osloenses,* 37 (1961), 88-95.

Klitzsch, C. I., *Kritischer Untersuchung über mehrere Stellen aus Plato's Gorgias*, Zwickau, 1845, 39 pp.

Kloch-Kornitz, P., "Der *Gorgias* Platons und die Philosophie Friedrich Nietzsches," *Zeitschrift für Philosophische Forschung*, 17 (1963), 586-603.

Koch, Konrad, "Platos *Gorgias* als Schullektüre," *Progr. des Gymn. Martino-Katharineum Braunschweig*, 4 (1892), 1-22.

Kolář, A., *Phaidros*. Prague, 1913, 81p.

Koller, H., "Die dihäretische Methode," *Glotta*, 39 (1960), 6-24.

Konvalina, L., *Die Prophetie in Platons Phaederus und Isokrates Rede gegen die Sophisten*. Marburg, 1866. 28p.

Kratz, H., *Gorgias*. Stuttgart: Metzler, 1864.

– "Exegetisch-Kritisches zu Platos *Gorgias*," *Correspondenzbl. für das Gelehrt. Realschulen in Württemberg*, 5 (1868), 30-36, 89-94; 123-136.

Kriegbaum, S., *Der Ursprung der von Kallikles in Platons Gorgias vertretenen Anschauungen*. Paderborn: Schöningh, 1913. 105p.

Krische, A. B., *Uber Platon's Phaedrus*. Göttingen, 1848.

Kucharski, P., "La 'méthode d'Hippocrate' dans le *Phèdre*," *Revue des Etudes Grecques*, 52 (1939), 301-57.

– "La rhétorique dans le *Gorgias* et le *Phèdre*," *Revue des Etudes Grecques*, 74 (1961), 371-406.

Kühner, Rud., *Platonis de eloquentia in Phaedro dialogo iudicium*. Slandow, 1868.

LaFrance, Yvon, "La Problematique morale de l'opinion dans le 'Gorgias' de Platon," *Revue Philosophique de Louvain*, 67 (1969), 5-29.

La Magna, G., *Gorgia. Introd., versione e note di G. La Magna*. Milano, 1936.

Lamberton, William, "Note on a passage in the *Gorgias* of Plato," *American Journal of Philology*, 5 (1884), 356-58.

Lang, Berel, "Presentation and Representation in Plato's Dialogues," *Philosophical Forum*, 4 (1972-1973), 224-40.

LaRusso, Dominic A., "A Neoplatonic Dialogue: Is Rhetoric an Art? An Introduction and Translation," *Speech Monographs*, 32 (1965), 393-440.

Lasso de la Vega, José S., "Notas al 'Gorgias'," *Emerita*, 35 (1967), 295-314.

Lebeck, Anne, "The Central Myth of Plato's *Phaedrus*," *Greek, Roman, and Byzantine Studies*, 13 (1972), 267-90.

Lemercier, A. P., *Le Gorgias*. Paris, 1888. 176p.

Levinson, R. B., "Plato's *Phaedrus* and the New Criticism," *Archiv für Geschichte der Philosophie*, 46 (1964), 293-309.

Levy, F., "Platon *Gorgias* 550c1," *Philologische Wochenschrift*, (1921), 115-17.

Liebhold, K. J., "Zu Platons *Symposium: Gorgias*," *Neue Jahrbücher für Philologie und Padägogik*, vol. 155, 499-503.

– *Die Bedeutung des platonischen Gorgias und dessen Beziehungen zu den übrigen Dialogen*. Progr. des Gymn. Rudolstadt, 1885. 26p.

Lillge, F., "Eine rhetorisches Schema in Platons *Kriton*," *Zeitschrift für das Gymnasialwesen*, (1916), 331-338.

Lindemann, M., *De prima, quae in convivio Platonico legitur, oratione*. Dresden. 1853. 41p.

— *De Agathonis oratione quae est in convivio Platonico.* Dresden, 1871.

Linforth, I. M., "Soul and Sieve in Plato's *Gorgias,*" *University of California Publications in Classical Philology,* 12 (1944), 295-314.

— "Telestic Madness in Plato, *Phaedrus* 244DE," *University of California Publications in Classical Philology,* 13 (1946), 163-72.

Lipke, G., *De Platonis Phaedri consilio.* Wesel, 1856. 20p.

— "Uber Plato's *Phädrus,*" (1870), 22p.

Lodge, Gonzalez, *Plato's Gorgias edited on the Basis of Deuschle-Cron's Edition by Gonzalez Lodge.* Boston and London, 1891. 308p.

Lodge, R. C., *Plato's Theory of Education.* New York, 1947.

Loebl, Friedrich, "Beiträge zur Textkritik des platonischen *Phaedrus,*" *Progr. des Gymn. Troppau,* (1882), 3-18.

Louis, Pierre, *Les métaphores de Platon.* Paris: Les Belles Lettres, 1945. 269 pp.

Luther, Wilhelm, "Die Schwäche des geschriebenen Logos. Ein Beispiel humanistischer Interpretation, versucht am sogenannten Schriftmythos in Platons *Phaidros,*" *Gymnasium,* 68 (1961), 526-48.

Marignac, Aloys de, *Imagination et dialectique, Essai sur l'expression du spirituel par l'image dans les dialogues de Platon.* Paris, 1951. 168p.

Märkinger, J., *Die Rhetorik nach dem Platon. Dialoge Gorgias.* Seitenstetten, 1877. 31p.

Marsh, Thomas H., "Aristotle versus Plato on Public Speaking," *Southern Speech Communication Journal,* 18 (March, 1953), 163-66.

Marten, R., *Der Logos der Dialektik. Eine Theorie zu Platons Sophistes.* Berlin, 1965. 260p.

McGibbon, D. D., "The Fall of the Soul in Plato's *Phaedrus,*" *Classical Quarterly,* 14 (1964), 56-63.

McKeon, Richard, "Plato and Aristotle as Historians: A Study of Method in the History of Ideas," *Ethics,* 51 (1941), 253-90.

Meixner, F. S., *Beweis, dass Platon's Urtheile über Perikles als Ethiker, Politiker und Rhetor im Gorgias, Menon und Phaedros ganz gleich sind.* München, 1836.

Menghini, D., *Il Gorgia.* Milano: Albrighi, 1912, 243p.

Merry, B., "Plato, *Gorgias* 468a," *Classical Review,* 14 (1964), 242.

Meunier, J., "Platon traduit par Cicéron. Une page célèbre du *Phèdre.*" *Nova et Vetera,* 24 (1945), 53-67.

Meyer, Peter, "Zu Platons *Gorgias,*" *Jahrbücher für classische Philologie,* 147 (1893), 401-402.

Milota, Alois, *Uber die Verschiedenheit des Standpunktes, von welchem aus die Kritik der Rhetorik im Platonischen Gorgias und Phädrus geübt wird und in wie weit sich aus der Ubereinstimmung und Verschiedenheit der beiden Dialoge bei Behandlung eines verwandten Gegenstandes Entscheidungsgründe ergeben für die Zeitfolge der Abfassung dieser beiden Dialoge.* Krems, 1857.

Modugno, G., *Phaedrus.* Bari, 1914, 191p.

— *Gorgia. Trad. e commento di G. Modugno.* Firenze: Ofiria, 1936, 240p.

Moore, J. D., "The Philosopher's Frenzy," *Mnemosyne,* 22 (1969), 225-30.

Monrad, Marcus Jacobus, "Nonnulla de Platonis philosophandi via et ratione. Oratio in circulo iuvenum antiquitatis studiosorum christianiensium habita a M.J.M." *Nordisk Tidskrift for Filologi,* 7 (1885-1887), 282-88.
Morrow, G. R., "Plato's Conception of Persuasion," *Philosophical Review,* 62 (1953), 234-50.
Mortley, R. J., "Plato on the Sophistic Heritage of Protagoras," *Eranos,* 67 (1969), 24-32.
Mras, K., "Platos *Phaedrus* und die Rhetorik," *Wiener Studien,* vol. 36, 295-319; vol. 37, 88-117.
Muche, Felix, "Der Dialog *Phädrus* und die platonische Frage," *Progr. des Marien-Gymn. Posen,* 4 (1885), 3-17.
Mueller, Gustav E., "Unity of the *Phaedrus,*" *Classical Bulletin,* 33 (March, 1957), 50-53.
Mühl, M., "Die Nachwirkung einer Antithese des Sophisten Gorgias," *Anzeiger für Altertumswissenschaft,* 6 (1953), 191-92.
Müller, H., *Platon Werke. Uebersetzt von Hieron. Müller, mit Einleitungen begleitet von Karl Steinhart.* Leipzig: Brockhaus, 1850-1873.
Müller, I., "Oratio de Platonis *Cratylo,*" *Acta philologor. Monacens.,* 4 (1829).
Münscher, W., *Ueber die Zeilbestimmungen in Plato's Gorgias.* Hersfeld, 1855.
— "Zur Erklärung und Kritik von Platons *Gorgias,*" *Jahrbücher für das classische Philologie,* 101 (1970), 153-81.
Murley, C., "Plato's *Phaedrus* and Theocritan Pastoral," *Transactions of the American Philological Association,* (1940), 281-95.
Murphy, James J., "The Metarhetorics of Plato, Augustine, and McLuhan: A Pointing Essay," *Philosophy and Rhetoric,* 4 (1971), 201-14.
Mutschmann, H., "Die ältesten Definition der Rhetorik," *Hermes,* (1918), 440-43.
Naber, S. A., *Observationes criticae in Platonem.* Leiden, 1862.
Natorp, P., "Plato's *Phaedrus,*" *Hermes,* (1900), 385-436.
Nestle, W., *Gorgias.* Leipzig, 1909. 194p.
Newhall, Barker, *The Dramatic and Mimetic Features of the Gorgias of Plato.* Baltimore: Johns Hopkins University Press, 1891, 26p.
Nobles, W. Scott, "The Paradox of Plato's Attitude Toward Rhetoric," *Western Speech,* 21 (Fall, 1957), 206-210.
North, Helen, "The Use of Poetry in the Training of the Ancient Orator," *Traditio,* 8 (1952), 1-33.
Norvin, William, *Olympiadori philosophi in Platonis Gorgiam commentaria ed. William Norvin.* Leipzig: Teubner, 1936. 250p.
Novák, Jan V., *Platon und die Rhetorik.* Leipzig: Teubner, 1883. 100p.
— "Jak muze recnictvi statí se umením dusevodným?," in *Sborník Prací filologickych vydaný na oslavu dvacetipeliteteho jubilea prof. Jana Kvícaly.* Prague, 1884. 137-148.
Neumann, Harry, "On the Comedy of Plato's Aristophanes," *American Journal of Philology,* 87 (1966), 420-426.
Nusser, Johann, *Inhalt und Reihenfolge vor sieben platonischen Dialogen.* 1882. 64p.
Oldenberg, Herm., *De Platonis arte dialectica.* Göttingae, 1873, 65p.

Olivet, G., *Phaidros ou la Beauté.* Prague: Otto, 1911. 105p.
Orsìer, J., *Le Phédon de Platon et le Socrate de Lamartine*, Paris, 1919. 149p.
Oscanyon, Frederick S., "On Six Definitions of the Sophist: *2210-231E*," *Philosophical Forum (Boston)*, 4 (1972-73), 241-59.
Paci, E., "Dialettica, metodo diairetico e rettorica nel *Fedro* di Platone," *Archivio di Storia della Filosofia italiana*, 4 (1935), 145-58.
Pagliaro, A., "La dottrina dell' analogia e i suoi precedenti," *Ricerche Linguistiche*, 4 (1958), 1-18.
Partee, M. H., "Plato's Banishment of Poetry," *Journal of Aesthetics and Art Criticism*, 28 (1970), 209-22.
Paul, L., *Zur Erklärung der Worte in Platon's Gorgias.* Kiel, 1874, 14p.
― "Zu Platons *Gorgias*," *Jahrbücher für classische Philologie*, 109 (1874), 43-47.
― "Ueber das Gesetz des Masses im Platonischen *Gorgias*," *Zeitschrift für das Gymnasialwesen*, 30 (1876), 593-603.
― "Das Gesetz des Masses im Platonischen *Gorgias*," *Zeitschrift für das Gymnasialwesen*, 32 (1878), 462-69.
Petersen, Hans, *Platon's ausgewählte Dialogen.* Berlin: Weidmann, 1896-98.
Petitjean, L., "Une phrase du *Gorgias*," *Faculté des lettres de Caen. Bulletin mensuel*, 2 (1886), 49-53.
Pfeiffer, W. M., "True and False Speech in Plato's *Cratylus* 385 B-C," *Canadian Journal of Philosophy*, 2 (1972), 87-104.
Philippson, Paula, *Untersuchungen über den griechischen Mythos.* Zürich, 1944.
Pieper, J., *Love and Inspiration. A Study of Plato's Phaedrus. Translated by R. & C. Winston.* London, 1965, 109p.
― *Enthusiasm and Divine Madness: On the Platonic Dialogue Phaedrus. Translated from the German by Richard and Clara Winston.* New York: Harcourt, Brace, and World, 1964. 109p.
Plaistowe, Francis Gifford, *Plato. Gorgias. A Translation with Test Papers.* London: W. B. Clive, 1894. 116p.
Plass, Paul, "The Unity of the *Phaedrus*," *Symbolae Osloenses*, 43 (1968), 7-38.
Platt, A., "Notes on Plato's *Phaedrus*," *Journal of Philosophy*, (1919), 162-64.
Pohlenz, Max, *Aus Platos Werdezeit: Philologische Untersuchungen.* Berlin, 1913.
Post, L. A., "Plato's *Euthydemus* and *Lysias*," *Classical World*, 20 (1926), 29-31.
Potempa, V., *Der Phaidros in der Entwicklung der Ethik und der Reformgedanken Platos.* Dissertation, Breslau, 1913. 68p.
Praechter, K., "Plato, *Gorgias* 521E," *Hermes*, (1916), 316-317.
Puech, A., "Le *Gorgias*," *Revue des Cours et Conférences*, 34 (1933), 606-15.
― "Le *Phèdre*," *Revue des Cours et Conférences*, 34 (1933), 699-708.
Purser, Louis Claude, "Note on Plato, *Gorgias*, 494B," *Classical Review*, 2 (1888), 225-26.
Purves, John, *Selections from the Dialogues of Plato with Introductions and Notes by John Purves and a Preface by Benjamin Jowett.* Oxford: Clarendon Press, 1883; 1891. 404p.
Räder, Hans, *Platons philosophische Entwicklung.* Leipzig, 1920, 245-79.
Radermacher, L., "Ein unbekanntes Zitat," *Philologische Wochenschrift*, (1921), 788-789.

Raeder, H., *Platon und die Rhetorik.* Danske Vidensk. Selskab, Filos. Medd. II,6. Köbenhavn: Munksgaard, 1956, 21p.
— "Platon und die Sophisten," *Proceedings of the Royal Danish Academy,* (Filos. Medd. Dan. Selsk.), 1938.
Re, Raffaello Del, *Gorgia. Trad., introd., e note, fi Raffaello Del Re.* Torino: Paravia, 1939. 140p.
Rechnitz, W., *Die Geistige Umwelt von Platos Phaidros.* Inselschrift, 1931, 254p.
Reinhardt, Carol, "Qua vice Nestoris et Ulixis personae in arte rhetorica functae sint," *Commentatt. in hon. Buecheleri et Useneri editae a societat. philol. Bonnens.* Bonnae, 1873, 12-19.
Reiner, H., "Unrechttun ist schlimmer als Unrechtleiden. Zur Beweisführung des Sokrates in Patons Gorgias," *Zeitschrift für Philosophische Forschung,* 11 (1957), 548-55.
Rettig, G. F., *De conviviorum Xenophontis et Platonis ratione mutua et de Socratis et Pausainiae apud utrumque auctorem orationibus commentatio.* Bern, 1864.
Richter, J., "In Platonis *Gorgiam,*" *Jahrbücher für classische Philologie,* 97 (1868), 232-36.
Riddell, James, "Order of Words and Clauses in Plato," in *Apology,* Oxford University Press, 1877, 236-246.
Riemann, Othon, "Note sur deux passages du *Gorgias* de Platon," *Revue de Philologie,* 8.(1884), 101-102.
Rieckher, J., "Kleine Beiträge zur Textgestaltung griechischen Schriftsteller," *Festschrift der Gymnasien zur 4. Säcularfeier der Univ. Tübingen, 4 (1877), 19-26.*
Ritter, Constantin, *Platon.* Munich, 1923. vol. II, 39-62.
— "Die Abfassungszeit des *Phaidros* ein Schibboleth der Platonerklärung," *Philologus,* vol. 83, 321-373.
Rivier, A., "Les horizons métaphysiques du *Gorgias,*" *Bulletin de la Société des Etudes de Lettres,* 21 (1947), 39-63.
Roberts, W. Rhys, "References to Plato in Aristotle's *Rhetoric,*" *Classical Philology,* 19 (1924), 342-46.
Roehl, H., *Protagoras, Laches, Menon, und Abschnitte aus dem Gorgias und dem Euthydemus.* Münster, 1910. 216 p.
Roland-Gosselin, M. D., "Le *Ménon* et le *Gorgias,*" *Revue des Sciences Philosophiques et Théologiques,* (1908), 308-313.
Roller, Hermann, *Die griech. Sophisten zu Sokrates' und Plato's Zeit und ihr Einfluss auf Beredsamkeit und Philosophie.* Stuttgart, 1832.
Rolleston, Thomas William, *Selections from Plato.* London: W. Scott, 1892. 281p.
Romilly, Jacqueline de, *Magic and Rhetoric in Ancient Greece.* Harvard University Press, 1975. 108p.
Rosen, Stanley, "The Non-Lover in Plato's 'Phaedrus'," *Man and World: An International Philosophical Review,* 2.(August, 1969), 423-37.
Rosenfeldt, C. F., *Ueber den inneren Gedankengang in Platons Phaedros.* Reval, 1865. 87p.
Rosenmeyer, T. G., "Plato's Prayer to Pan," *Hermes,* 90 (1962), 34-44.

Rostagni, A., "Un nuovo capitolo della retorica e della sofistica," *Studi Italiani di Filologia Classica,* 2 (1922), 148-201.
Routh, Mart. I., *Euthydemus et Gorgias, recens. vertit notasque suas adiecit Mart. Io. Routh.* Oxonii, 1784.
Ruiloba, Palazuelos, *Epilogo al Fedro.* Santa Cruz de Tenerife: Universidad de la Laguna, 1952.
Sánchez, Lasso De La Vega J., "Notas al *Gorgias,*" *Emerita,* 35 (1967), 295-314.
Sattler, William M., "Some Platonic Influences on the Rhetorical Works of Cicero," *Quarterly Journal of Speech,* 35 (1949), 164-69.
Schanz, Martinus, *Platonis opera quae feruntur Omnia.* Lipsiae, 1875-85.
Schlegel, I. H., *Platonis dialogum, qui Phaedrus inscribitur, exposuit atque explanavit,* Offenburg, 1854. 50p.
Schleiermacher, F., *Platon Werke. Uebers. von F. Schleiermacher.* Berlin, 1804-10; 1817-28; 1855-62.
– *Phaidros oder vom Schönen.* Leipzig, 1915. 109p.
Schmalzriedt, E., "Der Umfahrtsmythos des *Phaidros,*" *Der altsprachliche Unterricht,* 9 (1966), 60-99.
Schmelzer, C., *Studien zur Redekunst.* Guben: Ehrlich, 1869.
– *Platos ausgewählte Dialoge erklärt von Carl Schmelzer.* Berlin: Weidmann, 1882-84.
Schmidt, Ch., *Quid Plato de arte rhetorica senserit.* Strasbourg, 1855. 32p.
Schmidt, H., *Difficiliores aliquot Gorgiae Platonici loci accuratius explicati.* Wittenberg, 1860.
– *De quatuor Gorgiae Platonici locis disputatio.* Wittenberg, 1862.
Schmidt, Leop., "Die Rede des Lysias in Platon's *Phaedrus,*" *Verhandl. der 18. Versamml. deutscher Philologen und Schulmänner in Wien,* (1859), 93-101.
Schnakel, Peter J., "Plato's *Phaedrus* and Rhetoric," *Southern Speech Communication Journal,* 32 (1966), 124-32.
Schneidewin, W., *Das sittliche Bewusstsein. Eine Gorgiasanalyse. Mit einer Federzeichnung von G. D. S. Freydanck.* Paderborn, 1937. 54p.
Schnitzer, C. F., "Zu Platons *Gorgias* (449D)," *Eos,* 2 (1865), 620,
Schuhl, P. M., "Sur un passage du *Gorgias* (464-465)," *Revue des Etudes Grecques,* (1939), 19-22.
Schulthess, Geo., *Gorgias.* Zürich, 1775; 1838; 1857.
Schwind, A., "Der Mythus in Platons *Phaidros,*" *Blätter für das Bayerische Gymnasial-Schulwesen,* vol. 53, 25-34.
Segal, Charles P., "Gorgias and the Psychology of the Logos," *Harvard Studies in Classical Philology,* 66 (1962), 99-155.
Sesonske, Alexander, "To Make the Weaker Argument Defeat the Stronger," *Journal of the History of Philosophy,* 6 (1968), 217-231.
Shey, H. J., "Petronius and Plato's *Gorgias,*" *The Classical Bulletin,* 47 (1971), 81-84.
Shorey, Paul, "Emendation of Plato, *Gorgias* 503D," *Classical Philology,* (1915), 325-26.
– "On the Erotikos of Lysias in Plato's *Phaedrus,*" *Classical Philology,* (1933), 131-32.

— "On Plato *Phaedrus* 250D," *Classical Philology*, (1932), 280-82.
Shiller, F. C. S., *Plato or Protagoras, Being A Critical Examination of the Protagoras Speech in the Theaetetus with Some Remark upon Error.* Oxford: Blackwell, 1908.
— "Plato or Protagoras," *Mind*, (1908), 518-26.
Sicking, C. M. J., "Organische Komposition und Verwandtes," *Mnemosyne*, 16 (1963), 225-42.
Sidgwick, Arthur, *Easy Selections from Plato by Arthur Sidgwick*, London 1888. 146p.
Siebeck, Hermann, "Zu Plato's *Phädrus* und *Gorgias*," *Philologus*, 40 (1881), 175-79.
Sieveking, Wilhelm, "Bemerkungen zu einer neuen Schulausgabe von Platons *Gorgias*," *Neue Jahrbücher für Antike und deutsche Bildung* (Leipzig), 4 (1941), 251-57.
Sigall, Emil, "Platons Ethik im Dialoge *Gorgias*," *Progr. des Gymn. Suczawa*, 8 (1892), 3-40.
Silbiger, S. F., "Cicero Platonis aemulus (Ciceronis *Orator* et Platonis *Phaedrus* secum comparentur)," *Eos*, 37 (1936), 19-26.
Sinaiko, H. L., *Love, Knowledge, and Discourse in Plato: Dialogue and Dialectic in Phaedrus, Republic, Parmenides.* Chicago: University of Chicago Press, 1965. 314p.
Solmsen, F., "Aristotle and Cicero on the Orators' Playing Upon the Feelings," *Classical Philology*, 33 (1938), 390-404.
Sommer, Edouard, *Platon. Gorgias. Edition classique, publiée avec des arguments et des notes en français par Edouard Sommer.* Paris: Hachette et Cie, 1864; 1900, 195p.
Stallbaum, Gdf., *Lysiaca ad illustrandas Phaedri Platonici origines.* Lipsiae, 1851. 32p.
— *Artis rhetoricae in Phaedro Platonis expromptae iudicium.* Lipsiae, 1852.
Stark, Rudolf, "Bemerkungen zum Platontext," *Philologus*, 106 (1962), 283-90.
Stefanini, L., "L'amore platonico nel Fedro." *Civiltà Moderna.* (1934), 194-202.
Stender, J., *Gorgias.* Halle: Waisenhaus, 1900. 194p.
Stewart, J. A., *The Myths of Plato.* London, 1905. 532p.
Stolberg, F.L., *Phaedrus und Gorgias.* Königsberg: Nicolovius, 1796.
Stumpo, B., *Studi introduttivi al Gorgia.* Palermo: Trimarchi, 1931.
Susemihl, Franz, "Die Abfassungszeit des platonischen *Phaidros*," *Jahrbücher für classische Philologie*, 121 (1880), 707-724; 123 (1881), 657-670.
— *De Platonis Phaedro et Isocratis contra Sophistas oratione dissertatio cum appendice aristotelica.* Greifswald, 1887.
Sybrandi, N. S., *De Platon Gorgia.* Dissertation, Harlemi, 1829. 144p.
Takemiya, A., "Twofold Qualifications of τέχνη in Plato's *Gorgias*," *Journal of Classical Studies*, 11 (1963), 43-52. (In Japanese)
Teichmüller, G., *Literarische Fehden im Vierten Jahrhundert.* 2 vols. Breslau, 1881-84.
Thedinga, Friedrich, "Die Bedeutung der Reden in Platons *Phaedros*," *Progr. des Realgymn. und Gymn.*, 4 (1883).
Thompson, C. A., "Rhetorical Madness: An Ideal in the *Phaedrus*," *Quarterly Journal of Speech*, 55 (1969), 358-63.

Thompson, E. S., "The Preliminary Definitions in Plato's *Sophist,"Proceedings of the Cambridge Philological Society,* (1884), 2-3.
Thompson, Wayne N., "The *Symposium:* A Neglected Source for Plato's Ideas on Rhetoric," *Southern Speech Communication Journal,* 38 (1971), 219-33.
Thompson, William Hepworth, *The Gorgias of Plato with English Notes. Introduction and Appendix by William Hepworth Thompson.* London and New York: G. Bell and Sons, 1871, 1894. 278p.
— *Phaedrus, with English Notes and Dissertations.* London, 1868.
Thurot, F., *Gorgias, Traduit en français avec le texte en regard et des notes par Fr. Thurot.* Paris, 1864.
— *Platon. Gorgias. Expliqué litteralement et annoté par Edouard Sommer et traduit en français par François Thurot.* Paris: Hachette et Cie, 1864; 1896. 511p.
Trimpi, Wesley, "The Ancient Hypothesis of Fiction: An Essay on the Origins of Literary Theory," *Traditio,* 27 (1971), 1-78.
Usener, Hermann, "Abfassungszeit des platonischen *Phaidros,"Rheinisches Museum für Philologie,* 35 (1880), 131-51.
Vahlen, J., "Uber die Rede des Lysias in Plato's *Phaedrus,"Sitzungsberichte der Preussischen Akademie der Wissenschaften,* (1903), 788-816.
— "De Platonis *Gorgia," Wiederholt in des Verf. Opuscula academica,* 2 (1908), 1-20.
Vanhoutte, M., *La notion de liberté dans le Gorgias de Platon.* Studia Univ. Lovanium Fac. de Philos. & Lettres I Léopoldville Ed. de l'Univ., 1957, 43p.
— "Note sur la communauté des genres dans le Sophiste," *Revue Philosophique de Louvain,* 46 (1948), 177-87.
Vardaman, George T., "An Analysis of Some Factors Relating to the Dialectic of Plato, Aristotle, and Cicero." Unpublished doctoral dissertation, Northwestern University, 1952.
Verdam, H. D., "Quid Plato responderit ad Polycratis orationem in Socratem," *Mnemosyne,* vol. 45, (1917) 189-204.
— "Quo ordine Isocratis Busiris aduersus sophistas Helena orationes inter se succedant et quid Plato ad eas responderit." *Mnemosyne,* vol. 44, (1916) 373-95.
Verdenius, W. J., "Der Begriff der Mania in Platons *Phaidros," Archiv für Geschichte der Philosophie,* 44 (1962), 132-50.
— "Notes on Plato's *Phaedrus," Mnemosyne,* 8 (1955), 165-89.
Viano, C. A., 'Retorica, magia e natura in Platone," *Rivista di Filosofia,* 56 (1965), 411-53.
Vicaire, P., *Platon: Critique littéraire.* Paris, 1960.
— *Platon. Phèdre traduction avec une introduction et notes.* Paris, 1972.
Villa, E., *Gorgia, A cura di E. Villa.* Verona: La Scaligera, 1941. 269p.
Vlastos, G., "Was Polus Refuted? " *American Journal of Philology,* 88 (1967), 454-60.
Vollgraff, *Phaedrus.* Lugduni, 1912. 154p.
— *Dialogus qui inscribitur Phaedrus.* 1913.

Vonneilich, F., *De Phaedri Platonici aetate argumentoque.* Dissertation, Rostoch: Malchini, 1872. 31p.
Vries, G. J. de, *A Commentary on the Phaedrus of Plato.* Amsterdam: Hakkert, 1969. 244p.
— "A New Indication for the Date of the Phaedrus?" Mnemosyne, 16 (1963), 286-87.
— "Isocrates in the *Phaedrus*: A Reply," *Mnemosyne,* 24 (1971), 387-90.
Weaver, Richard, "The *Phaedrus* and the Nature of Rhetoric," in *The Ethics of Rhetoric,* Chicago, 1953, 3-26.
Weil, R., "Quelques nouveautés en philologie classique. Autour de Platon et de Démosthène," *L'Information littéraire,* 13 (1961), 104-08.
Wendt, G., "Vier Stellen in Plato's *Gorgias,*" *Zeitschrift für das Gymnasialwesen,* 30 (1876), 603-07.
Wenig, K., "Etudes sur l'histoire de l'art oratoire en Grèce," *Listy Filologicke,* vol. 41, 16-19; 102-104.
— *Die Conception der Ideenlehre im Phaedrus bildet den einheitlichen Grundgedanken dieses Dialoges und liefert den Schlüssel zum Verständnis der platonischen Ideenlehre überhaupt.* Breslau, 1883. 64p.
Wessely, Karl von, "Literarische Fragmente aus El-Faijûm; Platon *Gorgias,*" in *Mittheilungen aus der Sammlung der Papyrus Erzherzog Rainer,* 2 (1887), 74-82.
Wiechmann, G. R., *Platonis et Aristotelis de arte rhetorik doctrina inter se comparatur.* Dissertation, Berolini, 1864. 62p.
Wiehe, F. W., *Platons udvalgte dialoger bearbejdede til skolebrug af. F. W. Wiehe.* Kopenhagen: Reitzel, 1849; 1896.
Wilamowitz-Moellendorff, Ulrich, *Platon, sein Leben und seine Werke.* 3rd ed., Berlin, 1948.
Wimsatt, W. K., Jr., and Cleanth Brooks, "The Verbal Medium: Platon and Aristotle," *Literary Criticism: A Short History.* New York: Alfred A. Knopf, Inc., 1957. 57-76.
Winiewski, F., *De fontibus Graecorum de animarum post martem statu persuasionis.* Monasterii, 1845. 23p.
— *De loco Platonis disputatio.* Monasterii. 1853. 30p.
Wishart, D., and S. V. Leach, "A Multivariate Analysis of Platonic Prose Rhythm," *Computer Studies in the Humanities and Verbal Behavior,* 3 (1970), 90-99.
Wright, Josiah, *The Phaedrus, Lysis, and Protagoras of Plato.* London and New York: Macmillan and Company, 1848; 1888. 272p.
Wycherley, R. E., "The Scene of Plato's *Phaidros,*" *Phoenix,* 17 (1963), 88-98.
Yagüe, García, *Gorgias.* Buenos Aires, 1961. 181p.
Zilles, W., "Hippias aus Elis," *Hermes,* (1918), 45-56.
Zuccante, G., "Lisia e Platone. A propositio del discorso erotico di Lisia nel *Fedro,*" *Rendiconti del r. Istituto Lombardo di science e lettre,* 58 (1925), 132-36.
— "Die Platonis *Phaedro,* de Platonis *Protagora,* de Platonis *Protagora* et *Symposio,*" *Wiederhalt in des Verf. Opuscula academica,* 1 (1907), 470-86.

INDEX

Academy, 86, 296
accusations, 83
Achilles, 156, 334
Ackrill, J.L., 248
acting, 146
Acumenus, 229
Ad Demonicum, 271
Adeimantus, 344
Ad Femonicum, 268
adikia, 91
advantages, 133
Aeschines, 64, 156
aestheticism, 146
Against Eratosthenes, 281
Against the Sophists, 196, 245 247, 289
Agamemnon, 163, 340
Agathon, 107, 116, 121, 123, 125, 206, 223, 237, 243, 253, 269, 315, 316, 326, 327, 328, 332
Ajax, 65
Alcibiades, 64, 106, 140, 161, 163, 199, 216, 217, 224, 228, 232, 236, 253, 316, 317, 331, 334, 335
Alcibiades Major, 109, 119, 121
Alcidamas, 196, 209
aleitheia, 47, 48, 49, 54
Alleyne, S.F., 173
Ammon, G., 295
Amphibolous, 248
Amphion, 112
Anacreon, 206
Ananke, 50
Anaxagoras, 230, 277, 294
Anchinous, 250

Anderson, F.D., 299
Anderson, R.L., 299
Andocides, 67
andreious, 250
Antidosis, 199, 245, 253, 255, 259
Antigone, 263
antilogism, 289
antilogy, 155
Antiope, 112
Anti-Palamedes, 35
Antiphon, 32, 41, 47, 333
Antisthenes, 241
antithesis, 103, 153, 333
antitimesis, 59
Anytus, 26, 81, 92
Apelt, O., 127, 360
Aphrodite, 206, 207, 214, 225, 317, 318, 321
apodeictic, 198
Apollo, 41, 59, 60, 320
apologiai, 243
Apology, 31, 33, 35, 37, 41, 54, 59, 63, 67, 69, 77, 78, 81, 85, 89, 90, 124, 201, 217, 227, 376, 377
aporia, 91
appearances, 73, 104, 147, 300
appetite, 309
Archelaus, 154
arete, 94, 110, 121, 309
art, 28, 95, 121, 143, 144, 191, 342, 396
Athenaeus, 218
Athenian Stranger, 345, 347, 351, 353, 397

Athens, 34, 57, 78, 82, 85, 123, 200, 378
Archelaos, 104, 141
argument, 74, 76, 145, 148, 275, 300
Aristodemus, 326
Aristophanes, 199, 255, 330, 332, 334, 335, 351
Aristotle, 95, 111, 122, 191, 248, 262, 281, 298, 303, 325, 328, 329, 330, 339, 342, 348, 362
Arnim, H. von, 112
Ascham, R., 267
Ast, F., 195
audience, 167, 201, 301
authors, 195

Bacchic maidens, 231
Bacchus, 320
Baird, A.C., 299, 326
balance (psychological), 89
Ballard, E.G., 375
Barnes, J., 264
beautiful/ugly, 106, 201, 206, 211, 212, 241, 386, 396
being, 245, 359
belief, 97, 147
Bergua, J.B., 127
Bernays, J., 122
Bitzer, L., 332
blabe, 263
Black, E., 22, 171
Blass, F., 33
Bluck, R.S., 22, 55, 73
Boeotia, 200
Bonitz, J., 92, 99, 101, 105, 118, 173, 178, 212
Boreas, 230, 282, 319
boule, 254
Brown, M., 239
Brown, N.O., 313
Brownson, C.L., 394
Brownstein, O.L., 21, 336

Bruyn, J.C., 127
Bucheit, V., 260
Burkert, W., 155
Burnet, J., 65
Bury, J.B., 211
Bury, R.G., 246
Busiris, 268, 270

Callias, 72
Callicles, 28, 63, 72, 92, 94, 103, 106, 107, 110, 111, 115, 117-20, 129, 133, 136, 139-43, 150, 154, 156, 165, 166, 179, 180, 181, 250, 254, 381, 382, 387
Calliope-Urania, 205, 206
Calogero, G., 32
Calonge, J., 127
Canart, P., 207
Cassandra, 364
Categories, 248, 262
cave allegory, 188, 300, 301
Cephalus, 72, 91, 229
Chaerphon, 59, 93, 108
charioteer, 310, 322
charm, 159
Charmides, 253
Charmides, 72, 74, 121, 161, 162, 199, 201, 250, 300, 344
chatter, 375
Christ, W. von, 31
Chroust, A.H., 32, 38
Cimon, 141, 154
city, 154
Cleinias, 22, 23, 347, 397
Clouds, 34, 199, 210
Collingwood, R.G., 386
combatant (word), 75
comedy, 228
communication, 313, 315
community, 79, 375, 377
conjurers, 160, 168
content (speech), 147
conviction, 62

cookery, 27, 56, 178
Cooper, L., 127, 211, 297, 326
Cope, E.M., 173, 175, 178, 332
Corax, 212
Cornford, F.M., 177, 187, 209, 362
Corybantic ecstasy, 161, 215, 335
Coulter, J., 239, 241
Council, 154
courage, 266, 330
courtroom, 40, 46, 53, 54
Couvreur, P., 239
Cratylus, 120, 177, 247, 355-373, 388
Creon, 263
Critias, 107
Crito, 22, 354
Croiset-L.Bodin, A., 127
Crombie, I.M., 205, 251
Cronus, 206
cross-examination, 336
Ctesippus, 157
culture, 83, 103, 221, 241
Cyropaideia, 215

daimon, 225
Darius, 272
deception, 213
declamation, 389
De Demosthene, 244
defendant, 53-55
definitions, 25, 28, 163
Delphi (Oracle), 46, 59, 65, 282, 376
democracy, 281
Democritus, 215, 241, 365
demonstrations of talk, 132
demos, 35, 41, 254, 381
Demosthenes, 156
demotic, 241, 251
De Rerum Natura, 207
Derrida, J., 162
De Vries, G.J., 298

dialectic, 94, 114, 125, 177, 182, 184, 209, 213, 291, 293, 296, 301, 336
dialogue, 76, 194, 195, 203, 208, 233, 266, 375, 376
dianoia, 188
dicanic speech, 40
diegesis, 40
Diels, H., 212
Dike, 375
Diodotus, 263
Diogenes Laertus, 153, 217
Dionysus, 172, 208, 244, 320
Diotima, 225, 227, 237, 269, 325, 334, 336
discourse, 117, 182, 304, 305. 370
dispositio, 202, 299, 300, 302, 304, 307, 310
divided line simile, 131
divine, 234, 342
divisions of speech, 177, 299, 303
Dodds, E.R., 55, 114, 140
double entendres, 249
doxa, 47, 48, 52, 56, 61, 202, 240, 245, 251
doxopaideutike, 261
Duchemin, J., 127
Dümmler, F., 35, 164
Düring, I., 262

Edelstein, L., 201, 387
education, 95, 183, 240
Egyptians, 277
Ehrenberg, V., 200
eidolon, 250
Eidos, 121, 306, 310, 311
eikasia, 188
Eleatic, 289
electric fish, 160
Elis, 200
empeiria, 293
encomia, 243, 271
energesia, 45

enthymemes, 326, 331, 332
epekeina, 126
epideictic, 209, 333
epideixeis, 209
epilogos, 40
Epinomis, 308
episteme, 52, 53, 55, 188, 245
epistemology, 187, 194
Epistle VII, 131
epitaphios, 164
epithets, 327
epithymia, 240, 245
Erato, 205, 206
erga, 143
eristic, 382
eros, 194, 196, 197, 198, 199, 200
    201-204, 207-209, 212, 214, 215,
    217, 232, 234, 236, 244, 313-323,
    328, 330, 334, 336
erotesis, 42
Eryximachus, 223, 229, 314, 330,
    334
ethics, 54, 134, 147, 181, 194, 202,
    270
eudaemonia, 103, 121
Eudemian Ethics, 339
Euphemus, 263, 384
Eupolis, 341
Eurioides, 276
Euripides, 112, 294, 333, 341
Euthydemus, 22, 24, 92, 157, 241,
    344, 363, 368, 379, 388, 395
Euthyphro, 95, 108, 125
Evagoras, 253
Evagoras, 273
evil, 103
existentialists, 233

fakery, 323
Field, G.C., 22, 127
Finley, J.H., 31
flattery, 102, 165-66, 293, 315
force, 339

forensic, 82, 195
Forms, 73, 177, 179, 197, 211, 283,
    299
Fowler, H.N., 295
Freeman, K., 32
Frenkian, A.M., 298
Friedländer, P., 91, 257, 310

Geffcken, J., 127
Gercke, A., 196
Geryon, 111
Glaucon, 89, 161, 344
God, 87, 88, 157, 163, 188, 197,
    202, 203, 278, 295, 300, 306,
    314, 322
Goethe, 113
Gomperz, T., 31, 39, 64, 106, 172
"good", 112, 115-16, 278
Goodwin, A., 53
Gorgias, 25, 52, 103, 129, 133, 135-
    37, 154-56, 163-64, 167, 175,
    176, 178, 190, 243, 274, 341
Gorgias, 26, 29, 67, 99, 109-110,
    117, 119, 124, 134, 147, 160,
    150, 151, 165, 168, 170, 172,
    173-75, 178-81, 183, 185, 201,
    202, 245, 254, 265, 292, 293,
    294, 308, 328, 329, 336, 338,
    341, 380
governors, 27
"great speech," 239, 244
Greece, 43
Green, E., 335
Greene, N., 214
Grey, D.R., 395
Grote, G., 72
Grube, G.M.A., 21
guardian, 353
Guthrie, W.K.C., 305
gymnasia, 199
gymnastics, 24

Hackforth, R., 28, 29, 59, 182, 193,

237, 239, 297
Hall, R., 197
Hamberger, P., 40
handbooks, 303
Händel, P., 211
happiness, 104-06
harmony, 148, 149, 214
Hart, R.L., 388
Harward, J., 386
Havelock, E., 78, 80, 206
Heath, D.D., 370
hedonism, 233
Heinimann, F., 111
Helen, 34, 55, 270, 271, 283
Helen, 33, 153, 164, 166, 243, 244, 260, 266, 267, 268, 270, 274, 277
Hellas, 43
Hembold, W.C., 29, 184, 300
Heracleitus, 367
Herakles, 111
Hermias, 239
Hermogenes, 356, 357, 368, 369
Herodotus, 366
Hesiod, 205, 329, 340, 363, 364, 387
Highet, G., 203, 245, 299
Himera, 284
Himeros, 214
Hippias, 35, 71, 226
Hippias Major, 67, 95
Hippias Minor, 92, 156
Hippocrates, 24, 156, 294
Hoffmann, E., 126
Holther, W.B., 29, 184
Homer, 160, 161, 329, 340, 351, 363, 387
homilia, 199
honesty, 38
Horace, 207
Horn, F., 211
horses (black/white), 310, 311
Howland, R.L., 243, 265
Humbert, J., 127

humbleness, 149
Hunt, E.L., 21, 171, 299, 326, 336
hypothetical conversation, 333

ideal speech, 325
ignorance, 98
Iliad, 261
illusion, 155
imagining, 188
impressions, 50
incantation, 161
injustice, 103
inspiration, 94
intelligence, 113
interrogation, 42
inquiry, 76
invention, 305, 329, 332
Ion, 94, 166, 188, 205, 388
irony, 96
Isocrates, 33, 67, 196, 199, 203, 209, 241, 244, 245, 255, 258, 265, 268, 277, 297
Isthmian, 229

Jaeger, W., 93, 102, 173, 178, 200, 203, 255, 299
Jevons, F.B., 333
Joly, R., 201
Jowett, B., 23, 305
judges, 39, 378
jury, 42, 43, 61, 87
justice, 88, 98, 102, 124, 133, 144, 147, 149, 166, 210, 250, 330

Kahn, C.H., 31
kaiom, 340
Kallias, 97
kath'hautas, 249
Kelly, W.G., 313
Kennedy, G., 196, 256, 299, 333, 335
kill, 244
kingcraft, 244

Knights, 255
knowledge, 50, 56, 80, 95, 97, 115, 132, 167, 187, 197, 203, 275, 296
Krafft, F., 206
Kranz, W., 111

Lacedaemonian Constitution, 199
Laches, 72, 257
language, 82, 84, 108, 313, 370, 386, 395, 396
Lasky, M., 206
Lasserre, F., 200
laughing, 148
Laws, 73, 159, 162, 177, 179, 190, 256, 308, 339, 343, 345, 396, 398
law makers, 195, 297, 395
legislator, 190, 349
length (speech), 148
Levy, G.R., 390
Life of Apollonius of Tyana, 155
Linforth, I.M., 114, 186
listener, 75
literary theory, 299, 329
"living creature image," 299-311
Lobel, E., 206
logographos, 231, 287, 289, 325
logoi, 67, 97, 105, 121, 125, 162, 205, 218, 220, 231, 359, 370, 378
logic, 76, 149, 163, 177
logismoi, 177
logistikon, 245
Lord, A.B., 206
love, 183, 194, 195, 205-06, 210, 228, 284, 290, 314, 315, 332
lovers, 186, 233, 234, 315
Luce, J.V., 366
Lucretius, 207
Lycon, 81
Lycurgus, 272
Lysias, 28, 67, 72, 185, 193, 195, 196, 197, 199, 200, 201, 210, 215, 229, 232, 234, 237, 240, 241, 246, 252, 257, 267

madness, 186, 188, 227, 230, 283, 284, 291, 316
magic, 153, 155, 159, 160, 161, 163, 164, 169
Magnus, L., 172
mania, 198, 200, 208, 209, 211, 220, 221
manner, 149
Marrou, H.I., 246, 253
Marsyas, 161, 316
Marx, K., 233
mathesis, 52, 56
McBurney, J.H., 332
Meador, P.A., 332
Medea, 162, 341
medicine, 24, 29, 167, 168, 229, 230
Megillus, 397
Melesias, 155
Meletus, 41, 42, 58, 59, 65, 81, 85, 87, 124
Melissus, 266
Menander, 218
memory, 79, 85
Menexenus, 164, 305
Menexenus, 158, 335, 338
Meno, 160, 163, 217, 226, 253
Meno, 25-26, 36, 72, 73, 74, 92, 160, 188, 198, 256
metaphor, 9
metaphysics, 300
Metrodonus, 230
Meyerhoff, H., 91
Midias, 290
middle speech (*Phaedrus*), 239-65
Miltiades, 154
Minos, 225
Minucian, 332
monarchy, 349

money, 230
moral principles, 54, 97, 122, 123, 176, 203
Morgan, D., 391
moria, 42
Morr, J., 31, 32, 39
Morrison, J.S., 206
Morrow, G.R., 221, 339
Moss, L., 386
Mourelatos, A., 362
Mras, K., 196
Mudd, C.S., 332
muses, 201, 205, 207, 270, 284, 288, 297, 320
Myrrhinous, 284
myth, 112, 114, 125, 168, 329

names, 355-73
narrative style, 81
"nemo sua sponte peccat", 33
Nestor, 209, 274
Nicocles, 253
Nicomachean Ethics, 122, 175, 262
Ninus, 155
noble orator, 300, 304
noesis, 188
nomos, 107, 110, 349
non-lover, 321
nymphs, 201, 274

Odes, 207
Odysseus, 37, 41, 46, 47, 209
Odyssey, 205, 274
Oldfather, W., 141
oligarchs, 339
Olympiodorus, 172
On Interpretation, 248
On the Sacred Disease, 156
On the Sophists, 209
ontology, 194
ophelia, 263
opinion, 73, 257
oracle, 61, 63, 84

oral culture, 80-81
oral tradition, 83, 84
oratory, 96, 98, 101, 120, 146
Oreithuia, 230, 282, 319, 387
organic unity, 305
Orpheus, 156, 157
Orphic-Pythagorean, 114
ousia, 246, 250
Owen, G.E.L., 262

Page, D., 206, 214
paideia, 198, 199, 215, 376
painting, 94
pais, 216
Palamedes, 32, 33, 36, 40, 41, 44, 67, 209
Pan, 201
Panathenaicus, 248
panegyric, 95
Panegyricus, 276
paradeigma, 59
Parmenides, 225, 245, 289, 365
Partee, M.H., 385
passion, 149, 153, 233, 309, 316
Pater, W., 173, 174
pathos, 382
Pausanias, 200, 214, 237, 316, 317, 318, 334
pedantry, 172
pederasty, 207, 235
peitho, 214
penia, 44
percipi, 146
Pericles, 24, 26, 28, 97, 154, 216, 247, 255, 292-94, 334, 341
persuasion, 28, 53, 55, 75, 96, 141, 182, 196, 203, 212, 213, 219, 289, 317, 339-54
Pfeiffer, W.M., 355-73
Phaedo, 257
Phaedo, 73, 115, 158, 300, 308, 344, 387
Phaedrus, 185, 186, 193, 194, 197,

202, 204, 207, 208, 210, 211,
215, 220, 226, 228, 230, 231,
237, 241, 267, 268, 272-74, 285,
294, 297, 306, 316-17, 319, 334,
393
Phaedrus, 28, 31, 130, 131, 172,
173, 175, 177, 179, 181, 182,
183, 184, 185, 188, 193, 198,
200, 202, 210, 213, 217, 218,
225, 228, 252, 254, 261, 270,
273-4, 281, 293, 294, 305, 306,
309, 313-23, 336, 341
Pheidippides, 210
Philebus, 226
Philebus, 73, 115, 177, 215, 339
philodocia, 381
philodoxy, 240
philosopher, 83, 183, 219, 322, 394
philosopher-king, 143, 150
philosophia, 247, 251, 381
philosophical orator, 67
philosophy, 124, 131, 190, 193, 200,
241, 242, 283, 300, 302, 307,
337, 339
Philostratus, 155
Phoenician tale, 213
phronesis, 175
Phryne, 155
physician, 124, 149
physis, 107
Pieper, J., 258, 298
pietho, 309
Pindar, 111, 229, 364
pistis, 40, 41, 53, 188
plaintiff, 42
plane tree, 231
Plass, P., 193
pleasure/pain, 115, 134
pleonektic, 250
pleonexia, 244, 245
Plutarch, 155, 207
poets, 81, 205, 206, 297, 344
poetry, 79, 154, 155, 161, 186, 198,

205, 333, 337, 351, 385-98
Pohlenz, M., 209
polemic, 35, 134
polis, 123, 155, 229, 255
politics, 81, 102, 103, 104, 112, 135,
147, 159, 162, 168, 179, 189,
194, 254, 293, 375
Politicus, 159, 162, 177, 189, 213
Polus, 27, 93, 94, 95, 99, 101, 104,
105, 118, 119, 122, 129, 132,
133, 137-44, 179, 180, 381
Polycrates, 64, 123
Popper, K., 340, 347
Post, L.A., 304
Power (speech), 82, 97, 105, 132,
134, 138, 163
practice, 203
praise, 327
praxis, 202, 215, 219
prejudice, 58
premises, 74
pre-socratics, 83
Priam, 47
probability, 50, 62
Prodicus, 35, 317
Prometheus, 340
prooimion, 40
prose (homely), 82
protagonist, 148
Protagoras, 24, 25, 72, 92, 94, 155,
159, 160, 225, 246, 365
Protagoras, 24-26, 93, 95, 113, 166,
199, 203, 218, 265, 305, 371
Proteus, 156-57
proverbs, 333
prytaneum, 59
pseudo-arts, 120
psyche, 56
psychogogia, 182-84
psychology, 75, 181, 200, 219, 300,
302, 307, 341
public office, 316
punishment, 107

purpose, 149
Pyrilampes, 254
Pythagoras, 153
Pythagorean doctrine, 285
Pythocles, 284

Rabinowitz, W.G., 313
Raeder, H., 252
reality, 322, 359
reasoning, 164, 309-310
refutation, 74, 289
Regenbogen, O., 211
Reiner, H., 127
Reinhard, L., 120
Republic, 71, 73, 89, 98, 102, 106, 109, 117, 120, 122, 130, 137, 143, 145, 150, 154, 156, 158, 161, 189, 190, 193, 194, 196, 210, 212, 213, 231, 245, 247, 310, 339, 343, 350, 366, 386, 392
Rhetorica, 281, 329, 331
Rhetorica ad Alexandrum, 334
rhome, 240, 243-44
Riddle, J., 58
Ries, K., 242, 260
Rivier, A., 127
Roberts, W.R., 305
Robin, L., 267, 297
Robinson, R., 176, 247, 347, 355
Romilly, J. de, 153
Rosen, S., 223
Ross, W.D., 180
Rouse, W.H.D., 314
Rudberg, G., 127
Rufener, R., 87
Ruiloba, P., 298
ruler, 383
rules, 176, 349
Ryle, G., 22, 27

Sabbatucci, N., 127
Sandys, J.E., 298

Sappho, 206, 253
Sattler, W.S., 301
satyr, 316, 317
Schilling, K., 125
Schmelzer, C., 298
Schmid, W., 31-32
Schneidewin, W., 46
Schuhl, P-M., 102
Schwartz, E., 32, 47
sculpture, 94
Scythian, 73
seduction, 164, 218, 323
Segal, C.P., 221
self-importance, 150
self-praise, 49
Sesonske, A., 71
sex, 227, 315
sex-talk, 313
Sextus Empiricus, 241, 359
Shorey, P., 102, 127, 174, 175, 179, 394
Sicily, 25, 26
Sileni, 216, 218, 335
Simmias, 73, 257
Simonides, 71
siren, 161, 287
Skousgaard, S., 375
Smyth, H.W., 358
Snell, B., 112, 261
sobriety, 231
social organization, 79
society, 43, 44, 60
Socratic conversation, 100
Socratic dialogue, 93, 181
Socratic listener, 75
Socratic rhetoric, 131
Socratic schools, 65
Solmsen, F., 125
Solon, 272
somatic love, 240
sophia, 42, 381
Sophist, 106, 159, 177, 209, 234, 261, 275, 360, 361, 368, 389

Sophistry, 23, 24, 36, 45, 57, 72, 75, 84, 92, 123, 125, 157, 163, 184, 190, 256, 293, 321, 323, 326, 339, 379
Sophocles, 162, 193, 276
sophos, 250
sophron, 250
sophrosyne, 122, 202, 250, 263
soul, 87, 110, 137, 145, 196, 197, 202, 212, 220, 301, 302, 309, 311, 313, 391
speeches, 226, 227, 230, 314
Speusippus, 264
Spitzer, A., 129
Sprague, R., 241
Stählin, O., 32
state, 151, 349
Statesman, 102, 108, 123, 143, 339, 342, 343
Steidle, W., 199
Stesichorus, 271, 283
Stewart, J.A., 390
structure, 307
Stubbings, F., 206
Stumpo, B., 127
style, 130, 164, 181, 306
subjective impression, 62
substance, 148
syllogoi, 196, 203, 204
symbolism, 313
Symposium, 39, 73, 117, 137, 147, 160, 195, 196, 199, 200, 203, 205, 206, 211, 213, 216, 218, 223, 225, 228, 232, 236, 243, 313-18, 325-38
syntax, 80

talk, 314
Tate, J., 387
Taylor, A.B., 181, 182
teacher, 54, 84, 241, 246, 265, 294, 397
techne, 52, 136, 165, 226, 232, 235, 236, 287, 294, 302
Teichmuller, G., 35
Tejera, V., 281
testimony, 333
Thamus, 295
Theaetetus, 73, 187, 201, 370
Themistocles, 74, 97, 141, 154
Theodorus, 209
Theogony, 205, 340, 364
theoria, 155
therapeia, 133
Thessalonian, 25
Theuth, 277
thinking, 87, 188
Thompson, W.H., 172, 297
Thompson, W.N., 313
Thonssen, L., 299, 326
Thrasymachus, 91, 103, 109
Thrasymachus, 7, 98, 100, 111, 137, 161, 181, 209, 217, 252, 277, 292, 301
Thucydides, 155, 263, 333
Timaeus, 73, 187, 225, 257, 309, 310, 388, 395
Tisias, 52, 181, 212, 277
"to kalon", 244
To Nicocles, 243-46, 249, 254, 259, 273, 278, 279
"to on ontos", 245
topoi, 32, 34, 42, 43, 328, 329
tragedy, 293, 294, 375
treasury, 244
Tredennick, H., 300
Treves, P., 64
trial of Socrates, 112
Trojans, 46
true art, 129
true being, 111
true government, 102
true lover, 199
true rhetoric, 9, 28, 129, 146, 191, 197, 203, 204, 220, 293, 342
truth, 28, 61, 63, 72-74, 78, 82, 87,

148, 182, 256, 275, 301, 322, 323, 337, 364
trustworthiness, 38
Turyn, A., 111
Typhon, 230
tyranny, 104, 154, 281, 347, 381

übermensch, 142
Ullmann, S., 358

Vanhoutte, M., 127
vanity, 100
Verdenius, W.J., 367
Vicaire, P., 201
virtue, 348, 389
Voegelin, 127, 375
"vox propria", 58

Wace, A., 206
wantonness, 244
Warry, J., 390
Weaver, R., 172, 313
Wehrli, von Fritz, 211
Weingartner, R., 355
Wilcox, S., 196, 200
Wilhelm, F., 200
Will, 144
Wilson, N.L., 370
wisdom, 88, 162, 229, 266, 323
witchcraft, 155, 167
witnesses, 333
wizards, 159
Woodbury, L.E., 363
Woodhead, W.D., 127
words, 199, 203
writing, 195, 197, 226, 277, 278, 295, 297, 304, 389

Xenophon, 33, 34, 64, 119, 215, 218
Xenophanes, 365

youth, 150

Zeller, E., 173
Zeno, 209, 266, 274, 289
Zethos, 112
Zeus, 207, 214, 219, 341
Zurretti, C.O., 127

STUDIES IN CLASSICAL ANTIQUITY

Volume 1. Amsterdam 1979. 310p. XVIIp. Hfl. 65,–
FRITZ ERIK HOEVELS: Märchen und Magie in den Metamorphosen des Apuleius von Madaura
Inhaltsverzeichnis: Vorwort. A: Analytischer Teil, 1. Psyches Entrückung. 2. Psyche in Amors Palast. 3. Nach der Trennung. 4. Psyches Wanderungen. A: Synthetischer Teil.1. Das archaisch-rituelle Substrat des Psychemärchens. 2. Zur Psychoanalyse des Psychemärchens und des Apuleius. 3. Die Dichtung des Apuleius als Ausdruck des späatantiken Irrationalismus. Abkürzungen. Ausgaben und Kommentare. Literatur.

Volume 2. Amsterdam 1979. 251p. XXXp. Hfl. 60,–
WOLF-DIETER ALBERT: Darstellungen des Eros in Unteritalien
Inhaltsverzeichnis: Einleitung. 1. Götterbild und Erotenwagen. 2. Eros als Verfolger. 3. Der dionysische Eros. Abbildungen. Anmerkungen.

LIBRARY OF DAVIDSON COLLEGE

Books on regular loan may be checked out for **two weeks**. Books must be presented at the Circulation Desk in order to be renewed.

A fine is charged after date due.

Special books are
the library staff.

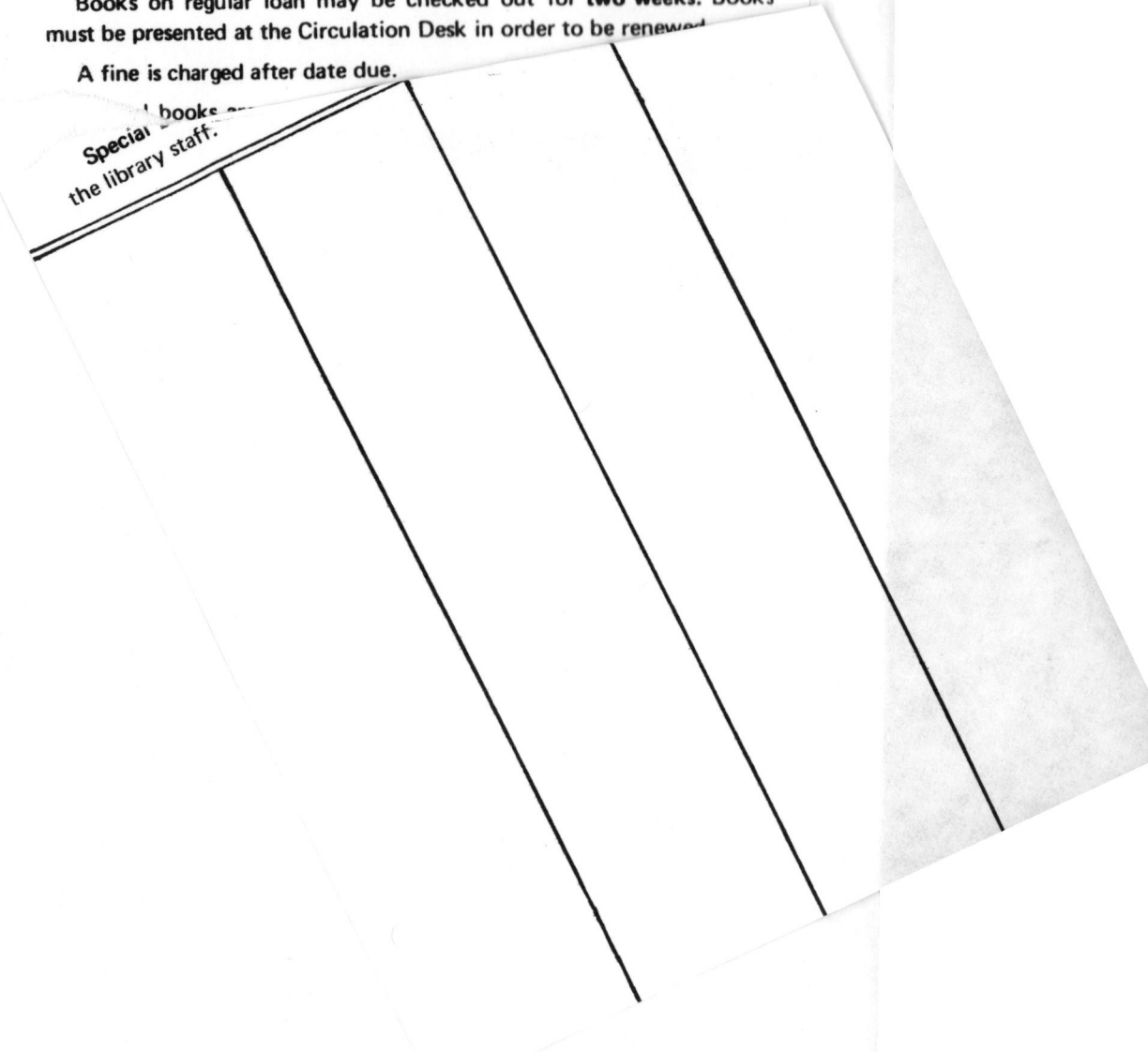